THE CONSUMER AND THE HEALTH CARE SYSTEM:
Social and Managerial Perspectives

Health Systems Management
Edited by **Samuel Levey, Ph.D.**, *City University of New York*, and **Alan Sheldon, M.D.**, *Harvard School of Public Health*

Volume 1:
Financial Management of Health Institutions
J.B. Silvers and C.K. Prahalad

Volume 2:
Personnel Administration in the Health Services Industry: Theory & Practice
Norman Metzger

Volume 3:
The National Labor Relations Act: A Guidebook for Health Care Facility Administrators
Dennis D. Pointer and Norman Metzger

Volume 4:
Organizational Issues in Health Care Management
Alan Sheldon

Volume 5:
Long Term Care: A Handbook for Researchers, Planners and Providers
Sylvia Sherwood, Editor

Volume 6:
Analysis of Urban Health Problems: Case Studies from the Health Services Administration of the City of New York
Irving Leveson and Jeffrey H. Weiss, Editors

Volume 7:
Health Maintenance Organizations: A Guide to Planning and Development
Roger W. Birnbaum

Volume 8:
Labor Arbitration in Health Care
Earl R. Baderschneider and Paul F. Miller, Editors

Volume 9:
The Consumer and the Health Care System: Social and Managerial Perspectives
Harry Rosen, Jonathan M. Metsch and Samuel Levey, Editors

Volume 10:
Long-Term Care Administration: A Managerial Perspective, I & II
Samuel Levey and N. Paul Loomba, Editors

THE CONSUMER AND THE HEALTH CARE SYSTEM:
Social and Managerial Perspectives

Edited by

Harry Rosen
City University of New York
New York, New York

Jonathan M. Metsch
Mount Sinai Services
City Hospital Center
Elmhurst, New York

Samuel Levey
City University of New York
New York, New York

S P Books Division of
SPECTRUM PUBLICATIONS, INC.
New York

Distributed by Halsted Press
A Division of John Wiley & Sons

New York   Toronto   London   Sydney

Copyright © 1977 Spectrum Publications, Inc.

SPECTRUM PUBLICATIONS, Inc.
175-20 Wexford Terrace, Jamaica, N.Y. 11432

Main entry under title:

The consumer and the health care system.

   (Health systems management ; 9)
   Bibliography: p.
   Includes index.
   1. Health services administration. 2. Community
health services--Citizen participation.
3. Community health services--United States–
Citizen participation. 4. Health planning--
Citizen participation. 5. Health planning--United
States–Citizen participation. I. Metsch,
Jonathan M. II. Rosen, Harry. III. Levey,
Samuel.
RA394.C68   362.1   76.47002
ISBN 0-89335-005-2

Distributed solely by the Halsted Press Division of John Wiley & Sons, Inc.
New York, New York
ISBN 0-470-99112-7

Preface

   In spite of the growing concern with consumer participation, the consumer interest, and consumerism in the health field, no single volume is currently available which provides the manager, researcher, or student with a broad perspective of the multidimensional issues and problems in this vital area. The evolution of this volume began with the editors' attempts to understand and describe the changing nature of consumerism and consumer participation in different kinds of health organizations for teaching purposes. While some of the readings may be of greater interest to one group than another, we believe there is sufficient balance to provide relevance to each.

   There are extant today myriad positions and opinions regarding the present and potential role of the consumer in America, and this situation obtains just as clearly in the health system. It seems self-evident that the future role of the consumer is an expanding one, and it is, therefore, vital to confront and elaborate upon the issues in order to insure that realistic approaches and methodologies for consumer-provider exchanges are adopted.

The volume is organized into an introductory section and four basic divisions. The introduction provides a conceptual framework for analysis of the growth and development of the consumer movement in America and includes a review of analogous trends in the health sector. The first group of readings provides background for understanding consumer participation in terms of organizational behavior and the difficulties inherent in bureaucratic management. The readings in the second section focus on the health care context and the broad issues pertaining to the role of the consumer in this sector. The third section presents a group of articles which portrays the mix of problems surrounding implementation of consumer participation in the health field. The concluding section includes papers which elaborate upon various methodologies to measure the effectiveness of consumer participation.

New York, New York   J.M.M.
                                                            H.R.
                                                            S.M.L.

Contents

SECTION IV — **RESEARCH ON CONSUMERISM**

THE CONSUMER AND THE HEALTH CARE SYSTEM:
Social and Managerial Perspectives

Introduction

HARRY ROSEN
SAMUEL LEVEY
JONATHAN M. METSCH

The primary objective of this discussion is to review briefly the set of evolving relationships between consumers and providers of products and services with special attention to the health services industry. Historical developments in the growth of industrial and governmental bureaucracies will be traced and the emergence of parallel trends in the health sector considered. A central conclusion which arises from examination of this anthology is that while the individual has benefited considerably from large-scale organization and technology, a major role for him in the formulation of public policy has not materialized; nor is it likely to in the short run because of the interplay of forces in society. This is due in large measure to the gap between individual and institutional values, apparently a natural consequence of the assignment of influence and power in a modern industrial framework.

Such discrepancies in conceptualizations of the needs of society are further exacerbated by insufficient attention to the nurturing of a revitalized philosophy of the individual. Altered definitions of individuality should reflect the necessity of responding psychologically and morally to opportunities created by technological innovations and organizational change. In addition, the new individuality should be expressed through adaptive and proactive organizational and governmental systems which are constructed to grapple with a rapidly changing environment and technology.

In the United States, where consumers have experienced the significant benefits of a nation endowed with great natural resources, economic and social power has gravitated toward large organizations whose views of the public or consumer interest do not always coincide with those of the individual. It should be noted, however, that significant progress has occurred in the consumer sector during the past decade, and business leadership has altered its attitudes about many subjects, including preservation of the environment, minority rights, and consumerism. Similar transformations in ways of examining other major issues, including health care, have emerged, to suggest that a more balanced approach in the recognition of individual and group needs is beginning to evolve. In the future, consumer participation in health care will be directly linked to the sophistication of an educated consumer in the market place, as well as his breakthroughs and attainments in the policy-making processes of major social institutions.

History of Consumerism

While the consumer protection issue arose as a "new" discovery in the 1960's, its apparent novelty was quite deceptive. Nadel (29) notes that although consumer protection had been a dormant issue for some thirty years, it has been the subject of intermittent public concern since the earliest years of the Republic. Prior to the sixties, the two most extensive and controversial periods of consumer-related activity involved attempts by the federal government to promulgate pure food and drug standards.

A burgeoning concern with consumerism, the consumer interest, and revision of the perceived role of the consumer in society began its upward momentum on March 15, 1962. In the first comprehensive statement to Congress on the consumer by an American President, John F. Kennedy proclaimed a "declaration of rights" for all Americans. On January 3, 1964, President Lyndon B. Johnson signed an executive order establishing the President's Committee on Consumer Interests and the Consumer Advisory Council. The functions of the committee were broad-ranged with respect to advice on federal policies and programs as they interfaced with the consumer interest and consultation with government agencies on issues of broad economic policy which were of primary concern to consumers. Under Johnson's leadership, consumer education programs grew rapidly, especially under the auspices of the Office of Economic Opportunity. On October 15, 1965, he stated that,

> ... the time has come to bury forever the myth that furthering the interest of the consumer must be at the expense of the producer. There is, I am convinced, a common interest between Americans in their capacity as producers and in their capacity as consumers. This mutuality must be emphasized.

He also discussed the necessity for adequate information and the need for particular attention to low-income consumers and other special groups including the elderly, teenagers, and new family units.

Approximately one year later on March 21, 1966, President Johnson in a message to the Congress on Consumer Interests stated that, "The consumer's interest is the American interest." He reiterated that new and progressive programs would be required in order to protect the consumer's rights in the marketplace, and he recommended that Congress enact comprehensive measures to secure these rights, including legislation regarding truth-in-lending, fair packaging and labeling, child safety, etc. Again he emphasized the lack of buyer "know-how" among the poor and the need for vastly improved consumer information and education. He believed that, ultimately, the job of furthering the consumer cause must lie in the hands of consumers themselves.

It is of historical significance that the above statement was made barely three months prior to the commencement of Medicare hospital benefits. This legislation contained stricter provisions relating to standards of health care delivery than at any time in history and set in motion a pattern for external control of health care organizations. The bolstering of requirements relating to patient care was, in effect, a direct response to the increased awareness within Congress of a need to protect the consumer interest even within institutions that were predominantly of eleemosynary origin.

On February 16, 1967, President Johnson gave his third and final message to Congress on advancing consumer interests. New areas for consumer protection were outlined—including provision for accurate and clear information on the cost of credit, provision for greater scrutiny of medical devices and laboratories, and laws dealing with hazardous household products.

In a message from the President regarding protection of consumer interests on October 30, 1969, Richard M. Nixon stated that "Consumerism is a healthy development that is here to stay." He emphasized that this did not mean that *caveat emptor* had been replaced by an equally harsh *caveat venditor*. But he did note that consumerism in the seventies would be a period of "buyers' rights" and reemphasized the right of the individual to make an intelligent choice among products and services; the right to accurate information on which to make a free choice; the right to expect that his health and safety be taken into account by those who seek his patronage; and the right to register dissatisfaction and have complaints "heard and weighed." (39)

On February 24, 1971, in an executive order, President Nixon reaffirmed the "Buyers' Bill of Rights," and on January 25, 1973, the Office of Consumer Affairs, which had been established in the Executive Office of the President, was transferred to the Department of Health, Education, and Welfare. Widespread interest in consumers as other than a formless constituency may thus be regarded as a phenomenon which began its momentum in the sixties.

Theory of the Consumer

Extensive literature exists regarding social, political, and economic issues surrounding the consumer in America. Industrial research groups have usually studied the consumer with particular emphasis on the introduction of new products and the effects of advertising campaigns on the habits of purchasers. The primary objective of these works has been to understand consumer behavior in order to improve marketing practices. Other studies have considered the impact of regulation, legal protection for the consumer, and the politics of consumer protection. Some of the major issues considered in such works are the rationality of consumer behavior, the utility of fulltime publicly employed consumer specialists, and the role of communications and media in controlling the intensity of consumer interest. (38) But a comprehensive theory of consumer behavior, which includes how he influences public policy, remains an elusive goal.

The actual role of the consumer in historical perspective has not corresponded with theoretical conceptualizations of his role. The traditional theory of consumer sovereignty, still prevalent in many quarters, holds that the principal obligation of the consumer is to lead the economy into the production of desired goods and services through selective purchasing. (25) Troelstrup (37) has pointed out that the theory of individual consumer sovereignty or consumer freedom of choice is outmoded:

> Playing umpire is not a new role for the consumer. In theory, consumer sovereignty—consumer freedom of choice—is indeed the keystone of our economic system. It is from this assumption that the free competition, private enterprise system derives social justification for its division of rewards for effort. Withdraw consumer sovereignty from this concept, and free competition resembles a

kind of economic jungle warfare. We are now fairly far along in the process of withdrawing true consumer sovereignty from the marketplace. The question is: Can we bring back into the marketplace a rational umpire—the consumer?

The evolution of many prominent sectors of society has been contradictory to the theory of consumer sovereignty in the view of a number of authors. Beard (5) argued provocatively that specifications of the United States Constitution were drawn to endorse the legal position of commercial, manufacturing, and land-holding interests. C. Wright Mills observed later that there exist relatively small numbers of individuals in each major sector who control the allocation and distribution of resources and, therefore, the general direction of society's major institutions. These views suggest that the existing power loci of society are in some ways inimical to the hypothetical consumer interest. (28)

Along a parallel vein, various periods in American history have also been described as being under the influence of institutionally-dominated special interests. The Federalist period of the early nineteenth century was considerably affected by central banking issues, and the Civil War has been described as a collision of commercial with agrarian interests. In the latter part of the nineteenth century, the rapid expansion and merger of industrial and banking enterprises into huge holding companies and trusts was pervasive, although some were subsequently broken up by anti-trust legislation. (33)

Thus, in spite of rhetoric which described the inherent power of the individual to control his environment, he could not generally effect a critical impact on social and public policy because of the prevailing distribution of power and the relationships between institutions and the public. The vast institutions of government and industry have been described as having, in effect, constructed an "every-man-for-himself" logic where individual consumer responses only were acceptable. (32) This issue leads to the question of whether—and in what specific areas—the consumer, acting alone, can assume a vital role in the restructuring of institutions and in the reordering of social priorities. The critical issue is thus whether "consumer sovereignty" requires the combined action of consumer organizations in order to sustain an effective countervailing force.

The Consumer and Corporate Power

Ralph Nader holds that modern corporate institutions are the most enduring generic managers of power in society. He points out that the inherently acquisitive nature of the corporation allows wide latitude and ready justification in the application of its multiple permutations of power. He argues that much of what passes as governmental power is derived from corporate power whose "advocacy or sufferance defines much of the direction and deployment of government activity." (36) Accountability of the modern corporation, or governmental bureaucracies assigned to regulate them, becomes an important consideration in the examination of the extent to which the consumer's role has been limited or eroded, and the directions it should assume.

To a significant degree, the consumer's power in the marketplace has been restricted by the wide variety of similar, if not identical, products and services that confront and confound him and by his lack of access to objective sources of information in order to improve his decision-making capabilities. As Galbraith (16) and Heilbroner (20) have noted, the major institutions of society operate with an identical, basic technology. Irrespective of the nature of the industry, the similarity of goods and services produced by different organizations is evident, even without overt collusion. In addition, modern marketing has been guilty of nefarious practices, and it is only recently that major inroads against such practices have been made through federal legislation. Management of ordinary household affairs is, therefore, increasingly arduous. (30) Advertising, oligopoly power, and shared technology have combined to accelerate the erosion of the traditional concept of consumer sovereignty.

An important requisite to bolster the consumer's capabilities for acting rationally in the marketplace, whether the product is health services or electronic gadgetry, is to improve his decision-making skills. Decision-making is a central and ubiquitous activity of all human beings. It is a deliberative process related to problem-solving and creativity. Frequently, the policies of industry have implied absence or limitation of such problem-solving abilities and skills and hence the lack of power of the average consumer. The position that has been assumed is that, because the consumer does not have ready access to information, he will usually rely upon his personal judgment, intuition, and rules-of-thumb for the majority of his decisions. In many instances, the consumer will actually make unintelligent choices because of incomplete, erroneous, or misrepresented information. To enable the consumer to select among alternatives, the evolution of educational systems, aimed specifically at improvement of his decision-making capacity, is mandatory. But it should be recognized that education of the public is an enormously costly and complicated undertaking that can only be realized through many years of major investment, for which the public will ultimately have to pay.

An anachronistic situation therefore exists. In a technocratic era in which the corporation has amassed vast assets, power, and influence, the philosophies of consumer sovereignty and *caveat emptor*, which espouse total personal responsibility on the part of consumers for their actions, are misguided. The average consumer often finds himself intimidated by a massive system of institutions and bureaucracies and does not comprehend the extent to which he is manipulated by existing social control systems, nor what actions he could take about his multiple dilemmas. A fundamental question which emerges from the above discussion is the extent to which the individual as consumer and citizen requires governmental intervention to protect him from the vagaries of institutions. Perhaps more importantly, how does government develop the mechanisms which reinforce impartiality and maintain uncooptable bureaucratic structures?

The Consumer and Regulation

The role of government as the desired regulator of the consumer interest is a controversial issue. How governmental regulatory bureaucracies impinge upon consumer choices and freedom in an increasingly "turbulent" environment requires study and debate. Their efficiency and effectiveness in regulation and in protection of consumer interests should also be questioned. In debating these issues the further question of balance between the federal and state bureaucracies within similar program jurisdictions arises. Peterson (31) has noted that regulations often result in the opposite of their intentions. Her position is that consumerism is too frequently a matter of right ends and wrong means. Nader has also observed that most regulatory agencies have made accommodations and philosophical coalitions with the industries they are supposed to regulate and that this has occurred at the expense of all consumers. The comments of Galbraith are also significant in this context. (16) To the extent that industries and their respective regulatory agencies share an identical technology, an independent consumer voice is precluded.

Questions regarding the processes of regulation are therefore vital. Peterson makes an important distinction between interventionistic regulation, which is detrimental to competition and growth, and neutral or benign regulation, which is either helpful to competition and growth or at least not harmful to it. She supports the role of consumerists such as the Nader group and the Consumer's Union in educating the individual but cautions them to be skeptical of the advantage of shifting from consumer sovereignty to governmental sovereignty. Governmental sovereignty, she believes, is eventually transmuted into producer sovereignty. The arguments illuminate the need for objectivity in an area that has been highly-charged and frequently subject to intense and often distorted rhetoric.

It has been argued that the institutions of industry and of government have acted upon their own interpretation of the concepts of consumer sovereignty and public interest. Although the belief has been pervasive that the individual can control his own destiny, large institutions have consistently shaped events and curtailed consumer alternatives. It has been indicated that consumers, in striving to maintain the individualist ethic, ultimately weaken self-determination because of an inability to realize and sustain a threshold of countervailing forces to established institutions. (17) In the consumer's view, there is an ongoing power struggle between the institutions of society with the consumer frequently emerging as a pawn in the process. Whether or not this situation will alter drastically in the future will depend largely upon the impact of the consumer movement.

Policy formulation which protects the public has been fought within Congress on an interminable basis. Much of the consumer legislation of the recent past took many years to accomplish when an objective was thought to be absolutely necessary. If one considers that a principal aim of regulation is to balance a variety of forces, including competing considerations of public policy, the difficulties of insuring even-handedness are clear. As has been previously intimated, policy formulation in the consumer area is also hampered by difficulties in evaluating the impact of regulation on the quality of life of consumers.

A critical question, which parallels that of the need for regulatory advocacy, is whether the consumer can develop the kind of broad-based countervailing political lobby that industry has held for many years. This will, no doubt, eventually become a long-term objective because of the time and resources that must be committed to learning the facts,to obtaining votes, to campaigning, and to mastering other nuances of the political process.

Lessons From the Labor Movement

Insight into the nature of the balance of power in the area of consumer rights can be gained from a brief recounting of the American labor movement. Early labor leaders also had to contend with a powerful set of institutions, as well as with a popular conception which held that individual action was the only appropriate course. Labor and living conditions for the common man at the turn of the twentieth century frequently bordered on the sub-human. Yet early organizing efforts achieved meager success among workers, and open hostility toward organizers was not infrequent. Workers were often convinced,that there was something inherently wrong with organizing for higher wages. (26) Corporations were treated by the courts and the public as if they were a single person, making price and wage decisions in accordance with conditions of the market. This view also reconciled corporate growth with an ingrained individualist ethic, while the personal alienation and physical discomforts created by the industrialization process were usually disregarded. (4)

Organization and collective action were vital to the success of the labor movement. Corporations had to be recognized as aggregations of resources and power. It became clear that individual actions for higher wages or improved working conditions were futile in view of the relative bargaining power of the individual as opposed to the large corporation. The principle of organizing groups to deal with a common problem ultimately proved successful. But it was a slow process, and almost fifty years were required for union-management relations to reach the relative equilibrium currently in existence. (8)

Today, consumer exploitation has replaced labor exploitation. The average consumer remains relatively unprepared to exercise objective judgment in an exceedingly complex, post-industrial society. (37) Analysis of the potential role of the consumer is further complicated by the fact that at any point in time an individual or a family unit has conflicting special interests as a result of multiple memberships in organizations, each of which has its unique set of objectives which may be in conflict with each other. Furthermore, each organization possesses a special set of consumer policies. These conditions have led to apparent inconsistencies in consumer behavior.

In spite of this problem, lessons of the labor movement are clear. Corporations, and government agencies which relate to them, are aggregates, not individuals. If the consumer movement is to be successful, it must be organized on a broad scale. It must develop sources of information to cope with the scale of technology inherent in modern industrial complexes. And finally it must also function as an independent force in the political arena to insure that government activities are in fact responsive to consumer needs and in balance with corporate viability requirements.

The Consumer and the Health Care System

Technologic advances in medicine in recent years have generated sharp increases in personal expectations for medical care and demands for health care services. As a result, the balance of power between consumers and providers of health care is also shifting. In the following pages a synopsis of views and events relating to this transformation will be presented.

McNerney (27) has noted that criticism and hostility toward institutions is wide-ranging and pervasive and that this climate has not left the health system unscathed. Much of the criticism of health institutions goes to the heart of the inadequacies in the organization and delivery of health care and to the high costs of medical care. Silver (35), in a parallel vein, emphasizes that widespread dissatisfaction with professional decision-making in the health system is part of the movement toward castigation and denigration of all social institutions. He notes the recent emergence of consumer demands for change and emphasizes that the political consequences of shifts in the decision-making processes have been relatively understudied. It is clear that alterations in the decision-making processes reflect directly upon, and are ultimately connected to changes within the power structure of the health services industry. (14)

According to Drucker, managing for *performance* is the single area in which the service institution does differ significantly from a business. (13) The health industry as a network of provider-service institutions differs in its purposes, values, and objectives from the industrial sector. Therefore, measurement of performance and results, normally a fairly uncomplicated series of tasks in most industries, is more complex due to the nature of the functions performed. Quantification of performance and thorough understanding of the components of quality in medical care have been relatively elusive objectives, due to the protean nature of the concept of "health" and the imprecision of existing outcome measures. Since the concept of performance is ambiguous, operational definitions vary according to the perspective of the definer. The practice of medicine is characterized by the extensive use of sophisticated technology; so process measures of health care, which stress the use of appropriate techniques and procedures, have usually prevailed. Current evaluative models generally exclude data regarding the extent of patient participation in therapeutic decisions or the degree to which care is found acceptable, because consumer assessments are frequently regarded as questionable by professionals.

Another part of the difficulty in obtaining adequate criteria for performance evaluation in the health services has been the reluctance of the physician to engage in self-criticism. This is changing as a result of the advent of public programs, such as Medicare and Medicaid, with their built-in utilization review mechanisms and the more recent Professional Standards Review Organizations legislation. The relative paucity of objective information regarding performance of health professionals and institutions is thus the critical factor which has impeded coherent, organized consumer responses.

The importance of the role of the physician in health institutions has been emphasized by Freidson. (15) He notes that the physician possesses both a legal monopoly and license to perform and prescribe therapies and holds considerable power over the division of labor and the establishment of priorities. Confronted by a fragmented network of provider institutions and a complex technology and jargon, it is therefore not surprising that the consumer has protested the shortcomings of institutions with which he must interact. Freidson, in considering the impact of professionalism in health care, notes that the opinions of laymen in the health area are usually subordinated to the opinions of professionals. The organization of health services revolves around professional authority, with the basic structure determined by the dominance of a single profession over a variety of other, subordinate occupations. He argues further that professional dominance is the analytical key to the present inadequacy of health services. While he restricts his discussion almost entirely to the field of health, his intent is to suggest that there are serious flaws in the nature of professionalism in general—flaws which can be shown to be responsible for difficulties in other services to consumers.

Another perspective of the balance of power equation in health care has been described by Kelman (22). He notes that "corporatization" of the health sector commenced with the formulation of medical research and teaching centers whose members moved to control professional societies and methods of reimbursement. From his perspective, the hospital, and particularly the affiliated teaching hospital, lies at the epicenter of institutional influence in the health system, due largely to the reliance by the medical profession on sophisticated costly technology.

Alford (1) assumes a slightly different position. He describes the historical power balance in the health sector as the result of interplays between three groups. Biomedical researchers, physicians in private or group practice, and salaried physicians are categorized as "professional monopolists." These individuals are vitally concerned with developing and strenthening those institutional mechanisms which reinforce professional control of projects and programs. Medical school officials, insurance companies, and hospital administrators, whom he categorizes as "corporate rationalizers," have primarily been concerned with subordinating professionals to "coordinated" delivery systems. Heterogeneous "community populations" attempt to make health professionals responsive to their concerns. The "professional monopolists" and the "corporate rationalizers" accuse each other of creating inadequacies in the health care system. Each group attempts to promote reforms which would increase control over resources or to legitimize

control over medical practice. Alford states that "community populations" have not acted independently, and in their support of either
"professional monopolists" or "corporate rationalizers" have accomplished a disservice to their own ends. He suggests that much of the
disorganization and inefficiency in health care is the result of efforts of
"professional monopolists" to protect their turf in research, teaching,
and care, in contrast to parallel efforts of "corporate rationalizers" to
extend their control over the organization of services.

But in spite of the enormous power and influence of professional
forces in the health sector, their unquestioned legitimacy is wavering.
Sheps (34) notes that a major effect of implementation of public programs has been to focus attention on gaps in services. He also argues that
public programs seem to be altering the nature of responsibility for
planning in health. Challenges to traditional decision-making processes
in the health sector thus are present to a degree which did not exist
before.

Alterations in decision-making described by Sheps are the result of
a number of factors including rapid aggregate growth in the health
sector, multiple sources of financing, and a host of federally funded
special programs and demonstration projects. Some of these programs
have created what Grodzins terms "cracks in the system," or entry points
for consumer participation in the decision-making process. (19) But,
while such "cracks" might become opportunities for further inputs on
the part of the consumer, they do not necessarily result in programmatic
changes. Every constituency represents a potential for consumer participation and a challenge to institutional priorities, but consumer organization in health care does not exist in profusion; and each constituency, catchment area, or neighborhood is usually oriented to its own
service needs. The result of these diversified interests is that when
changes occur, they are most likely to be incremental and narrowly
program specific.

At the community level, leaders, who are often incorrectly assumed
to speak for the consumer, have been more concerned with costs, cost-
effectiveness, and allocation of resources in the hospital arena rather
than with the total community health system. Elling believes, however,
that community spokesmen will expand their interests to other organizations, and to manpower and quality of care issues. (14) The extent to
which eventual national health legislation encompasses consumer-
related goals will determine the future power balance for many decades
to come.

Recent attempts have been made by consumers to organize and
publicize their views about requirements for change in the health care
system. Examples of organizations involved in such actions are the

Citizens Board of Inquiry Into Health Service for Americans and the Health Policy Advisory Center. The Citizens Board of Inquiry was established jointly by the Universities of North Carolina and California "to study America's health services from the point of view of the consumer not from the viewpoint of the professional." (9) A report of the Board dramatically describes obstacles which confront the consumer in his search for health care services. Among the issues discussed are insensitivity of many practitioners to patients' personal needs and the impact of increasing cost of care on families. The report also emphasizes that health professionals have benefited from increasing subsidies but have failed to demonstrate desirable responsibility, accountability, or responsiveness. A series of recommendations are called for, including public accountability for health professionals; a consumer role in establishing delivery system goals; mechanisms to enhance consumer skills; and attainment of resources to facilitate consumer participation in the decision-making process.

Health-PAC is a health consumer advocacy organization which, through publications, workshops, a speaker program, and technical assistance, seeks to promote radical change in the health care system. It is devoted to the organization of health workers and patients in a collective effort to reform the health system. Organizers have repeatedly excoriated medical schools, major teaching hospitals, and third parties for their insensitivity to consumers. They are highly critical of health providers, many of whom are regarded as operating for profit and aggrandizement while ignoring the rights and needs of patients.

A number of segments in the health care industry have responded positively to demands for a greater consumer role in formulating goals and objectives and in evaluating programs. The American Hospital Association's "Statement on Consumer Representation in Governance of Health Care Institutions" (2) recognizes the right of users of service to become involved in policy-making even if credentials traditionally assumed necessary for this role are lacking. The 1972 "Patient's Bill of Rights" of the American Hospital Association proposes that patient relationships with health care institutions are two-way affairs and affirms the consumer's right to participate in decision-making relative to treatment. (3) This statement also identifies patient rights, in relation to the teaching and research objectives of the institution. Also, consumer participation in hospital accreditation has been made possible. Consumer organizations "can learn when a hospital's biannual accreditation survey is scheduled and can be present at an information interview to state complaints as they relate to the commission's standards." (21)

Various levels of government are also facilitating consumer-provider interaction through the provision of information guides and through mandating a consumer role in policy-making. An example of the former is the "Shopper's Guide to Health Insurance" prepared by the Pennsylvania Department of Insurance. This publication provides facts regarding limits in coverage and compares premiums for all major health insurance packages. (12) The Department has also issued a patients' guide to evaluating the need for surgery. Another example of government activity is a requirement of the New York City Department of Health that voluntary hospitals who receive special ambulatory care program funds consult with community advisory boards. (6) At the regional and local levels, federal legislation specifies that Health Systems Agency boards be comprised of a majority of consumer members and that they function on the working committees of the agencies. (39) The P.S.R.O. legislation requires public representation on each State's Professional Standards Review Council, and physicians must be recommended by consumer groups in order to serve on the National Standards Review Council. (40) The Health Maintenance Organization Act of 1973 mandates consumer participation in H.M.O. planning and policy-making and requires grievance procedures for enrollees and documentation of consumer support for the H.M.O. prior to award of federal funds. (42)

CONCLUSION

This introduction has recognized the ambiguities in some conceptions of the doctrines of consumer sovereignty and *caveat emptor* as the foundation for achieving a balance of power between consumers and producers. Improved understanding of the consumer, his role in society, and a well-informed, organized consumer public is more crucial than ever as the philosophy underlying *caveat venditor* expands. Although various mechanisms exist to assist the consumer, and spokesmen are more prevalent than at any previous time, the need for greater decision-making capability and responsibility on the part of the consumer in purchasing goods and services and in his voting behavior must be recognized.

In the short run, the consumer of health care cannot expect major breakthroughs in the reorganization of health services, nor can he expect his role to be considerably enhanced. The historical inability of government at the federal, state, and local levels to develop planning networks is a principal barrier. Another problem is the fact that the majority of promises which are made by legislators result in rising expectations without a proportionate increase in efficiency and effectiveness. The dilemma which arises is obvious. To relieve the pressures on government, while deflecting them to the community level, is unworkable. What is necessary is continuing pressure on politicians, particularly at the federal and state levels, to insure that the consumer interest is protected. The form and substance underlying such pressure is crucial to the success of consumer-oriented enterprises. In order to attain a higher order of responsiveness and accountability, several ingredients are required. First, health planning, evaluation, and information systems must be upgraded. Second, health professionals must be held individually accountable for their actions to a greater degree than before through a broadening of their political and value orientations. Finally, more universities must include institutes which are focused not only on health services research, but also on public policy and its interface with human and health services.

REFERENCES

1. Alford, Robert R. "The Political Economy of Health Care: Dynamics Without Change." *Politics and Society*, (Winter, 1972): 127-164.
2. American Hospital Association, "Statement on Consumer Representation in Governance of Health Care Institutions," *Hospitals, JAHA*, 47 (Feb. 16, 1973).
3. American Hospital Association, "Statement on a Patient's Bill of Rights," *Hospitals, JAHA*, 47 (Feb. 16, 1973)
4. Arnold, Thurman *The Folklore of Capitalism* (1937) Oxford University Press, New York.
5. Beard, Charles *An Economic Interpretation of the Constitution of the United States*, (1929) The MacMillan Company, New York.
6. Bellin, Lowell E., Florence Kavaler and Al Schwarz "Phase One of Consumer Participation in Policies of all Voluntary Hospitals in New York City." *American Journal of Public Health*, 61 (October 1972) 1370-1378.
7. Bennett, Peter D. and Kassarjian, Harold H. *Consumer Behavior*, (1972) Prentice-Hall, Englewood Cliffs, New Jersey.
8. Bloom, Gordon F. and Northrup, Herbert *Economics of Labor Relations* (1973) Richard D. Irwin Inc., Homewood, Illinois.
9. Citizens Board of Inquiry Into Health Services. *Heal Yourself* Chapel Hill, North Carolina.
10. Cohen, M.F. and Stigler, G.J. *Can Regulatory Agencies Protect Consumers?* (1971) American Enterprise Institute for Public Policy Research, Washington, D.C.
11. Connolly, W.E. *The Bias of Pluralism* (1969) Atherton Press, New York.
12. Denenberg, Herbert S. *A Shopper's Guide to Health Insurance* (1971) Insurance Department of the Commonwealth of Pennsylvania.
13. Drucker, Peter F. "On Managing the Public Service Institution," *The Public Interest* 29 (Fall 1973).

14. Elling, Ray H. "The Shifting Power Structure in Health" *Milbank Memorial Fund Quarterly* (January 1968).
15. Freidson, Eliot *Professional Dominance* (1970) Atherton Press, Inc., New York.
16. Galbraith, John K. *The New Industrial State* (1967) Houghton Mifflin Company, Boston.
17. Galbraith, John K. *The Affluent Society* (1958) Houghton Mifflin Company, Boston.
18. Graham, G.A. and Reining, H. Jr. *Regulatory Administration* (1943) John Wiley and Sons, Inc., New York.
19. Grodzins, Morton *The American System* (1969) Rand McNally, New York.
20. Heilbroner, Robert L. *The Limits of American Capitalism* (1966) Harper Torchbooks, The Academy Library, Harper and Row, Publishers, New York.
21. *Joint Commission on Accreditation of Hospitals*. Policy and Procedure on Information Interviews with Public Representatives During Facility Accreditation Survey. April 26, 1975.
22. Kelman, Sander "Towards a Political Economy of Medical Care," *Inquiry*, 8 (September 1971).
23. Kohlmeier, L.M. *The Regulators* (1969) Harper and Row, New York.
24. Leder, L.H. *Liberty and Authority* (1968) Quadrangel Press, Chicago.
25. Leftwich, Richard H. *The Price System and Resource Allocation* (1970) Dryden Press, Hinsdale, Illinois.
26. Manchester, William *The Glory and The Dream* (1974) Little, Brown and Company, Boston.
27. McNerney, Walter J. "Medicine Faces the Consumer Movement," *Prism* (September 1973).
28. Mills, C. Wright *The Power Elite* (1959) Oxford University Press, New York.
29. Nadel, Mark V. *The Politics of Consumer Protection* (1971) Bobbs-Merrill Company, Inc., New York.
30. Packard, Vance *The Hidden Persuaders* (1957) D. McKay Company, New York.
31. Peterson, M.B. *The Regulated Consumer* (1971) Nash Publishing Company, Los Angeles.
32. Reich, Charles A. *The Greening of America* (1970) Random House, New York.
33. Schlesinger, Arthur *New Viewpoints in American History* (1928) The MacMillan Company, New York.
34. Sheps, Cecil G. "The Influence of Consumer Sponsorship on Medical Services" in Irving K. Zola and John B. McKinlay (eds.), *Organizational Issues in the Delivery of Health Services* (1973) Prodist, New York.
35. Silver, George A. "Community Participation and Health Resource Allocation" *International Journal of Health Services*, 3 (Spring 1973).
36. Taylor, Jack L. and Troelstrup, Arch W. *The Consumer in American Society: Additional Dimensions* (1974) P. 5 McGraw-Hill Book Company, New York.

37. Troelstrup, Arch W. *The Consumer in American Society* (1974) p. 10 McGraw-Hill Book Company, New York.

38. Tucker, W.T. *Foundations for a Theory of Consumer Behavior* (1967) Holt, Rinehart, and Winston, New York.

39. U.S. Congress. PL 93-641, "National Health Planning and Resources Development Act of 1974"

40. U.S. Congress PL 92-603, "Social Security Amendments of 1972."

41. U.S. Congress, *House of Representatives*, Document No. 91-188, First Session.

42. U.S. Congress PL.93-222, "The Health Maintenance Organization Act of 1973."

THE ORGANIZATIONAL ENVIRONMENT

Consumer participation exists in an environment dominated by complex organizations. It is important to gain some insights into the strategies employed by institutions in coping with consumer demands.

Katz and Georgopoulos note that pressures from leftist reformers of the sixties have forced organizations to confront the question of democratic values, in addition to more traditional issues relating to organizational structure and function. They believe that organizational reform requires a rethinking of values as a guide for action.

Lindblom argues persuasively that policies of organizations evolve through a system of successive comparisons with existing situations. This incrementalist view of the process of adaptation is pragmatic and assumes the necessity of relative organizational stability. In order to maintain balance, a mix of organization members, who hold traditional and innovative viewpoints, seems to be appropriate.

Drucker examines the management of service organizations. He believes that the lack of agreement on performance standards prevents adoption of the styles of management practiced in the commercial sector.

Organizations in a
Changing World

DANIEL KATZ
BASIL S. GEORGOPOULOS

Our nation has been aptly characterized as an *organizational society* (Presthus, 1962). Most of our working hours are spent in one organizational context or another. If the dominant institution of the feudal period was the church, of the early period of nationalism the political state, the dominant structure of our time is the organization. Even among those in revolt the old union line still works: "Organize the guys."

But the organization forms today are under challenge and without creative modification may face difficulties in survival. On the one hand they are growing in size and complexity, with criss-crossing relationships with other systems and with increasing problems of coordination, integration, and adaptation. The traditional answer in organization structure is on the technical side, *more* computerized programs for feedback and coordination, *more* specialization of function, *more* centralization of control. Yet the social and psychological changes in the culture are increasingly at odds with the technological solution calling

Reprinted, with permission, from *The Journal of Applied Behavioral Sciences.*, Vol. 7, Number 3, 1971, pp. 343-370.

for more and more of the same. Technological efficiency far surpasses social efficiency in most cases, even though neither is a substitute for the other from the standpoint of organizational effectiveness; and the gap is widening so as to generate serious conflict within the system.

THE MAINTENANCE AND INTEGRATION OF THE SYSTEM

Before exploring this conflict and its implications in greater detail, let us examine briefly the structure and functioning of organizations as open social systems. We can distinguish among the subsystems which comprise the larger structure (Katz & Kahn, 1966). The production, or instrumental, subsystem is concerned with the basic type of work that gets done, with the "throughput"—the modification of inputs which result in products or services. Attached to the productive subsystem are the supportive services of procurement of supplies, material and resources, and the disposal of the outputs.

The maintenance, or social, subsystem is concerned not with the physical plant but with the social structure, so that the identity of the system in relation both to its basic objectives and the environment is preserved. People not only have to be attracted to the system and remain in it for some period of time but they have to function in roles which are essential to the mission of the organization. The maintenance subsystem is concerned with rewards and sanctions and with system norms and values that ensure the continuity of the role structure. In short, its function has to do with the psychological cement that holds the organizational structure together, with the integration of the individual into the system. The channeling of collective effort in reliable and predictable pathways is the basis of organizational structure.

The managerial subsystem cuts across all other subsystems as a mechanism of control, coordination, and decision making and as a mechanism for integrating the instrumental and maintenance functions of the organization. To meet environmental changes both with respect to inputs and receptivity for outputs and to handle system strains, the managerial subsystem develops adaptive structures of staff members as in the case of research, development, marketing, and planning operations.

Let us look at the maintenance function more closely, however, before considering the adaptation problem in the light of major societal changes. Over time it requires more than sheer police power and coercive sanctions. It depends upon some degree of integration or involvement of people in terms of their own needs. Values, norms, and roles tie people into the system at different psychological levels and in different ways (Parsons, 1960).

Values provide the deepest basis of commitment by their rational and moral statement of the goals of a group or system. To the extent that these values are accepted by individuals as their own beliefs, we speak of the internalization of group goals. The degree of internalization will vary among the members of any group, but it is important for all organizations to have some hard core of people dedicated to their mission both for accomplishment of many types of tasks and as models for others. Such value commitment can come about through self-selection into the system of those possessing beliefs congruent with its goals, through socialization in the general society or in the organization, and through participation in the rewards and decision making of the group. The internalization of group goals is facilitated by the perception of progress toward these objectives. Such progress is interpreted as an empirical validation of values.

Normative involvement refers to the acceptance of system requirements about specific forms of behavior. These requirements are seen as legitimate because rules are perceived as necessary and because in general the rules are equitable. A particular demand by a particular officer may be seen as unjust, but in general there is acceptance of the need for directives from those in positions of authority, provided that they have attained their positions properly and they stay within their areas of jurisdiction in the exercise of their authority. In complex organizations, such as universities, hospitals, and industrial firms, the rules of the game can be improved, but they are universalistic and do not permit particularistic favoritism or discrimination.

At the level of *role behavior* people make the system function because of their interdependence with others, the rewards for performing their roles, and the socio-emotional satisfactions from being part of a role-interdependent group. In carrying out their roles, organizational members at all times but in varying degrees are interdependent both functionally and psychologically. Not all role performance provides expressive gratifications, however, and hence other rewards such as monetary incentives and opportunities for individual achievement, as well as group accomplishment and socio-emotional satisfactions, can be linked to adequate behavior in the given role. In most large organizations extrinsic rewards of pay, good working conditions, and so on are relied on heavily.

It is apparent that these three levels of member involvement are not necessarily intrinsically related. The values of a particular organization may have little to do with many of the roles in the system, and the norms of legitimacy are not necessarily specific to organizational values. A research organization may furnish a nice fit among values, norms, and roles for its research workers but a poor fit for its supportive personnel. Few organizations, however, can rely on value commitment alone to hold their members, and hence they maximize other conditions and rewards to compete with other systems. The development of universalistic norms under the impact of bureaucratic organization forms has provided great mobility for people in an expanding economic society, and thus has contributed to its growth—at the expense of value commitment.

In a well-integrated system, however, there is some relationship among these levels so that they are mutually reinforcing. In an ideal hospital, even the attendant can be affected by the values of saving lives and improving health, can perceive the normative requirements as necessary and fair, and derive satisfaction from his role, particularly if he is made part of a therapy team. Values can contribute to the strength of the normative system in providing a broader framework of justifiable beliefs about the rightness of given norms. Thus norms can be seen not only as equitable rules but as embodiments of justice and of equality. The strength of maintenance forces lies in the many mechanisms for supporting the role structure and for some degree of mutual reinforcement.

ACT OF SOCIETAL CHANGES ON NATIONS

The problem of how to organize human effort most effectively in complex, specialized organizations within a rapidly changing sociocultural environment, while maintaining the integrity of the system, is of utmost significance and concern everywhere in our time. Its solution generally demands greater social-psychological sophistication, however, rather than a more sophisticated work technology (Georgopoulos, 1970). It requires social organization innovations and the testing of new forms and patterns of organization, or at least significantly modified organizational structures than those now in operation (Georgopoulos, 1969; Likert, 1967). It will not be achieved at acceptable levels simply by an even more perfect technology at our disposal. As profound changes continue to occur in society at rapid but uneven rates, organizational viability and effectiveness are in jeopardy unless the social efficiency of the system can more clearly match its technological efficiency in the vast majority of organizations, and unless the adaptability of organizations can be improved well beyond current levels.

Four major changes have occurred in our society which challenge both the production and social subsystems of organizations: (a) a break, at first gradual and now pronounced, with traditional authority and the growth of democratic ideology; (b) economic growth and affluence; (c) the resultant changes in needs and motive patterns; and (d) the accelerated rate of change. These changes are significant for organizations, since as open systems organizations are in continuing interaction with their environment both with respect to production inputs of material resources and social inputs from the culture and from the larger social structure.

Weakened Traditional Authority Forces

The break with the older pattern of authority has eroded some of the formerly dependable maintenance processes of organizations. Bureaucratic systems had long profited from the socialization practices of traditional society, in which values and legitimacy had a moral basis of an absolutist character. It was morally wrong to reject in word or deed the traditional teachings about American institutions. It was wrong to seek change other than through established channels. Not everyone, of course, lived up to the precepts, but deviance was easy to define and highly visible, and those who deviated generally felt guilty about their misconduct. If they did not, they were considered to be psychopaths. Organizations had the advantage of a degree of built-in conformity to their norms and in some cases to their values because of the general socialization in the society about agreed-on standards. This consensus, moreover, made nonconformity a matter of conscience. There was an all-or-none quality about virtue, honesty, and justice, and these values were not seen as relativistic or empirical generalizations. Member compliance with organizational norms and values no longer can be sustained on the basis of authority (Etzioni, 1964; Georgopoulos, 1966; Georgopoulos & Matejko, 1967).

The very growth of bureaucratic systems helped to demolish absolutist values of a moral character. As conscious attempts to organize collective enterprises, organizations were guided by rational objectives and empirical feedback. Pragmatism replaced tradition. Results and accomplishment were the criteria rather than internal moral principle. Furthermore, the normative system shifted, as Weber (1947) noted, from traditional authority to rational authority. Rules and laws were the instruments of men to achieve their purposes and lacked any transcendental quality. They could be changed at will as situations and needs changed or they become ineffective. Having undercut the traditional basis of authority, the bureaucratic system can no longer rely upon the older moral commitment to its directives.

The growth of organizations affected the larger society and its socialization practices and in turn was affected by it. The training of children in a rational and democratic framework further increased a nontraditional orientation to values and norms.

The decline of traditional authority has been accompanied by the growth of the Democratic Ethic and democratic practices. The source of power has been shifting from the heads of hierarchies and from oligarchies to the larger electorate. This process can be observed in the political system where restrictions have been removed on suffrage. Nonproperty owners, women, and now blacks are eligible to vote. Indirect mechanisms of control from above are changing as in the political conventions of major parties. Democratic ideas of governance have extended into other institutions as well.

Growth and performance

The tremendous technological advances which have increased the productivity of the nation need no documentation. We are already using the phrase "postindustrial society" to characterize our era. This development raises questions about the basic functions of colleges and universities. Havighurst (1967) has pointed out that in the past, two functions have been dominant: the *opportunity function* and the *production function*. Education was a means of social mobility, the opportunity function. On the production side, education provided the training for professional, technical, and industrial roles in the society. Today, however, when we are over the economic hump, these two functions are less important and a third function comes to the fore: the *consumption function*. "Education as a consumption good is something people want to enjoy, rather than to use as a means of greater economic production" (Havighurst, 1967, p. 516). This means not only greater attention to the arts but also greater concern with education as it relates to living here and now.

One reason why the demands of black students are often easier to deal with in spite of the rhetoric is that they are directed in good part to the opportunity and production functions. These are understandable issues in our established ways of operating. Demands on the consumption side present new problems. For the blacks, however, there is sometimes the complexity of attempting to achieve all three objectives at the same time.

The case of educational institutions, moreover, is not unique. The interests and expectations of consumers of goods and services no longer remain disregarded either by industry or government. Outside pressures and demands are increasingly responded to with greater attention by most organizations, however inadequately or belatedly. In the health care field, for example, hospitals slowly are becoming more responsive to the health care expectations of an increasingly better educated and more demanding clientele who now see comprehensive health care as a right. At the same time, as the costs of care continue to rise at staggering rates, the quest for quality care is accomplished by demands for public controls, higher organizational efficiency, and even reorganization of the entire health system (Bugbee, 1969; McNerney, 1969; Sibery, 1969; TIME, 1969; U.S. News and World Report, 1969). Hospitals are being pressured from all directions to innovate and experiment with new patterns of internal social organization and more effective forms of operation in the areas of administration, staffing, organizational rewards for members, community relations, and the utilization of both new health knowledge and new social-psychological knowledge (Georgopoulos, 1964, 1969). As a consequence, they are being forced to be not only more community-oriented but also more sensitive to the interests and contributions of their various groups of members at all levels (Georgopoulos & Matejko, 1967). More generally, partly as a result of affluence and economic growth, organizations in all areas are becoming more open systems and less immune to social forces in their environment.

Resultant Changes in Motive Patterns

Economic affluence and the decline in traditional authority are related to a shift in motive patterns in our society. Maslow (1943) developed the notion years ago of a hierarchy of motives ranging from biological needs, through security, love, and belongingness, to ego needs of self-esteem, self-development, and self-actualization. His thesis was that the motives at the bottom of the hierarchy were imperative in their demands and made the higher level motives relatively ineffectual. Once these lower level needs are assured satisfaction, however, the higher level needs take over and become all-important.

Maslow's thesis has abundant support among the young people in our educational system. They are less concerned with traditional economic careers than was once the case. A recent study reported only 14 per cent of the graduates of a leading university planning business careers, compared with 39 per cent five years earlier and 70 per cent in 1928 (Marrow, Bowers, & Seashore, 1967). Engineering schools similarly are experiencing falling enrollments.

Our society has been called, with considerable justification, the *achieving society* (McClelland, 1961). The content analysis of children's readers by de Charms and Moeller (1962) shows that a great rise in achievement themes occurred in the last part of the 19th century, but a great decline in this emphasis has occurred in recent decades.

The decline in the older motive patterns has one direct consequence for all organizations. Extrinsic rewards such as pay, job security, fringe benefits, and conditions of work are no longer so attractive. Younger people are demanding intrinsic job satisfactions as well. They are less likely to accept the notion of deferring gratifications in the interests of some distant career.

In most organizations today the dominant motives of members are the higher-order ego and social motives—particularly those for personal gratification, independence, self-expression, power, and self-actualization (Argyris, 1964; Blake & Mouton, 1968; Georgopoulos, 1970; Georgopoulos & Matejko, 1967; Herzberg, 1968; Likert, 1967; Marrow, Bowers, & Seashore, 1967; McGregor, 1960; Schein, 1965). Increasingly, expressive needs and the pursuit of immediate and intrinsic rewards are outstripping economic achievement motives in importance, both in the work situation and outside. Correspondingly, the dominant incentives and rewards required for member compliance, role performance, and organizational effectiveness are social and psychological rather than economic (Blake & Mouton, 1968; Etzioni, 1964; Georgopoulos, 1970; Georgopoulos & Matejko, 1967; Herzberg, 1968; Likert, 1967; Marrow, Bowers, & Seashore, 1967; McGregor, 1960). Even at the rank-and-file level, where economic motives are especially strong, there is now more concern on the part of unions for other than bread-and-butter issues, and contract negotiations often stall on matters of policy, control, and work rules rather than money. As a result of these shifts, there is pressure for a place in the decision-making structure of the system from all groups and members in organizations, and there is a growing need for meaningful participation in the affairs of the organization by all concerned at all levels.

The forms which newly aroused ego motives take can vary, but at present there are a number of patterns familiar to all of us. First there is the emphasis upon self-determination or self-expression, or "doing one's thing." Second is the demand for self-development and self-actualization, making the most of one's own talents and abilities. Third is the unleashing of power drives. The hippies represent the first emphasis of self-expression, some of the leftist leaders the emphasis upon power. Fourth is the outcome of the other three, a blanket rejection of established values—a revolutionary attack upon the existing system as exploitative and repressive of the needs of individuals.

With the need for self-expression goes the ideology of the importance of spontaneity; of the wholeness of human experience; the reliance upon emotions; and the attack upon the fragmentation, the depersonalization, and the restrictions of the present social forms. It contributes to the anti-intellectualism of the student movement and is reminiscent of the romanticism of an older period in which Wordsworth spoke of the intellect as that false secondary power which multiplies delusions. Rationality is regarded as rationalization.

Accelerated Rate of Change

Not only are we witnessing significant shifts in the economic and value patterns of society but they are happening at a very fast rate. Probably there has always been some conflict between the older and younger generations, but in the past there has been more time to socialize children into older patterns and the patterns were of longer duration, thus preventing serious lags and social dislocation. History is becoming less relevant for predicting change. It is difficult to know what the generation now entering high school will be like when they enter college.

All organizations face a period of trouble and turmoil because of these changes, which affect all three levels of integration in social systems. Some of the basic values of the social system are under fire, such as representative democracy of the traditional, complex type, the belief in private property, conventional morality, the importance of work and of economic achievement, the good life as the conventional enjoyment of the products of mass culture. The Protestant Ethic (Weber, 1958) is no longer pervasive and paramount in our society.

The norms legitimized by societal values of orderly procedures and of conformity to existing rules until they are changed by socially sanctioned procedures are also brought into question. The rebels emphasize not law and order but justice, and justice as they happen to see it. It is interesting that President Nixon, the spokesman for the Establishment, modified his plea for law and order by stressing law, order, and justice. The challenge to the norms of any system is especially serious, since it is genuinely revolutionary or anarchistic in implication, whether voiced by official revolutionaries or reformers. If the legitimate channels for change are abandoned and the resort is to direct action, then people are going outside the system. If enough do, the system collapses.

At the level of role integration there is also real difficulty. As has already been noted, extrinsic rewards have lost some of their importance in our affluent society. Moreover, the usual set of roles in an organization segmentalize individuals, and our ever-advancing technology adds to the problem. A role is only partially inclusive of personality at most levels of the organization. This fractionation runs counter to the needs for wholeness and for self-expression. Inreasing specialization everywhere exacerbates the problem (Etzioni, 1964; Georgopoulos, 1966; Georgopoulos, 1970; Georgopoulos & Mann, 1962; Likert, 1967; J.D. Thompson, 1967; V. Thompson, 1961). It engenders coordination and integration difficulties for organizations and their members because it results in greater organizational complexity and more intensive inter-dependence among unlike participants who must relate to one another and to the system and whose efforts must be collectively regulated (Georgopoulos, 1966; Georgopoulos & Mann, 1962; Morton, 1964; V. Thompson, 1961; Wieland, 1965). Role specialization is the main social invention available with which man can cope with the problems of the explosion of knowledge in our times, for specialization makes possible both the utilization of available knowledge and the development of new knowledge. But, at the same time, specialization leads to fractionation and diversity that make the integration of members into the system all the more difficult to attain.

In linking the changed patterns of many of the younger generation to societal changes, we want to emphasize that it is an error to simplify the problem as a younger-older generation conflict. It is broader and deeper than that, and many of the developing trends predate the present student generation. In fact, the revolt started with people now in their sixties, if not earlier. We were the ones to attack the inequities of bureaucratic society, the ones to raise children in democratic practices and to think for themselves. The older generations furnished the ideol-ogy of the present student movements. Try to find any ideology in these movements which is not a bastardized version of old revolutionary and romantic doctrines. We started the rebellion and now we are astonished to find that we are the "establishment."

This is one reason why organizations have been so vulnerable to attack. Older citizens do not rally to their support because they feel that the rebels are in good part right. Or else why should we so often hear it stated, 'We agree with your objectives but we don't like your tactics?" Nathan Glazer (1969) has shown, however, that this vague sentiment is based upon a failure to come to grips with the significant issues.

THE PROBLEM OF ADAPTATION

The dynamic nature of our society makes imperative greater attention to processes of adaptation. In the past, industrial organizations, because of their dependence upon a market, have developed adaptive subsystems of planning, research, and development. The major emphasis has been, however, upon production inputs, upon product development, upon finding new markets and exploiting old ones, upon technology in im-proving their productive system. Only minor attention has been placed upon social inputs or upon restructuring the organization to meet the psychological needs of members. Technological innovation without social innovation has been the rule, and exclusive concern with technical and economic efficiency has undermined the social and psychological efficiency of the system to the detriment of organizational effectiveness and adaptability.

Traditionally, organizations have shown much more concern for the technology of work than for their social inputs and human assets. They have been more concerned with providing a safe and attractive physical work environment than with creating and maintaining an equally attractive social and psychological work climate for the members. With the emphasis for technical and economic efficiency, they have paid much more attention to recruiting and selecting members with the "proper" training and aptitude for filling inflexibly defined jobs than to problems of member attitudes, needs, and values. The approach has been to fit the man to the job rather than the other way around, and organizational role redefinition has been largely disregarded as a problem-solving mechanism. Organizational restructuring to improve the adaptability of the system has been abhorred and resisted. Most organizations have avoided social innovation and renovation and have sought technological innovation as the answer to all their problems. Correspondingly, in relating to their members, they have been concerned with authority-based, superior-subordinate relations more than with social relations, relying more on economic incentives and rewards and less on social-psychological motivation and compensation.

Because of the changes in society just discussed, however, the situation is now changing within organizations as well. The conditions for effective role performance, job satisfaction, member integration into the system, and organizational effectiveness and adaptability demand different organization-member relations than in the past. For organizations to survive and perform their functions effectively in the future, some sizable proportion of their resources wil have to be committed to enlarging their adaptive subsystems to deal more adequately with external relations and new social inputs. Social effectiveness will have to be added to productive efficiency as an important objective.

Better adaptive subsystems are now needed not only in industrial organizations but in all complex organizations, including educational and health institutions. The case of hospitals is instructive. Continuous progress in medicine, nursing, and allied health professions and occupations, advances in medical technology, the professionalization of hospital administration, and the explosion of knowledge witnessed inside and outside the health field have made a strong impact upon the traditional social organization of the hospital system. The result is a gradual redefinition of the institutional role of the hospital as the health center in the total framework of health-related institutions. Such redefinition, however, is being forced by public expectations and demands from without and pressures from non-medical members on the prevailing power structure, rather than from planned social innovation within the system (Georgopoulos, 1969; Georgopoulos, 1970; Georgopoulos & Matejko, 1967). Redefinition is taking place and must be accomplished along with proper internal organizational restructuring, however, in the context of current health trends and societal health conceptions—for example, the Medicare program, the recent development of regional medical programs, the growing emphasis on comprehensive health planning, the promulgated national goal of adequate health care for all, and the widespread concern for improvements in care coverage, quality, and cost.

These recent changes in the health field, along with the major changes in society discussed earlier, have strong and concrete implications for the kind of organizational restructuring that is feasible and appropriate for the hospital as a complex, sociotechnical, problem-solving system. Today's hospital is still ruled by three dominant decision-making centers—trustees, physicians, and administrators (Georgopoulos & Mann, 1962; Georgopoulos & Matejko, 1967). The above trends argue, however, for better recognition of the contributions of nurses and nonmedical groups and for a broader base of decision making. They argue for an interaction-influence structure which transcends the conventional tripartite arrangement and which can truly encompass all participants regardless of their professional affiliation or hierarchical position in the system. The traditional maintenance mechanisms and adaptive structures of the organization (formal authority, rule enforcement, medical dominance, identification with the system primarily on the basis of moral values and service motives, influence and rewards according to professional status and hierarchical position) which have been successful in the past are clearly becoming less and less effective (Georgopoulos, 1969; Georgopoulos & Matejko, 1967). Inside and outside the system the premises of the traditional structure no longer remain unchallenged, and new bases for organizational adaptation are therefore required.

Similar problems, evident in all large-scale organizations, await solution. Without an adequate adaptive subsystem to modify and filter new inputs leading to planned change, two things can happen: The new potential inputs can be summarily rejected; the organizational structure becomes rigid and the problems are postponed and often intensified. Or the inputs slip into the system and are incorporated in undigested fashion; there is erosion of basic values and the system loses its identity. It does not acquire a formal death certificate but for practical purposes it has been replaced. If a university were to accept research inputs uncritically from the Defense Department, for example, it could end up as a branch of the military and not as an institution for advancing science. Sometimes it happens that in organizations the first response of blanket rejection and rigidity cannot be maintained over time and the opposite reaction of wholesale acceptance of any and all demands follows. For example, a university may show rigidity to suggested reforms at first, and then, as pressure mounts, capitulate completely without critical evaluation of the suggested changes. To complicate matters, both rigidity and uncritical incorporation can occur in different parts of the same organization.

Most organizations suffer from a lack of adequate adaptive and integrative structures concerned with their maintenance subsystems. We should like to indicate some of the lines of inquiry which adaptive subsystems should follow and some directions in restructuring organizations which seem consistent with the present state of knowledge in the field. The views of our critics from the left are at times helpful, though not original, in pointing up vulnerable aspects of bureaucratic structures, but they are singularly lacking in constructive suggestions for reform. Some of them, of course, are not interested in reform, but are committed to destruction of the system. In short, they make no attempt to come to grips with the problems of the one and the many or with the fact that the individual doing his "thing" may interfere with other individuals doing their "thing." Anarchy may have its philosophic appeal, but it cannot be practiced in crowded settings where millions of people live in constant interdependence.

The young dissenters have focused upon some fundamental weaknesses in organizational structure which have been recognized before but which become more critical as the majority of the younger generation no longer finds them acceptable. In the first place, there is a growing dissatisfaction with the fragmentation of life in an organization, with the difficulties of being a whole personality and of finding personal satisfactions in relating to others in impersonal role relationships. The major point is that many organizational arrangements and procedures in our society cut the individual into segments in his various role responsibilities. This is especially true once we leave the more satisfying roles for the elite groups at the top of the structure. In this process we move toward a disintegrated personality. Once his wholeness and unity are violated, the individual may become alienated or seek personality expression outside his role responsibilities (Argyris, 1964; McGregor, 1960). Then we attempt artificial devices such as mass leisure pursuits of sports, movies, and television, of company programs of recreation, or even human relations training for supervisors or recreation, or even human relations training for supervisors to remedy the weaknesses in the system. But this is the organizational fallacy *par excellence*. Once we have destroyed the integrated individual we no longer have the unified pieces to provide a truly integrated system. It is not like making an automobile out of pieces of steel, rubber, and other materials. One cannot have a truly integrated social system if the human pieces are not themselves integrated. It is not possible to have a moral society made up of immoral men.

The second major criticism concerns the exploitative character of bureaucratic structures: namely, that the rewards of the system, both intrinsic and extrinsic, go disproportionately to the upper hierarchical levels and that the objectives of organizations are distorted toward the immediate interests of the elite and away from desirable social goals of the many.

ADAPTATION THROUGH STRUCTURAL REFORM

One important line of structural reform which can be significant with respect to the above weaknesses is the fuller extension of democratic principles to the operation of organizations. Many writers on organizations fail to address themselves to this problem in structural terms, but talk about improvement of interpersonal relations, sensitivity training, and consultative practices. The extreme left is also not concerned with democratic reform. Nonetheless, we believe that much can be done in organizational settings through democratic restructuring to improve their social effectiveness—i.e., their psychological returns to their members.

Two issues must be faced in the extension of democratic principles to organizational functioning. One is direct or representative democracy. The second is the appropriate area of decision making for various subgroups in different types of complex systems.

Representative democracy has been under fire because it can be elaborated through complex mechanisms to distort the wishes of the electorate and to give top decision makers great power. Such abuses do not negate its potential virtues. What is critical here is the number of hierarchical levels in the form of a pyramid similar to the administrative structure: for example, what has been the older practice in some states of the elected state legislators in turn electing senators. The general rule of never allowing more than two levels, that of the electorate and that of their duly chosen representatives, is gaining recognition in political organizations and can be applied to other organizations as well since it ensures more responsible and more responsive decision making.

Direct democracy of the town meeting sort is a cumbersome and ineffective mechanism for many purposes, once the electorate is numbered in hundreds and thousands. In many of our universities, however, we still persist in town meetings of a faculty of over a thousand. It is small wonder that such meetings get stalemated on details and often fail to come to grips with the central issue. Representative assemblies of a smaller number of democratically elected delegates would be a more effective mechanism for decision making.

Direct democracy, however, is still a necessary part of the picture. In the first place, the full electorate should have the opportunity to veto major policy changes suggested by their elected leaders. In the second place, direct democracy can be more adequately utilized in smaller units of the system. Within a university, for example, there is a greater role for direct democracy at the departmental level than at the university level—although we still have a long way to go to achieve this goal. The great advantage of direct democracy within the smaller unit is that it ties the individual into his own group on matters of direct concern to him and thus permits the possibilities of tying him into the larger system of representative democracy. If he is not integrated through participation in his own group, then he is more likely to be apathetic toward or alienated from the larger structure. Democracy, like charity, begins at home, and in most organizations, home is the functional group where the individual spends most of his time.

An esoteric example of this model of combining direct and indirect democracy is embodied in the kibbutzim of Israel (Golomb, 1968). These utopian communities are remarkable in that they have survived, even prospered, for 60 years under the most difficult circumstances. Each kibbutz is a community with a great deal of autonomy, run by direct democracy, with town meetings, with direct election of all decision-making officers including the farm manager, and with rotation of such officers. In addition, the individual kibbutz belongs to a larger movement which can include 40 or 50 similar communities. The larger movement operates training centers, banking facilities, and other services which the individual community could not afford. The management of the movement is handled through representative democracy. The sense of community achieved in the small kibbutz contributes to the integration of the individual into the larger system. Remote as this example is from the size and complexity of the American scene, it is of some interest in that the 230 communities of the kibbutz federation involving 90,000 persons have no problems of violence, delinquency, crime, or unemployment. Psychotic breakdown is an unusual event and crime a rare occurence. Farm productivity is higher than the productivity of private farms in Israel.

A model of this sort combining direct and representative democracy has obvious limitations in its application to large-scale organizations which restrict areas of decision making in many ways. In the first place, a complex system tends to reduce the decision-making powers of any component group, including the top echelon. Even the president of a university will feel that his margin for decision making is within a fairly narrow band of possibilities; the same is true, only more so, of the hospital administrator. And the individual member will feel less room for meaningful participation for determining policy. In the second place, the administrative agency of a public institution has to operate within the legislation of a representative democracy in which it has had little say. In the third place, activities that have to be thoroughly coordinated on a rigorous time schedule, as in the military or space program, or in the operating room of a hospital, heavily restrict the areas of decision making for component groups.

Nevertheless, we do not take full advantage of the opportunities available within these limitations, nor do we examine the nature of these restrictions to see to what extent they can be made less rigid. Though coordination by experts may be necessary after a policy decision, there is still room for the involvement of people in making that decision and reviewing its outcomes. Though legislation determines objectives there is often considerable leeway in how these directives can be implemented. Though size and complexity limit the amount of decision making possible for any one group, matters that are not of significance to the overall system may loom large for individuals in their own work setting. For example, we are constantly expanding the plant in many organizations with new buildings and new construction. Yet the people who have to use these facilities are frequently not consulted about them with respect to their own needs and the uses to which the buildings will but put. There are instances of windowless structures dictated by considerations of economy and standardizations from above which turn out to be frightfully inefficient. We need to analyze the assumptions about coordination and centralization as demanding decisions only from the top echelons.

The facts are that centralization *de jure* often leads to decentralization *de facto*. We need to be more critical of the whole centralization concept to see where tight controls are really necessary and whether they will be genuinely effective. Even with centralized controls in large organizations it is sometimes true that the right hand does not know what the left hand is doing. Hence the criterion should not be some abstract concept of centralization but objective data about how it operates in practice.

Moreover, we need to distinguish among the types of organizations and their objectives, as between mass-producing and other organizations, and particularly among organizations whose primary output is a physical product, some service, or information.

In some organizations there is a necessary coordination of all effort so that there is a convergence of activities upon one outcome, as in the space program's objective of getting men on the moon or in a heart transplant operation. But many organizations do not have single products which require such convergence of the energies of all members of the system. In a university, for example, where we are concerned with training people and extending knowledge, there is a great variety of outcomes and hence much more freedom and degrees of autonomy within the total system. The traditional model of organizational structure deriving from the military and industry is not necessarily the appropriate model for all organizations, nor even for all aspects of industry of the military.

For example, the concept of job enlargement, or that of job enrichment (Herzberg, 1968), as it is more recently described, has been limited primarily to single roles. There are, however, serious limits beyond which we cannot go with a single job. What is possible is group responsibility for a meaningful cycle of work involving a number of related work roles simultaneously. It has been demonstrated by the Tavistock researchers that a cohesive group can be created about a task objective. With some reduction in specialized roles within the group, some rotation of roles, removal of status differences, and responsibility given to the group to get the job done, the results in such widely separated industries as a calico mill in India (Rice, 1958) and a coal mine in Great Britain (Trist, Higgin, Murray, & Pollock, 1963) have been spectacular in the improvement of productivity and morale. The findings are particularly important because they give us new leverage on an old problem. Many jobs in themselves are routine and without challenge. Overall they add up to something significant in the way of performance. If they are not rigorously delimited and assigned to particular people, they can be given to a group with the group itself assuming responsibility for the outcome. Thus the advantages of collective accomplishment become not the ideal of top management but the objective and psychological reality for group members.

Another structural reform to make roles more meaningful has to do with organizational divisions based upon process specialization. Supportive activities today are often separated off from production activities, as when we set apart persons performing a service such as personnel recruitment or typing services in a bureau or section of their own. We organize on the basis of process rather than purpose, to use a distinction made by Aristotle. Then we proceed to institutionalize the separation by removing the given service unit from is production counterpart physically and psychologically. The service people may in fact never have direct personal contact with production people. This separation, which results in overspecialization and unnatural interdependence at work, may be particularly damaging to the morale of various service units since the major production functions enjoy the greater prestige and often the more rewarding types of work. It is difficult for the girls in a typing pool to identify with their task or with organizational objectives when they have no meaningful relationship to them. Moreover, the service unit split off from major functions develops a compensatory defensive posture which often interferes with the effective functioning of the larger system. Staff-line conflicts in complex organizations are another familiar problem (Dalton, 1950). More generally, as Morton (1964) points out, where organizational members whose work is related are separated with physical barriers, social bonds are essential to effective organizational functioning, and physical bonds are important when members are socially separated.

The type of restructuring that needs to be considered here is the creation of teams and groups for accomplishing an objective in which service people have primary membership in the production unit and secondary membership in a service unit, and sometimes the secondary membership can be dispensed with. Inclusive, common membership at the workgroup level may be similarly desirable for staff and line personnel in most organizations.

We may need more subgroups than we now have because people can identify more readily with one another and with the group task in small settings than in large. What is important, however, is that the subgroups are broadly enough designed with respect to an objective so that people with different skills can cooperate with one another and identify with the group goal. Groups should be small but their task responsibility large. This runs counter to the traditional way of organizing for turning out automobiles, but it may be more appropriate for many types of organizations not mass producing a physical product.

For example, general hospitals in the future may profit greatly from a self-governing structure that would give every professional and occupational group and member of the opportunity to participate meaningfully in the decision-making processes of the organization, taking fully into account both the functional and the social-psychological interdependence of the participants (Georgopoulos, 1969; Georgopoulos, 1970; Georgopoulos & Matejko, 1967). It would seem advantageous to develop decision-making mechanisms on an organization-wide basis, built on the principles of representative democracy and multilevel federalism of semiautonomous small groups that are highly attractive to their members and can contribute effectively to the solution of system problems at the same time. Such an organizational structure would provide for effective representation of all individual members and their respective groups in the system. It could be established so as to take account of group size; the specialized competencies, functions, and interests of members; and of their location in the system in relation to major problems but not solely on the basis of traditional power or formal position in the authority hierarchy. Every new unit probably should consist of a relatively small number of members who would choose their own representative to the next level. The highest unit in the organization would be a Board of Participants (Georgopoulos, 1969).

This Board of Participants, representing the interests of all hospital personnel, and the conventional Board of Trustees, representing the community's interests, would work cooperatively and on a continuing basis on matters of organizational policy, external relations, priorities and objectives for the institution, and major decisions affecting the hospital, its members, and the public (Georgopoulos, 1969). Hospital administration would function as an executive body , charged with the principal managerial, planning, financial, personnel, and coordinative functions, following and implementing the general policies and decisions made jointly by the Board of Trustees and the Board of Participants (on which the administration would be properly represented, as would doctors, nurses, and other groups) of the institution. Other structural models built on the same organizing principles also would be appropriate. The same applies to organizations other than hospitals, of course.

In general, the changes we have been discussing all point toward a looser role system with broader role definitions, more flexibility and openness of subsystem boundaries, with group responsibility for task objectives. Admittedly, such debureaucratization may add to the noise in the system, but some of what appears to be noise from the point of view of the formal chart maker may be meaningful activity directed toward important goals. It is doubtful whether the true volume of uncertainty in the system would rise very significantly. It should also be remembered that in supposedly tight structures the empirical system may be at variance with the formal organization, with real noise that goes undetected because the formal channels do not code it. What matters is that the facts of functional as well as social-psychological interdependence among the participants in the organization both be taken fully into account.

In a change process the techniques of sensitivity training and of organizational development can be utilized for the full implementation of social reform. These techniques are directed primarily at the improvement of interpersonal relationships and do not in themselves provide for permanent changes in social structure. What is critical is the legitimation of change in institutional arrangements and a restructuring of formal patterns to permit more democratic processes to function. After this has been achieved, methods for improving self-understanding and the understanding of others can help to ensure the success of the structural reforms. To a limited extent they can even prepare the way for these basic changes.

REFORMULATION OF VALUES
FOR SOCIAL REINTEGRATION

We have left to the last the most difficult problem of all: the system values which can bind the individual to the organization and furnish the ideology to justify organizational norms and requirements. Values seldom are static, and our dynamic period with its accelerated changes has seen fundamental challenges to the older belief structure. The task for the adaptive processes of an organization is one of the creative adaptation of central values to changing inputs. Such adaptations means the preservation of the basic nature of the system with modifications which clarify issues but do not destroy the system. Adaptation through genuine participation and active involvement based upon democratic principles and processes can still be successful.

The great need of our time is a reformulation of social values that would make possible a higher level of integration for all social systems. Organizational leaders should play a much more vigorous role as the responsible agents of the adaptive mechanisms in their social structures. In many instances they have given much time and energy to the adaptive function but generally in terms of mediation, negotiation, and compromise in crisis situations. Negotiation and compromise are important, but they are far from a complete answer. Compromise without consideration of principle can merely lead to a new round of demands. Various factions within and without an organization interpret concessions and compromises as an invitation to mobilize their forces for a new offensive. Politics has been called the art of compromise; yet if we rely wholly upon this process we leave everything to power and power-driven individuals. The conceptualization of values and the enunciation of basic principles should not be left to the extremists on either the left or the right. Organizational leadership has a challenge in meeting the rhetoric of the dissidents with a compelling statement of principles and an implementation of them in practice. Many people today are eager for such a formulation of values. When Senator Eugene McCarthy took a clear position on foreign policy, the popular response was of such magnitude as to confound political analysts.

In the past we have been mainly a pragmatic nation, and leaders as well as followers have tended to shy away from ideological discussion. And some of this pragmatic emphasis is to be found in the present demands for relevance and in the anti-intellectualism of the New Left. Nonetheless, values and principles which transcend the single case—the single individual, the single organization, the single faction—are critical to the maintenance of social order. The facts are that there are many assumptions, as well as practices of a moral character in contemporary society, which need reemphasis and reformulation. Without attempting to catalog them, may we cite a few examples?

In the first place, research and observation show that the norm of reciprocity (Gouldner, 1960), of cooperation, of mutual helpfulness, runs wide and deep. Organizations could not exist without many uncounted acts of cooperation which we take for granted. If people operated merely on a basis of role prescription, organizations would run poorly. And role prescriptions also take account of mutual interdependence. Berkowitz and Daniels (1963) have shown experimentally that people will respond to others who need their help. Hospital studies (Georgopoulos & Mann, 1962; Georgopoulos & Matejko, 1967; Georgopoulos & Wieland, 1964; Wieland, 1965) have shown the importance of this norm for group performance, organizational coordination, and patient care. Studies of citizenship orientation have shown that individuals see themselves as good citizens not if they are flag wavers but if they are cooperative and helpful toward their fellows. We cite this basic value of mutual helpfulness because we lose sight of it in the self-oriented push of some protesters.

In the second place, justice and fairness are not outmoded values. Justice as a value is evident in many forms of social exchange (Blau, 1964), and the underdog elicits sympathy partly because there is an assumption that he has not been fairly treated. In fact, justice and fairness are the ideological weapons of the dissenters, but they have no monopoly on them. It is essential to emphasize the importance of justice and fairness in the operation of an organization and to introduce reforms where inequity is the practice.

In the third place, social responsibility or involvement in matters of more than local concern has a potential that remains to be developed. It is no longer acceptable to brag about one's nonparticipation in political affairs. It is apparently less difficult to recruit candidates for public office than was once the case. There seems to be more concern about national decisions which the "little" people were once content to leave to the authorities. Again, the New Left has taken advantage of this broadened conception of political and social responsibility to urge direct action by students on all types of issues. But again the doctrine of social concern can be formulated to make people more aware of the social consequences of their actions. This social concern, which transcends the individual's own self-oriented needs, is reflected in the positive esteem achieved by leaders who show humanitarian values. Part of the late Robert Kennedy's popular appeal was the conviction that he was concerned — that he cared about the fate of others.

All of these values are related to, if not an integral part of, the Democratic Ethic which is still our basic creed. We have already noted the development of democratic practices in our political system and their extension to other social institutions. The democratic doctrine is invoked by the left in its attack upon the establishment but not in its own operations and program. With this group the use of democratic phrases seems to be more of a tactic than an ideological commitment. As the right mobilizes, there is some revival of reactionary beliefs. With the increasing polarization, the middle of the spectrum could profit greatly from a reformulation of the democratic creed by those who believe that democracy is not an outmoded concept—in spite of inadequacies in its application. Organization reform needs such a value base both as a set of social principles and as guidelines for action.

REFERENCES

Argyris, C. *Integrating the individual and the organization.* New York: Wiley, 1964.

Berkowitz, L., & Daniels, Louise R. Responsibility and dependency. *J. abnorm. soc. Psychol.,* 1963, *66,* 429-437.

Blake, R. R., & Mouton, Jane S. *Corporate excellence through grid organization development.* Houston, Tex.: Gulf, 1968.

Blau, P.M. Justice in social exchange. *Sociolog. Inquiry,* 1964, *24,* 199-200.

Bugbee, G. Delivery of health care services: Long range outlook. The Univer. of Michigan *Medical Center J.,* 1969, *35,* 75-76.

Dalton, M. Conflicts between staff and line managerial officers. *Amer. sociolog. Rev.,* 1950, *15,* 342-351.

de Charms, R., & Moeller, G. H. Values expressed in children's readers. *J. abnrom. soc. Psychol.,* 1962, *64,* 136-142.

Etzioni, A. *Modern organizations.* Englewood Cliffs, N.J.: Prentice-Hall, 1964.

Georgopoulos, B.S. Hospital organization and administration. *Hospital Admin.,* 1964, *9,* 23-25.

Georgopoulos, B.S. The hospital system and nursing: Some basic problems and issues. *Nursing Forum,* 1966, *5,* 8-35.

Georgopoulos, B.S. The general hospital as an organization: A social-psychological viewpoint. The Univer. of Michigan *Medical Center J.,* 1969, *35,* 94-97.

Georgopoulos, B.S. An open-system threory model for organizational research: The case of the contemporary general hospital. In A.R. Negandhi and J.P. Schwitter (Eds.), *Organizational behavior models.* Kent, Ohio: Kent State Univer., 1970. Pp. 33-70.

Georgopoulos, B.S., & Mann, F.C. *The community general hospital.* New York: Macmillan, 1962.

Georgopoulos, B.S., & Matejko, A. The American general hospital as a complex social system. *Health Services Res.,* 1967, *2,* 76-112.

Georgopoulos, B.S. & Wieland, G.F. *Nationwide study of coordination and patient care in voluntary hospitals,* No. 2178. Ann Arbor, Mich.: Institute for Social Research, The Univer. of Michigan, 1964.

Glazer, N. The campus crucible. 1. Student politics and the university. *Atlantic Monthly,* July 1969, *224,* 43-53.

Golomb, N. Managing without sanctions or rewards. *Mgmt of Personnel Q.,* 1968, *7,* 22-28.

Gouldner, A.W. The norm of reciprocity: A preliminary statement. *Amer. sociolog. Rev.,* 1960, *25,* 161-178.

Havighurst, R.J. The social and educational implications of interinstitutional cooperation in higher education. In L.C. Howard (Ed.), *Interinstitutional cooperation in higher education.* Milwaukee: Univer. of Wisconsin, 1967. Pp. 508-523.

Herzberg, F. One more time: How do you motivate employees? *Harvard bus. Rev.,* 1968, *46,* 53-62.

Katz, D., & Kahn, R.L. *The social psychology of organizations.* New York: Wiley, 1966.

Likert, R. *The human organization: Its management and value.* New York: McGraw-Hill, 1967.

Marrow, A.J., Bowers, D.G., & Seashore, S.E. *Management by participation.* New York: Harper and Row, 1967.

Maslow, A.H. A theory of human motivation. *Psycholog. Rev.,* 1943, *50,* 370-396.

McClelland, D. *The achieving society.* New York: D. VanNostrand, 1961.

McGregor, D.M. *The human side of enterprise.* New York: McGraw-Hill, 1960.

McNerney, W.J. Does America need a new health system? The Univer. of Michigan *Medical Center J.,* 1969, *35,* 82-87.

Morton, J.A. From research to technology. *Int. Sci. & Technol.,* May 1964, Issue No. 29, 82-92.

Parsons, T. *Structure and process in modern society.* Glencoe, Ill.: Free Press, 1960.

Presthus, R. *The organizational society.* New York: Knopf, 1962.

Rice, A.K. *Productivity and social organization.* London: Tavistock Publications, 1958.

Schein, E.H. *Organizational psychology.* Englewood Cliffs, N.J.: Prentice-Hall, 1965.

Sibery, D.E. Our social responsibilities as health professionals and university center hospitals. The Univer. of Michigan *Medical Center J.,* 1969, *35,* 88-93.

Thompson, J.D. *Organizations in action.* New York: McGraw-Hill, 1967.

Thompson, V. *Modern organization. New York: Knopf, 1961.*

TIME Magazine, Medicine—the plight of the U.S. patient. February 21, 1969, 93, 53-58.

Trist, E.L., Higgin, G.W., Murray, H., & Pollock., A.B. *Organizational choice.* London: Tavistock Publications, 1963.

U.S. News & World Report. How to improve medical care. March 24, 1969, 66, 41-46.

Weber, M. *The theory of social and economic organization* (A.M. Henderson & T. Parsons transl.). New York: Oxford Univ. Press, 1947.

Weber, M. *The protestant ethic and the rise of capitalism* (T. Parsons transl.). New York: Scribner, 1958.

Wieland, G.F. Complexity and coordination in organizations. Unpublished doctoral dissertation, The Univer. of Michigan, 1965.

The Science
Of Muddling Through

CHARLES E. LINDBLOM

Suppose an administrator is given responsibility for formulating policy with respect to inflation. He might start by trying to list all related values in order of importance, e.g., full employment, reasonable business profit, protection of small savings, prevention of a stock market crash. Then all possible policy outcomes could be rated as more or less efficient in attaining a maximum of these values. This would of course require a prodigious inquiry into values held by members of society and an equally prodigious set of calculations on how much of each value is equal to how much of each other value. He could then proceed to outline all possible policy alternatives. In a third step, he would undertake systematic comparison of his multitude of alternatives to determine which attains the greatest amount of values.

In comparing policies, he would take advantage of any theory available that generalized about classes of policies. In considering inflation, for example, he would compare all policies in the light of the theory of

Reprinted, with permission, from *The Public Administration Review*, V. 19, Spring 1959, pp. 79-88.

prices. Since no alternatives are beyond his investigation, he would consider strict central control and the abolition of all prices and markets on the one hand and elimination of all public controls with reliance completely on the free market on the other, both in the light of whatever theoretical generalizations he could find on such hypothetical economies.

Finally, he would try to make the choice that would in fact maximize his values.

An alternative line of attack would be to set as his principal objective, either explicitly or without conscious thought, the relatively simple goal of keeping prices level. This objective might be compromised or complicated by only a few other goals, such as full employment. He would in fact disregard most other social values as beyond his present interest, and he would for the moment not even attempt to rank the few values that he regarded as immediately relevant. Were he pressed, he would quickly admit that he was ignoring many related values and many possible important consequences of his policies.

As a second step, he would outline those relatively few policy alternatives that occurred to him. He would then compare them. In comparing his limited number of alternatives, most of them familiar from past controversies, he would not ordinarily find a body of theory precise enough to carry him through a comparison of their respective consequences. Instead he would rely heavily on the record of past experience with small policy steps to predict the consequences of similar steps extended into the future.

Moreover, he would find that the policy alternatives combined objectives or values in different ways. For example, one policy might offer price level stability at the cost of some risk of unemployment; another might offer less price stability but also less risk of unemployment. Hence, the next step in his approach—the final selection—would combine into one the choice among values and the choice among instruments for reaching values. It would not, as in the first method of policy-making, approximate a more mechanical process of choosing the means that best satisfied goals that were previously clarified and ranked. Because practitioners of the second approach expect to achieve their goals only partially, they would expect to repeat endlessly the sequence just described, as conditions and aspirations changed and as accuracy of prediction improved.

BY ROOT OR BY BRANCH

For complex problems, the first of these two approaches is of course impossible. Although such an approach can be described, it cannot be practiced except for relatively simple problems and even then only in a somewhat modified form. It assumes intellectual capacities and sources of information that men simply do not possess, and it is even more absurd as an approach to policy when the time and money that can be allocated to a policy problem is limited, as is always the case. Of particular importance to public administrators is the fact that public agencies are in effect usually instructed not to practice the first method. That is to say, their prescribed functions and constraints—the politically or legally possible—restrict their attention to relatively few values and relatively few alternative policies among the countless alternatives that might be imagined. It is the second method that is practiced.

Curiously, however, the literatures of decision-making, policy formulation, planning, and public administration formalize the first approach rather than the second, leaving public administrators who handle complex decisions in the position of practicing what few preach. For emphasis I run some risk of overstatement. True enough, the literature is well aware of limits on man's capacities and of the inevitability that policies will be approached in some such style as the second. But attempts to formalize rational policy formulation—to lay out explicitly the necessary steps in the process—usually describe the first approach and not the second.[1]

The common tendency to describe policy formulation even for complex problems as though it followed the first approach has been strengthened by the attention given to, and successes enjoyed by, operations research, statistical decision theory, and systems analysis. The hallmarks of these procedures, typical of the first approach, are clarity of objective, explicitness of evaluation, a high degree of comprehensiveness of overview, and wherever possible, quantification of values for mathematical analysis. But these advanced procedures remain largely the appropriate techniques of relatively small-scale problem-solving where the total number of variables to be considered is small and value problems restricted. Charles Hitch, head of the Economics Division of RAND Corporation, one of the leading centers for application of these techniques, has written:

> I would make the empirical generalization from my experience at RAND and elsewhere that operations research is the art of suboptimizing, i.e., of solving some lower-level problems, and that difficulties increase and our special competence diminishes by an order of magnitude with every level of decision-making we attempt

---

James G. March and Herbert A. Simon similarly characterize the literature. They also take some important steps, as have Simon's recent articles. To describe a less heroic model of policy making see *Organizations* (John Wiley & Sons, 1958) p. 13.

to ascend. The sort of simple explicit model which operations researchers are so proficient in using can certainly reflect most of the significant factors influencing traffic control on the George Washington Bridge, but the proportion of the relevant reality which we can represent by any such model or models in studying, say, a major foreign-policy decision, appears to be almost trivial.[2]

Accordingly, I propose in this paper to clarify and formalize the second method, much neglected in the literature. This might be described as the method of *successive limited comparisons.* I will contrast it with the first approach, which might be called the rational-comprehensive method.[3] More impressionistically and briefly—and therefore generally used in this article—they could be characterized as the branch method and root method, the former continually building out from the current situation, step-by-step and by small degrees; the latter starting from fundamentals anew each time, building on the past only as experience is embodied in a theory, and always prepared to start completely from the ground up.

Let us put the characteristics of the two methods side by side in simplest terms.

Assuming that the root method is familiar and understandable, we proceed directly to clarification of its alternative by contrast. In explaining the second, we shall be describing how most administrators do in fact approach complex questions, for the root method, the "best" way as a blueprint or model, is in fact not workable for complex policy questions, and administrators are forced to use the method of successive limited comparisons.

INTERTWINING EVALUATION AND EMPIRICAL ANALYSIS (1B)

The quickest way to understand how values are handled in the method of successive limited comparisons is to see how the root method

---

[2]"Operations Research and National Planning — A Dissent," *Operations Research* 5 (October 1957): 718. Hitch's dissent is from particular points made in the article to which his paper is a reply; his claim that operations research is for low-level problems is widely accepted.

For examples of the kind of problems to which operations research is applied see C.W. Churchman, R.L. Ackoff and E.L. Arnoff, *Introduction to Operations Research* (John Wiley and Sons, 1957); and J.F. McCloskey, and J.M. Coppinger (eds.). *Operations Research for Management,* Vol. II (The Johns Hopkins Press, 1956).

[3]I am assuming that administrators often make policy and advise in the making of policy and am treating decision-making and policy making as synonomous for purposes of this paper.

Rational-Comprehensive (Root)	Successive Limited Comparisons (Branch)
1a. Clarification of values or objectives distinct from and usually prerequisite to empirical analysis of alternative policies.	1b. Selection of value goals and empirical analysis of the needed action are not distinct from one another but are closely interwined.
2a. Policy-formulation is therefore approached through means-end analysis: First the ends are isolated, then the means to achieve them are sought.	2b. Since means and ends are not distinct, means-end analysis is often inappropriate or limited.
3a. The test of a "good" policy is that it can be shown to be the most appropriate means to desired ends.	3b. The test of a "good" policy is typically that various analysts find themselves directly agreeing on a policy (without their agreeing that it is the most appropriate means to an agreed objective).
4a. Analysis is comprehensive; every important relevant factor is taken into account.	4b. Analysis is drastically limited: i) Important possible outcomes are neglected. ii) Important alternative potential policies are neglected. iii) Important affected values are neglected.
5a. Theory is often heavily relied upon.	5b. A succession of comparisons greatly reduces or eliminates reliance on theory.

often breaks down in *its* handling of values or objectives. The idea that values should be clarified, and in advance of the examination of alternative policies is appealing. But what happens when we attempt it for complex social problems? The first difficulty is that on many critical values or objectives, citizens disagree, congressmen disagree, and public administrators disagree. Even where a fairly specific objective is prescribed for the administrator, there remains considerable room for disagreement on sub-objectives. Consider, for example, the conflict with respect to locating public housing, described in Meyerson and Banfield's study of the Chicago Housing Authority[4] disagreement which occurred despite the clear objective of providing a certain number of public housing units in the city. Similarly conflicting are objectives in highway location, traffic control, minimum wage administration, development of tourist facilities in national parks, or insect control.

Administrators cannot escape these conflicts by ascertaining the majority's preference, for preferences have not been registered on most issues; indeed, there often are no preferences in the absence of public discussion sufficient to bring an issue to the attention of the electorate. Furthermore, there is a question of whether intensity of feeling should be considered as well as the number of persons preferring each alternative. By the impossibility of doing otherwise, administrators often are reduced to deciding policy without clarifying objectives first.

Even when an administrator resolves to follow his own values as a criterion for decision, he often will not know how to rank them when they conflict with one another, as they usually do. Suppose, for example, that an administrator must relocate tenants living in tenements scheduled for destruction. One objective is to empty the buildings fairly promptly, another is to find suitable accommodations for persons displaced, another is to avoid friction with residents in other areas in which a large influx would be unwelcome, another is to deal with all concerned through persuasion if possible, and so on.

How does one state even to himself the relative importance of these partially conflicting values? A simple ranking of them is not enough; one needs ideally to know how much one value is worth sacrificing for some of another value. The answer is that typically the administrator chooses—and must choose—directly among policies in which these values are combined in different ways. He cannot first clarify his values and then choose among policies.

A more subtle third point underlies both the first two. Social objectives do not always have the same relative values. One objective may be highly prized in one circumstance, another in another circumstance. If, for example, an administrator values highly both the dispatch with which his agency can carry through its projects *and* good public relations, it matters little which of the two possibly conflicting values he favors in some abstract or general sense. Policy questions arise in forms which put to administrators such a question as: Given the degree to

[4]Martin Meyerson and Edward C. Banfield, *Politics, Planning and the Public Interest* (The Free Press, 1955).

which we are or are not already achieving the values of dispatch and the values of good public relations, it is worth sacrificing a little speed for a happier clientele, or is it better to risk offending the clientele so that we can get on with our work? The answer to such a question varies with circumstances.

The value problem is, as the example shows, always a problem of adjustments at a margin. But there is no practicable way to state marginal objectives or values except in terms of particular policies. That one value is preferred to another in one decision situation does not mean that it will be preferred in another decision situation in which it can be had only at great sacrifice of another value. Attempts to rank or order values in general and abstract terms so that they do not shift from decision to decision end up by ignoring the relevant marginal preferences. The significance of this third point thus goes very far. Even if all administrators had at hand an agreed set of values, objectives, and constraints, and an agreed ranking of these values, objectives, and constraints, their marginal values in actual choice situations would be impossible to formulate.

Unable consequently to formulate the relevant values first and then choose among policies to achieve them, administrators must choose directly among alternative policies that offer different marginal combinations of values. Somewhat paradoxically, the only practicable way to disclose one's relevant marginal values even to oneself is to describe the policy one chooses to achieve them. Except roughly and vaguely, I know of no way to describe—or even to understand—what my relative evaluations are for, say, freedom and security, speed and accuracy in governmental decisions, or low taxes and better schools than to describe my preferences among specific policy choices that might be made between the alternatives in each of the pairs.

In summary, two aspects of the process by which values are actually handled can be distinguished. The first is clear: evaluation and empirical analysis are interwined; that is, one chooses among values and among policies at one and the same time. Put a little more elaborately, one simultaneously chooses a policy to attain certain objectives and chooses the objectives themselves. The second aspect is related but distinct: the administrator focuses his attention on marginal or incremental values. Whether he is aware of it or not, he does not find general formulations of objectives very helpful and in fact makes specific marginal or incremental comparisons. Two policies, X and Y, confront him. Both promise the same degree of attainment of ojbectives, a, b, c, d, and e. But X promises him somewhat more of f than does Y, while Y promises him somewhat more of g than does X. In choosing between them, he is in fact offered the alternative of a marginal or incremental amount of f at the expense of a marginal or incremental amount of g. The only values that are relevant to his choice are these increments by which the two policies differ; and, when he finally chooses between the two marginal values, he does so by making a choice between policies.[5]

As to whether the attempt to clarify objectives in advance of policy selection is more or less rational than the close interwining of marginal evaluation and empirical analysis, the principal difference established is that for complex problems the first is impossible and irrelevant, and the second is both possible and relevant. The second is possible because the administrator need not try to analyze any values except the values by which alternative policies differ and need not be concerned with them except as they differ marginally. His need for information on values or objectives is drastically reduced as compared with the root method; and his capacity for grasping, comprehending, and relating values to one another is not strained beyond the breaking point.

RELATIONS BETWEEN MEANS AND ENDS (2B)

Decision-making is ordinarily formalized as a means-ends relationship: means are conceived to be evaluated and chosen in the light of ends finally selected independently of and prior to the choice of means. This is the means-ends relationship of the root method. But it follows from all that has just been said that such a means-ends relationship is possible only to the extent that values are agreed upon, are reconcilable, and are stable at the margin. Typically, therefore, such a means-ends relationship is absent from the branch method, where means and ends are simultaneously chosen.

Yet any departure from the means-ends relationship of the root method will strike some readers as inconceivable. For it will appear to them that only in such a relationship is it possible to determine whether one policy choice is better or worse than another. How can an administrator know whether he has made a wise or foolish decision if he is without prior values or objectives by which to judge his decisions? The answer to this question calls up the third distinctive difference between root and branch methods: how to decide the best policy.

---

[5]The line of argument is, of course, an extension of the theory of market choice, especially the theory of consumer choice, to public choices.

THE TEST OF "GOOD" POLICY (3B)

In the root method, a decision is "correct," "good," or "rational" if it can be shown to attain some specified objective, where the objective can be specified without simply describing the decision itself. Where objectives are defined only through the marginal or incremental approach to values described above, it is still sometimes possible to test whether a policy does in fact attain the desired objectives; but a precise statement of the objectives takes the form of a description of the policy chosen or some alternative to it. To show that a policy is mistaken one cannot offer an abstract argument that important objectives are not achieved; one must instead argue that another policy is more to be preferred.

So far, the departure from customary ways of looking at problem-solving is not troublesome, for many administrators will be quick to agree that the most effective discussion of the correctness of policy does take the form of comparison with other policies that might have been chosen. But what of the situation in which administrators cannot agree on values or objectives, either abstractly or in marginal terms? What then is the test of "good" policy? For the root method, there is no test. Agreement on objectives failing, there is no standard of "correctness." For the method of successive limited comparisons, the test is agreement on policy itself, which remains possible even when agreement on values is not.

It has been suggested than continuing agreement in Congress on the desirability of extending old age insurance stems from liberal desires to strengthen the welfare programs of the federal government and from conservative desires to reduce union demands for private pension plans. If so, this is an excellent demonstration of the ease with which individuals of different ideologies often can agree on concrete policy. Labor mediators report a similar phenomenon: the contestants cannot agree on criteria for settling their disputes but can agree on specific proposals. Similarly, when one administrator's objective turns out to be another's means, they often can agree on policy.

Agreement on policy thus becomes the only practicable test of the policy's correctness. And for one administrator to seek to win the other over to agreement on ends as well would accomplish nothing and create quite unnecessary controversy.

If agreement directly on policy as a test for "best" policy seems a poor substitute for testing the policy against its objectives, it ought to be remembered that objectives themselves have no ultimate validity other than they are agreed upon. Hence agreement is the test of "best" policy in both methods. But where the root method requires agreement on what elements in the decision constitute objectives and on which of these objectives should be sought, the branch method falls back on agreement wherever it can be found.

In an important sense, therefore, it is not irrational for an administrator to defend a policy as good without being able to specify what it is good for.

NON-COMPREHENSIVE ANALYSIS (4B)

Ideally, rational-comprehensive analysis leaves out nothing important. But it is impossible to take everything important into consideration unless "important" is so narrowly defined that analysis is in fact quite limited. Limits on human intellectual capacities and on available information set definite limits to man's capacity to be comprehensive. In actual fact, therefore, no one can practice the rational-comprehensive method for really complex problems, and every administrator faced with a sufficiently complex problem must find ways drastically to simplify.

An administrator assisting in the formulation of agricultural economic policy cannot in the first place be competent on all possible policies. He cannot even comprehend one policy entirely. In planning a soil bank program, he cannot successfully anticipate the impact of higher or lower farm income on, say, urbanization—the possible consequent loosening of family ties, possible consequent eventual need for revisions in social security and further implications for tax problems arising out of new federal responsibilities for social security and municipal responsibilities for urban services. Nor, to follow another line of repercussions, can he work through the soil bank program's effects on prices for agricultural products in foreign markets and consequent implications for foreign markets and consequent implications for foreign relations, including those arising out of economy rivalry between the United States and the U.S.S.R.

In the method of successive limited comparisons, simplification is systematically achieved in two principal ways. First, it is achieved through limitation of policy comparisons to those policies that differ in relatively small degree from policies presently in effect. Such a limitation immediately reduces the number of alternatives to be investigated and also drastically simplifies the character of the investigation for each. For it is not necessary to undertake fundamental inquiry into an alternative and its consequences; it is necessary only to study those respects in which the porposed alternative and its consequences differ from the status quo. The empirical comparison of marginal differences among alternate policies that differ only marginally is, of course, a counterpart of the incremental or marginal comparison of values discussed above.[6]

Relevance as well as realism

It is a matter of common observation that in Western democracies public administrators and policy analysts in general do largely limit their analyses to incremental or marginal differences in policies that are chosen to differ only incrementally. They do not do so, however, solely because they desperately need some way to simplify their problems; they also do so in order to be relevant. Democracies change their policies almost entirely through incremental adjustments. Policy does not move in leaps and bounds.

The incremental character of political change in the United States has often been remarked. The two major political parties agree on fundamentals; they offer alternative policies to the voters only on relatively small points of difference. Both parties favor full employment, but they define it somewhat differently; both favor the development of water power resources, but in slightly different ways; and both favor unemployment compensation, but not the same level of benefits. Similarly, shifts of policy within a party take place largely through a series of relatively small changes, as can be seen in their only gradual acceptance of the idea of governmental responsibility for support of the unemployed, a change in party positions beginning in the early 1930's and culminating in a sense in the Employment Act of 1946.

Party behavior is in turn rooted in public attitudes, and political theorists cannot conceive of democracy's surviving in the United States in the absence of fundamental agreement on potentially disruptive issues, with consequent limitation of policy debates to relatively small differences in policy.

Since the policies ignored by the administrator are politically impossible and so irrelevant, the simplification of analysis achieved by concentrating on policies that differ only incrementally is not a capricious kind of simplification. In addition, it can be argued, that given the limits on knowledge within which policy-makers are confined, simplifying by limiting the focus to small variations from present policy makes the most of available knowledge. Because policies being considered are like present and past policies, the administrator can obtain information and claim some insight. Non-incremental policy proposals

---

[6]A more precise definition of incremental policies and a discussion of whether a change that appears "small" to one observer might be seen differently by another is to be found in my "Policy Analysis", *American Economic Review* 48, (1959), 298.

are therefore typically not only politically irrelevant but also unpredictable in their consequences.

The second method of simplification of analysis is the practice of ignoring important possible consequences of possible policies, as well as the values attached to the neglected consequences. If this appears to disclose a shocking shortcoming of successive limited comparisons, it can be replied that, even if the exclusions are random, policies may nevertheless be more intelligently formulated than through futile attempts to achieve a comprehensiveness beyond human capacity. Actually, however, the exclusions, seeming arbitrary or random from one point of view, need be neither.

Achieving a degree of comprehensiveness

Suppose that each value neglected by one policy-making agency were a major concern of at least one other agency. In that case, a helpful division of labor would be achieved, and no agency need find its task beyond its capacities. The shortcomings of such a system would be that one agency might destroy a value either before another agency could be activated to safeguard it or in spite of another agency's efforts. But the possibility that important values may be lost is present in any form of organization, even where agencies attempt to comprehend in planning more than is humanly possible.

The virtue of such a hypothetical division of labor is that every important interest or value has its watchdog. And these watchdogs can protect the interests in their jurisdiction in two quite different ways: first, by redressing damages done by other agencies; and, second, by anticipation and heading off injury before it occurs.

In a society like that of the United States in which individuals are free to combine to pursue almost any possible common interest they might have and in which government agencies are sensitive to the pressures of these groups, the system described is approximated. Almost every interest has its watchdog. Without claiming that every interest has a sufficiency powerful watchdog, it can be argued that our system often can assure a more comprehensive regard for the value of the whole society than any attempt at intellectual comprehensiveness.

In the United States, for example, no part of government attempts a comprehensive overview of policy on income distribution. A policy nevertheless evolves, and one responding to a wide variety of interests. A process of mutual adjustment among farm groups, labor unions, municipalities and school boards, tax authorities, and government agencies with responsibilities in the fields of housing, health, highways, national parks, fire, and police accomplishes a distribution of income in which particular income problems neglected at one point in the decision processes become central at another point.

Mutual adjustment is more pervasive than the explicit forms it takes in negotiation between groups; it persists through the mutual impacts of groups upon each other even where they are not in communication. For all the imperfections and latent dangers in this ubiquitous process of mutual adjustment, it will often accomplish an adaptation of policies to a wider range of interests than could be done by one group centrally.

Note, too, how the incremental pattern of policy-making fits with the multiple pressure pattern. For when decisions are only incremental—closely related to known policies, it is easier for one group to anticipate the kind of moves another might make and easier too for it to make correction for injury already accomplished.[7]

Even partisanship and narrowness, to use pejorative terms, will sometimes be assets to rational decision-making, for they can doubly insure that what one agency neglects, another will not; they specialize personnel to distinct points of view. The claim is valid that effective rational coordination of the federal administration, if possible to achieve at all, would require an agreed set of values[8]—if "rational" is defined as the practice of the root method of decision-making. But a high degree of administrative coordination occurs as each agency adjusts its policies to the concerns of the other agencies in the process of fragmented decision-making I have just described.

For all the apparent shortcomings of the incremental approach to policy alternatives with its arbitrary exclusion coupled with fragmentation, when compared to the root method, the branch method often looks far superior. In the root method, the inevitable exclusion of factors is accidental, unsystematic, and not defensible by any argument so far developed, while in the branch method the exclusions are deliberate, systematic, and defensible. Ideally, of course, the root method does not exclude; in practice it must.

Nor does the branch method necessarily neglect long-run considerations and objectives. It is clear that important values must be omitted in considering policy, and sometimes the only way long-run objectives can be given adequate attention is through the neglect of short-term considerations. But the values omitted can be either long-run or short-run.

---

[7]The link between the practice of the method of successive limited comparisons and mutual adjustment of interests in a highly fragmented decision-making process adds a new facet to pluralist theories of government and administration.

[8]Herbert Simon, Donald W. Smithburg and Victor A. Thompson. *Public Administration* (Alfred A. Knopf, 1950). p. 434.

Succession of comparisons (5b)

The final distinctive element in the branch method is that the comparisons, together with the policy choice, proceed in a chronological series. Policy is not made once and for all; it is made and re-made endlessly. Policy-making is a process of successive approximation to some desired objectives in which what is desired itself continues to change under reconsideration.

Making policy is at best a very rough process. Neither social scientists, nor politicians, nor public administrators yet know enough about the social world to avoid repeated error in predicting the consequences of policy moves. A wise policy-maker consequently expects that his policies will achieve only part of what he hopes and at the same time will produce unanticipated consequences he would have preferred to avoid. If he proceeds through a *succession* of incremental changes, he avoids serious lasting mistakes in several ways.

In the first place, past sequences of policy steps have given him knowledge about the probable consequences of further similar steps. Second, he need not attempt big jumps toward his goals that would require predictions beyond his or anyone else's knowledge, because he never expects his policy to be a final resolution of a problem. His decision is only one step, one that if successful can quickly be followed by another. Third, he is in effect able to test his previous predictions as he moves on to each further step. Lastly, he often can remedy a past error fairly quickly—more quickly than if policy proceeded through more distinct steps widely spaced in time.

Compare this comparative analysis of incremental changes with the aspiration to employ theory in the root method. Man cannot think without classifying, without subsuming one experience under a more general category of experiences. The attempt to push categorization as far as possible and to find general propositions which can be applied to specific situations is what I refer to with the word "theory." Where root analysis often leans heavily on theory in this sense, the branch method does not.

The assumption of root analysis is that theory is the most systematic and economical way to bring relevant knowledge to bear on a specific problem. Granting the assumption, an unhappy fact is that we do not have adequate theory to apply to problems in any policy area, although theory is more adequate in some areas—monetary policy, for example—than in others. Comparative analysis, as in the branch method, is sometimes a systematic alternative to theory.

Suppose an administrator must choose among a small group of policies that differ only incrementally from each other and from present policy. He might aspire to "understand" each of the alternatives—for example, to know all the consequences of each aspect of each policy. If so, he would indeed require theory. In fact, however, he would usually decide that, *for policy-making purposes,* he need know, as explained above, only the consequences of each of those aspects of the policies in which they differed from one another. For this much more modest aspiration, he requires no theory (although it might be helpful, if available), for he can proceed to isolate probable differences by examining the differences in consequences associated with past differences in policies, a feasible program because he can take his observations from a long sequence of incremental changes.

For example, without a more comprehensive social theory about juvenile delinquency than scholars have yet produced, one cannot possibly understand the ways in which a variety of public policies—say on education, housing, recreation, employment, race relations, and policing—might encourage or discourage delinquency. And one needs such an understanding if he undertakes the comprehensive overview of the problem prescribed in the models of the root method. If, however, one merely wants to mobilize knowledge sufficient to assist in a choice among a small group of similar policies—alternative policies on juvenile court procedures, for example—he can do so by comparative analysis of the results of similar past policy moves.

Theorists and practitioners

This difference explains—in some cases at least—why the administrator often feels that the outside expert or academic problem-solver is sometimes not helpful and why they in turn often urge more theory on him. And it explains why an administrator often feels more confident when "flying by the seat of his pants" than when following the advice of theorists. Theorists often ask the administrator to go the long way round to the solution of his problems, in effect ask him to follow the best canons of the scientific method, when the administrator knows that the best available theory will work less well than more modest incremental comparisons. Theorists do not realize that the administrator is often in fact practicing a systematic method. It would be foolish to push this explanation too far, for sometimes practical decision-makers are pursuing neither a theoretical approach nor successive comparisons, nor any other systematic method.

It may be worth emphasizing that theory is sometimes of extremely limited helpfulness in policy-making for at least two rather different reasons. It is greedy for facts; it can be constructed only through a great collection of observations. And it is typically insufficiently precise for application to a policy that moves through small changes. In contrast, the comparative method both economizes on the need for facts and directs the analyst's attention to just those facts that are relevant to the fine choices faced by the decision-maker.

With respect to precision of theory, economic theory serves as an example. It predicts than an economy without money or prices would in certain specified ways misallocate resources, but this finding pertains to an alternative far removed from the kind of policies on which adminis-trators need help. On the other hand, it is not precise enough to predict the consequences of policies restricting business mergers, and this is the kind of issue on which the administrators need help. Only in relatively restricted areas does economic theory achieve sufficient precision to go far in resolving policy questions; its helpfulness in policy-making is always so limited that it requires supplementation through comparative analysis.

Successive comparison as a system

Successive limited comparisons is, then, indeed a method or sys-tem; it is not a failure of method for which administrators ought to apologize. Nonetheless, its imperfections, which have not been exp-lored in this paper, are many. For example, the method is without a built-in safeguard for all relevant values, and it also may lead the decision-maker to overlook excellent policies for no other reason than that they are not suggested by the chain of successive policy steps leading to the present. Hence, it ought to be said that under this method, as well as under some of the most sophisticated variants of the root method—operations research, for example—policies will continue to be as foolish as they are wise.

Why then bother to describe the method in all the above detail? Because it is in fact a common method of policy formulation, and is, for complex problems, the principal reliance of administrators as well as of other policy analysts.[9] And because it will be superior to any other decision making method available for complex problems in many cir-cumstances, certainly superior to a futile attempt at superhuman com-prehensiveness. The reaction of the public administrator to the exposi-tion of method doubtless will be less a discovery of a new method than a better acquaintance with an old. But by becoming more conscious of their practice of this method, administrators might practice it with more skill and know when to extend or constrict its use. (That they sometimes practice it effectively and sometimes not may explain the extremes of opinion on "muddling through," which is both praised as a highly sophisticated form of problem-solving and denounced as no method at all. For I suspect that in so far as there is a system in what is known as "muddling through," this method is it.)

One of the noteworthy incidental consequences of clarification of the method is the light it throws on the suspicion an administrator sometimes entertains that a consultant or adviser is not speaking relevantly and responsibly when in fact by all ordinary objective evidence he is. The trouble lies in the fact that most of us approach policy problems within a framework given by our view of a chain of successive policy choices made up to the present. One's thinking about appropriate policies with respect, say, to urban traffic control is greatly influenced by one's knowledge of the incremental steps taken up to the present. An administrator enjoys an intimate knowledge of his past sequences that "outsiders" do not share, and his thinking and that of the "outsider" will consequently be different in ways that may puzzle both. Both may appear to be talking intelligently, yet each may find the other unsatisfactory. The relevance of the policy chain of succession is even more clear when an American tries to discuss, say, antitrust policy with a Swiss, for the chains of policy in the two countries are strikingly different and the two individuals consequently have organized their knowledge in quite different ways.

If this phenomenon is a barrier to communication, an understanding of it promises an enrichment of intellectual interaction in policy formulation. Once the source of difference is understood, it will sometimes be stimulating for an administrator to seek out a policy analyst whose recent experience is with a policy chain different from his own.

This raises again a question only briefly discussed above on the merits of like-mindedness among government administrators. While much of organization theory argues the virtues of common values and

---

[9]Elsewhere I have explored this same method of policy formulation as practiced by academic analysts of policy ("Policy Analysis,' *American Economic Review* 48 [June, 1958]: 298). Although it has been here presented as a method for public administrators, it is no less necessary to analysts more removed from immediate policy questions, despite their tendencies to describe their own analytical efforts as though they were the rational-comprehensive method with an especially heavy use of theory. Similarly, this same method is inevitably resorted to in personal problem-solving, where means and ends are sometimes impossible to separate, where aspirations or objectives undergo constant development, and where drastic simplification of the complexity of the real world is urgent if problems are to be solved in the time that can be given to them. To an economist accustomed to dealing with the marginal or incremental concept in market processes, the central idea in the method is that both evaluation and empirical analysis are incremental. Accordingly I have referred to the method elsewhere as the incremental method."

agreed organizational objectives, for complex problems in which the root method is applicable, agencies will want among their own personnel two types of diversification: administrators whose thinking is organized by reference to policy chains other than those familiar to most members of the organization and, even more commonly, administrators whose professional or personal values or interests create diversity of view (perhaps coming from different specialties, social classes, geographical areas) so that, even within a single agency, decision-making can be fragmented and parts of the agency can serve as watchdogs for other parts.

Managing the
Public Service Institution

PETER F. DRUCKER

Service institutions are an increasingly important part of our society. Schools and universities; research laboratories; public utilities; hospitals and other health-care institutions; professional, industry, and trade associations; and many others—all these are as much "institutions" as is the business firm, and, therefore, are equally in need of management.[1] They all have people who are designated to exercise the management function and who are paid for doing the management job—even though they may not be called "managers," but "administrators," "directors," "executives," or some other such title.

[1]Government agencies and bureaus are also "service institutions," of course, and have management problems which are comparable to those of the institutions I have mentioned. But because they also partake of a general "governmental" purpose, not usefully defined in management terms, I shall not be dealing with them in this article. I shall feel free, however, to include such quasi-governmental organizations as the TVA or the post office in my discussion.

Reprinted from The Public Interest (1973) Condensation of chapters 11-14 in Management: Tasks, Responsibilities, Practices (1974) Copyright © 1973 by Peter F. Drucker. By permission of Harper and Row, Publishers, Inc.

These "public service" institutions—to give them a generic name—are the real growth sector of a modern society. Indeed, what we have now is a "multi-institutional" society rather than a "business" society. The traditional title of the American college course still tends to read "Business and Government." But this is an anachronism. It should read "Business, Government, and Many Others."

All public service institutions are being paid for out of the economic surplus produced by economic activity. The growth of the service institutions in this century is thus the best testimonial to the success of business in discharging its economic task. Yet unlike, say, the early 19th-century university, the service institutions are not mere "luxury" or "ornament." They are, so to speak, main pillars of a modern society, load-bearing members of the main structure. They *have* to perform if society and economy are to function. It is not only that these service institutions are a major expense of a modern society; half of the personal income of the United States (and of most of the other developed countries) is spent on public service institutions (including those operated by the government). Compared to these "public service" institutions, both the "private sector" (i.e., the economy of goods) and the traditional government functions of law, defense, and public order, account for a smaller share of the total income flow of today's developed societies than they did around 1900—despite the cancerous growth of military spending.

Every citizen in the developed, industrialized, urbanized societies depends for his very survival on the performance of the public service institutions. These institutions also embody the values of developed societies. For it is in the form of education and health care, knowledge and mobility—rather than primarily in the form of more "food, clothing, and shelter"—that our society obtains the fruits of its increased economic capacities and productivity.

Yet the evidence for performance in the service institutions is not impressive, let alone overwhelming. Schools, hospitals, universities are all big today beyond the imagination of an earlier generation. They all dispose of astronomical budgets. Yet everywhere they are "in crisis." A generation or two ago, their performance was taken for granted. Today, they are being attacked on all sides for lack of performance. Services which the 19th century managed with aplomb and apparently with little effort—the postal service, for instance—are deeply in the red, require enormous and ever-growing subsidies, and yet give poorer service everywhere. In every country the citizen complains ever more loudly of "bureaucracy" and mismanagement in the institutions that are supposed to serve him.

Are service institutions manageable?

The response of the service institutions to this criticism has been to become "management conscious." They increasingly turn to business to learn "management." In all service institutions, "manager development," "management by objectives," and many other concepts and tools of business management are becoming increasingly popular. This is a healthy sign—but no more than that. It does not mean that the service institutions understand the problems of managing themselves. It only means that they have begun to realize that, at present, they are not being managed.

Yet, though "performance" in the public service institutions is the exception rather than the rule, the exceptions can perform. Among American public service agencies of the last 40 years, for instance, there is the Tennessee Valley Authority (TVA), the big regional electric-power and irrigation project in the Southeastern United States. (TVA's performance was especiallly notable during its early years, in the 1930's and 1940's, when it was headed by David Lilienthal.) While a great many—perhaps most—schools in the inner-city, black ghettos of America deserve all the strictures of the "deschooling" movement, a few schools in the very worst ghettos (e.g., in New York's South Bronx) have shown high capacity to make the most "disadvantaged" children acquire the basic skills of literacy.

What is it that the few successful service institutions do (or eschew) that makes them capable of performance? This is the question to ask. And it is a *management* question—of a special kind. In most respects, the service institution is not very different from a business enterprise. It faces similar—if not precisely the same—challenges in seeking to make work productive. It does not differ significantly from a business in its "social responsibility." Nor does the service institution differ very much from business enterprise in respect to the manager's work and job, in respect to organizational design and structure, or even in respect to the job and structure of top management. *Internally*, the differences tend to be differences in terminology rather than in substance.

But the service institution is in a fundamentally different "business" from business. It is different in its purpose. It has different values. It needs different objectives. And it makes a different contribution to society. "Performance and results" are quite different in a service institution from what they are in a business. "Managing for performance" is the one area in which the service institution differs significantly from a business.

Why service institutions do not perform

There are three popular explanations for the common failure of service institutions to perform:
1) Their managers aren't "businesslike";
2) They need "better men";
3) Their objectives and results are "intangible."
All three are alibis rather than explanations.

1) The service institution will perform, it is said again and again, if only it is managed in a "businesslike" manner. Colbert, the great minister of Louis XVI, was the first to blame the performance difficulties of the non-business, the service institution, on this lack of "businesslike" management. Colbert, who created the first "modern" public service in the West, never ceased to exhort his officials to be "businesslike." The cry is still being repeated every day—by chambers of commerce, by presidential and royal commissions, by ministers in the Communist countries, and so on. If only, they all say their administrators were to behave in a "businesslike" way, service institutions would perform. And of course, this belief also underlies, in large measure, today's "management boom" in the service institutions.

But it is the wrong diagnosis; and being "businesslike" is the wrong prescription for the ills of the service institution. The service institution has performance trouble precisely because it is not a business. What being "businesslike" usually means in a service institution is little more than control of cost. What characterizes a business, however, is focus on results—return on capital, share of market, and so on.

To be sure, there is a need for efficiency in all instututions. Because there is usually no competition in the service field, there is no outward and imposed cost control on service institutions as there is on business in a competitive (and even an oligopolistic) market. But the basic problem of service institutions is not high cost but lack of effectiveness. They may be very efficient—some are. But they then tend not to do the right things.

The belief that the public service institution will perform if only it is put on a "businesslike" basis underlies the numerous attempts to set up many government services as separate "public corporations"—again an attempt that dates back to Colbert and his establishment of "Crown monopolies." There may be beneficial side effects, such as freedom from petty civil service regulation. But the intended main effect, performance, is seldom achieved. Costs may go down (though not always; setting up London Transport and the British Post Office as separate "businesslike" corporations, and thereby making them defenseless against labor union pressures, has led to skyrocketing costs). But services essential to the fulfillment of the institution's purpose may be slighted or lopped off in the name of "efficiency."

The best and worst example of the "businesslike" aprɔach in the public service institution may well be the Port of New York Authority, set up in the 1920's to manage automobile and truck traffic throughout the two-state area (New York and New Jersey) of the Port of New York. The Port Authority has, from the beginning, been "businesslike" with a vengeance. The engineering of its bridges, tunnels, docks, silos, and airports has been outstanding. Its construction costs have been low and under control. Its financial standing has been extremely high, so that it could always borrow at most advantageous rates of interest. It made being "businesslike"—as measured, above all, by its standing with the banks — its goal and purpose. As a result, it did not concern itself with transportation policy in the New York metropolitan area, even though its bridges, tunnels, and airports generate much of the traffic in New York's streets. It did not ask: "Who are our constituents?" Instead it resisted any such question as "political" and "unbusinesslike." Consequently, it has come to be seen as the villain of the New York traffic and transportation problem. And when it needed support (e.g., in finding a place to put New York's badly needed fourth airport), it found itself without a single backer, except the bankers. As a result the Port Authority may well become "politicized"; that is, denuded of its efficiency without gaining anything in effectiveness.

"Better people"

The cry for "better people" is even older than Colbert. In fact, it can be found in the earliest Chinese texts on government. In particular, it has been the constant demand of all American "reformers," from Henry Adams shortly after the Civil War, to Ralph Nader today. They all have believed that the one thing lacking in the government agency is "better people."

But service institutions cannot, any more than businesses, depend on "supermen" to staff their managerial and executive positions. There are far too many institutions to be staffed. If service institutions cannot be run and managed by men of normal—or even fairly low—endowment, if, in other words, we cannot organize the task so that it will be done on a satisfactory level by men who only try hard, it cannot be done at all. Moreover, there is no reason to believe that the people who staff the managerial and professional positions in our "service" institutions are any less qualified, any less competent or honest, or any less hard-working than the men who manage businesses. By the same token, there is no reason to believe that business managers, put in control of service institutions, would do better than the "bureaucrats." Indeed, we know that they immediately become "bureaucrats" themselves.

One example of this was the American experience during World War II, when large numbers of business executives who had performed very well in their own companies moved into government positions. Many rapidly became "bureaucrats." The men did not change. But whereas in business they had been capable of obtaining performance and results, in government they found themselves producing primarily procedures and red tape—and deeply frustrated by the experience.

Similarly, effective businessmen who are promoted to head a "service staff" within a business (e.g., the hard-hitting sales manager who gets to be "Vice President—marketing services") tend to become "bureaucrats" almost overnight. Indeed, the "service institutions" within business—R&D departments, personnel staffs, marketing or manufacturing service staffs, and the like—apparently find it just as hard to perform as the public service institutions of society at large, which businessmen often criticize as being "unbusinesslike" and run by "bureaucrats."

"Intangible" objectives

The most sophisticated and, at first glance, the most plausible explanation for the non-performance of service institutions is the last one: The objectives of service institutions are "intangible," and so are the results. This is at best a half-truth.

The definition of what "our business is" is always "intangible," in a business as well as in a service institution. Surely, to say, as Sears Roebuck does, "Our business is to be the informed buyer for the American family," is "intangible." And to say, as Bell Telephone does, "Our business is service to the customers," may sound like a pious and empty platitude. At first glance, these statements would seem to defy any attempt at translation into operational, let alone quantitative, terms. To say, "Our business is electronic entertainment," as Sony of Japan does, is equally "intangible," as is IBM's definition of its business as "data processing." Yet, as these businesses have clearly demonstrated it is not exceedingly difficult to derive concrete and measurable goals and targets from "intangible' definitions like those cited above.

"Saving souls," as the definition of the objectives of a church is, indeed, "intangible." At least the bookkeeping is not of this world. But church attendance is measurable. And so is "getting the young people back into the church."

"The development of the whole personality" as the objective of the school is, indeed, "intangible." But "teaching a child to read by the time he has finished third grade" is by no means intangible; it can be measured easily and with considerable precision.

"Abolishing racial discrimination" is equally unamendable to clear operational definition, let alone measurement. But to increase the number of black apprentices in the building trades is a quantifiable goal, the attainment of which can be measured.

Achievement is never possible except against specific, limited, clearly defined targets, in business as well as in a service institution. Only if targets are defined can resources be allocated to their attainment, priorities and deadlines be set, and somebody be held accountable for results. But the starting point for effective work is a definition of the purpose and mission of the institution—which is almost always "intangible," but nevertheless need not be vacuous.

It is often said that service institutions differ from businesses in that they have a plurality of constituencies. And it is indeed the case that service institutions have a great many "constituents." The school is of vital concern not only to children and their parents, but also to teachers, to taxpayers, and to the community at large, Similarly, the hospital has to satisfy the patient, but also the doctors, the nurses, the technicians, the patient's family—as well as taxpayers or, as in the United States, employers and labor unions who through their insurance contributions provide the bulk of the support of most hospitals. But business also has a plurality of constituencies. Every business has at least two different customers, and often a good many more. And employees, investors, and the community at large—and even management itself—are also "constituencies."

Misdirection by budget

The one basic difference between a service institution and a business is the way the service institution is paid. Businesses (other than monopolies) are paid for satisfying the customer. They are only paid when they produce what the customer wants and what he is willing to exchange his purchasing power for. Satisfaction of the customer is, therefore, the basis for performance and results in a business.

Service institutions, by contrast, are typically paid out of a budget allocation. Their revenues are allocated from a general revenue stream that is not tied to what they are doing, but is obtained by tax, levy, or tribute. Furthermore, the typical service institution is endowed with monopoly powers; the intended beneficiary usually has no choice.

Being paid out of a budget allocation changes what is meant by "performance" or "results." *"Results" in the budget-based institution means a larger budget. "Performance" is the ability to maintain or to increase one's budget.* The first test of a budget-based institution and the first requirement for its survival is to obtain the budget. And the budget is, by definition, related not to the achievement of any goals, but to the *intention* of achieving those goals.

This means, first, that efficiency and cost control, however much they are being preached, are not really considered virtues in the budget-based institution. The importance of a budget-based institution is measured essentially by the size of its budget and the size of its staff. To achieve results with a smaller budget or a smaller staff is, therefore, not "performance." It might actually endanger the institution. Not to spend the budget to the hilt will only convince the budget-maker—whether a legislature or a budget committee—that the budget for the next fiscal period can safely be cut.

Thirty or 40 years ago, it was considered characteristic of Russian planning, and one of its major weaknesses, that Soviet managers, towards the end of the plan period, engaged in a frantic effort to spend all the money allocated to them, which usually resulted in total waste. Today, the disease has become universal, as budget-based institutions have become dominant everywhere. And "buying-in"—that is, getting approval for a new program or project by grossly underestimating its total cost—is also built into the budget-based institution.

"Parkinson's Law" lampooned the British Admiralty and the British Colonial Office for increasing their staffs and their budgets as fast as the British Navy and the British Empire went down. "Parkinson's Law" attributed this to inborn human perversity. But it is perfectly rational behavior for someone on a budget, since it is the budget, after all, that measures "performance" and "importance."

It is obviously not compatible with *efficiency* that the acid test of performance should be to obtain the budget. But *effectiveness* is even more endangered by reliance on the budget allocation. It makes it risky to raise the question of what the "business" of the institution should be. That question is always "controversial"; such controversy is likely to alienate support and will therefore be shunned by the budget-based institution. As a result, it is likely to wind up deceiving both the public and itself.

Take an instance from government: The U.S. Department of Agriculture has never been willing to ask whether its goal should be "farm productivity" or "support of the small family farm." It has known for decades that these two objectives are not identical as had originally been assumed, and that they are, indeed, becoming increasingly incompatible. To admit this, however, would have created controversy that might have endangered the Department's budget. As a result, American farm policy has frittered away an enormous amount of money and human resources on what can only (and charitably) be called a public relations campaign, that is, on a show of support for the small family farmer. The effective activities, however—and they have been very effective indeed—have been directed toward eliminating the small farmer and replacing him by the far more productive "agribusinesses," that is, highly capitalized and highly mechanized farms, run a s a business and not as a "way of life." This may well have been the right thing to do. But it certainly was not what the Department was founded to do, nor what the Congress, in approving the Department's budget, expected it to do.

Take a non-governmental example, the American community hospital, which is "private" though "non-profit." Everywhere it suffers from a growing confusion of missions and objectives, and the resulting impairment of its effectiveness and performance. Should a hospital be, in effect, a "physician's facility"—as most older American physicians still maintain? Should it focus on the major health needs of a community? Or should it try to do everything and be "abreast of every medical advance," no matter what the cost and no matter how rarely certain facilities will be used? Should it devote resources to preventive medicine and health education? Or should it, like the hospital under the British health service, confine itself strictly to repair of major health damage after it has occurred?

Every one of these definitions of the "business" of the hospital can be defended. Every one deserves a hearing. The effective American hospital will be a multi-purpose institution and strike a balance between various objectives. What most hospitals do, however, is pretend that there are no basic questions to be decided. The result, predictably, is confusion and impairment of the hospital's capacity to serve any function and to carry out any mission.

Pleasing everyone and achieving nothing

Dependence on a budget allocation militates against setting priorities and concentrating efforts. Yet nothing is ever accomplished unless scarce resources are concentrated on a small number of priorities. A shoe manufacturer who has 22 per cent of the market for work shoes may have a profitable business. If he succeeds in raising his market share to 30 per cent, especially if the market for his kind of footwear is expanding, he is doing very well indeed. He need not concern himself too much with the 78 per cent of the users of work shoes who buy from somebody else. And the customers for ladies' fashion shoes are of no concern to him at all.

Contrast this with the situation of an institution on a budget. To obtain its budget, it needs the approval, or at least the acquiescence, of practically everybody who remotely could be considered a "constituent." Where a market share of 22 per cent might be perfectly satisfactory to a business, a "rejection" by 78 per cent of its "constituents —or even by a much smaller proportion—would be fatal to a budget-based institution. And this means that the service institution finds it difficult to set priorities; it must instead try to placate everyone by doing a little bit of everything—which, in effect, means achieving nothing. thing.

Finally, being budget-based makes it even more difficult to abandon the wrong things, the old, the obsolete. As a result, service institutions are even more encrusted than businesses with the barnacles of inherently unproductive efforts.

No institution likes to abandon anything it does. Business is no exception. But in an institution that is being paid for its performance and results, the unproductive, the obsolete, will sooner or later be killed off by the customers. In a budget-based institution no such discipline is being enforced. The temptation is great, therefore, to respond to lack of results by redoubling efforts. The temptation is great to double the budget, precisely because there is no performance.

Human beings will behave as they are rewarded for behaving—whether the reward be money or promotion, a medal, an autographed picture of the boss, or a pat on the back. This is one lesson the behavioral psychologist has taught us during the last 50 years (not that it was unknown before). A business, or any institution that is paid for its results and performance in such a way that the dissatisfied or disinterested customer need not pay, has to "earn" its income. An institution that is financed by a budget—or that enjoys a monopoly which the customer cannot escape—is rewarded for what it "deserves" rather than for what it "earns." It is paid for good intentions and for "programs." It is paid for not alienating important constituents rather than for satisfying any one group. It is misdirected, by the way it is paid, into defining 'performance" and "results" as what will maintain or increase its budget.

WHAT WORKS

The exception, the comparatively rare service institution that achieves effectiveness, is more instructive than the great majority that achieves only "programs." It shows that effectiveness in the service institution is available—though by no means easy. It shows what different kinds of service institutions can do and need to do. It shows limitations and pitfalls. But it also shows that the service insititution manager can do unpopular and highly "controversial" things if only he makes the risk-taking decision to set priorities and allocate resources.

The first and perhaps simplest example is that of the Bell Telephone System. A telephone system is a "natural" monopoly. Within a given area, one supplier of telephone service must have exclusive rights. The one thing any subscriber to a public telephone service requires is access to all other subscribers, which means territorial exclusivity for one monopolistic service. And as a whole country or continent becomes, in effect, one telephone system, this monopoly has to be extended over larger and larger areas.

An individual may be able to do without a telephone—though in today's society only a prohibitive inconvenience. But a professional man, a tradesman, an office, or a business *must* have a telephone. Residential phone service may still be an "option." Business phone service is compulsory. Theodore Vail, the first head of the organization, saw this in the early years of this century. He also saw clearly that the American telephone system, like the telephone systems in all other industrially developed nations, could easily be taken over by government. To prevent this, Vail thought through what the telephone company's business was and should be, and came up with his famous definition: "Our business is service."[2] This totally "intangible" statement of the telephone company's "business" then enabled Vail to set specific goals and objectives and to develop measurements of performance and results. His "customer satisfaction" standards and "service satisfaction" standards created nationwide competition between telephone managers in various areas, and became the criteria by which the managers were judged and rewarded. These standards measured per-

---

[2]This was so heretical that the directors of the telephone company fired Vail when he first propounded his thesis in 1897—only to rehire him 10 years later when the absence of clear performance objectives had created widespread public demand for telephone nationalization even among such non-radicals as the Progressive wing of the Republican Party.

formance as defined by the customer, e.g., waiting time before an operator came on the line, or time betweeen application for telephone service and its installation. They were meant to direct managers' attention to results.

Vail also thought through who his "constituents" were. This led to his conclusion—even more shocking to the conventional wisdom of 1900 than his "service" objectives—that it was the telephone company's task to make the public utility commissions of the individual states capable of effective rate regulation. Vail argued that a national monopoly in a crucial area could expect to escape nationalization only by being regulated. Helping to convert the wretchedly ineffectual, corrupt, and bumbling public utility commissions of late 19th-century populism into effective, respected, and informed adversaries was in the telephone company's own survival interest.

Finally, Vail realized that a telephone system depends on its ability to obtain capital. Each dollar of telephone revenue requires a prior investment of three to four dollars. Therefore, the investor too had to be considered a "constituent," and the telephone company had to design financial instruments and a financial policy that focused on the needs and expectations of the investor, and that made telephone company securities, whether bonds or shares, a distinct and preferred financial "product."

THE AMERICAN UNIVERSITY

The building of the American university from 1860 to World War I also illustrates how service institutions can be made to perform. The American university as it emerged during that era was primarily the work of a small number of men: Andrew D. White (President of Cornell, 1868-1885); Charles W. Eliot (President of Harvard, 1869-1909); Daniel Coit Gilman (President of John Hopkins, 1876-1901); David Starr Jordan (President of Stanford, 1891-1913); William Rainey Harper (President of Chicago, 1892-1904); and Nicholas Murray Butler (President of Columbia, 1902-1945).

These men all had in common one basic insight: The traditional "college"—essentially an 18th-century seminary to train preachers—had become totally obsolete, sterile, and unproductive. Indeed, it was dying fast; America in 1860 had far fewer college students than it had had 40 years earlier with a much smaller population. The men who built the new universities shared a common objective: to create a new institution, a true "university." And they all realized that while European examples, especially Oxford and Cambridge and the German university, had much to offer, these new universities had to be distinctively American institutions.

Beyond these shared beliefs, however, they differed sharply on what a university should be and what its purpose and mission were. Eliot, at Harvard, saw the purpose of the university as that of educating a leadership group with a distinct "style." His Harvard was to be a "national" institution rather than the parochial preserve of the "proper Bostonian" the Harvard College had been. But it also was to restore Boston—and to New England generally—the dominant position of a moral elite, such as in earlier times had been held by the "Elect," the Puritan divines, and their successors, the Federalist leaders in the early days of the Republic. Butler, at Columbia—and, to a lesser degree, Harper at Chicago—saw the function of the university as the systematic application of rational thought and analysis to the basic problems of a modern society, from education to economics, and from domestic government to foreign affairs. Gilman, at Johns Hopkins, saw the university as the producer of advanced knowledge; indeed, originally Johns Hopkins was to confine itself to advanced research and was to give no undergraduate instruction. While, at Cornell, White aimed at producing an "educated public."

Each of these men knew that he had to make compromises. Each knew that he had to satisfy a number of "constituencies" and "publics," each of whom looked at the university quite differently. Both Eliot and Butler, for instance, had to build their new university on an old foundation (the others could build from the ground up) and had to satisfy—or at least to placate—existing alumni and faculty. They all had to be exceedingly conscious of the need to attract and hold financial support. It was Eliot, for instance, with all his insistence on "moral leadership," who invented the first "placement office" and set out to find well-paying jobs for Harvard graduates, especially in business. It was Butler, conscious that Columbia was a late-comer and that the millionaire philanthropists of his day had already been snared by his competitors (e.g., Rockefeller by Chicago), who invented the first "public relations" office in a university, designed—and most successfully—to reach the merely well-to-do and get their money.

The founders' definitions did not outlive them. Even during the lifetime of Eliot and Butler, for instance, their institutions escaped their control, began to diffuse objectives and to confuse priorities. In the course of this century, all these universities—and many others, like the University of California and other major state universities—have converged towards a common type. Today, it is hard to tell one "multiversity" from another. Yet the imprint of the founders has still not been totally erased. It is hardly an accident that the New Deal picked faculty members primarily from Columbia and Chicago to be high-level advisors and policy makers; for the New Deal was, of course, committed to the application of rational thought and analysis to public policies and problems. And 30 years later, when the Kennedy Administration came in with an underlying belief in the "style" of an "elite," it naturally turned to Harvard. For while each of the founding fathers of the modern American university made compromises and adapted to a multitude of constituencies, each had an objective and a definition of the university to which he gave priority and against which he measured performance. Clearly, the job the founders did almost a century ago will have to be done again for today's "multiversity," if it is not to choke on its own services.

SCHOOLS, HOSPITALS, AND THE TVA

The English "open classroom" is another example of a successful service institution. It is being promoted in this country as the "child-centered" approach to schooling, but its origin was in the concern with performance, and that is also the secret of its success. The English "open classroom" demands that each child—or at least each normal child—acquire the same measurable proficiency in the basic skills of literacy at roughly the same time. It is then the teacher's task to think through the learning path best suited to lead each child to a common and pre-set goal. The objectives are perfectly clear; the learning of specific skills, especially reading, writing, and figuring. They are identical for all children, measurable, and measured. Everything else is, in effect, considered irrelevant. Such elementary schools as have performed in the urban slums of this country—and there are more of them than the current "crisis in the classroom" syndrome acknowledges—have done exactly the same thing. The performing schools in black or Puerto Rican neighborhoods in New York, for instance, are those that have defined one clear objective—usually to teach reading—have eliminated or subordinated everything else, and then have measured themselves against a standard of clearly set performance goals.

The solution to the problem of the hospital, as is becoming increasingly clear, will similarly lie in thinking through objectives and priorities. The most promising approach may well be one worked out by the Hospital Consulting Group at Westinghouse Electric Corporation, which recognizes that the American hospital has a multiplicity of functions, but organizes each as an autonomous "decentralized" division with its own facilities, its own staff, and its own objectives. There would thus be a traditional care hospital for the fairly small number of truly sick people who require what today's "full-time" hospital offers; an "ambulatory" medical hospital for diagnosis and outpatient work; an "ambulatory" surgical hospital for the large number of surgical patients—actually the majority—who, like patients after cataract surgery, a tonsilectomy, or most orthopedic surgery, are not "sick" and need no medical and little nursing care, but need a bed (and a bedpan) till the stitches are firm or the cast dries; a psychiatric unit—mostly for out-patient or overnight care; and a convalescent unit that would hardly differ from a good motel (e.g., for the healthy mother of a healthy baby). All these would have common services. But each would be a separate health care facility with different objectives, different priorities, and different standards of performance.

But the most instructive example of an effective service institution may be that of the early Tennessee Valley Authority. Built mainly during the New Deal, the TVA today is no longer "controversial." It is just another large power company, except for being owned by the government rather than by private investors. But in its early days, 40 years ago, the TVA was a slogan, a battle cry, a symbol. Some, friends and enemies alike, saw in it the opening wedge of the nationalization of electric energy in the United States. Others saw in it the vehicle for a return to Jeffersonian agrarianism, based on cheap power, government paternalism, and free fertilizer. Still others were primarily interested in flood control and navigation. Indeed, there was such a wealth of conflicting expectations that TVA's first head. Arthur Morgan, a distinguished engineer and economist, completely floundered. Unable to think through what the business of the TVA should be and how varying objectives might be balanced, Morgan accomplished nothing. Finally, President Roosevelt replaced him with an almost totally unknown young lawyer, David Lilienthal, who had little previous experience as an administrator.

Lilienthal faced up to the need to define the TVA's business. He concluded that the first objective was to build truly efficient electric plants and to supply an energy-starved region with plentiful and cheap power. All the rest, he decided, hinged on the attainment of this first need, which then became his operational priority. The TVA of today has accomplished a good many other objectives as well, from flood control and navigation to fertilizer production, and, indeed, even balanced community development. But it was Lilienthal's insistence on a clear definition of the TVA's business and on setting priorities that explains why today's TVA is taken for granted, even by the very same people who, 40 years ago, were among its implacable enemies.

THE REQUIREMENTS FOR SUCCESS

Service institutions are a most diverse lot. The one and only thing they all have in common is that, for one reason or another, they cannot be organized under a competitive market test.[3] But however diverse the various kinds of "service institutions" may be, all of them need first to impose on themselves the discipline practiced by the managers and leaders of the institutions in the examples presented above.

1) They need to answer the question, *"What is our business and what should it be?"* They need to bring out into the open alternative definitions and to think them through carefully, perhaps even to work to (as did the presidents of the emerging American universities) the balance of different and sometimes conflicting definitions. What service institutions need is not to be more "business-like." They need to be more "hospital-like," "university-like," "government-like," and so on. They need to be subjected to a performance test—if only to that of "socialist competition"—as much as possible. In other words, they need to think through their own specific function, purpose, and mission.

2) Service institutions need to derive *clear objectives and goals* from their definition of function and mission. What they need is not "better people," but people who do the management job systematically and who focus themselves and their institutions purposefully on performance and results. They do need efficiency—that is, control of costs. But, above all, they need effectiveness—that is, emphasis on the right results.

3) They then have to think through *priorities* of concentration which enable them to select targets; to set standards of accomplisment and performance (that is, to define the minimum acceptable results); to set deadlines; to go to work on results; and to make someone accountable for results.

4) They need to define *measurements of performance*—the "customer satisfaction" measurements of the telephone company, or the figures on reading performance by which the English "open classroom" measures its accomplishments.

5) They need to use these measurements to *"feed back"* on their efforts—that is, *they must build self-control from results into their system.*

---

[3]This may no longer be necessarily true for the postal service. At last an independent postal company in the U.S. is trying to organize a business in competition to the government's postal monopoly. Should this work out, it might do more to restore performance to the mails than the recent setting up of a postal monopoly as a separate "public corporation" which is on a "businesslike" basis.

6) Finally, they need an organized audit of *objectives and results*, so as to identify those objectives that no longer serve a useful purpose or have proven unattainable. They need to identify unsatisfactory performance, and activities which are obsolete, unproductive, or both. And they need a mechanism for *sloughing off* such activities rather than wasting their money and their energies where the results are not.

This last requirement may be the most important one. The absence of a market test removes from the service institution the discipline that forces a business eventually to abandon yesterday's products—or else go bankrupt. Yet this requirement is the least understood.

No success lasts "forever." Yet it is even more difficult to abandon yesterday's success than it is to reappraise failure. Success breeds its own *hubris*. It creates emotional attachments, habits of thought and action, and, above all, false self-confidence. A success that has outlived its usefulness may, in the end, be more damaging than failure. Especially in a service institution, yesterday's success becomes "policy," "virtue," "conviction," if not indeed "Holy Writ," unless the institution imposes on itself the discipline of thinking through its mission, its objectives, and its priorities, and of building in feedback control from results over policies, priorities, and action. We are in such a "welfare mess" today in the United States largely because the welfare program of the New Deal had been such a success in the 1930's that we could not abandon it, and instead misapplied it to the radically different problem of the black migrants to the cities in the 1950's and 1960's.

To make service institutions perform, it should by now be clear, does not require "great men." It requires instead a system. The essentials of this system may not be too different from the essentials of performance in a business enterprise, as the present "management boom" in the service institutions assumes. But the application will be quite different. For the service institutions are not businesses; "performance" means something quite different for them.

Few service institutions today suffer from having too few administrators; most of them are over-administered, and suffer from a surplus of procedures, organization charts, and "management techniques." What now has to be learned—it is still largely lacking—is to manage service institutions for performance. This may well be the biggest and most important management task for the remainder of the century.

SECTION II

VIEWPOINTS ON CONSUMERISM

This section is intended to focus on the range of opinion regarding consumer roles in the health sector, with particular emphasis on hospitals. A pertinent review of the literature is provided by *Metsch and Veney.*

Silver takes a very positive stance toward consumer input and insists that giving the consumer a voice will not damage the professional's role but will, in fact, enhance it by limiting claims of institutional racism, class discrimination, and poor responsiveness by bureaucracies.

Elling examines the nature of institutionalized power formations in the health field and the importance of power analysis in planning for regionalized health systems. He believes that consumer groups will exert an increasing impact on delivery decisions through participation on governmental agency and institutional advisory boards.

McNerney believes that consumers and professionals must be candid with each other if they are to resolve the mutual resentments which prevail. A shift to consumer power is well under way and should be accepted by professionals, who must foster communication patterns with their patients which serve to interpret the complexities of clinical technology.

Feingold offers a broad review of the key issues of consumer participation. He argues that the hospital administrator has a personal stake in increased participation and must, therefore, seek to structure it in a way which is valuable to both the consumer and the institution.

Cathcart states that consumers must be included in hospital governance to avoid radical and catastrophic change. However, consumer inclusion in governance is not tantamount to abdication of administrative responsibility. He also believes that consumer participation is essentially problematic, so each solution must take account of the local situation.

Pomrinse believes that voluntary hospitals currently maintain a high level of public accountability generated by audits conducted by various third parties, governmental agencies, and institutional boards of trustees. Further, placing responsibility for the management of multi-million dollar institutions into the hands of individuals who do not possess necessary training and experience is not in the best interests of the community. All groups should be heard, but ultimate responsibility rests with management.

Sade believes that the philosophy of medical care as a right, supported by government, represents a serious infringement of the physician's right to make professional choices. Threats of force by government to obtain physician compliance are by their very nature anti-democratic and immoral.

Consumer Participation
and Social Accountability

JONATHAN M. METSCH
JAMES E. VENEY

INTRODUCTION

Consumer participation as a mandated component of federally funded health care programs is accepted to the extent that some form is unquestionably included in any new legislative proposal. It is apparently assumed that by requiring consumer participation and/or establishing mechanisms through which consumers can be involved in planning, managing and evaluating programs, the provider sector will become increasingly responsive to health care needs as perceived by the recipients of services. In a broader sense it might be inferred, with legislation of consumer participation taken as prima facie evidence, that the system which evolves will assure social accountability, be functional in facilitating the accomplishment of program objectives and accepted as legitimate by the community at large.

It is our contention that it remains problematic whether, in fact, consumer participation contributes substantially to the attainment of

Reprinted, with permission, from *Medical Care*, V. 14, April 1976, pp. 283-291.

program objectives or the promotion of social accountability. Moreover, the current trend in federal legislation and a growing body of knowledge about the effects of that legislation raises cause for concern that possible consumer expectations about their potential influence in shaping the health care delivery system through participatory planning may be quite naive.

Recent health care legislation, when mandating consumer participation has been unclear as to what the role of the consumer is to be, when compared to earlier legislation mandating consumer participation. For example, in the legislation which produced O.E.O. Neighborhood Health Centers, consumer participation was encouraged as a goal of the funding agency, as a way of determining health center policy, as a method for service evaluation and as the means of program implementation.[35] In contrast the mandate for consumer participation in more recent legislation has been largely non-specific. For example the Emergency Medical Services Systems Act (P.L. 93-154, November 16, 1973) states only that an emergency medical services system shall "be organized in such a manner that provides persons who reside in the system's service area and who have no professional training or financial interest in the provision of health care with an opportunity to participate in the making of policy for the system". Moreover, this lack of specificity has not as yet been clarified by the administering agency.

The National Health Planning and Resources Development Act (P.L. 93-641, January 4, 1975) requires that each health systems agency have a governing body with a majority comprised of area residents who are not providers of health care and "who are broadly representative of the social, economic, linguistic and racial populations, geographic areas of the health service area, and major purchasers of care." Without further clarification, conflict over who fits this definition and how the different consumer groups are represented may displace health planning as the principal focus of some health systems agencies.

At the same time the increasingly sophisticated assessment of the process and efficacy of consumer participation by researchers, consumer participants, providers and governmental program planners has identified a number of stumbling blocks in the effort to establish effective consumer participation. These obstacles include conceptualization of the consumer role, definition of the consumer as well as measurement of the impact of consumer input on policy development.

Taken together these two trends portray a complex situation. On the one hand, research findings clearly suggest the need for a high degree of specificity in the mandating of consumer participation if the consumer sector is to be a real and viable force. The trend toward vague or non-specific statements in recent legislation, however, is likely to assure that the consumer participation will not only fail to produce social accountability but may also serve to reinforce the divisions between providers and consumers in health care delivery system management. If consumer participation is to be a positive force in health care delivery specific guidelines defining the consumer participants' roles and responsibilities must be delineated and the resources necessary for successful participation must be identified. In addition we conclude that overemphasis on the restructuring of the participatory process will result only in incremental rather than substantive change unless a complementary strategy is developed which dramatically destabilizes the current power balance between government, providers and consumers. In this case, as the system seeks a new equilibrium it may be possible for the consumer sector to negotiate changes in the consumer participation process which will enhance the consumer role in health sector decision making.

ISSUE AREAS

There are a number of issues involved in the successful participation of consumers in health programs, even when specifically mandated. To focus on these issues it is appropriate to classify them into categories which relate first to the actors involved and secondly to the integrative process necessary for collaborative decision making. Therefore these issues will be discussed by focusing on characteristics of provider participants, consumer eligibility and selection processes, consumer-provider interaction and defining the outcome of consumer participation. A clarification of concepts in each of these areas will be critical to better definition of what consumer participation is and better performance of this activity.

THE PROVIDER PARTICIPANTS

Review of the literature suggests that the values, predisposition and agendas that define the strategies that provider organizations and their representatives bring to the participatory setting may be a key factor in determining the outcome of that participation. These predisposing characteristics may become manifest in provider attitude toward consumer participation and provider perception of the consumer's participatory role as well as in efforts to transform consumer participation into an administrative strategy of cooptation.

It should be expected, but is nevertheless worthy of documentation, that provider attitudes toward consumer participation is a critical determinant of the impact of consumer participation on the delivery of health care services. For example, in a study of nine Neighborhood Health Centers, Chenault and Brown found that administrative professionals who were consumer oriented were likely "to provide support and guidance on technical matters, and advice in general, but with the specific aim of community self determination in mind."[12] Douglass[20] found providers more influential than consumer participants in the planning of eight Model Cities Health Programs and a direct relationship between provider attitude toward consumer participation and the community orientedness of the final plan developed. Interestingly, however, Douglass[21] found that formal representatives of provider organizations involved in the planning process held attitudes which were less consumer oriented than providers serving in informal or unaffiliated capacities. Finally, in a study of nineteen consumer advisory boards mandated under the Ghetto Medicine Program in New York City, Metsch and Veney[16] found the attitude of hospital administrators toward consumer participation to directly influence the level of input attributed to consumer representatives.

Provider attitude toward consumer involvement in decision making is undoubtedly influenced by the process of professional training and professional socialization they experience. Salber[59] has pointed out that health professionals often find it difficult to accept consumers as decision makers because they cannot separate the role of consumer-as-patient from citizen. Other researchers have noted that professional education runs directly counter to the notion of sharing decision making responsibility with non professionals.[33,34,35] The main objective of provider involvement with consumers is often to maintain control over their work.[15,36,39] At the same time, the mandate for consumer participation is most often attached to legislation aimed at altering or modifying the present delivery system. In this environment providers are likely to resist demands for participation which often appear to them to have the purpose of organizational change. Every major professional group will seek a part in the decision making process in an effort to gain veto power over those decisions which directly affect them.[13,19]

Given the motivations of the provider, it is not difficult to see that attempts to operationalize consumer participation as an administrative strategy of cooptation will follow in many cases. Moreover, efforts at cooptation are possible since the mandate to incorporate consumer participation as a program component is given to the grantee and not to the community itself.

The sharp edge of consumer participation can be effectively blunted by administrative strategies such as shifting the objectives for participation to ones of altering community attitudes about the program or institution, elevating less militant community leadership into official status while using minor or symbolic concessions to offset the challenge of radical groups, and developing participatory structures which have minimal impact on agency operations.[10,11,16]

From this discussion it is not unjustified to suggest that factors which affect the manner in which providers participate with consumers are critical determinants of the long term impact consumer participation has on the health care delivery system. For effective consumer participation to take place it will be necessary to confront the problem of provider attitudes head on. Admittedly, these attitudes are not subject to change overnight, but the task of making providers more receptive to consumer input must be undertaken before the effect of consumer participation mandates can be expected to be seriously felt in any way.

THE CONSUMER REPRESENTATIVES

Provider domination of the implementation phase of consumer participation raises a series of interesting issues on how certain decisions are made during this process. These issues relate to how and why "consumer" is defined and how consumer representatives are selected. Taken together it becomes understandable how cooptation can take place and how certain types of provider determined implementation decisions can influence the capacity for consumer representatives to organize themselves effectively.

The issue of who the consumer is, given an unclear mandate to implement consumer participation, is a significant one.[1,65] Subsumed under this conceptual question of how one, in fact, identifies a community[38] is how one defines eligibility for becoming a consumer representative. Alternative criteria for determining eligibility have generally included anyone who does not make a living in the health care industry, those who obtain services from a given program, residency in a specified catchment area or income level.[28,33,67] Obviously the criterion finally selected determines the skills, resources, and constituencies that consumer representatives bring to the decision arena.

Given a decision on eligibility criteria, the method of selecting consumer representatives further defines capacity for playing a strong advocacy role. In general, there is no best way for selecting consumer representatives[62] and consumer representatives have been selected by election, appointment, self-selection and designation by community organizations.[6,10,28] It has been suggested, however, that the community itself should determine how representatives will be selected[41] and that the community should manage the selection process.[32] It is likely that consumer representatives not selected through a publicly determined process will have their legitimacy challenged by both other consumers and providers.[57] Experience suggests as well that lack of attention to the appropriateness of the selection process can lead to a selection advantage to those who shout the loudest even if they are not the most representative.[52,61] Other examples of resulting distortions include high status minority residents capturing a minority representation allocation in one community[25] and a focus on process rather than substantive issues where consumer participants are not program clients.[8]

Numerous studies have shown that in order for consumers to be effective participants they should have previous participatory experience.[22,37,46,49,50] Daniels[15] has also shown that effective consumer representatives require a constituency to support their activities while Graves[31] notes the importance of access to resources capable of balancing the power and influence that organizational strength brings to providers. To the extent that eligibility criteria and selection processes limit or exclude the participation of consumer representatives with these strengths it is likely that the impact of consumer participation in shaping health care programs will be minimal.

CONSUMER - PROVIDER INTERACTION

Over and above the issues which can be categorized as relating principally to provide participation and identifying and selecting consumer participants are those issues which relate to the interaction of these two groups. In particular, it is likely that providers and consumers will have differing objectives for consumer participation. Provider representatives and program staff are likely to implement consumer participation in a way which is designed to socialize consumers to a traditional point of view.

Salber[59] maintains that consumers must be involved in making key decisions if consumer participation is to be viable on a long-term basis. It has been noted that decisions about program structure, staff, and program priorities are often made before consumer involvement begins.[1,5] At the same time Hatch[32] points out that effective consumer participation depends on precisely an involvement in these types of key decisions. Clearly, if health professionals, community residents and political figures are to develop an ongoing and constructive relationship it must be based on "early and consistent community involvement."[41]

In any particular program development there are several points at which the community can become involved including for example; preparation of the grant application; after the grant is approved but before key program decisions are made; and well after program development has begun. Obviously, the importance of early consumer involvement is magnified by the fact that consumer and provider goals for any program are often in conflict.[7,17,23,34,48] Early involvement of consumers is also suggested so goals for their participation can be set. If realistic goals cannot be specified early in the process, little in the way of substantive participation follows.[46,54,61] Partridge[54] and Aleshire[1] both have shown that lack of goal clarity often leads to concentration on procedural rather than substantive matters with consequent "dropping-out" of consumer representatives who feel they have no impact on program operations. This often produces precisely what providers have sought, a paper consumer majority but an operative provider majority as a consequence of variable consumer attendance patterns.[6]

Staff roles and perceptions further confound the situation. It has been reported for example, that staff/consumer communication is not often well developed[7] and that staff put more value on the opinions and judgments of providers than consumers because of similar professional ideologies.[34] It has also been suggested that staff serving in bureaucratic positions cannot alter their overemphasis on rules and adherence to hierarchical decision making in order to collaborate with consumers.[27,56] This potential for conflicting perceptions and objectives among consumers, providers and staff may influence how processes which might integrate these three groups are developed. In particular, while it is part of the conventional wisdom of consumer participation that consumer representatives benefit from training, many critical questions about training remain unanswered.

Parker[53] has suggested that training will increase consumer confidence in the legitimacy of their participatory role, increase the ability of consumer representatives to work together, increase substantive knowledge and improve planning skills. In fact, a recent study of consumer training concluded that at the study sites observed, the training experience helped consumers to redefine their role and move on to higher levels of activity.[44] However, training can also be used to socialize consumers to a point of view divergent from the values and goals of the constituencies they represent. Clearly we do not know enough about training to state what forms are most effective.[29,49] It has been suggested that consumers benefit most from training programs which are sustained efforts rather than short term stabilizing devices[29] and which they themselves have helped to plan.[31] Nonetheless a debate exists over the correct sponsorship for training with proponents of outside groups whom the consumers trust[1,53] and the health care agency or institution itself.[17,42] At the time previous note has been made of the notion that providers often need training as well if they are to be able to share decision making responsibility with consumers.[33,34,35,59]

A similar lack of clarity exists over whether or not consumer representatives should be paid for their services. Opinions vary from payment of stipends for attendance at meetings, reimbursement for expenses, payment for consumer representative "education and development",[10,17,18] to the notion that any kind of payment is unnecessary if the program is relevant to the community.[65]

Providers and staff usually control the process through which consumer participation is implemented. It is likely in this climate that goal conflict will generate the development of processes which serve to orient consumer representatives to traditional and provider oriented viewpoints. This powerful lever in the hands of providers is likely to negate much of the influence consumer representatives have in modifying the delivery of health care services to better reflect community needs.

OUTCOME OF CONSUMER PARTICIPATION

Perhaps the most complex issue surrounding consumer participation is the difficulty of conceptualizing what the outcome should be in specific cases. Numerous outcome criteria have been proposed including: increased client identification with a program;[26] increased client utilization of services;[30] and increased provider sensitivity to consumer perspectives on the delivery of health care services.[66,67] Others have suggested that outcome should be viewed in terms of: improved patient care outcomes;[36] better informed consumers more aware of the complexities of the health care system;[43] consumer influence in the shaping of final decisions about health care programs;[40,60] and more coordinated planning process.[37] Finally, proposed criteria also include: the community orientedness of final programs;[20] the development of leadership and administrative skills in the community;[30,38,41] the consumers' sense of adequacy and confidence about controlling their own destinies;[59] and an end to racism in the planning and delivery of health services.[14,63]

The goals stated for a specific program of consumer participation would appear to be shaped by the numerous interrelated factors already discussed and in themselves be a result of the positive or negative interactions that have occurred between providers and consumers.

Government itself may have unintentionally set up situations where consumers compete among themselves through multiple overlapping consumer boards with unclear jurisdictional areas.[4]In New York City, for example, consumers sit on Comprehensive Health Planning District Boards, Ghetto Medicine Program Consumer Advisory Boards, Department of Mental Health and Mental Retardation Service Sub-Regional

Planning Boards, Health and Hospital Corporation Community Boards and City Planning Commission Community Planning Boards. Consumer representatives serving on several of these boards at once often fail to remember which hat they are wearing at a particular meeting and that the different boards may have conflicting objectives.

DISCUSSION

The issues identified here have been raised because they call into question the efficacy of vague mandates to implement consumer participation as adjuncts to health care programs. One conclusion might be to suggest that the appropriate means of implementing consumer participation have not as yet been found and that the current assumptions about organization of the participatory process need rethinking. Another conclusion might be that the notion of consumer participation as a vehicle for increasing provider accountability to the consumer sector remains unsubstantiated and that, in fact, the implementation problems noted in this review are symptomatic of an underlying contradiction between assumptions about consumer participation and the realities of the decision making processes dominant in the health care sector.[45]

The first conclusion, focusing on the inadequacies of the implementation proceess, assumes that consumer participation will be a visible mechanism for fostering social accountability if efforts are made to deal with obstacles identified in this report. Such a conclusion suggests two approaches to "fine tuning" the process.

First, the variations in consumer participation structures, processes and outcomes that have been reported, suggest that guidelines for implementing consumer participation cannot be generic but must be program specific and reflect program goals, settings and complexity. Further research would then be needed to develop comprehensive models of the consumer participation process so that specific and generalizable propositions about consumer participation could be identified. Much progress has been made which can serve as the foundation for this model building process.[3,20,21,46,47,54,55,64]

On a more immediate level movement in several directions is called for. The trend in mandating undefined consumer participation should be discontinued and replaced, at a minimum, with statements on the specific objectives for consumer participation and specificity on the consumers' role. It is evident that where no clear role exists, little in the way of substantive participation follows no matter what other facilitating activity takes place. Even if we have not reached the level of sophistication where we can explicate specific behavioral guidelines, enough has been learned that certain types of behavior can be precluded or prohibited.

Careful attention should be paid to defining "consumer" or "community" for a funded program and specifying eligibility criteria. Preferably, this should be done collaboratively with consumer, provider and program manager involvement.

Key program decisions should be identified and it should be made certain that they are made with consumer involvement. The nature of these decisions may vary across program categories, yet be consistent within a program.

Training should not be viewed as a panacea, but be planned for the specific needs of each consumer group. Careful evaluation protocols should also be developed and used. Provider training and staff development may be necessary for competent training for consumer representatives.

The impact of having multiple centers of consumer participation within a geographic, service or catchment area should be further investigated. Either specific decisional territories for each board should be identified or mechanisms for collaboration between groups should be developed. Too much consumer participation should not be allowed to become the root of its own failure.

The second conclusion, that implementation problems are indicative of an underlying contradiction between the tenets of consumer participation and established values and priorities related to decision making in the health care sector has several bases. In general consumer participation has had little impact to date on the redistribution of health care resources through such programs as Comprehensive Health Planning and Regional Medical Program[51,58] and has served primarily to legitimize the role of existing power centers in the health care sector.[2] Although there have been numerous examples of consumer participation, its failure to promote fundamental changes in the health care delivery system should be assessed within the political context of the health care sector.

The role of government in mandating consumer participation has fallen short of substantive efforts to monitor if consumers are appropriately involved in the planning process[48] to the point where consumer participation is often implemented to prevent other types of government intervention[43] such as regulation. This approach would only be selected by providers with the knowledge that minimal risk in terms of loss or sharing of power actually existed. Evidently government sees its role as the establishment of broad policy with final results determined by the resources and capabilities which each participating group of consumers and providers brings to the participatory process.

Even where mechanisms have been developed for an ongoing consumer role, the potential for major change in the health care delivery system is minimal. While consumer participation may alter the health planning process and lead to the development of categorical programs in such areas as maternal and child health, alcoholism or drug abuse, this is not equivalent to gaining control over resources or establishing a collaborative role in decision making. The latter might include involvement in the reordering of organizational values and priorities.

Although consumer participation may be used by providers to legitimize intervention in a new area and prompt the awarding of governmental grants for demonstration projects, these same consumers are usually unable to later withdraw their approval if and when the actual program is unsatisfactory to them. While the participation of consumers in the planning process may make it easier for government to allocate resources in a non-conflictual atmosphere, government does not create communication channels for direct consumer feedback on program implementation or impact and usually adheres to provider developed evaluation criteria. The result is often an essentially superficial commitment by government to consumer participation which leads to minimal or strategic action by providers and frustration on the part of consumers.

In this light one can reassess the frequent reports of successful provider/consumer interaction in certain settings. Closer scrutiny of these cases will reveal that success occurs most often in demonstration projects where providers are made aware of the high value placed on consumer participation *before* they join the system. Thus, for the most part, the provider characteristics noted above are not evident and provider behavior is consumer oriented. These cases should not lull program planners into generalizing that a normative consumer/provider relationship will exist in all settings and that specific guidelines for consumer participation are not needed.

CONCLUSION

The political scientist David Easton has developed an equilibrium model of how the political system responds to stress. This model can serve as a useful framework for understanding the current status of consumer participation.

Easton[24] explains that stress on a political system is comprised of increased demands on and/or decreased support of the system (inputs) by forces in the system's environment. A political system compensates for these pressures through decisions and actions (outputs) which seek to decrease the demands on and/or increase the support of the system. For the most part such decisions vary only incrementally from existing policy to a new equilibrium near the one which preceded it.[9]

In this context, govermental mandates to implement consumer participation in health sector decision making can be viewed as an output resulting from consumer expectations heightened, for example, by the community development programs of the 1960s such as Model Cities and the Office of Economic Opportunity[35,50] and the Civil Rights movement.[14,63]

Consumer participation through advisory boards was an incremental adjustment to environmental conditions which served to reestablish the equilibrium of health care system relationships without a major alteration in power relationships. By mandating consumer participation yet failing to promote or evaluate its purpose, and by assigning the implementation process, for the most part to providers, government has apparently made the adjustment necessary to diminish consumer demands on the system. More simply stated, it has been possible to decrease demand by creating participatory structures without the necessity of allocating resources which the consumer sector would need to be effective within these structures.

Similarly, by allowing consumers to participate superficially in the hospital accreditation process the provider sector is accommodating consumer demand without giving up provider dominance of the accreditation process.

Perhaps the consumer movement in health care will become a major influence only when it identified strategies which affect the support component of the equilibrium equation rather than by simply accepting new structures which reduce the credibility of its demands. Given the lack of homogeniety and discipline in the consumer sector it may be simplistic to presume that a strategy could be developed in this direction which would generate responses which are more than incremental and cosmetic.

This discussion should suggest however that consumer leaders may be jeopardizing the potential for consumer influence by concentrating solely on structural changes in the participatory process such as those suggested above. These changes may be significant only if they are built on a foundation which will enhance the possibility that negotiated change will be more than illusory. Only when the consumer sector can convince the other actors, government and providers, that it is capable of appreciably reducing the support for the current mode of resource allocation will its demands for participation be answered substantively. Concentration on this agenda therefore should be the current priority if consumer participation in health sector decision making is to be effective in the long run.

REFERENCES

1. Aleshire, R.A.: Power to the People: An Assessment of the Community Action Model Cities Experience. Pub. Admin. Rev. XXXII:428, 1972.
2. Alford, R.R.: The Political Economy of Health Care: Dynamics Without Change. Pol. and Soc. Winter:127, 1972.
3. Anderson, D.M. and Kerr, M: Citizen Influence in Health Services Programs. Am. J. Publ. Health 61:1518, 1971.
4. Ardell, D.B.: Public Regional Councils and Comprehensive Health Planning: A Partnership? J. Am. Inst. Plan. XXXII:393, 1970.
5. Austin, D.: Resident Participation: Political Mobilization or Organizational Co-optation? Pub. Admin. Rev. XXXII:409, 1972.
6. Bellin, L.E., Kavaler, F. and Schwartz, A.: Phase One of Consumer Participation in Policies of 22 Voluntary Hospitals in New York City. Am. J. Pub. Health 62-1370, 1972.
7. Bradbury, R.C.: A Comprehensive Health Planning Board of Directors. Health Serv. Rep. 87:905, 1972.
8. Bradshaw, B.R. and Mapp, C.B.: Consumer Participation in a Family Planning Program. Am. J. Pub. Health 62:969, 1972.
9. Braybrooke, D. and Lindblom, C.E.: A Strategy for Decision. New York, The Free Press, 1963.
10. Brieland, D.: Community Advisory Boards and Maximum Feasible Participation. Am. J. Pub. Health 61:292, 1971.
11. Burke, E.M.: Citizen Participation Strategies. J. Am. Inst. Plan. XXXIV:287, 1968.
12. Chenault, W.W. and Brown, D.K. Consumer Participation in Neighborhood Health Care Centers — Volume I — Interpretive Report. Washington, D.C., Department of Health, Education and Welfare, 1971.
13. Colt, A.M.: Elements of Comprehensive Health Planning. Am. J. Pub. Health 60:1194, 1970.
14. Cornely, P.B.: Community Participation and Control — A Possible Answer to Racism in Health. Mil. Mem. Fund Quart. XLVIII:347, 1970.
15. Daniels, R.S.: Governance and Administration of Human Services in Urban Low-Income Communities. Am. J. Pub. Health 63:715, 1973.
16. Davis, J.W.: Decentralization, Citizen Participation, and Ghetto Health Care. Am. Beh. Scient. 15:94, 1971.
17. Davis, M.S. and Tranquada, R.E.: A Sociological Evaluation of the Watts Neighborhood Health Center. Med. Care VII:105, 1969.
18. de Diaz, S.D.: Beyond Rhetoric — The NENA Health Center After One Year. Am. J. Pub. Health 62:64, 1972.

19. de Vise, P.: Planning Emphasis Shifts to Consumers. Mod. Hosp. 113:133, 1969.
20. Douglass, C.W.: Effect of Provider Attitude in Community Health Decision-Making. Med. Care XI:135, 1973a.
21. Douglass, C.W.: Representation Patterns in Community Health Decision-Making. J. Health Soc. Beh. 14:80, 1973b.
22. Douglass, C.W.: Health Services Planning in the Urban Ghetto: A Comparative Analysis of Eight Model Cities Programs. Ann Arbor, Michigan: Program in Health Planning, School of Public Health, University of Michigan, 1971.
23. Duvall, W.L.: Consumer Participation in Health Planning. Hosp. Admin. 16:35, 1971.
24. Easton, D.: A Framework for Political Analysis. Englewood Cliffs, New Jersey, Prentice-Hall, 1965.
25. Evans, R.D.: Representational Patterns in Comprehensive Health Planning. Am. J. Pub. Health 64:549, 1974.
26. Falkson, J.L.: An Evaluation of Alternative Models of Citizen Participation in Urban Bureacracy. Ann Arbor, Michigan, Program in Health Planning, School of Public Health, University of Michigan.
27. Fauri, D.P.: The Limits of Consumer Participation in Public Social Programs. Pub. Wel. 31:16, 1973.
28. Feingold, E.: Citizen Participation: A Review of the Issues. The Citizenry and the Hospital, Durham, N.C., Duke University, 1974.
29. Galiher, C.B., Needleman, J. and Rolfe, A.J.: Consumer Participation. HSMHA Health Rep. 86:99, 1971.
30. Glogow, E.: Community Participation and Sharing in Control of Public Health Services. Health Serv. Rep. 88:442, 1973.
31. Graves, J.G.: Involvement of Consumers. Hospitals, JAHA 44:46, 1970.
32. Hatch, J.: Community Shares in Policy Decisions for Rural Health Center. Hospitals, JAHA 43:109, 1969.
33. Hochbaum, G.M.: Consumer Participation in Health Planning: Toward Conceptual Clarification. Am. J. Pub. Health 59:1968, 1969.
34. Holton, W.E., New, P.K. and Hessler, R.M.: Citizen Participation and Conflict. Admin. Ment. Health Fall:96, 1973.
35. Howard, L.K.: Decentralization and Citizen Participation in Health Services. Pub. Admin. Rev. XXXII:701, 1972.
36. Johnson, E.: Giving the Consumer a Voice in the Hospital Business. Hosp. Admin. 15:15, 1970.
37. Kaplan, M.: The Model Cities Program — A Comparative Analysis of the Planning Process in Eleven Cities: Washing, D.C., Department of Housing and Urban Devopment, 1070.
38. Levin, H.: Power and Conflict — Key Concepts in Community Dynamics. The Citizenry and the Hospital, Durham, N.C., Duke University, 1974.
39. Maddox, G.L. and Stead, E.A.: The Professional and Citizen Participation. The Citizenry and the Hospital, Durham, N.C., Duke University, 1974.

40. McNamara, J.J.: Communities and Control of Health Services. Inquiry IV:64, 1972.
41. McGee, T. and Wexler, S.: The Evolution of Municipally Operated, Community Based Mental Health Services. Comm. Men. Health J. 8:303, 1972.
42. McNerney, W.J.: Medicine Faces the Consumer Movement: PRISM September: 13, 1973.
43. Medalia, N.: Citizen Participation and Environmental Health Action: The Case of Air Pollution Control. Am. J. Pub. Health 59:1385, 1969.
44. Metsch, J.M., Berson, A. and Weitzner, M.: The Impact of Training on Consumer Participation in the Delivery of Health Services. Health Education Monographs, forthcoming.
45. Metsch, J.M. and Rosen, H.: The Paradox of Consumer Participation in Health Delivery Systems. N.Y.U. Educ. Quart. (forthcoming).
46. Metsch, J.M. and Veney, J.E.: A Model of the Adaptive Behavior of Hospital Administrators to the Mandate to Implement Consumer Participation. Med. Care 12:338, 1974.
47. Metsch, J.M. and Veney, J.E.: Measuring the Outcome of Consumer Participation. J. Health Soc. Beh. 14:368, 1973.
48. Milio, N.: Dimensions of Consumer Participation and National Health Legislation. Am. J. Pub. Health 64:357, 1974.
49. Mogulof, M.B.: Citizen Participation: The Local Perspective. Washington, D.C., The Urban Institute, 1970.
50. Mogulof, M.B.: Coalition to Adversary: Citizen Participation in Three Federal Programs. J. Am. Inst. Plan. XXXV:225, 1969.
51. Navarro, V.: The City and the Region. Am. Beh. Scient. 14:865, 1971.
52. Notkin, H. and Notkin, M.S.: Community Participation in Health Services: A Review Article. Med. Care Rev. 27:1178.
53. Parker, A.W.: The Consumer as Policy Maker — Issues of Training. Am. J. Pub. Health 60:2139, 1970.
54. Partridge, K.B.: Community and Professional Participation in Decision Making at a Health Center. Health Serv. Rep. 88:527, 1973.
55. Partridge, K.B. and White, P.E.: Community and Professional Participation in Decision Making at a Health Center. Health Serv. Rep. 87:336, 1972.
56. Perlmutter, F.: Citizen Participation and Professionalism: A Developmental Relationship. Pub. Wel. 31:25, 1973.
57. Peterson, P.E.: Community Representation and the 'Free Rider' Question. The Citizenry and the Hospital. Durham, N.C., Duke University, 1974.
58. Rushing, W.A.: Public Policy, Community Constraints, and the Distribution of Medical Resources. Soc. Prob. 19:21, 1971.
59. Salber, E.J.: Consumer Participation in Neighborhood Health Centers. New Eng. J. Med. 283:515, 1970.
60. Schwartz, J.L.: Medical Care Plans and Health Care. Springfield, Ill., Charles C. Thomas, 1968.
61. Sheps, C.G.: The Influence of Consumer Sponsorship on Medical Services. Irving V. Zola and John B. McKinlay (eds.), Organizational Issues in the

Delivery of Health Services. New York, Prodist, 1974.

62. Silver, G.A.: Community Participation and Health Resource Allocation. Internat. J. Health Serv. 3:117, 1973.

63. Skinner, H.: Citizen Participation and Racism. Pub. Admin. Rev. XXXII: 210, 1972.

64. Sparer, G., Dines, G.B. and Smith, D: Consumer Participation in OEC Assisted Neighborhood Health Centers. Am. J. Pub. Health 60:1091, 1970.

65. Thomson, R.: The Whys and Why Nots of Consumer Participation. Comm. Men. Health J. 9:143, 1973.

66. Tischler, G.L.: The Effects of Consumer Control on the Delivery of Services. Am. J. of Orth. 41:501, 1971.

67. Wells, B.B.: Role of the Consumer in Regional Medical Programs. Am. J. Publ. Health 60:2133, 1970.

Community Participation and Health Resource Allocation

GEORGE A. SILVER, M.D.

For more than 200 years now, efforts have been devoted to improving and increasing the professional content of social decisions. In place of caprice, charity, religious motivation, personal prejudice, or economic vested interest, rational professional considerations have been attempted in allocating scarce resources for social ends. It is only recently that attention has been directed to the problem of adjusting these professional considerations to the needs or demands of clients. In part this is because it is only recently that clients—the community served—have begun to assert such demands or protest the purely professional decisions. Because of the recency of this phenomenon, the political implications and consequences of community decision making and community control of human service organizations have been little studied. Statistical data or formal political science studies in this area are rare if they exist at all. Yet some few case studies have been published and anecdotal material is available [1-9]. The comments that follow are in

Reprinted, with permission, from The International Journal of Health Services, V. 3, 1973, pp. 117-131.

the nature of observations and descriptions rather than analysis. Wider circulation of such presentations will no doubt encourage officials and students to seek more rigorous expression and more formal data collection.

HISTORICAL DEVELOPMENT

The earlier trend toward professionalism in social decision making was facilitated by the growth of scientific knowledge, technology, and industrial competence. Collection of statistical information was started in the 17th and 18th centuries. Causes of death, relative longevity, and health factors related to morbidity were correlated with places and substances. The burgeoning science of epidemiology accompanied an awakening of interest in and concern for public health action.

As public health grew in scientific esteem and public importance, professionalism in its activities was increasingly sought and encouraged. Qualifications were introduced for health officers on the assumption that formal training was necessary to carry out the duties. Educational programs were designed to serve these ends and schools of public health specializing in such training became a worldwide phenomenon. In the United States particularly, university degrees reflecting special competence were established and requisite qualifications for specialists were established. We now have accrediting agencies for the schools, the special fields, and the jobs within the fields.

In the 20th century, obsession with management techniques has advanced in pace with industrialization. These techniques relate successful operations to the planning, evaluation, and modification of production methods and distribution mechanisms. Business, to be competitive, has to be rapidly responsive to market effects. Manufacturing processes are constantly modified to increase their productivity. The competitive character of these enterprises demands managerial expertise.

Out of this milieu grew the science of economic analysis, planning, and decision making, indicating that priorities have to be determined before choices could be made. The analogy was then extended to the service fields: health, education, and welfare. Unfortunately, far less information was available about input and output in these fields than in business, especially concerning what constituted a "good" outcome. Thus as management theory and measures were introduced into these service fields, data were collected to be fed into the economic analysis models for the decision making process in the service areas.

Health Planning

Planning in the health field took two forms: social planning and resource allocation. Social planning determined the proportion of social resources to be assigned to health, distinct from education and welfare, while resource allocation, within the health field, determined what proportion of health resources should go to develop new knowledge, or produce manpower, or provide services. In both cases, in the United States, the planning process was unworkable. Since the bulk of the expenditures for health services in the United States has been, and continues to be, from the private sector, not subject to public or official decision making, the "planning" was essentially theoretical, without the opportunity for implementation. Clearly, planning is only as effective as the penalties which can be imposed for failure to comply. Not merely was the private sector in control of most expenditures, limiting the potential for public penalties, but actually the public sector did not, or would not, apply penalties for violation of the plans that were promulgated. Nor need one accept at face value that planning which is practiced in the public sector. Gorham, who initiated PPBS (planning-programming-budgeting system) into the Department of Health, Education, and Welfare, recognizes the dependence of planning on political factors:

> . . .some people now imagine that "cost-benefiters," using computers, are taking over decision-making in the Federal government. . . . Such a notion . . . is silly. . . . Anyone in government knows that most decisions on spending emerge from a political process . . .[10]

At the same time and in this context, unconscious planning was taking place. It was of a negative nature but it had the effect of positive planning. For example, failing to put sufficient funds into medical education resulted in fewer physicians being produced than would otherwise have been the case, while putting huge sums of money into medical research drove large numbers of trained people into that field and away from practice and medical service responsibilities. In time the failure to provide enough medical resources resulted in the inflation of cost as demand exceeded supply, and in maldistribution as resources flocked to the dollar.

No significant legislative action to remedy this situation was undertaken until recently, when the poor and minority groups were visibly at an increasing disadvantage and even the moderately well-off began to suffer the consequences of increasing health resource shortages and inefficiencies. Indeed, the rapid inflation in the cost of medical care over the past few years results largely from inept legislative efforts to remedy the inaccessibility of care for the poor (Medicaid) and the elderly (Medicare) by putting more funds into the medical marketplace. That this lesson has not yet been learned is evident from the fact that it is almost a certainty at this point that the U.S. Congress will soon promulgate a national plan at least for payment for health services, and possibly for some reorganization of health services. This may well result in further inflation, still however without attacking the basic problems.

In any case, since the tools for planning and design of health services have now been available for years, building on techniques from other fields, any health system reorganization will unquestionably be of a highly professional character.

Given the temper of the times, will this be acceptable? Will it be workable?

THE NEED FOR CONSUMER PARTICIPATION

With the drive for social equity has arisen a demand for more consumer or client participation in the planning and design of social mechanisms for improvement of social conditions. That demand had its inception in 1964 with the creation of the Office of Economic Opportunity. At the time, consumer participation was defined as "maximum feasible participation" of the poor or of the residents of the area to be served. It gradually came to have a broader connotation—not only that those who are served must share in decision making, but that decision making has to have local power of enforcement—a call for consumer or client *control* rather than simply participation. The problems of planning generally, considered above, contributed to the dissatisfaction which gave rise to the demand for consumer participation and eventually, control[11].

De Tocqueville's observation remains as pertinent as it was a century ago: "The evils which are endured with patience as long as they are incurable, seem intolerable as soon as a hope can be entertained of escaping from them." Over the last decade, conferences, rhetoric, and political platforms have emphasized the possibility, temptingly described the opportunity, and promised the reality of health services to the poor and deprived. Other social factors have played their part in enhancing the need and demand for more consumer participation. First among these is the fact of the immobility of large systems, as one writer has noted:

> It is the unresponsiveness of such mammoth systems and the
> poor quality of mass services which lead to frustration. . . . One of the

main functions of the various forms of community control is to provide a new kind of accountability of professionals to constituents or consumers.[1]

Yet another writer has called attention to the lack of political accountability implicit in racism: "What, then, does political theory have to say when basic institutions have lost their legitimacy in the eyes of a *minority* because for too long a time to be borne, the majority is thought to have done wrong or to have been oppressive?"[7] And finally there is the problem of the unwieldy bureaucracies:

> The human rights revolution has been a major theme of the domestic history of the U.S. since the end of WW II. . . . This recent emphasis upon community control emerged rather suddenly. . . . As an expression of poor-people power, neighborhood control grew under the Community Action Program . . . [of] the Economic Opportunity Act. . . . As a reaction to the ineffectiveness of programs controlled by stagnant, big-city bureaucracies, neighborhood control became a major interest of most big cities[8].

In addition to noting the problem of unwieldy bureaucracies, Hallman points out that the original programs in which poor people were involved derived not so much from the need to modify the professional input as to "provide for them a greater stake in society and thus reduce their alienation"[8]. In a sense, this involvement was designed to be a rejuvenation of the political structure, reviving the stultified bureaucracies. Thus this same writer goes on to define and justify a special kind of planning involving the poor:

> Advocacy planning . . . is founded upon the premise that many planning decisions are the expression of values and interests of certain groups and that therefore planning policy is never wholly objective. Therefore, each planning group should have its own planning advocate to give it the necessary technical competence to participate in the decision-making process[8].

He quotes also Marshall Kaplan's thesis on advocacy and urban planning: "His [the planning advocate's] role is to defend or prosecute the interests of his clients . . . when the facts interpreted by others overlook, minimize, and/or negatively affect his client's interests"[8].

Community participation thus emerges as a powerful political force:

> The citizen who is the target of Federal involvement is *not* every man . . . he is a special segment of the population whose participation can be instrumental in achieving certain purposes . . . (a) decrease alienation, (b) engage the "sick" individual, (c) create an organized societal force capable of protecting aggrieved groups and winning for them a fairer share of the resources, and (d) develop a constituency and engineer its consent[2].

These general dissatisfactions and the consequences have their counterpart in the health field. In one of the papers presented recently before the New York Academy of Medicine, the author notes gloomily: "The only way in which consumer interests appear to have been adequately represented is when people have been paid to protect the consumer's interests . . ."[12].

Another writer recommends for health planning the same frame of reference noted above[8]. "(1) Improving image of black male in poverty communities. (2) Stimulating and maintaining solidarity among migrant Chicano farm workers. (3) Pacification of hostile communities by colonial powers. (4) Discharging missionary service obligations of the medical-hospital establishment. (5) Filling a political void in social and economic action. (6) Politicization/radicalization of youth"[13].

Still others see the problem in a class perspective: "The American health care system is a middle class system, and as far as the poor are concerned, it needs to be altered if it is to serve them"[14]. A few writers recognize historic trends and see community participation today as a renewed emphasis of the democratic promise of the U.S., responding to community demands and community needs:

> No matter where they come or how they get their jobs, public health officers, like other public officials, can be sure of one thing: the day they assume office they will become the focal point of pressures from a variety of sources. . . . The pattern of public health services is an outcome of settlements and understandings tacit and explicit, among all the groups and interests concerned[15].

One writer puts this drive in the context of the older efforts to place consumers on voluntary hospital boards, public school boards, and university boards[16]. However, the class relations of voluntary hospital boards and neighborhood centers are quite different and this argument is less persuasive. The following description of the situation of a farm worker underlines the need for participation of the poor in health service organization. This is what a Mexican-American indigent patient had to do to obtain health care in Monterey County in 1965.

> . . . most of the hospital's clinics opened at 8 a.m. . . . The patient would . . . have to start his journey at 1 a.m. (from King City) boarding a Greyhound bus for the one hour trip to Salinas. He would then have to sit up the balance of the night, waiting for the clinic to open. Even if he were seen early in the morning, he still had to wait for a bus back, as the first bus for King City did not leave until afternoon. The status degradation and "mortification process" of county hospital care was perhaps the most significant hardship. Being classified as a second-class citizen, submitting to uncomfortable tests of financial means, suffering liens on property, and enduring long waits before appointments are implemented are all parts of the invidious class categorization of the indigent and denigrate his self-image[14].

It is true that the health center movement can be described as having its origin and development in many places in the world: Russia, Chile, Yugoslavia, Puerto Rico, Peckham in England, Pholela in South Africa[17]. But the key difference between these local health center innovations and the community participation or community control development in the United States is the demand for intervention on the part of the consumer himself to control a bit of his destiny through his actions in the center. This is not just a government or professional effort. Indeed, ". . . the delivery of medical care must meet the needs of the community served and must address itself to its aspirations"[12]. It should be recognized that the grievances which have accumulated are medical as well as social. From the social standpoint, planning is more urgently demanded for assignment of priorities to health for the deprived and for a consumer share in the health process. From the medical standpoint, more participation in the design and accessibility of the health system is required.

Among the poor there is rising resentment and anger at their exploitation in the medical setting as "teaching material" (expressed by some unknown critic as white middle-class kids learning on black bodies) and as "research material." Study after study of various kinds (clinical, community, social, or cultural) has been carried on among the poor. But while some of the research was theoretically not just for the benefit of mankind (or the researcher) but for the benefit of the community itself, even this created resentment. Why couldn't community people receive the money and do the studies on themselves? Couldn't they hire the technical help? They are demanding an end to this kind of exploitation. They are insisting on informed consent, for one thing, and on being paid for their services as "guinea pigs," for another[12,14,15,18,2]. They certainly do not want to be research subjects for investigations from whose results they will not benefit. And they do not want to be the subjects of research from which they might benefit unless they are to be involved in asking the questions and interpreting the results. Most of all, they expect to be employed to carry out the investigations themselves, among themselves. Even when a community is being studied for its own good, the investigators decide on the questions, interpret the answers, and apply judgment generally on selection of the data. The community wants participation because the results would also describe and affect the community.

CONSUMER CONTROL

The stage has been set, therefore, for a confrontation between consumers and professionals for control of health programs and, in the larger arena, between consumers and professionals for control of the planning and decision making machinery as well as how much money is to go into the health field altogether. If a national health plan were to come into being and the total money spent came from the public sector via tax funds, public decisions would determine how much was to be spent. Within such limits, the partition of funds among research, services, and resource development (personnel facilities, and knowledge) would also become a public (nonprofessional) decision.

It is widely recognized that professionals have been a little cavalier in their acceptance of social responsibility:

> Medicine is the only enterprise, private or public, in which it has not been considered essential to equate effectiveness and cost. . . . All that is necessary to satisfy public scrutiny or private conscience is to insure that a procedure is well intended and has some claim to consideration, at least in the judgment of the doctor who uses it. Doctors defend vigorously their right to make up their own minds about what is good for their patients and the claim is endorsed by most patients[21].

However, the movement for consumer control is being vigorously promoted. A number of questions remain to be answered:

- Is this an insoluble conflict situation?
- If not, what are the models for resolution?
- What are the values in consumer participation and/or consumer control?
- Who is a consumer? How is he selected?
- What are the dangers or difficulties inherent in reducing professional participation in decision making?

Broadly viewed, there is no need for controversy or conflict. Both professional and consumer can be well served and the decision making shared equitably. In order for this to come to pass, however, the aspirations of the consumer have to be met and the aspirations of the professionals recast to conform with public expectations. Tools are now available for planning on a scientific and rational basis. Information may be lacking for decision making, but a great deal more information is available than has ever been used. Further, mechanisms for using the information in a rational way can be developed and applied since penalties for failure to observe planned goals can now be imposed.

The missing ingredient which created the impasse to begin with is *accountability*. Professionals have shirked this responsibility in the past. Now that human and mechanical systems can be devised to obtain necessary information and share it, accountability is possible. The added information in planning and evaluation is the consumer's concept of what it is he wants and how he wants it delivered. The responsibility then revolves upon the professional to add this information to the professional knowledge. Here we speak only of the design of programs, not yet of policies.

Examples of Planning with Consumers

Health professionals seek to identify the causes of illness, prevent them where possible, and treat them when they do occur, utilizing modern knowledge, trained manpower, equipment, and facilities. Nonmedical professionals seek to maximize the economic capability of medical care by introducing management efficiency into facility operation and by training, and assign personnel in rational, orderly ways for most efficient use. To the planner, hospitals need to be of a certain size, so far apart, and have a staff of so many people with a variety of skills and training. As patients come or are brought to the institution for care, they receive the best and most efficient service possible under those conditions.

Economists then develop programs for paying for the system, or for collecting funds to pay for this system based on other models of paying for services. If the tradition and mode of practice are entrepreneurial, the economists and professionals devise methods based on entrepreneurial practice. Consequently system values, such as the savings possible from reduced inpatient service costs if there were better ambulatory care systems, are recognized but not considered.

What can the patient as consumer offer in planning differently? Primarily, he can compel a description of alternatives. If his wishes are to be met when, for example, he chooses to have a hospital not more than 40 minutes' travel from his workplace or home, the burden will be upon the professionals to design the system so that it will be economical, fair to professionals, and meet institutional demands as well as the client's demand. It is no different from what architects have been used to from time immemorial. The client announces his wish. The architect designs. The client demands certain kinds of changes or amenities in the design. The architect tries to comply, and if he fails, announces added costs. The client then has the option of lesser convenience, more cost, or another architect. The profession has the responsibility of creating new ideas and possibilities out of professional experience; the client has the option of accepting or rejecting the new ideas. So far, in the health field, options have not been open to the consumer.

In assessing the role consumers might or should play in the decision making process with regard to health services or medical care delivery, the customary conflict situation as described actually misstates the case. It is not participation versus control that is at issue. The issue is recognition of the client's wishes.

Poor people or minority groups, accustomed to being bypassed or, at most, condescendingly solicited and then ignored, have no patience with advisory roles. Further, they have no patience with devices whereby they are given a seat even on controlling bodies—planning, policy, or operating. They know that one vote can't swing the board for one thing. For another, they are increasingly skeptical, one might even say cynical, as to how one poor or minority person will react on a board of twenty or thirty members, most of whom are accustomed to the political situation in which they find themselves and accustomed to take command or follow signals of leadership or self-interest.

On the other hand, a board on which the poor or minority group makes up a majority is also viewed with some skepticism. In this case, the more sophisticated community groups know that the majority will place obstacles in the way of minority group decisions (and perhaps even rightly so, since the decision may affect not only the minority involved, but the majority as well, particularly in the health field). Furthermore, where there may be more than one minority group involved, much more complex representation will need to be developed lest political conflict polarize and paralyze the board's actions. In general, it may be that placing a majority of the minority in control is to obstruct the board's effective functioning.

Consumer Participation and Accountability

What the minority seeks is satisfaction and in most health delivery situations this can be accomplished through *accountability*. Since at present there is no real health care system and no office or organized group to whom grievances can be presented, or from whom satisfaction can be obtained, the groups affected and deprived feel that the only recourse is control of administration. Such control by nonprofessionals has its negative aspects as well. While professionals must operate within social constraints, it is usually better to allow decisions on medical care—diagnosis and treatment—to be professionally decided and not part of an administrative "plan." Since illness and human reaction to illness are varied and idiosyncratic, a great deal of leeway and flexibility must be provided professionals[22].

Perhaps as important in the determination of how much control can be exercised over professionals is the size of the professional "labor pool" and the alternative opportunities available for professionals. For example, so long as physicians can be self-employed or find other kinds of employment (in hospitals, health centers, or group practices) in which they are not subject to community review or control, they will either not join organizations that give them no leeway, or will leave them as the constraints begin to bind. Accountability has then to be developed without interfering with this concept of professional freedom. At the same time, sufficient representation from the serviced community must be evident to provide the grievance channel and mechanism for redress.

One avenue that suggests itself is the Yugoslav model of worker management. In the model that might be applied to the U.S. situation, there would actually be four moving parts:

- The worker committee managing the "enterprise," i.e. medical care system or an element of it;
- The community health committee, with a majority of minority representatives;
- The professional committee of physicians and associated health workers representing the professional interests;
- The grievance committee, with equal representation from the three above to whom the community can appeal and within which the evaluation of the performance of the unit, its professional members, and the patient's responses will be monitored.

Under such a rather elaborate model, the matter of control will be thinned out so as to take away the onus of direct pressure on professionals; the grievance channel will be open for the community to redress grievances; and accountability will be public and open. Indeed,

> Yugoslavia . . . introduced social self-management as a deliberate and systematic effort to shift from the orthodox, highly centralized, bureaucratic Soviet-style socialism toward a socialism that would be more democratic, liberal, humane and decentralized. . . . In conjunction with other aspects of the Yugoslav system . . . the workers' councils seem to have produced not only a relatively decentralized economy but a substantial amount of participation by workers in the government of the enterprise[23].

Consumer Selection and Representation

Some thought has gone into defining consumers, how a consumer board should be selected or its influence exerted, and how consumer participants should be selected or elected, but the situation is still far from clear. As Hallman has stated, ". . . to gain a representative governing body there is no adequate substitute for the use of democratic procedures that achieve widespread citizen participation"[8]. For community participation agencies, this writer mentions the possibility of direct elections, the use of membership corporations, indirect elections (organizational delegates choosing a governing board) sometimes with reservation of a third or more of the seats for the poor (to overcome the possibility of the middle class preempting the seats), or a board simply selected by a small leadership group, and of course some combination of these. Hallman goes on to say, "There is no clear evidence that one selection method is superior to another in all places at all times, but whatever procedures are used, the mandate of the electorate should be renewed regularly"[8].

On the other hand, some writers give up on democratic forms: "It is a truism, perhaps, to say that democratic theory has not really solved the problem of legitimacy and consent"[7].

Altshuler settles for satisfaction, rather than a reasoned position: "So long as a particular electoral method gives each vote equal weight and conduces to peace, why carp?"[9]. But he does come to grips with major problems: Who is a consumer? And why not let the professionals run it? As to who is a consumer, he plumps for the deprived: ". . . racial prejudice, ethnic nationalism, and dissatisfaction with the size, unresponsiveness and impersonality of modern public bureaucracies are worldwide phenomena."

Further, Altshuler cites other authors to the effect that "we are in the grip of a movement against bureaucracy and centralization": Flemings/Walloons; French speaking/German speaking in Bern, Switzerland; Welsh, Scottish, French Canadian nationalism; Hindu/Moslem; Catholic/Protestant in Ulster; Arab/Jew; African tribal resurgence in newly independent countries. He adds, ". . . and irrational demand that the 'foreigners' and 'others' . . . be removed . . . a demand, now coming from the ostensibly dominated rather than the domineering groups, for the clearing out of the dominators, so that the formerly inferior group can conduct its own life, without involvement with others"[9]. He equates this movement with "the long history of efforts by lower class groups to acquire greater control over their immediate environments (e.g. factory working conditions) and to improve their socioeconomic circumstances"[9].

While we may admit that defining a "community" or "neighborhood" or "representative" may be difficult, "users of services" is a perfectly good definition from which to start. Altshuler further points out that political decentralization has been an historically American effort and he is impatient with historians and social critics who are "Federalist" as opposed to "localist"[9]. While the class struggle is the model counterpart for today's efforts to obtain community control, as union organization was a generation ago, he does recognize the danger of factionalism, whereby power would be fragmented by numerous single-purpose agencies, and urges multipurpose neighborhood action groups[9]. This process, called "Balkanization of services," by another writer [1] is a serious problem; since community people may want multiple boards to give more people opportunity for participation.

A number of writers discuss these issues with one or another gloss on the approach ([2,6,18,24,25]; also Denise in reference 4 and Cahn in reference 12). Several others also point out that without more powerful financial and educational support behind these selection efforts for community participation and control, the result will be sterile (Piven in reference 4; references 20 and 26).

Still others have made analogies between traditional politics and community organizations: "The neighborhood center is an attempt to institutionalize many of the services performed by local political bosses"[27]. One author[28] sees in community control the wish to control jobs and other patronage elements customarily in the control of politicians.

Whatever the problems implicit in developing community control, there seems to have grown up among professionals who deal with the community a recognition that this is an idea whose time has come. Strategically, it is important to give community people a power base for controlling their own destiny[29]. And even if the question asked by Schorr and English[28], "Can poor people exercise control over institutions they share with the middle class?" has not been answered, it is worth the effort. Cahn[4] adds, ". . . values of consumer participation . . . the mobilization of additional resources . . . to do a job that cannot possibly be done by a profession . . . provide a source of knowledge, of unique insight and feedback about the failure or inadequacy of the present health-care delivery system."

Schwartz[14] discusses the fact that consumer involvement will not necessarily guarantee success, even as professional design without consumer input does not necessarily fail: "Consumer participation provided a general benefit in the form of heightened communication between consumers and staff members around specific improvements in the program."

Added Values in Community Participation and Control

Another value inherent in a community-related medical or health center, aside from the political or psychologic benefits, is in the broader use of services. Writers looking at a specific Boston center noted that families with the least access to other medical care were most attracted to the center[30]. Goering and Coe[31] note,

> . . . it is misleading to believe that giving more care to the poor would be wasted because they really do not want it. The poor both desire and need more and better care. . . . The restructuring of the medical care delivery system, to recognize the importance of the context of poverty rather than the characteristics of the poor, seems a necessary conclusion.

These authors studied factors influencing use of services: 'Time and cost, income and race appear as more or less explicit situations constraining the use of medical services'[31].

THE URBAN COALITION EXPERIENCE

With the riots in so many large cities in the U.S. in the summer of 1967, a group of concerned Americans decided that the job of changing the nation over to greater responsiveness toward the poor and minorities was just as much a private as a public responsibility. The Urban Coalition was thus organized to assemble and focus the strengths of the private sector—the business and banking community, civil rights and religious organizations, professional and voluntary social action groups. More than a year passed before this Coalition turned its attention to health as a community problem and as a recognized opportunity for private sector action.

Utilizing the experience of the poverty programs and the evidence of failure of professional groups to make change and move sufficiently swiftly in the direction of meeting urgent health needs of the poor, the elderly, the minorities, and the geographically deprived, the Urban Coalition took the step of forming a Health Task Force to meet the challenge of health needs. The added step in the Coalition's action was to include the poor and deprived, the client, the resident of the deprived community, along with professional students among the task force membership.

When this national Health Task Force issued a report[32], the Coalition moved to make the report more than a shelf item by creating pilot community programs of the sort recommended in the report. In these pilot programs, too, the same sort of community participation was urged and provided. The methodology of the approach was simple. The community was asked to develop a local health task force, including in its membership professionals, officials, businessmen and bankers, and voluntary agency representatives along with representatives of the poor and deprived for whom the health program improvement was principally to be designed.

Rx for Action, the report of the Health Task Force of the National Urban Coalition[32], was basically a "menu," a collection of descriptions of the kinds of problems and the broad categories of solutions available or under trial. Sample chapter headings will demonstrate the approach: "Where to Start—Adjusting Services to Human Needs"; "Paying the Piper—Financing Health Services." Other sections touched on health facilities, health manpower, nutrition, the environment, transportation, and special rural health problems. The report was used to stimulate community interest. Consultation was offered to the communities served. It was emphasized that the role of the local health task force was not to preempt the role of any other local health agency, but to help make existing agencies work. The local health task force was not to replace or displace the health department or, if one existed, the comprehensive health planning agency. It was not intended to go into the business of health program operation except where no agency existed or could be brought into being. Thus, the aim of existing legislation and professional aspiration—comprehensive health planning and eventually comprehensive health services—was to be brought about by the concerted action of the community itself.

Such an approach already begins to postulate subordination of the professional role to the community mandate or, even further, to the mandate of the deprived. The poor and the minorities were able to sit in on the planning and to decide whether the plans were suitable or what should be done to make them suitable. It was an effort to provide not only "input" in the classical political sense, but an element of control.

What happened?

In different cities different approaches to problem solving and different problems were attacked. In San Diego, California, the Mexican-American community had been without access to medical services: no hospitals or clinics in their areas, practically no transportation to such services. They demanded a clinic of their own. Professionals argued for application to federal sources for additional funds; the community obtained volunteer services until such added financing could be obtained. Although the situation had been known for years, only after the meeting of community representatives and formation of an Urban Coalition Health Task Force did the action take place.

In El Paso, Texas, the community was even poorer and the state welfare and social services more limited and desultory than in California. The Chicano community there demanded funds to attempt to help itself. It sought a store-front clinic, its own transport, and the funds to train local people to fulfill culturally acceptable rather than professionally described health roles. As a result of Coalition action, El Paso has received a mixture of funds to carry this out: federal funds, funds from the Coalition itself, and funds from a private foundation stimulated by the Coalition.

In New Orleans, Louisiana, the situation was again different. While there is in New Orleans a large network of services that might be stretched, little money was available. Here the effort was directed at trying to synthesize available resources, uniting them with added funds sought for this specific purpose. The state-supported Charity Hospital, representatives of the Tulane Medical School (particularly the maternal and child health professionals), the City Health Department, the vice chancellor of the Louisiana State University, a group of wealthy and influential citizens, black neighborhood organizations, community groups, Model City officials, and school board representatives—all agreed to cooperate. A person agreeable to all of them was selected as special advisor to the Mayor on health planning, and funds were provided by the Urban Coalition. Since he was basically a community organizer, the Coalition offered to give him indoctrination in the health field. He spent a month of concentrated study in the field of health services needs and organization, including a week in Washington where he was introduced to the officials in government departments whose activities touched upon the activities that would be considered or acted upon in New Orleans.

In other cities there were other approaches. In Providence, Rhode Island, the effort was directed toward including the poor within a prepaid group practice system that was on the point of becoming operative. Lesser health organizational activities were unnecessary in the community with the wealth, resources, and opportunities for a true comprehensive health program already in being in Providence. The same was true of efforts on behalf of poor black people in San Diego. While the Chicanos in San Diego had almost nothing, the blacks there had a bit more in the way of resources. There was a group of black medical practitioners, for example, and with some money and technical assistance, there was no reason why a prepaid group practice of black physicians for black patients could not be organized. Funds for prepayment could be made available for a segment of the community through the premium method of utilizing Title XIX funds (Medicaid) for which at least a third of the black community of San Diego was eligible.

In sum, the Urban Coalition undertook to give communities a voice in program design for health services by setting up a power center (the Health Task Force) and giving the poor and deprived an important role in its deliberations. The Coalition then proceeded to use the power of this community structure to influence existing health decision-making bodies. In the background of this effort was the fact that professionals had failed: the community was ill-served, and planning, in the legislated, authoritative sense, was not operative. Further, by relying wholly on professionals for future action, successful programs to meet community needs were years away and the likelihood of innovation, either in program or manpower, was remote. Community action *created* health programs.

SUMMARY

To date, the discussions in the area of community and consumer participation have been very largely polemical and academic. What is required now is evidence of the value—or lack of it—in consumer participation and control. There is evidence that the traditional system of planning and design of health services is inappropriate, irrelevant, and unsatisfactory. We must study the impact of consumer-oriented planning where it is in use, and assure ourselves of its capability. As Gorham[10] has pointed out, "In order to measure the benefits, we have to find out what actually happened to the people affected by the program." And he adds, "The problems of benefits measurement, however, are not just technical; they are conceptual."

These evaluations will have added benefits for program managers, feedback into the system itself, and benefit patient care generally[33,34]. But, at the moment, in planning health care systems, among the situations for which community participation can offer better and more meaningful contributions in the decision making on plans for health services are:

- location and size of the medical care center, or whether there is to be a center at all;
- whether solo or group practice is desired and which is more feasible;
- the number and types of physicians needed, or new types of substitute health workers if there are to be such;
- recruitment procedures for health workers within and without the community;
- the share of representation in admission policies in the training institutions;

- the duration and content of the curriculum of various health professional education institutions;
- the employment practices and personnel policies in the service units; and
- the nature of financing and resource allocation.

Determination of health services needs and satisfaction of community requirements for health services are now recognized as demanding participation of consumer groups, in order to obtain information from clients. In the United States this has arisen in part from social forces, such as the struggle for justice for the poor, the disadvantaged, and minority groups in aiding them to express their needs and end their powerlessness; from practical political reasons, such as to establish new constituencies; from reassertion of some traditional values, like decentralization; and from professional reasons as well.

The professional reasons include: (a) realistic assessment of priorities as seen by the consumer and efforts needed to accommodate to those priorities; (b) ensuring the acceptability of the decisions as they are made by planning or controlling bodies, elected officials, or professionals; and (c) evidence of failure of professionals alone to solve problems despite their duration and the existence of public monies to meet those needs. In a sense, all the elements are political corollaries of one another: injustice and failure to meet glaring, desperate health needs; establishment of realistic priorities to assure consumer satisfaction and acceptance of programs.

REFERENCES

1. Hillman, A. Community Control. Paper presented at National Conference on Welfare, June 1970.
2. Mogulof, M. B. Citizen Participation, Vol. 1, Federal Policies. Urban Institute, Washington, D.C., January 1970.
3. Mogulof, M. B. Citizen Participation, Vol. 2, Local Perspective. Urban Institute, Washington, D.C., March 1970.
4. Spiegel, H. B. C., editor. Citizen Participation in Urban Development, Vol. 1, Concepts and Issues. National Institute for Applied Behavioral Science, Washington, D. C., 1970.
5. Spiegel, H. B. C., editor. Citizen Participation in Urban Development, Vol. 2, Cases and Programs. National Institute for Applied Behavioral Science, Washington, D. C. 1970.
6. Brieland, D. Community advisory boards and maximum feasible participation. Am. J. Public Health 61:292-296, February 1971.
7. Green, P., and Levinson, S., editors. Power and Community, pp. 249-250. Vintage, New York, 1970.

8. Hallman, H. W. *Neighborhood Control of Public Programs*, pp. 4, 170, 214, 216. Praeger, New York, 1970.
9. Altshuler, A. *Community Control*, pp. 34, 35, 67, 69, 96. Pegasus, New York, 1970.
10. Gorham, W. PPBS: Its scope and limits. *The Public Interest* 8: 4-8, Summer 1968.
11. Navarro, V. The city and the region. *American Behavioral Scientist* 14(6): 865-892, 1971.
12. Community Participation for Equity and Excellence in Health Care. Special issue of *Bull, N. Y. Acad. Med.* Vol. 46, December 1970.
13. Elinson, J., and Herr, C.E. A Sociomedical View of Neighborhood Health Centers. Paper presented at annual meeting of American Public Health Association, November 11, 1969.
14. Schwartz, J. L. Early histories of selected neighborhood health centers. *Inquiry* 7: 3-16, December 1970.
15. Kaufman, H. The political ingredient of public health services. *Milbank Mem. Fund Q.* 44 (part 2): 13-33, October 1966.
16. Notkin, H., and Notkin, M. S. Community participation in health services. *Medical Care Review* 27: 1178-1201, December 1970.
17. Stoeckle, J. D., and Candib, L. M. The neighborhood health center. *New Engl. J. Med.* 280: 1385-1391, June 19, 1969.
18. Gordon, J. B. The politics of community medicine projects. *Med. Care* 7: 419-428, 1969.
19. Sparer, G., Dines, G. B., and Smith, D. Consumer participation in OEO assisted neighborhood health centers. *Journal of the American Public Health Association* 60: 1091-1102, June 1970.
20. Goldberg, G. A., Trowbridge, F. L., and Buxbaum, R. C. Issues in the development of neighborhood health centers. *Inquiry* 6: 37-47, March 1969.
21. McKeown, T. *Medicine in Modern Society*, p. 13. Allen & Unwin, London, 1965.
22. Freidson, E. *Professional Dominance*. Atherton, New York, 1970.
23. Dahl, R. A. *After the Revolution?*, pp. 130-131. Yale University Press, New Haven, 1970.
24. Perucci, R., and Pilisuk, M. Leaders and ruling elites. *American Social Revolution* 35: 1040-1057, December 1970.
25. Geiger, J. Community control or community conflict. *Bulletin of the National Tuberculosis and Respiratory Disease Association* 4-10, November 1969.
26. Goldberg, J. H. Anatomy of a hospital takeover. *Medical Economics* 156-157, December 1970.
27. O'Donnell, E. J., and Sullivan, M. M. Service delivery and social action through the neighborhood center. *Welfare Review* 7: 1-11, November/December 1969.
28. Special Issue, *Milbank Mem. Fund Q.* Vol. 46, part 1, July 1968.
29. Davis, M. S., and Tranquada, R. E. A sociological evaluation of the Watts neighborhood health center. *Med. Care* 7: 105-117, March-April 1969.
30. Salber, E. J., Feldman, J. J., Offenbacher, H., and Williams, S. Characteristics

of patients registered for service at a neighborhood health center. *Am. J. Public Health*, 60: 2273-2283, December 1970.

31. Goering, J. M., and Coe, R. M. Cultural versus situational explanations of the medical behavior of the poor. *Social Science Quarterly* 309-319, September 1970.
32. *Rx for Action*. National Urban Coalition, Washington, D. C., 1969.
33. Wholey, J. S., Scanlon, J.W., Duffy, H. G., Fukumoto, J. S., and Vogt, L. M. *Federal Evaluation Policy*. Urban Institute, Washington, D. C. 1970.
34. Shuval, J. T. Methods of assessing public attitudes toward health. *Int. Dent. J.* 17: 63-74, March 1967.

The Shifting Power
Structure in Health

RAY H. ELLING

This paper deals with a complex, difficult topic about which little is known. The paper considers social power in a general way; makes some observations on power changes internal to the health establishment, including observations on "the" physician's role and the university health center; examines the increasing role of government, particularly at the federal level; the changing role of lay community leaders; and the awakening, but as yet relatively inactive, consumer public. Following these considerations, the conclusion will present some thoughts on the central problem of the paper: the implications of power analysis for structuring the planning and administration of regionalized health services and facilities and the preparation of persons for this endeavor. To grasp these problems, a brief examination will first be made of social power and certain broad changes in the health systems of complex, technological societies.[1]

Reprinted, with permission, from *The Milbank Memorial Fund Quarterly*, (Health and Society). January 1968, pp. 83-107.

SOCIAL POWER

Social power is here defined as the ability to influence the orientation and behavior of others. How does an individual or group obtain social power in a social system? Individual and group power is given through the consent of others in the social system.[2] That consent is dependent upon certain recognized bases or sources of power that are described below. An individual may "hold" power or "exercise" influence, but he can do so only if others do his bidding. The power structure in health (or any other sphere) changes, as does the control of different individuals and groups over the bases of power.

Some authors differentiate between power and influence on the basis of resistance versus acquiescence in the relationship. For example, friends are said to influence each other, while opponents wield power.[3] Since social interaction is always redefining some situation or reducing some ambiguity from a situation,[4] the above distinction between power and influence is rejected. For no matter how much in accord two persons or groups may be, if they emerge in symbolic exchange, the resistance of prior definitions must be overcome. Thus the category of no resistance is essentially a null category in human intercourse and the problem of a substantive basis for distinguishing between power and influence is not a useful one.

If it is not important to make a distinction between power and influence on the basis of resistance being present or not (since it is always present to some degree), it may be more valid and useful to make a distinction on a temporal basis. Thus, one might suggest that power applies only to potential, or undemonstrated realization of an actor's influence.[5] Influence then is actualized power. Instances of influence are evidence that power existed and has been employed. Power is always present in a situation and will show itself as influence before a particular "scene" or other bit of interaction is completed.[6]

To more fully understand social power and have some way of assessing or "toting up" what Norton Long calls "the power budget"[7] of the health administrator or other persons and interest groups in the health system, the bases on which power rests must be studied. Some or all of the following bases of power may be involved in a given interaction between a staff physician and the hospital administrator, between a hospital and a planning agency and so on:

1. The interpretation of traditions, philosophies and history is one important tool by which men may be moved. The administrator who can remind board members of past traditions of delivering

maternity care, when some members of the board were themselves born in the hospital, has considerable power in opposing a planning agency's moves to consolidate maternity services in another hospital.

2. The ability to generate believable myths, whether intentionally mythical or not, is another idea tool of some importance. Simply mentioning the Orson Wells-directed radio broadcast of the Invasion from Mars, during which some people jumped into the Hudson River to save themselves, validates W. I. Thomas' aphorism, "When men define things as real, they are real in their consequences." The same phenomenon is seen in the health field (usually with less frightening results) when justification is sought in "magic numbers"—one public health nurse per 5,000 population, 4.5 general hospital beds per thousand population, and so on. Often such figures are justified very little in terms of function and need; yet plans are drawn, budgets passed and building programs launched in response to such calculations.

3. Reasoning ability or the power of logic seems clear enough not to need illustration.[8] However, it differs from "force of presentation" in the sense of personal style or other valued social characteristics. One can illustrate that distinction by "the brains of the outfit" (a person with knowledge as well as reasoning ability), who may act from a relatively hidden position of the state health department where some abrasive personal characteristics cannot do much harm, while his influence is felt through the actions and programs he suggests to others.

4. In most community (and other) power structures the expert who controls technical knowledge or skills fills an essential place. He may or may not constitute an initiating and perpetuating force, but he is essential at some point to certify the soundness of a program.

5. Control of economic resources is a major base of power. To Marx, this factor was important enough to base a theory of history on control over the means of economic production. Indeed, it may be that regional health services planning structures can have their major impact on coordination of services through control over the channeling of both operating and capital funds. But at least four conditions limit the power of the person or group who controls resources: those to be influenced may have resources the controller badly desires; they may obtain the same resources elsewhere; they may have power on other grounds to force relinquishment; they may resign themselves to do without.[9] Some of these limiting conditions reflect the operation of other bases of power.

6. The authority one has as a function of his office in a formal organization may be a source of far-reaching influence. This source of power has increased in importance and to some extent changed hands as the administrative function in hospitals, health departments and other organizations has emerged as a special endeavor.
7. Apart from holding an office, control over an organization of men through formal or informal means is a familiar, but nonetheless important part of accomplishing tasks, especially large-scale ones. One or more nonelected power figures may control a political party, a government bureaucracy, even a health services planning agency from "behind the scenes." Such control may involve a formal office, as in the case of a large employer who is asked to head the United Fund drive; or it may not involve formal office, as in the case of the racketeer who moves into the nursing home field.
8. Position in the social structure (aside from prestige as discussed below) can be an important determinant of power. It is not impossible, but very much less likely, that the "lower-class" patient will have as great access to or control over any of the sources of power as will the health professional who seeks to influence his behavior. The health organization that is primarily "plugged in" to the "lower class" will be similarly short in its power budget.[10]
9. Prestige can be thought of as the combined impression of a person or organization due to valued social characteristics. Whatever causal role these characteristics play in the generation of power, considerable evidence may be found of their association with those identified as powerful. This has been regularly noted among community leaders.[11] It has also been noted for high-prestige occupational roles such as that of the physician. Outwardly, given some native intelligence, training makes the physician. But this is not all, for he is expected to have certain of what Everett Hughes terms "auxiliary characteristics."[12] In the United States, these expectations operate to exclude many women, Negroes and others from these roles.[13] That condition may change, however, in the face of manpower shortages and public demands.
10. Direct popular or political support is an important power base to which public health professionals have given inadequate attention while attempting to justify their programs to political figures on economic grounds. Within certain limits, the costs do not matter if the people in general are sophisticated enough about health problems and services to vigorously demand adequate care as a basic human right.
11. The "miraculous cure" lends charisma to the one seen by the patient as responsible, for the event breaks all expectations of

disaster. Charisma is not a mystical source of power. It can be empirically indexed by behavior that violates rules or expectations with good results. Some community health leaders acquire charisma as they demonstrate ability to ignore various bureaucratic labyrinths while achieving results for their followers.

12. The power of violence is gone as soon as it is unleashed. Only in the potential of its use are men moved out of fear to do the bidding of its wielder. To a considerable degree, the potential of violence on the mental patient's part structures the whole mental hospital, even to some of the fine points of architecture. In some institutions this is seen as the ultimate problem. Even if the threat of violence achieves negative results, it can influence the behavior of others.

13. But even violence, to have its effect, requires, as Simmel pointed out, the reciprocity of the threatened preson.[14] The narcotized patient has no ability to influence the surgeon, but we could not say that social power is involved in this relationship. The matter of hypnosis is an interesting and problematic relationship from this point of view.

To distinguish these several foundations upon which social power rests may be arbitrary and no doubt overlaps occur, which a better categorization might eliminate. Nevertheless, an inventory of these sources of power for a given health administrator or planner and his organization, as compared with the same assessment for those to be influenced, would yield a reasonably adequate estimate of the "power budget" available to develop and institute plans.

Plans, of course, have their own definitional power when developed throughout the system to be affected. Further, the various sources of power may be differentially weighted and these weightings may vary with the context of opposition or encouragement faced by the planning organization. Clearly, the power budget is no static entity granted within some fiscal period. The total budget may increase or decrease and its component parts shift depending on changing definitions, new enthusiasms, crises and other events.

THE CHANGING HEALTH SYSTEM

The relevance of the size and complexity of a social system will be seen if certain broad shifts in the health system are considered that have altered access to and control over the bases of power and have thus changed its power relationships.

First, in recent years a vast proliferation of new health specialists has taken place. By way of illustration, Dochez examined the records of two cases of heart disease in the same hospital, one in 1908 and the second in 1938. The first case developed a written record of two and one-half pages reflecting the observatons of three professionals—an attending physician and a house officer, with consultation from a pathologist-bacteriologist. In the later case, the record occupied 29 pages reflecting the contributions of 32 professionals, more than ten times the number involved in the first case. These included three attending men, two residents, three interns, ten specialists, and 14 technicians.[15]

New groups continue to enter the field. "The trend toward new careers is yet to be fully appreciated. Among the 200 plus careers listed by title in the *Health Careers Guide Book*, the majority represented but a small segment of total health manpower prior to World War II. Many careers, e.g., inhalation therapist, nuclear medical technologist, radiologic health technician, cytotechnologist and medical engineering technician, did not exist."[16]

Within the once relatively unified, single profession of medicine, numerous specialties now operate in effect as independent occupational groups.[17] Whereas, in 1931, five general practitioners were found for every full-time specialist in active private practice, 30 years later one-half were specialists. "Between 1931 and 1959 the number of full-time specialists more than tripled, increasing from 22,158 to 78,635. On the other hand, the number of general practitioners (including part-time specialists) decreased from 112,116 to 81,957."[18]

Increased complexity is also evident for health organizations. In his book, published in 1945, covering 95 national health agencies of the nongovernmental, promotional type (National Tuberculosis Association, American Child Health Associaton, etc.), Cavins noted that no attempt was made to deal with all national voluntary health organizations. Further, none of the organizations dealt with was formed before 1904. In the following two decades they sprang up "mushroom-like."[19]

In 1961, a report for the Rockefeller Foundation by an ad hoc citizen's committee counted, aside from hospitals, over 100,000 national, regional and local voluntary health and welfare agencies that solicit contributions from the general public.[20] The growing complexity of governmental organizations in the health field is not much, if any, less striking. For example, in recent federal legislation granting 256 million dollars in addition to matching state and local monies for activities in the field of mental retardation, Congress provided for no less than 12 federal agencies to disburse these funds.[21]

In 1950, Roemer and Wilson examined this problem from a new perspective. In the words of Joseph W. Mountin, they "Attempted to set down systematically the structure and function of all organized health services having an impact on the people of one county."[22] In this semi-rural county of what is now identified as "Appalachia," they found no less than 604 agencies involved in organized health service that had some impact on health care in that county. Locally based health-relevant organizations numbered 155.[23]

In addition to increasing complexity, the health system shows striking evidence of increased size, change in relative size of different components and change in position in society generally. As regards occupational groups, "It is estimated that the health professions requiring college education or professional preparation accounted for approximately 200,000 persons in 1900. The number of individuals in these same categories increased to 409,000 in 1920; 692,000 in 1940; and 1,140,000 in 1960. . . . Individuals in the health occupations accounted for 1.2 per cent of the experienced civilian labor force at the turn of the century. This proportion increased to 2.1 per cent by 1940; 2.4 per cent by 1950; and 3.0 per cent by 1960."[24] Relative to other groups, physicians have lost dominance simply in terms of numbers. "Whereas at the turn of the century, three out of five health professionals were physicians, by 1960 rapid growth in other disciplines reduced the proportion of physicians to one of five professional health workers. A continued decline is to be anticipated as other disciplines experience more rapid rates of growth and new categories of personnel emerge."[24] According to another estimate, the present ratio of physicians to all health personnel is less than one to ten.[25]

From fear-inspiring, segmental units serving only the displaced and disinherited of society, some of the most essential health organizations, such as clinics and hospitals, following the development of scientific secular medicine, became more effective, highly desired and generally used.[26] The rate of admissions to general hospitals, for example, rose from about one in every 18 persons in 1931, to approximately one in seven in 1962. Modern health care has come to be regarded as a basic human right.[27] Health institutions have moved squarely into the community. They have become community institutions.

CHANGING POWER RELATIONS

General

It is not possible to detail the impacts on power relations in the health system of the increased complexity, size, change in relative size of certain components (e.g., physicians relative to other health workers) and overall shift in the place of the health services industry in society.

Yet several observations seem evident. First, with the rate of technological and social change in this field the power structure is certainly very fluid. That is not news. But perhaps it is this very fluidity throughout modern society that seems to accentuate the striving of occupational groups and organizations to protect or increase their autonomy, gain greater support and generally hold or improve their "place in the sun." Perhaps, too, this complexity and fluidity of power relations is what makes the problem of planning health services so important, yet at once frustrating and fascinating. In any case, it is not anything that could be characterized as a stable structure; the power budget is fluid. Thus, rather than carrying the assigned title, this paper should have "power relations" in its title.

Second, some growth has taken place in the power of the total health system. In these perilous, warring times, health has not achieved, and may never approach, the concentraton of power C. Wright Mills found combined in the "defense" establishment as it serves the interests of "Big Business," "Big Labor," Government and The Military.[28] But with the generally high regard in which health services have come to be held, increased utilization and greater proportions of personnel and funds, health now occupies a more substantial place in society. For this, and other reasons to follow, health affairs have become matters of important public concern and political action. For example, see the conflicts between groups of elderly voters, the American Medical Association and other interest groups as detailed in Richard Harris' series on the legislative process involved in the development of Medicare.[29]

Third, although the system overall may be more powerful (at least when overwhelming budgets for international conflict do not intervene), power is more dispersed, shared as it is among a myriad of health occupations and organizations in different public and private jurisdictions. That entails unnecessary inefficiency, expense and suspected lower effectiveness. Certain reactions have occurred to the dispersal of power within the health system. Government has begun to play a larger part as have various quasi-governmental health bodies. Consumers too, particularly in poverty areas have begun to insist on a role in determining the character of health services delivered to them.

In the Health System

Although the position of "the" physician in society may have remained relatively constant and high in the view of the general public,[30] insiders are beginning to realize that "the" physician is a myth. Not only do medical schools differ in their emphases in the two, four or five years their programs run, but differentiation within specialties has progressed to such an extent that when someone collapses in a gathering it no longer makes sense to shout. "Is there a doctor in the house?" Doctors in a range of specialties who really treat patients might answer the call (if they are not afraid of malpractice suit as a consequence of treating someone outside their usual, well-equipped work setting). But what of the administrator, the researcher, specialists in "thing-oriented" fields such as radiology. What of epidemiologists? Or psychiatrists who have only *talked* to patients for years? Could they do much more for the victim than the nurse or even the lay person trained in first-aid?

The specialization and development of new health occupations is not limited to physicians.

What are the consequences of specialization for the power of a given occupational group or representative thereof? On the one hand is a tremendous increase in esoteric, technical knowledge and, in situations where it is relevant, it affords tremendous power. On the other hand, the monopoly the physician once had in the health field is gone.[31] Not only is his own house often divided against itself, with different specialties having different associations and making different representations, but many newcomers are on the scene. Often the newcomers are as vital as any particular type of physician in the provision of care. For example, a radiologist recently complained that he was leaving his practice in a community hospital in part because he was no longer in complete control of therapy—a physicist now determines the use of the cobalt unit. It is this "functional equality" that is beginning to make one member of the health team as vital as another.

Although the colleague rather than leader-follower relationship among health workers has not been given wide recognition, to some extent it is a fact and it makes some health workers uneasy. After imperialistically referring to "sub-professionals" for years and recently modifying this to "ancillary professionals," the vogue among physicians now is to speak of "allied professionals."

Of course, prestige and income differentials suggest that the label may only be a sop. The left-hand column of Table 1 shows a ranking of several listed groups according to "how professional" their members are judged to be by a general sample of public health workers (members of the American Public Health Association or one of its state or regional affiliates).[32] In the right-hand column are the median incomes determined from reports by members of these occupational groups in the same mailed questionnaire. Although new words like "allied professionals" may only be a cover for continued exploitation, they probably reflect change in power relations.

In the struggle for position, now with particular reference to occupational groups, various strategies and means are employed.[33] But one

TABLE 1. Professional Rank and 1964 Incomes of Selected Occupational Groups in Public Health, by Self Identity, Degree and Self-Identified Basic Discipline*

Work Group	Professional Rank**	Under $5,000 N	Under $5,000 %	5,000–9,999 N	5,000–9,999 %	10,000–14,999 N	10,000–14,999 %	15,000 and Over N	15,000 and Over %	Total N	Total %	No Resp.	Not Appl.	Median Income	Income Ranking
Physicians†	1	37	8.0	40	8.6	80	17.2	308	66.2	465	100	39	10	17,850	1
Public health dentists	2	4	6.8	22	37.3	25	42.3	8	13.6	59	100	3	3	10,700	4
Veterinarians	3	2	2.8	28	37.8	28	37.8	16	21.6	74	100	5	4	11,250	3
Laboratory scientists	4	47	13.0	207	57.3	84	23.3	23	6.4	361	100	14	24	8,200	9
Health officers	5	9	3.7	52	21.5	104	43.0	77	31.8	242	100	14	18	12,850	2
Public health engineers	6	6	2.0	154	52.1	111	37.5	25	8.4	296	100	10	15	9,550	6
Biostatisticians	7	36	28.6	63	50.0	21	16.7	6	4.7	126	100	4	14	7,100	11-13
Public health nurses	8	760	58.9	513	39.7	18	1.4			1,291	100	59	174	4,200	16
Other nurses	9	77	56.7	55	40.4	4	2.9			136	100	4	15	4,400	15
Hospital administrators	10	27	6.1	181	40.8	133	30.1	102	23.0	443	100	26	37	10,500	5
Other public health administrators	11	69	13.4	240	46.4	109	21.1	99	19.1	517	100	25	13	8,900	8
Health educators	12	42	21.8	128	66.7	18	9.4	4	2.1	192	100	7	19	7,100	11-13
Nutritionists	13	23	20.5	77	68.8	9	8.0	3	2.7	112	100	4	12	7,100	11-13
Public health social workers	14	12	10.7	84	75.0	14	12.5	2	1.8	112	100	1	3	7,600	10
Sanitarians	15	273	48.8	279	49.8	7	1.2	1	.2	560	100	25	29	5,100	14
Occupational hygienists	16	5	2.4	121	57.3	65	30.8	20	9.5	211	100	6	3	9,150	7
Others**	unranked	964	27.6	1,194	34.2	595	17.0	741	21.2	3,494	100	184	363	8,250	unranked
Total		2,393		3,438		1,425		1,435		8,691		430	756		

*Exact means of delimiting groups furnished on request.

**See reference 32 for derivation of this ranking.

†These are largely clinical physicians in public health, epidemiologists, specialists in preventive medicine and occupational health physicians. Excludes M.D.s who identified themselves in other categories, such as health officer, hospital administrator, etc.

††Includes a number of "professional" categories with only a few members as well as secretaries, clerks and certain other "nonprofessional" categories plus those unemployed or not in the labor force.

that comes under myth making should be examined briefly as it is so pervasive, ubiquitous and consequential for the question of health manpower. That is the master myth of "professionalization." If a group can become known as "professional," as seen in table 1, it is more likely (though the rank-order correlation is only .57) to enjoy a better income. Other conditions lending prestige and power to the group are also correlated with this appellation. Indeed, after a careful analysis of available studies and theoretical discussions, Becker has concluded that "professional" is only a term of approbation, and does not clearly distinguish one work group from another except possibly in terms of power and prestige.[34] Yet, a great deal is made of the term with extensive ideologies and much effort is invested in "becoming professional." Aside from a certain assurance of quality to the public, the net result may be narrowness of outlook, special jargon, restricted supply, higher costs, sloughing off of necessary but "dirty" tasks, divorce from those most in need of service (such as poverty, "lower-class" and certain ethnic groups)[35] and expensive machinery to license, accredit, lobby and otherwise protect secrets and domains. In short, as has been seen in various parts of the world, "when the chips are down," doctors and nurses are not so different from other work groups; they make use of the ultimate labor weapon like anyone else; that is, the strike, though it may be called "mass sick leave" or "a professional holiday."[36]

Control of the health organization, too, is changing. In the hosptial, particularly, a new breed of non-medical administrator has entered upon the scene in the past 30 years.

Sharply prepared in quantitative aspects of management, personnel relations and organization theory and other aspects of the social sciences, they are in a better position to respond to the problem of the complex health organization than is the case-oriented, biologically prepared physician, however much he enjoyed (or did not) his preventive medicine and public health courses. Over the years, the administrator has also learned the value of having the board in his corner. Through his board, if it has the right composition, the administrator has access to the community leadership—the industrial, financial, legal people. Physicians and other health professionals listen when and if these men become interested in "a new wing," "a new professorship in surgery," "a hospital planning agency" and so on.

Public health organizations are also showing signs of change, even at the very top of the structure. A blue-ribbon committee composed largely of public health physicians concluded the following:[37].

> To say, however, that the departments of health are the logical agencies to take on major responsibility for the planning and coordination of the delivery of these [personal health] services is not to say

that they are now ideally equipped for the job. A responsibility of this breadth will of course require special personnel to meet it, and this brings us back again to the problems of education for public health, especially in the schools of public health. The simple fact is that very few people are being prepared in schools of public health today, or anywhere else, who could justifiably be presented to a community as qualified for this task. . . .

The schools of public health should give immediate attention to establishing a doctoral curriculum which would blend the contributions of economics, political science, sociology, the health sciences, certain of the physical sciences and other fields of study.

Although the power of formal position and control over an organization have accrued to the administrator's balance to an ever increasing degree as the hospital has taken on greater central importance in the health system, important counter trends have appeared. With the increasing size of the health system (in terms of overall budget, personnel and other matters) and complexity of modern care and consequent rising costs, no health organization is an island unto itself. If, as Martin Cherkasky has indicated, the hospital must become "a sharpened instrument" used in the right way for the right case at the right time, it must be integrally tied in to preventive services, ambulatory care, domiciliary care and diagnostic services, home care, nursing care and other extended care and rehabilitation units. That means a sharing of power and the likelihood of numerous interorganizational problems.[38] In any case, it is no longer fruitful to look at the hospital as an autonomous unit with definite boundaries outlined by its walls. Instead, it has become a kind of point of intersection for several functions that must be carried out by the community or regional health system as a whole.

The development of organizational networks, as well as other conditons that will be discussed presently, has turned the organization outward. The Surgeon General, William Stewart, has reflected on this trend as it affects medical schools by pointing out that after developing two faculties, the so-called "basic" science faculty and the clinical faculty, medical schools have begun to develop a third faculty—a community medicine faculty. Growing community awareness is in no way limited to or particularly characteristic of medical faculties. Other patient care professionals, the administrators and board members of the university-based health center are becoming community conscious. Since the Flexner report, the medical school particularly, but other schools of the health professions as well, have served increasingly as the establishers of new knowledge and legitimators of values in the health system. In addition, the university-based health center has gathered, in most cases, the most elaborate and effective armamentarium of personnel, equipment and facilities of any organization in the immediate vicinity. To the extent of these occurrences, the university health center has become the power center of the local health system. Now, in addition, the Regional Medical Care Program, even if it is interpreted as primarily educational in character, may add major impetus to the abilities of the centers to reach into the surrounding networks of health organizations and occupational groups.

Changes in the Environment

Four general developments seem noteworthy: the efforts of organized occupation groups; the increasingly political nature of health issues; the increasing interest of lay community leadership in health planning; and a slowly awakening desire of consumers of health services to determine policy with regard to local service institutions.

As mentioned in the previous section, occupational groups, of which numbers are increasing in the health field, are on the move toward establishment. Their efforts are sometimes carried out within the health organization and could have been treated as part of the internal analysis as one examination of the "negotiated order" suggests. But many of these efforts are frank moves in the larger body politic to gain legislative support for higher salaries, a different more advantageous system of payment, higher stipends to aid recruitment and stricter licensure to maintain better control over a domain of work.

That health issues have achieved political status indicates a reaction to rising costs, fractionation, inefficiency, impersonality, suspected ineffectiveness and the dispersal of power among the units of the complex health system. The engagement of political power in the determination of health policy has of necessity held in view the action of government, particularly the federal government.[10] The state, after all, is, at any level of government, the only institution of society that covers or intends to cover all elements of the society no matter how disparate and diverse. The larger part that government plays in health policy is not only a matter of payment and decisions as to criteria and standards for these expenditures. Government is also an adjudicator, a guardian of the public interest as regards licensure of individual practitioners and health organizations. The hearings conducted by Commissioner Smith of Pennsylvania on Blue Cross rates demonstrated that even where a private insurance organization is concerned, the state may inquire into the public interest.

As effective and desirable as modern health care has become, the public has an ambivalent attitude. On the one hand is the possibility of saving life, preventing disability, even realizing and enhancing human potential. On the other hand are fantastically rising costs,[11] and impersonality and disjointedness in a family's care, which is difficult for even the most sophisticated to tolerate.[42] Thus, health services have become matters of public concern, particularly to large, so-called "third-party" payers (Government, labor, industry, insurance organizations), but also to community leaders, philanthropic interests and consumers. As a result, health issues have become key political issues with government at all levels entering the health care picture to an increasing degree.

Since Bismarck's time, politicians have seen that they can protect their power or obtain election in part by making adequate health services more available. Although the determination of health policy has always been to some degree external to the health system because the actions of health agencies and professionals require the support and acceptance of the surrounding society. Such determination is currently moving into the conscious scrutiny of mass politics and could easily mean the setting of goal and priorities that "professionals" would not choose. The bulk of the voters are not health professionals, although the sizable interest group, particularly the large "third-party" is likely to have the expertise of health workers at its command.

Sometimes a lack of correspondence is noted between the general public mandate for action to improve health services as expressed in the election of officials and legislators and the specifics of health legislation and administration of such legislation. No exact correspondence exists, for example, between the Debakey Report, representing an expression of broad public interest in the receipt of "the latest" medical care, and the Regional Medical Program Legislation. On the one hand, the pressures of public demand and political promise build up relevant to very general health goals. On the other, the expertise of health officials is applied to specific measures in a context of what is possible in Congress and the political arena generally.

Political parties as such have not as yet engaged themselves in the health sphere to any great degree at any level. True, the major parties have included health concerns in their platforms and presidential candidates have included issues such as Medicare in their campaigns. But good health care is an amazingly nonpartisan issue and detailed questions of financing and organizing are generally too complex to make good public issues. Although it is difficult for political parties as such to develop and take positions on health questions, they can be expected to do so increasingly as good health care is more and more regarded as a fundamental human right. Furthermore, politicians, as individual campaigners and as policy makers, can be expected to take greater interest in the details of health issues in the future. Men like Hill and Fogarty have already become expert guides to their congressional colleagues on health policy.

At the local level, health questions—especially when they involve the determination of the location for a new hospital or other facility, or the expenditure of public funds for programs and improvements—often become points for political action; sometimes rather acrimonious as Banfield's analysis of the Cook County Hospital expansion plans indicates.[43] But, again, these are seldom developed into party issues with one party vigorously supporting one side and so on. Instead the local party leader is called upon to meet the demands of various organized interests that do not fall along strict party lines. Of course, when a hospital rests under the control of the party in power, a continuing struggle occurs between patronage and appointment and promotion for merit. But, again, the Cook County case is instructive. Although the hospital administrator, Meyer, had built up "an organization" it was not for party politics.[44]

On occasion a local party will adopt a program of economy, perhaps even focusing on welfare and indigent care. The mayoral candidate may run on that issue with success (the case of Newburg, New York, comes to mind). Or the issue may be improvement of services in city or county health institutions, a situation that may be developing now in New York, where state legislators and others have made tours of Bellevue and other public hospitals and found appalling conditions. These developments obviously have important implications for retaining personnel and for general ability to deliver services. Usually the issues depend less on party competition than on other organized interest groups (welfare association, medical or dental society, trade unions) or civic leadership. By common consent political parties tend to avoid "stirring up fights" on religion, schools, and hospitals.

Another reaction in the environment of the health system has been the establishment of new, sometimes quasi-governmental systems of planning and control that cut across health occupations, organizations and even communities where "area-wide" or regional planning is envisioned. Lay community leaders have begun to assume an increasing role in these endeavors. One official of a powerful planning agency, composed of nonelected financial and industrial leaders (and two ministers to lend a sense of contact with the populace), was asked from where his board derived its authority. His answer: "They asserted it."

With the colossal capital and operating expenses required by the modern hospital in an urban region, the men who control the large economic and organizational resources that are likely to be financially bled to death, have begun to band together to seek economies. So far the emphasis of community leaders has been on the costs of bricks and mortar rather than on sophistication about people and service programs. They have also concentrated their interests on those organizations requiring the most private capital (hospitals) with little awareness of the total community health sytem.[45] But one can expect community leaders to expand their interests to other organizations, supply of manpower and concern for services, including their quality and controls, in a continuing and expanding search for an answer to the question. "Are we getting our money's worth?"

With the activities of the Office of Economic Opportunity, particularly the Community Action Programs that arose in response to the poverty-civil rights revolution now in progress, a larger voice is demanded by consumer groups. These are mainly "lower-class," neighborhood-based groups with social structural characteristics similar to those Gans described for the once vibrant West End of Boston.[46] It is evident that on the local scene where a direct confrontation can take place between health professionals and those they serve, or should serve (a confrontation even the political system or some vast and distant bureaucracy of the state does not provide), "the forgotten" may develop a contribution to determine the policy for operating a given network of health service agencies. New forms of nonbureaucratic organization may evolve in which these populations will exercise control and learn to seek health care before it is too late. The present wilderness of outpatient clinics may be particularly anachronistic in this context.[47]

In summary, thus far, to assess the power budget available to the health planner, one must realize how the bases of power have come to be distributed through complex changes, internal and external, to the health system. These have entailed fluidity in power relations; a more prominent place for health concerns generally in society, but dispersal of power among occupational groups and organizations in the system, including a less exclusive and dominant role for "the" physician and a more prominent role for administrators and planners; the development of organizational networks in which hospitals and university health centers play key roles; and certain public reactions including a vast politicalization of health policy issues, sometimes with political party involvement and greater involvement of "third-party" payers, community leaders and the consumer generally.

IMPLICATIONS

Research

From this brief and necessarily abstract overview of a complex topic, one thing is clear: knowledge, even an adequate framework, is lacking in the field. This is not the place to specify a long list of research opportunities and needs, but a few examples are called for.

What is the relative contribution of each of the bases of power to the outcome of various issues in the health field? Is "professional magic" (myth making), scientific knowledge, tradition, economic and organizational resources, official authority, charisma or some other source of power the dominant factor in resolving various issues?

How do power relationships alter with changes in organizational complexity, size and arrangement?

What is the relative contribution of various types of health experts and lay leaders to decisions at the policy-planning level in the local community and at regional, state and national levels?

How do lay leaders' connections with and understandings of the health system and its component organizations differ according to the socioeconomic composition of the community and the structure of the leadership itself? What places do health and particular health endeavors hold in the value hierarchies of lay leaders such that the position of health in the priorities of public policy is affected?

Must the "value" of health be expressed in economic terms or is a potent political force that is desirous of better and more health services enough to assure health a high priority in public policy?

If the health system is to be regionalized, how does "community power structure" relate to regional power structure" (if such exists) and what effect does crossing local and state jurisdictions have on regionalization?

The Organization of Regional Health Planning

The accomplishment of efficient, effective delivery of health services to all segments of the population within a specific geographical region will require special personnel and special organization to accomplish the task. The concluding section will discuss the preparation of community-wide health services administrators and planners. All aspects of the organizational question will not be considered, for that involves a determination of 1. the potential of the population, given adequate health care; 2. the relative place of health in the overall endeavors of the region and the investment that can be made in health; 3. sociocultural variations in the population; 4. the available resources including manpower; 5. the setting of priorities among health activities; 6. delegation of responsibility and authority for assigned, functionally interrelated tasks; 7. two-way (center—periphery—center) flow of communication, patients, staff; 8. evaluation, and so forth. Here, interest is limited to power relationships.

Much discussion has centered around the "locus" of the health planning effort in the future. Will it be the hospital? Will it be the Health and Welfare Association? Will it be the Health Department? Will it be the university-based health center? Will it be public or private? These questions cannot be answered in any final sense at this time. In fact, the problems should be treated in experimental fashion across different regions. Nevertheless, if the foregoing analysis is at all accurate, and since the effective power is now dispersed throughout many organizations and occupational groups in the local system, no present single component will be adequate to carry out planning.

Some new organization will be required that, above all, will have to bring to bear the effective power structure of the region. The "power budget" must be adequate to the task. Where the power structure is fractionated and uninformed as to the overall health system, planning will be little more than several unheeded staff functions located where they cannot become an embarrassment. Where the power structure is united in the achievement of well-understood specific goals, the planning process will be integral to the total endeavor of the system. Under these ideal conditions, planning would not be exclusively assigned to a given unit. Instead, the development and institution of plans would go on throughout the system to be affected.

Major contributions to the power structure as regards health are: 1. government and legal authority; 2. lay community leaders, particularly financial and industrial figures, depending somewhat on the composition of the community;[48] 3. increasingly, consumer groups who may have an impact through local government, health organization boards or neighborhood groups; 4. the university-based health center; 5. large "third-party" payers; 6. particular organizations, such as dominant hospitals that are well connected with lay community leaders; 7. particularly well-organized occupational groups.

Although the pattern of regional health planning for the future cannot be envisioned, it is possible to suggest that this become a problem for the design and evaluation of planned change. With a legal mandate and the engagement of the effective power system, along with health planners, health service personnel, social scientists and other researchers to aid in the design and evaluation, various health planning systems can be tried out in different regions. Careful research methods involving before-after and cross-regional comparisons will be necessary. In some settings, nothing should be undertaken other than the before-after measurement of the efficiency and effectiveness of the local health system. The most sophisticated theory will be required to develop the design, with deliberate variation on key points to "test" the impact of crucial factors on the operation of various regional health planning structures. Under this plan the region will become a laboratory for the design, institution and evaluation of planned change.

Preparation of Regional Health Administrators and Planners

It was of major concern to the Joint Committee on Education for Public Health that nowhere in this country today is an adequate effort consciously being put forth to provide the kind of persons required for the above task.[37] What would such preparation involve?

Several components of the university would be required to carry out a program at the doctoral level in regional health services administration and planning. It would be necessary for the student to become acquainted with the subculture of the health world, its occupations, its organizations, its traditions and patterns generally. That could be done in part through reading and class work, but more through varied field experiences. The student would need to have social science theories and methods at his command, the tools of quantitative management, an understanding of the place of science in society, knowledge of political and economic systems and an understanding of, if not expertise in, epidemiological research. He would give special attention to the planning process and to the design and evaluation of planned change.

For the student to develop ability in practice, teaching and research, the school or health center that prepares him would ideally have responsibility for the planning and delivery of health services in the surrounding region. As suggested above, community leaders and consumers might play determining policy-making roles to assure that the health center carry out its responsibilities to the public. Through this means, students could be assigned in such a manner that the teaching would be beneficially focussed, and in turn the teaching would be altered to confront realities seldom imagined in the insulated classroom.

It is not necessary that students in such a program be of any particular health discipline or profession. Excellence in a liberal arts and sciences background should be adequate. Nor should a certain amount of experience be required, since practice in regional health services administration and planning would be gained in the program itself. It should be clear that persons of any health discipline or profession and any amount of experience would also be admitted on grounds of ability and interest in pursuing such a program.

REFERENCES

1. By a system is meant a collection of identifiable units interrelated in their effects on some outcome. The many health agencies, occupational groups and individuals involved in them make up the health system of a community or region (some geographically bounded place containing a human

population) for these units act to affect for good or ill the level of disability in the population.

2. Bierstedt, Robert, An Analysis of Social Power, *American Sociological Review*, 15, 730-738, December, 1959.

3. Weber, Max, THEORY OF SOCIAL AND ECONOMIC ORGANIZATION (Trans. A. M. Henderson and T. Parsons), New York, Oxford University Press, 1947, p. 152. Most modern sociologists accept the essentials of Weber's definition and have only slightly qualified it—e.g. Schermerhorn, R. A. SOCIETY AND POWER, New York, Random House, Inc., 1961, pp. 9-10. Blau also excludes power from "intrinsically rewarding" relationships and reserves its applicability to relationships that are unilateral (as opposed to reciprocal) and involve extrinsic elements, i.e. those which can be detached from the persons supplying them. Blau, Peter M. EXCHANGE AND POWER IN SOCIAL LIFE, New York, John Wiley & Sons, Inc., 1964, pp. 312-313. But this seems unnecessarily complicated. It implies (as the author recognizes) a static theory of social life and structure, and good theoretical grounds in the symbolic interaction school of thought indicate that some ambiguity or "resistance" must be overcome in any human interaction. Thus, some "extrinsic" or general social element is always in the relationship, almost be definition, so long as one remains at the human, social level and is not concerned simply with any unsymbolized biological aspects that probably are involved in the most ideal reciprocal, love relationship.

4. A classic experiment identifying the element of ambiguity and some factors associated with its removal in one direction or another is given *in* Sherif, Muzafer, Group Influences Upon the Formation of Norms and Attitudes, *in* Macoby, E., Newcomb, T. and Hartley, E. (Editors), READINGS IN SOCIAL PSYCHOLOGY, Third edition, New York, Henry Holt and Company, 1960, pp. 219-232.

5. To Bierstedt, power is always potential, Bierstedt, *op cit.* Weber's use of the term "probabilities" suggests the same. A different kind of distinction that may be useful reserves power for intentional effects on another's behavior while influence is broader, including unintended effects. Van Houten, Donald R., Opportunity and Influence: A Study of Medical Leadership in Community Hospitals, Ph.D. thesis, University of Pittsburgh, 1967.

6. It may be on this basis that a basic unit of social interaction could be identified; something comparable to the atom, various subparticles, or "quanta" (whatever is current in physics these days). Various frameworks have been suggested for the social sciences with the recognition of this problem in view. For example, Foote, Nelson N., Anachronism and Synchronism in Sociology, *Sociometry*, 21, 17-29, March, 1958.

7. The lifeblood of administration is power. Its attainment, maintenance, increase, dissipation, and loss are subjects the practitioner and student can ill afford to neglect. Loss of realism and failure are almost certain consequences. . . . Power is only one of the considerations that must be weighed in administration, but of all it is the most overlooked in theory and the most dangerous to overlook in practice. . . . Analysis of the sources from which power is derived and the limitations they impose is as much a dictate of

prudent administration as sound budgetary procedure. The bankruptcy that comes from an unbalanced power budget has consequences far more disastrous than the necessity of seeking a deficiency appropriation." Long, Norton E., Power and Administration, in THE POLITY, Chicago, Rand McNally & Co., 1962, pp. 51-52.

8. These may be the formal rules of logic recognized in disciplined intercourse or the "folk logic" of everyday interchange. See Rose, Arnold M., Popular Logic in the Study of Covert Culture, in THEORY AND METHOD IN THE SOCIAL SCIENCES, Minneapolis, University of Minnesota Press, 1954, pp. 320-326.

9. Blau, op cit., pp. 118-119.

10. The author and co-workers suggested that different relations to the class structure would explain the lower support received by local governmental hospitals as compared with voluntary hospitals. Elling, R. and Halebsky, S., Organizational Differentiation and Support, A Conceptual Framework, in Scott, W. R., and Volkart, E. (Editors), MEDICAL CARE—READINGS IN THE SOCIOLOGY OF MEDICAL INSTITUTIONS, New York, John Wiley & Sons, Inc., 1966, pp. 543-557.The paper by Robb Burlage included in this volume analyzes the working of a program in New York City designed to upgrade the public hospitals by affiliating them with voluntary hospitals.

11. For example, Freeman, Linton, et al., LOCAL COMMUNITY LEADERSHIP, Syracuse, University College, 1960. A recent study in Pittsburgh also found a great predominance of male, white, Anglo-Saxon, Protestants among those reputed to be leaders of the community. Elling, R. H. and Lee, O. J., Formal Connections of Community Leadership to the Health System, Milbank Memorial Fund Quarterly, 4, 294-306, July, 1966.

12. Hughes, Everett C., Dilemmas and Contradictions of Status, The American Journal of Sociology, 50, 353-59, March, 1945.

13. These trends seem particularly marked among industrial physicians. Shepard, W. P., Elling, R. H. and Grimes, W. F., Study of Public Health Careers: Some Characteristics of Industrial Physicians, Journal of Occupational Medicine, 8, 108-119, March, 1966.

14. Simmel, George, THE SOCIOLOGY OF GEORGE SIMMEL, Glencoe, The Free Press, 1950.

15. As cited by Rosen, George, The Hospital: Historical Sociology of a Community Institution, in Freidson, Eliot (Editor), THE HOSPITAL IN MODERN SOCIETY, New York, the Macmillan Company, 1964, p. 27.

16. Kissick, William L., Health Manpower in Transition, in this volume.

17. Bucher, R. and Strauss, A., Professions in Process, American Journal of Sociology, 66, 325-334, January, 1961.

18. Stewart, W. H. and Pennell, M. Y., Physicians' Age, Type of Practice, and Location, in Health Manpower Source Book No. 10, Washington, Public Health Service Publication No. 263, section 10, 1960, p. 4.

19. Cavins, H. M., NATIONAL HEALTH AGENCIES, Washington, Public Affairs Press, 1945.

20. Hamlin, R. H., VOLUNTARY HEALTH AND WELFARE AGENCIES IN THE UNITED STATES, New York, Schoolmasters' Press, 1961.

21. These funds and organizational arrangements were provided by the Mills-

Ribicoff Act (Public Law 88-156) and the Mental Retardation and Community Health Centers Construction Act (Public Law 88-164). A study of coordination resulting from planning for mental retardation activities in several states has been funded and carried out by Conrad Seipp, Edward Suchman, Ray H. Elling and research associates Edmund Ricci and Malcolm MacNair.

22. From the preface of Roemer, M. I. and Wilson, E. A., *Organized Health Services in a County of the United States*, Public Health Service Publicatin No. 197, 1952.

23. *Ibid.*, p. 77 and Table I, p. 78.

24. Kissick, *op cit.*, p. 4.

25. Somers, Anne R., Some Basic Determinants of Medical Care and Health Policy: An Overview of Trends and Issues, in this volume.

26. Sigerist, H. E., An Outline of the Development of the Hospital, *in* Roemer, M. I. (Editor), HENRY E. SIGERIST ON THE SOCIOLOGY OF MEDICINE, New York, M.D. Publications, 1960.

27. "Health care, like education, should be available to everyone in the United States, and it can be. Whether looked at from the standpoint of a good life for the individual or the excellence of the society, its absence causes a large, measurable loss—one an affluent, civilized nation cannot, morally or economically, afford." *The New Republic*, Supplement: "Health: Are We the People Getting Our Money's Worth?" November 9, 1963, p. 37. Also, Roemer, M. I., Changing Patterns of Health Service: Their Dependence on a Changing World, *The Annals*, 346, 53, March, 1963.

28. Mills, C. Wright, THE POWER ELITE, New York, Oxford University Press, 1959. For a sharpened, even if disturbing version of Mills' analysis , see THE CAUSES OF WORLD WAR III, New York, Simon and Schuster, Inc., 1958. In this connection, recall also President Eisenhower's parting speech in which he identified the combination of business and military as almost overhwelming of civilian control in government. Senator Fulbright has recently issued similar warnings.

29. *See The New Yorker*: Annual of Legislation, Medicare, Part I: All Very Hegelian, July 2, 1966, pp. 29-62; Part II: More Than a Lot of Statistics, July 9, 1966, p. 39-77; Part III: We Do Not Compromise, July 16, 1966, pp. 35-91; Part IV: A Sacred Trust, July 23, 1966.

30. Hodge, Robert W., Siegel, Paul M. and Rossi, Peter H., Occupational Prestige in the United States, 1925-1963, *American Journal of Sociology*, 70, 286-302, November, 1964.

31. Wilson, R. N., The Physician's Changing Hospital Role, *Human Organization*, 18, 117-183, Winter, 1959-60.

32. The prestige ranking in Table 1 is based on useable replies to the question: "People differ in their opinion with regard to the Professional status of various occupational groups. In your own judgment, how professional is each of the following groups?" The number of responses to this question varied by occupational group. The usable replies from the general sample ranged from 4879 to 4769, or an average of 4634 usable responses. A rank

was obtained for each group by scoring responses as follows and obtaining an average: "highly professional, " 4; "professional," 3; "somewhat professional," 2; "not professional at al," 1. "Don't know" responses were fairly evenly distributed and were not scored. On the average, 234 cases responded "don't know" to the question of professional ranking. Since other ways of manipulating the scoring system are possible and since different samples might give different results, this ranking cannot be viewed as final. Further, it is supposed here that change may occur in the position of any of these groups over time.

32. For other methodological details of the study *see* Shepard, Elling and Grimes, *op cit.*
33. These strategies and means have been discussed elsewhere: Elling, R. H. Occupational Group Striving and Administration in Public Health, to appear *in* Arnold, M., Blankenship, L. V. and Hess, J. (Editors), HEALTH SERVICES ADMINISTRATION, Atherton Press, forthcoming.
34. Becker, Howard S., The Nature of a Profession, *in* EDUCATION FOR THE PROFESSIONS, Sixty-first Yearbook, Chicago, The National Society for the Study of Education, 1962, Chapter 2.
35. Walsh, James L., Professional Group Striving and the Orientations of Public Health Professionals Toward Lower Class Clients, Ph.D. Thesis, University of Pittsburgh, 1966.
36. Badgley, Robin F. and Wolfe, Samuel, DOCTOR'S STRIKE, New York, Atherton Press, 1967.
37. Fry, H. G., Shepard, W. P. and Elling, R. H., EDUCATION AND MANPOWER FOR COMMUNITY HEALTH, based on the Report of the Joint Committee on the Study of Education for Public Health, Pittsburgh, University of Pittsburgh Press, 1967.
38. Not the least interesting of these is the question, "With more than one hospital in town, which one becomes the center of the health center?" Of course they might all be if specialization and division of labor were shared among hospitals, but that assumes a degree of personal and institutional selflessness yet to be achieved. At present, competition for support is to acute to permit such functional specialization and integration. See Elling, R. H., The Hospital Support Game in Urban Center, *in* Freidson, Eliot, THE HOSPITAL IN MODERN SOCIETY, the Macmillan Company, 1963, pp. 73-111.
39. Strauss, A., *et al.*, *The Hospital and its Negotiated Order, in* Freidson, *op. cit.*, pp. 147-169.
40. "Not every political power as such is state power, but in the eyes of its incumbents at least, every political power is potentially state power." Heller, H., Power, Political, ENCYCLOPEDIA OF THE SOCIAL SCIENCES, New York, the Macmillan Company, 1933, Vol. 12, p. 301.
41. "In 1929 total expenditures for health and medical care, including health-facility construction and medical research, amounted to $3.6 billion and accounted for 3.6 per cent of the gross national product. By 1963 such expenditures came to over nine times this amount—some $33.8 billion—and represented 6.0 per cent of the gross national product."

Folsom, M. B., *Responsibility of the Board Member of Voluntary Health Agencies,* second Michael M. Davis Lecture, University of Chicago, Graduate School of Business, 1964 (pamphlet). At present, health is a $40 billion enterprise with the Social Security Administraton's projections for the next fiscal year at $44 billion. And indications are that it will probably increase by 7.5 per cent per year within the next decade. Experts do not doubt that the ratio of health expenditures to GNP "will eventually move to 8-10 per cent." Somers, *op cit.*

42. *For a humorous, but still tragi-comic account of an "upper-class" person's experience, see* Franken, Rose, You're Well Out of a Hospital, New York, Doubleday & Company, Inc., 1966. For a less humorous account of "lower-class" experiences, see Strauss, A., Medical Ghettos, *Transactions,* 4, 7-15, May, 1967.

43. Banfield, E. C., Political Influence, New York, the Macmillan Company, 1961.

44. *Ibid,* p. 26

45. Elling and Lee, *op cit.*

46. *Gans, Herbert,* The Urban Villagers: Group and Class in the Life of Italian-Americans, New York, The Free Press, 1962.

46. By comparing the known characteristics of "middle-class," bureaucracies and "lower-class' neighborhood residents, the appearance of an effective organization has been theorized elsewhere: Elling, R. H., The Design and Evaluation of Planned Change in Health Organization, *in* Shostak, A. (Editor), Sociology in Action, Chicago, Dorsey Press, 1966.

48. Walton, John, Substance and Artifact: The Current Status of Research on Community Power, *The American Journal of Sociology,* 71, 430-38, January, 1966.

Medicine Faces the
Consumer Movement

WALTER J. MCNERNEY

The average physician is likely to blame government for many of his problems when, in fact, much of what he reacts against is simply an outgrowth of the growing consumer involvement in health affairs in which the government is merely one channel among several. As the chief producers of health services, physicians are vexed not only by what they see as a shift in power between producers and consumers, but also by their uncertainty as to what the new balance of power will be or how it will be determined. This article focuses on one important element of the overall issue of balance: the content and nature of consumer involvement.

THE CONSUMER'S ROLE

First, it should be established that the consumer has played an essential role in the health field—as he has in all fields—from the

Reprinted, with permission, from *Prism*, September, 1973, pp 13-16.

beginning. If it is true that appendicitis cannot exist without the confirmation of a doctor, it is equally true that the ailment requires a patient. And beyond the core patient-doctor relationship, the consumer has acted in a variety of roles, e.g., as institutional trustee, fringe benefit negotiator, and member of the electorate.

Over the years, through the financing and operation of a wide variety of institutions and through the passage of laws and regulations, he has made an important impact on the delivery of health care in the United States. Further, it should be noted that neither the scope nor the quality of consumer involvement should be denigrated by casual application of today's standards against the problems of yesterday, when fewer tools and insights were available.

Second, it is important to understand that the increase and changes in consumer involvement in the financing and delivery of health care are not passing fancies; they reflect fundamental changes in our economy and society as a whole.

The roots of increased consumer involvement are many and diverse; all the underlying causes for this growth are not clearly understood.

There are now more than 1,000 federal government consumer programs in operation. Twenty-three states have consumer protection departments, 39 have consumer fraud units, and 50 cities sponsor or operate other agencies designed to protect the consumer. In my opinion, these grew in direct response to shoddy products and services emanating from both big business and big government.

SOCIAL RESPONSIBILITIES

In a recent statement, "Social Responsibilities in Business Corporations," the Committee for Economic Development (CED), a premier spokesman for American management, dealt at length with the nature of social responsibilities: "Business functions by public consent, and its basic purpose is to serve constructively the needs of society . . . to the satisfaction of society." While businessmen agree that they cannot reform the nation alone—they must join government, labor, and the professional community—the CED's statement shows that they see the contract between industry and society including service to a wider range of human values and an obligation to members of the public with whom they have no commercial transactions. How far does this commitment go? Henry Ford II has stated: "How much freedom business will retain in the closing decades of this century depends on the quality of management's response to the changing expectations of the public." In essence, the business corporation is becoming politicized. Examples of social programs promulgated by such corporations are numerous, whether dealing with ugly surroundings, infested water, dirty air, or land redevelopment.

CONCERNED CITIZEN MOVEMENT

The movement of concerned citizens has spread to our religious organizations. Among the churches, programs are determined significantly more often by laymen now than ever before, resulting in changes never thought possible even a decade ago. This development is contested by some, but many laymen want the faith to be active outside the churches. As a result, the coming of the laymen has changed the role of the clergyman, regardless of creed.

In the health field, the symptoms are manifold. Hospitals are trying to broaden and intensify community representation on their boards. Patient ombudsmen have been established in some institutions. The American Hospital Association recently published a patient's Bill of Rights. Blue Cross Plans now have a majority of consumer or public representatives on their boards, while maintaining significant input from providers, and a public advisory committee reviews the Blue Cross system's national policy and programs. Federal law calls for consumer majorities on areawide planning boards. Malpractice suits and class suits in behalf of aggrieved consumers have increased significantly, in number and ingenuity. Outrage has been directed against hospitals whose trustees sanction the depositing of funds in interest-free accounts in banks run by some of the same trustees, instead of, for example, applying the money toward mortgages. Laws and regulations have been designed to come forcibly to grips with access and other health care delivery problems.

Although all the causes underlying reform are not clear, an important few can be identified.

Today, the American public is better educated and has more material wealth than previous generations. The average worker is no longer a relatively untutored newcomer to the United States, accustomed to strict authority on the job and in his home. Nor is his wife. His education has led to higher expectations and a desire for greater control over his own destiny. Quite importantly, he is less likely to accept society as it is and blame himself for personal or societal shortcomings, and he is more likely to try to change the institutions with which he deals. Maladaption to life's difficulties is perceived more as a social condition and less as a personal problem. The mass media plays a role here, throwing various problems and options into bold relief, enabling the average citizen to see issues as part of a broader context and not only as the aberrations of a particular neighborhood.

Accelerated technology has out-stripped the ability of many of our institutions to cope with social problems, and the resulting tensions and anxiety have at times given rise to intense public criticism of all our institutions, including the courts, the military and industry. Workers are deeply concerned about inflation and the effects of rising costs on the purchasing power of their earnings. They are also worried about urban unrest and international troubles. Many complain about deteriorating services in the economy, whether in the form of power cutbacks, computer mistakes, or appliances that don't work. Their mood is reflected in state legislatures and in Congress, where the structure, as well as the performance, of various institutions is now under sharp scrutiny.

Institutionalization is seen as a major problem. Too many companies seem more preoccupied with the economic or social purposes they are supposed to serve. The end of our involvement in Vietnam showed clearly that the war could not be held accountable for the entire problem. The cease-fire revealed that ennui, lack of productivity, and other problems have a broader base.

In the health field, it suddenly became apparent that the delivery system in 1970 was designed to meet the conditions of 1950. And the distortions were great. For example, there was undue emphasis on expensive care when less costly care would do the job as well or better, and there was a notable lack of ingenuity in using health manpower effectively.

Institutionalization produces societal disease; and beyond a certain stage, it can be cured only by the intervention of consumers. If U.S. Steel now lists the indirect interests of directors and officers in its annual report, it does not take much imagination to see that hospital trustees must soon follow suit and that there will be greater consumer interest evidenced in the relations of physician owners to proprietary hospitals and to their subcontractors.

Of course, accountability cannot be achieved or approached only by structural reforms and disclosure techniques. It must include the workings of the institutions and extend to its mood, if not its soul. In the hospital, for example, accountability must revolve around such fundamental considerations as the responsible involvement of physicians in the management of the institution.

In the shifts of power, there is an element of egalitarianism. The poor want to be more equal; women are seeking economic equality with men; the young want a broader franchise; black people want to be on an equal footing with whites.

EGALITARIANISM

This attitude is bound to have leveling effects and to involve greater consumer participation through contracts, negotiation, or legislation. But there are few signs that egalitarianism will become an overriding political philosophy. Nor will elitism. The middle ground will probably be explored in a series of relatively pragmatic decisions and progams. Given a reasonable degree of social justice, the public may well stand for the achievement of certain minimum standards of service for all, provided that the inequalities beyond those standards encourage innovation and produce a larger gross national product.

Thus, in the quest for a better balance between social justice and efficiency, the consumer will play a stronger role—and only he or his surrogates can address such major questions. It does not follow that extremes will be struck that are unacceptable to providers or producers. After all, the ingenuity of such schemes forms an important part of the equation.

This and other trends have been sifted and evaluated by many observers in an effort to explain the new emphasis on consumerism in our society, including the health field. But we should not forget that there were earlier trends in the same direction.

During the 1930s and 1940s, management, which had thought of itself by and large as a technical system, began to see itself as a social system as well as an agent of policy formulation that had many relations with external constituencies. Hence, *morale, participation,* and *accountability* joined *efficiency* as operating concepts, and although it was overused at times, the idea that workers had to have some voice in the conditions surrounding them, if optimum productivity was to be achieved, took hold.

Also, in the 1940s and 1950s, social scientists began to evaluate hospitals and drew certain parallels from the doctor-patient relationship, i.e., the patient wanted to know more about his condition and to participate in certain decisions regarding it. Accordingly, in the context of industrial and health service management, some of the seeds of the 1960s were sown.

This recollection should reinforce the idea that the health field is now being affected by consumer forces that are substantive, not illusionary or transitory—forces that must be dealt with, not wished away.

Given a larger measure of consumer involvement, how do consumers feel about health providers and professionals? The evidence is fragmentary, but it indicates that the public feels the hospitals and doctors are less interested in many facets of access and productivity than they should be. Surveys that show the individual essentially satisfied with his own physician should not be misread; many of these surveys do not probe fully or objectively. A positive response may be only a form of selfjustification on the part of the patient or an attempt to reaffirm his faith in his physician. In fact, throughout the civilized world, people interviewed about their health system generally support it despite wide ranges in the effectiveness of those systems. Indeed, many of these same people have been active in changing their health care systems in recent years, sometimes markedly.

Accordingly, it is important to concentrate on what people do, not just on what they say. Presently, they are busy changing the shape of the same U.S. system that 84 percent (a national sample) essentially endorsed in 1971, according to Stephen P. Strickland in *U.S. Health care: What's Wrong and What's Right?* Some of the consumer advocate language is harsh; words like "fraud' and "self-righteous" are applied to health carriers.

But importantly, consumers have not chosen up sides. They assail physicians and hospitals, big business and big government. And the issue is not ideology—it is performance.

SEVERAL ROLES

We need to remember that there are consumers and consumers, and that one person can play several roles. For example, a sick consumer is quite different from one who is well. When ill, the patient allies himself with hospital's search for the best; when well, he complains about costs. A local businessman is likely to express great concern over the rise in expenses for health fringe benefits. Sitting as a hospital trustee, he may join forces with the hospital administration and medical staff to fill empty beds or keep supporting services busy.

Physicians and others working in the health field should not be deceived by the actions of such captive consumers as trustees. Probably one of the most naive tactics in the health field is the relatively uncritical camaraderie among too many trustees, medical staffs, and administrators, when, in fact, each needs precisely the honest input of the other if voluntary effort is to be legitimized. Physicians should appeal to trustees to identify with the larger community so that institutional versus professional issues can be clearly defined and dealt with close to the everyday problems involved.

On the other hand, physicians and health institutions are not one and the same for institutions have goals that do not necessarily reflect the goals or values of any given patient; so the doctor may often be caught in the dilemma of choosing which to serve. Both the institution and the patient can demand consumer recognition from him. The inherent conflict of interest for the doctor is, in some cases becoming serious. He may be influenced, subtly or otherwise, by the institution to conform to its concept of acceptable behavior, but how does this square with his responsibility to the patient?

Should the transplant team be allowed to determine when a patient donor is dead? In a university hospital setting, how are educational, research, and care loyalties identified and monitored? In a health maintenance organization (HMO) where bonuses sometimes depend upon under-budget performance, is the patient put at risk?

As medical science expands and we face the increasingly sophisticated functional as well as organic diseases of middle and advanced age, the problems will expand. The conveniences of institutions and individuals subtly interact, particularly when mental aberration becomes involved. And we are all aware of how personal freedom can be manipulated when vigilance is lax. The consumer and the hospital depend upon and determine the actions of the physician. All parties must learn to work together.

As confusing as it may seem, pointing out these complications tends to clarify one thing: The consumer revolution refers to the public at large, with its myriad minority interests; yet it is precisely the public at large that many physicians do not seem to understand.

PERCEPTION GAP

It is within this larger body, incidentally, that such major health issues are being debated: In what framework should national health insurance be instituted, and what associated control strategies should be implemented? Organized medicine has sponsored a bill that leaves much the way it is. The real battle centers around the relative worth of a public utility versus a moderated market format and such bold interventions as Professional Standards Review Organizations (PSRO), HMOs, and incentive reimbursement. Such a perception gap tends to confirm a misunderstanding or perhaps an underestimation of consumer interest (and influence). It is interesting to note that even the PSRO program is essentially a consumer initiative. And many consumers who are involved feel a bit uncomfortable watching medicine, so clearly on the defensive, trying to gain control of its own initiative.

What can be done to ease the confrontations among consumers, providers, and professionals? There are no easy remedies, but a few observations may help.

Consumerism, as we know it in its various forms, will not go away. Physicians must accept it and understand it as an outgrowth of the total economy and society, responding to several strong mid-century forces. Further, we must accept the idea that consumers are better than professionals at several key tasks, such as setting institutional goals and devising economic or political sanctions. They do not wish to compromise quality as is often alleged. The trick is how to join relative assets unpatronizingly. Both consumers and physicians have key roles to play, and balance is of the essence.

However, the assertion of consumer responsibility does not connote unqualified eminence. In some communities, the take-over of a health institution by inexperienced consumers has been little short of calamitous. But the professional who points to these situations to justify anticonsumer feeling misses the point. These consumers need to be educated and trained—their role is in question; their status is not. Sophisticated and supportive health administrators and physicians can go a long way toward educating the public in matters of health care and realistic medical goals.

RESENTMENT

Differences should be honestly recognized and negotiated, not treated brittlely or ignored. Since the provider and the professional often fear loss of control and prerogative, let them state in what way and why. Consumers, for their part, are genuinely troubled about their institutions and systems and are saying so. They are disillusioned with sweeping programs (such as the Great Society measures of the 1960s) and unfulfilled promises. Moreover, they are beginning to sense the severe limitations of technology and to appreciate human values. We are entering a phase of public policy and social management in which professional arrogance or technical solutions offered to solve complex issues will be deeply resented. Also, the resentment will be felt at all levels of society.

Welfare recipients and the population as a whole share far more similar life aspirations than many people may realize.

CONFLICT OF INTEREST

The medical profession and the patients must be candid with one another. This should start with a ready identification by the physician of a conflict of professional interest, whenever it may exist. But it should go to other matters, too.

Many patients are bad consumers because they have been taught to be that way by the health profession: "Getting care from anyone other than a physician is unsafe" — yet substitute skills under supervision could suffice in many cases. "Keep coming back for treatment" — yet the problem and its solution may be one of life style, which too often, unfortunately, lies outside the limited definitions of health care. "Many conditions are preventable" — in fact, the evidence is that few are, and there is little consensus regarding the worth of pre-symptomatic screening. No wonder the consumer seeks relief from the wrong system or is apt to pursue expensively unrealistic expectations.

If the health system is to work reasonably well, the consumer must be motivated (by the physician, among others) to come to grips with his life situation, and he must be sympathetically retaught about what is real and what is not in modern medicine—what pays off in improved functional capacity and what does not. If all physicians were to accept this challenge, a contract between professional and consumer would be struck that would go a long way toward cutting down on patient turnover and restoring faith in the system and its institutions. Technological medicine, which is often effective, would then have a more solid base upon which to operate.

Thus the consumer must be seen as someone properly concerned with and involved in what are essentially community health problems, and he must be accepted as a mature adult when under care. Physicians who threaten not to participate in Medicare or Medicaid or who resist the worth of trained assistants while vociferously protesting blame for rising costs and system malfunctions are a disgrace to the profession! Such behavior is not only less than professional, it addresses an imagined or distorted problem from an era that has long-since passed.

A shift of power to the consumer is underway. It could result in too many strictures on medicine, but this need not be the case if the physician will remember the value inherent in wholesome professional relationships with his patients. If he cultivates such relationships, he will, in the process, be giving up his long-held defensive posture.

REASSURANCE

Some years ago, a young mother brought her little girl, who seemed about the age of my own seven-year-old daughter Rosalyn, into my clinic. This little girl was screaming, crying, and kicking. She fought her mother every step of the way.

With the help of a nurse, the mother got the frightened child half-way down the hall, at which time I was able to hear what was going on.

As I started to rise from my desk, I heard the mother trying to reassure her daughter. "Mary, you shouldn't be scared of the doctor—he's Rosalyn's father."

The cries and screams stopped. She thought a moment about what had just been said, then turned her tear-stained face toward her mother and sobbed, "Poor Rosalyn."

Citizen Participation: A Review of the Issues

EUGENE FEINGOLD

Citizen participation, community control, consumer invovlement, and other related ideas have been much talked about in the last ten years, and have had much conflict centering around them. Those who advocate citizen participation do so for different reasons and have differing concepts of what they mean by citizen participation. It is this difference in motivation and meaning which in large part causes the conflict that has been attendant on efforts to achieve citizen participation.

Why are people demanding more citizen participation when our government system already builds opportunities for such participation through elections, legislative hearings and other mechanisms for individuals and organized groups to press their interests?

There are several reasons. First, even if governmental mechanisms were totally satisfactory as a means of pursuing citizen interests, the pursuit of those interests cannot be confined to government alone.

Reprinted, with permission, from The Citizenry and the Hospital, Department of Health Care Administration, Duke University, Durham, North Carolina, 1974, pp 8-16.

Social policy, decisions of social importance, decisions which affect the daily lives of citizens, are made by *private* institutions, including hospitals, and some citizens, at least, want to be able to affect those decisions.

Secondly, the existing mechanisms for citizen participation are primarily involved in the selection of elected officials and in the operations of legislative bodies. Yet important decisions in our society are increasingly being made by administrators, in a process which is much less amenable to citizen participation. The advance of technology and the accompanying bureaucratization of society have increasingly placed the typical individual in a position where he has little influence on social policy, whether publicly or privately made. People feel that administrators, public and private, are not publicly accountable, either directly or through existing representative institutions. Thus, the new demands for participation have been focused primarily on administrators, rather than elected officials.

The mechanisms that exist for consumer participation through the electoral process and the legislative process are predominantly used by middle-class and upper-class citizens, and not by lower-class citizens. The lower class is now demanding that it too participate. The situation is somewhat different in health than in other fields where the demands for the community participation have been heard. In the field of health, there has been little participation by laymen, upper or lower class, except for limited participation by the elite on governing boards of hospitals and community agencies. Thus, the demand from lower-class people for participation in medical care decision-making is more radical than is the similar demand for participation in other fields—they are not simply asking for extension of participation from other consumers to themselves, but rather they are demanding something that is largely new.

But the demand for consumer participation is really more than simply a demand for inclusion in the *process* of making decisions. It also is concerned with—and indeed stems primarily from concern about—the *content* of the decisions.

The inability to control the bureaucracy has probably been felt less by the middle and upper class, because they share the values of the administrators, and because social policies have largely been shaped in a way that is congruent with their interests and values. However, there are substantial groups in the population—both the poor and the working class—who feel that the system has not provided them with a fair share of the available benefits. Thus, they are not concerned simply with participation, but rather with power or control. They want enough power to be able to change the distribution of benefits and costs. They want new mechanisms for this purpose because their past experience has led them to the conclusion that they can't get their fair shares through existing mechanisms.

Related to the powerlessness of the poor is the powerlessness of minority ethnic groups. These groups see "white" control of major social institutions resulting in both conscious racism and perhaps unconscious institutional patterns that are antagonistic to the interests of both minority individuals and the minority community as a whole. We thus have the call for Black power, Brown power, Red power—the effort to build self-pride within the minority community and use it as a base for organizing to press for the interests of the minority group. Minority group activists see citizen participation as a means of transferring power to themselves and their communities. Although the demand for increased participation does not come exclusively from them, they are a major element in its advocacy.

That, then, is one set of reasons for citizen participation, a desire on the part of citizens, and especially low-income and minority group citizens, for what they define as their fair share of society's goods and services. Closely related to this is the view of their spokesmen who see citizen participation as a means of gaining power, either for themselves or for the group they represent.

Those who have responded favorably to this demand have done so for a number of reasons. In no special order of priority, these include, first, a commitment to democratic ideology, which says that the citizen should have a voice in controlling his own life:

> Citizen participation is part of our democratic heritage, often proclaimed as a means to perfect the democratic process. Stated most simply, it views the citizen as the ultimate voice in community decision-making. Citizens *should* share in decisions affecting their destinies.[1]

Secondly, many have been concerned that the programs carried on by their organizations indeed are deficient in that they have been formulated by insiders, by experts, who are not adequately sensitive to the needs of the persons for whom the programs are being planned. Thus, consumer participation is seen as a means of improving the information received by the organization about its environment, and thus creating better programs.

Third, there is a set of therapeutic goals. Some of the originators of the Community Action Program saw that program as a vehicle for organizing the poor, and in the process changing them. Their thinking was that "indigenous, locally based and locally led conflict and protest organizations, fighting for power and control over jobs, services, money and programs, involve the uninvolved; that they are in themselves educational, provide the necessary first step for other and later kinds of involvement with the larger social order, train leadership and at once provide a fight for an end to alienation, institutionalized dependency, failure, withdrawal, and frustration."[2] In the long run, then, citizen participation was seen by conservatives as a means of socializing the poor into the existing political, economic, and social order, and by the more radical as providing " . . . new aspirations . . . new skills . . . and a new determination . . . that will eventually cleanse, purge, purify and reform society as a whole."[3]

Fourth, there is a set of manipulative reasons. People are more willing to go along with decisions in the making of which they have participated, or in the making of which they think they have participated. Citizen participation therefore is a means of coopting the citizenry and defusing opposition.

Thus, there is widespread *rhetorical* agreement in favor of increased citizen participation—but the *practice* is very different from the *rhetoric*. The conflict and disagreement in practice stems from the different motives of those uttering the rhetoric—a community leader who wants citizen participation in order to gain power and change the nature of a hospital's programs will have a very different view of the meaning of citizen participation from that of the administrator who is seeking a means of convincing the citizenry that it should support him.

What are their differences about the *meaning* of citizen participation? The phrase has two words and there is disagreement about the meaning of both of them.

The first conflict is over the meaning of "citizen." Who is it who is going to participate, whatever we mean by "participate"? Those being served by the institution, i.e., its present clients? Those who could potentially be served by it, i.e., the residents of the catchment area? All the citizens? Only *low-income* citizens? Only laymen? Only ethnic minority groups? All of these definitions have been used at one time or another.

Let us suppose we are agreed on the group of citizens who are to participate. It is not likely that they will be able to participate directly, and they thus must be represented some way in the participation process, whatever that will be. How will they be represented?

There is no one community but "a bewildering array of self-styled leadership personalities, each claiming to represent the community."[4] How does one make sure that the community "representatives" truly represent the community? More likely, there are differing interests within the community—how to determine which are the relevant interests and make sure they are represented?

A prior question may be just what we mean by representation. Are we concerned primarily with making sure that the formal arrangements by which a representative is selected are appropriate? Our society has typically felt that election is the most democratic manner of selecting citizen representatives. Yet, the special elections of model cities boards, community action boards, and the like, have never attracted great turnout. The low-income groups for whom these elections are designed are sufficiently alienated and distrustful that they don't participate. The saliency of the election and the candidates for potential voters is low, and is matched by low turnout.

An alternative to election is appointment. But, who does the appointing? Whom do they appoint? If they choose "established leaders," these leaders may very well turn out not to have grass-roots support. Faced with this dilemma, there has been some tendency to accept self-selected representatives of the community.

Yet, these self-selected representatives may be atypical of those they claim to represent. Are we concerned that the representatives reflect accurately the characteristics of those whom they represent? If so, which are the relevant characteristics that we want represented? In general, people with more education, with more money and leisure, tend to be more interested in participating. They are thus likely to be more effective spokesmen. If our concern is with effectiveness, we should opt for highly educated, knowledgeable consumers, regardless of their constituency, and give them long terms of office, so that they can become more knowledgeable. On the other hand, if we are concerned about accurately reflecting the demographic makeup of the population, such consumers are not the best choice.

Are we concerned that the representatives act on behalf on the interests of those they are representing? If so, how do we assure that?[5]

Let me turn from the problems involved in defining "citizen," to those involved in defining "participation". To the consumer making the demand, "participation" means either sharing power significantly or complete citizen control. To the administrator, however, citizen participation does not mean that he gives up power, but rather that he listens to consumers. One writer has suggested a "ladder of citizen participation,"[6] which I have modified into the following five rungs: informing, consultation, partnership, delegated power, and citizen control.

In the lowest degree of participation, *informing,*

> ... the emphasis is placed on a one-way flow of information—from officials to citizens—with no channel provided for feedback and no power for negotiation. Under these conditions, particularly when information is provided at a late stage in planning, people have little opportunity to influence the program designed 'for their benefit.'[6]

Consultation, the next degree of participation, attempts to ascertain citizens' views, rather than simply giving them the organization's views.

Inviting citizens' opinions, like informing them, can be a legitimate step toward their full participation. But if consulting them is not combined with other modes of participation, this rung of the ladder is still a sham since it offers no assurance that citizen concerns and ideas will be taken into account.[6]

With *partnership:*

. . . power is in fact redistributed through negotiation between citizens and power-holders. They agree to share planning and decision-making responsibilities through such structures as joint policy boards, planning committees, and mechanisms for resolving impasses. After the ground rules have been established through some form of give and take, they are not subject to unilateral change.

Partnership can work most effectively when there is an organized power base in the community to which the citizen leaders are accountable; when the citizens' group has financial resources to pay its leaders reasonable honoraria for their time-consuming efforts, and when the group has the resources to hire (and fire) its own technicians, lawyers, and community organizers. With these ingredients, citizens have some genuine bargaining influence over the outcome of the plan (as long as both parties find it useful to maintain the partnership).[6]

In the case of delegated power,

Negotiations between citizens and public officials can also result in citizens' achieving dominant decision-making authority over a particular plan or program. Model city policy boards or CAA delegate agencies on which citizens have a clear majority of seats and genuine specified powers are typical examples. At this level, the ladder has been scaled to the point where citizens hold the significant cards to assure accountability of the program to them. To resolve differences, power-holders need to start the bargaining process rather than respond to pressure from the other end.[6]

Finally, *citizen control is*

"that degree of power (or control) which guarantees that participants or residents can govern a program or an institution, be in full charge of policy and managerial aspects, and be able to negotiate the conditions under which 'outsiders' may change them. A neighborhood corporation with no intermediaries between it and the source of funds is the model most frequently advocated."[6]

Once there is agreement on the nature of participation, on the citizens to be represented, and on the identity of their representatives, what do we expect those representatives to do? Do they have the time, the knowledge and the skills to carry on their function? Is there a trade-off between efficient delivery of service and participation?

Will the citizen representatives be unduly influenced by the real and asserted expertise of the physician and, to a lesser extent, the other professionals with whom they deal? Even when the structures exist for consumer control, where consumers have control over budget and personnel, over planning and services, they are still often limited by their deference to the professional experts with whom they deal. Moreover, they must retain those professionals (especially physicians) because they are essential to the program; yet this need surely makes it difficult to overrule the professional, even where the consumer wishes to do so. "At stake is the proper relationship between expert authority and democratic accountability in an increasingly bureaucratized society."[7]

Once the citizen representatives have gained experience, they may no longer be true representatives of their constituents. Rather, they develop interests different from those of their constituency—they become coopted. Or, perhaps, they do pursue their constituency's demands, but those demands are not in that constituency's long-run interests (assuming that there is some way of knowing what is in their long-run interest).

Does citizen participation actually provide the more equitable distribution of social goods that underlies the demand for participation? Or, is citizen participation in the hospital a diversion because it is concerned primarily with the allocation of resources within the hospital, whereas the larger problem of the allocation of resources between the hospital and other social institutions is left untouched?

I have provided many questions and few, if any, answers, which was my understanding of my assignment. Let me close with an argument that, despite all the difficulties I have outlined, it is in the interests of hospital and hospital administrators to effectuate greater consumer participation. First, the expectations of the poor and underprivileged, which were heightened during the past decade, are now being undercut with the Administration's message that they are on their own. The alienation and frustration which results may very well have violent expression, which may be limited if hospitals and other institutions show themselves capable of accommodating to their needs and desires. Moving beyond the poor to the citizenry at large, one way to mobilize support for hospitals is to open membership on their boards to a wider range of citizens. Note, however, that "the symbolism of giving power to new constituencies can lead to explosive results when the reality falls short of expectations."[8]

The hospital administrator also has a personal stake in increased citizen representation. Much of his time is spent in open or subterranean conflict with a medical staff that attempts to arrogate a monopoly of influence for itself. The interests of the administrator and those of the community will often be compatible in their contest with the physicians. The consumer, then, can strengthen the hand of the administrator—although we should not forget that the consumer may also work against the administrator.

Hospital administrators view themselves as resource managers and are trained for this role. They may not find it congenial to deal with the politics of community relations. Yet, if they do not, they will fail to be successful.[9] The question is not whether there should be consumer participation, but rather how it can be structured so as to meet the needs and goals of both consumers and administrators in an effective manner.

REFERENCES

1. Edmund Burke, "Citizen Participation Strategies." *Journal of the American Institute of Planners*, September 1968. p. 287.
2. H. Jack Geiger, "Of the Poor, By the Poor, or For the Poor: The Mental Health Implications of Social Control of Poverty Programs." In M. Greenblatt *et al.*, eds., *Poverty and Mental Health*. Washington: American Psychiatric Association, 1967.
3. Avedis Donabedian, "An Examination of Some Directions in Health Care Policy." *American Journal of Public Health*. Vol. 63, No. 3, March 1973, p. 246.
4. Leonard W. Cronkhite, Jr., "What are the Conflicts Involved in Community Control?" In John C. Norman, ed., *Medicine in the Ghetto*. New York: Appleton-Century-Crofts, 1969. p. 288.
5. Hanna Pitkins's *The Concept of Representation* (Berkeley, University of California Press, 1967) discusses these and other concepts of representation. See also Paul E. Peterson's "Forms of Representation: Participation of the Poor in the Community Action Program," *American Political Science Review*, Vol. 64, No. 2, June 1970. pp. 491-507.
6. Sherry R. Arnstein, "A Ladder of Citizen Participation, *Journal of the American Institute of Planners*, July 1969, pp. 216-223. See also Edmund Burke, *op. cit.*
7. Judith V. May, "The Relationship Between Professionals and Clients: A Constitutional Struggle," unpublished paper, p. 1.
8. Bruce, L.R. Smith, "Introduction," *American Behavioral Scientist*, Vol. 15, No. 5, May-June 1972, p. 11.
9. Two recent discussions of the managerial skills necessary for effective administration in an environment of extensive citizen participation are Adam W. Herbert, "Management Under Conditions of Decentralization and Citizen Participation," *Public Administration Review*, Vol. 32 (October 1972 Special Issue), pp. 631-633, and Eli Glogow, "Community Participation and Sharing in Control of Public Health Services," *Health Services Reports*, Vol. 88, No. 5 May 1973, pp. 446-447.

Including the Community
in Hospital Governance

H. ROBERT CATHCART

It may well be that the 1970s will be remembered as the decade of the articulate consumer. He is no longer the dull and colorless fellow depicted by economists during the past two centuries. He is alert, outspoken, and fickle. He lacks reticence, is suspicious of tradition, and is always ready to challenge the establishment. Hospitals that are anxious to continue offering relevant services must be responsive to this new breed of consumer and find ways to permit his needs to influence institutional policies.

Society has chosen a toally imperfect word, "hospital," to label a very human organization. Today, hospitals are multi-purpose institutions that engage in a variety of outreach activities, frequently having satellite characteristics. The hospital is the one community health agency adequately meeting those public needs which have not been met by public health units, categorical health agencies, medical schools, professional associations, and solo practitioners. These agencies have

Reprinted, with permission, from *Hospital Progress*, October 1970, pp. 72-76.

failed because they lack the almost magical combination found in hospitals: A collection of highly talented, organized professional personnel, vast amounts of sophisticated equipment, an accomplished management staff, some degree of quality control over professional and administrative affairs as the result of internal audits, and a tradition of policy formation by a community board of trustees. The hospital organizations under review in this article are generally noted for their service to inner-city, heterogeneous populations.

DEMOGRAPHY

The turmoil of the inner city has been well-documented. Results of the population turnover that occurs when the middle-class, white collar group moves out and the rural-based, black-, brown- and red-skinned peoples move in are alarming. Crime rates multiply, disease rates increase, hunger becomes a bigger problem each day, more grime and trash clutter the streets daily, housing deteriorates, public transportation becomes more costly as it grows less and less effective, and public educational goals become more difficult to achieve each year. The one thing that does not seem to decline is the infant mortality rate.

In September, 1970, the nation's inner cities are a study of tragedy, hopelessness, deprivation, and neglect—the home of angry, unhappy, and volatile people. Typically, these people have been unrecognized and uninvolved in the governance of the institutions available to serve them. Increasingly, they want a piece of the action; they want to be involved and to be recognized. Inner-city hospitals would do well to acknowledge this situation with care and sincerity. To do otherwise could result in a breakdown in the institution's ability to deliver services.

Full involvement in community health services contributes to the self-interest of both the citizens of the community and the hospital itself. Such involvement will assure citizens of better health service, rendered with greater continuity, and will enable the hospital to provide such services more effectively and efficiently. If its direct service needs are being satisfied, the community will more readily endorse hospital projects that are less closely identified with community projects (e.g., education and research). On the other hand, if community wants are not satisfactorily met, community tolerance and support for the more traditional hospital efforts will be withdrawn, and these efforts may come to be considered irrelevant to the immediate and visible needs of the community. In effect, consumers are saying that the implied franchise to operate may well be restricted or withdrawn if the priorities they identify are not met.

Great management skill and judgment are required in order to convert general principles and philosophies into a successful institutional change. Many administrative personnel, involved in both daily management responsibilities and the formation of major policy directions, can report from first-hand knowledge that the execution of policy to bring about organizational and operational change may well be even more taxing and require even more judgment and skill than the actual policy-making process.

The governance of the hospital, or the exercise of authority therein, involves many diffuse elements, even before the new consumer element as considered. These power points can be grouped in a variety of ways. One convenient method is to separate them into three different groups: Internal forces, organized external forces, and unorganized external forces (**Figure 1**).

This listing of forces that exercise authority in the hospital organization does not purport to be comprehensive. Depending upon how the elements are counted, there are from 22 to 35 such forces in this list. Some authorities have identified as many as twice this number. The list is of value, however, because it stresses the widespread authority which must be considered when examining the governance of the hospital.

The various power points are not necessarily of equal influence or importance. For example, the power of the women's auxiliary is frequently less than that of the medical staff. However, this is not always true, and, in some limited areas of hospital activity, the auxiliary might be of greater influence than the medical staff. It is entirely possible that a single patron might have more real influence than either the board of trustees or the medical staff.

Because the authority pattern in hospital governance is materially different from institution to institution and, within a single institution, from day to day, introducing the new element of greater consumer participation into this pattern will have different results in each hospital.

In most instances, the changes effected by this new influence can be quite modest, and the institution can accommodate the new input without major interruptions. Of course, if greater consumer participation is to be meaningful, there must be some results—generally in the form of change. If change and modification did not occur, there would be little reason for the new representation and it would be identified, with much scorn, as tokenism. Such action should be avoided at all costs.

In other instances, however, consumer participation can be most

Hospital "Power Points"

A. Internal Forces
  1. Trustees
  2. Medical staff
  3. Employees
     a. by professional association
     b. by unionization
     c. by ad hoc committee or
        action interests
  4. Women's auxiliary
  5. Faculty or educational interests
  6. Research interests
  7. House staff and student groups
  8. Advisory committees
  9. Administration

B. Organized External Forces
  1. Government—all levels
  2. Accreditation—"voluntary"
     a. education
     b. service
  3. Personnel mechanism
     a. credentialism
     b. licensure

  4. Consumer organizations
     a. Blue Cross and Blue Shield
        plans
     b. Labor union groups
     c. Neighborhood groups
  5. Coordinating agencies
     a. Health facility planning
        agency
     b. Regional medical programs
     c. Comprehensive health
        planning
     d. Community mental health
        planning

C. Unorganized External Forces
  1. Tradition
  2. Legal (customary and reasonable
     standards for the community)
  3. Economic
  4. Social
  5. Folk ways
  6. Patrons
  7. Scientific developments
  8. Marketing pressures

FIGURE 1

traumatic, and, when such input gets out of control, it can become violently traumatic. If institutional change is essential, perhaps some non-violent trauma will be necessary in order to effect the desired results. The degree of change and the method by which it is accomplished depend upon the individual institution and those wishing to effect the change.

RESPONSIVE TO DESIRES

There is ample evidence that many health care institutions could be more responsive to the desires of consumers. (Note, the term is "desires," not "needs.") The fact that consumers' needs may not have been neglected does not excuse the health system's failure to recognize that consumers have many desires that should be considered. After reviewing these desires with the consumer, a hospital might appropriately fulfill some, defer others, and reject still others. The key point, in fact the essential point, is that the hospital must be responsive to not only the needs but also the desires of the consumer.

If a hospital is truly responsive, and very few can demonstrate optimal responsiveness, no change in organizational make-up to influence the governance of the institution need be undertaken. However, if change is required, it can be undertaken in a number of ways. Each change must be tailored to the individual institution and situation. There is no single right way to effect change. What is good in one place may be folly in another. The test of effectiveness is whether the change makes the institution more responsive. If not, the change is of little value.

Whatever change is undertaken, it should be adopted with utmost care. The institution's ability to continue to render service or improve service must be maintained. If a change that makes an institution more responsive also bankrupts it, the victory is, indeed, hollow.

BOARD UNDER ATTACK

The most frequently suggested method of altering institutional makeup to improve responsiveness is to modify the characteristics of the board of trustees, either by enlarging it, changing terms of office, or adding new members. Although this is one way and, in the right place at the right time, perhaps the proper way to bring about change, it is not necessarily the best or only way to do so.

The power and influence of the larger, urban hospital board of trustees have been under severe attack. The impact of the board of trustees has been eroded and its powers diluted and delegated to many others. A national committee or commission may soon be needed to protect and lobby for the interests of boards of trustees. This change in the board's status takes place at a time when legal authority has not been transferred from the trustees. As a result, many new complex and serious issues are developing.

It is necessary to emphasize the fact that, while society must struggle to make the hospital more responsive, it must not compound existing problems. Until and if the legal status of the trustee is changed or the board of trustees becomes more of an "in-house" board, strong trustee involvement and leadership is essential to maintain an institution that properly serves the local constituency. Strength at this level is also essential if other necessary changes are to be made in additional areas of the hospital. If it is possible to maintain the board of trustee's role, hospitals may escape the anarchy which has developed in the university systems, public schools, and some church establishments.

Increased responsiveness is achieved when boards become something more than mere ratifying bodies and are permitted to channel their efforts and energies on selected issues. Board committee organization is unusually well-suited for this task. The issues facing larger hospitals today are so complex and varied that boards cannot be expected to respond to all of them with originality. They can and do react to proposals; they can and do audit performance; and they do arbitrate conflicting interests within the institution. But their responsibilities must be equitably divided and well-defined, and they must have able staff support.

Increasingly, the board committee level is becoming the place to influence institutional policy. At this level, subjects can be explored in greater depth, opinions can be formed, attitudes can be shaped, and policies can be developed. More basic policy-making can be accomplished at the committee level in two hours than at 12 official trustee meetings. It is here that consumer participation and interest should be encouraged. Consistent, formalized consumer attendance at board committee functions can often be the most valuable means of achieving wider consumer participation.

Many articulate consumers fail to distinguish between trustee and management policy issues. Frequently, a close examination of what consumers interpret as a trustee policy issue reveals that it is really a management policy decision. Once a decision is identified as a management decision, it is important for the consumer to exert pressure on management rather than the board.

Management's governance of the hospital can also be influenced by hospital employees. Presumably, employees are drawn from the community, and they can represent an important point of view to management. Good personnel practices, good supervisory talent, and alert personnel staff support for administration can convert this body of opinion into an important thermometer to gauge community temperament. It should be utilized.

PHYSICIAN INFLUENCE

The rapport characteristic of the best physician-patient relationship is another channel that can be used by consumers to influence the policies and activities of health care institutions. The physician, without breaking the confidentiality of the doctor-patient relationship, can often effect many changes of major consequence.

Consumer influence in institutional affairs can often be achieved if management simply listens. Effective listening is difficult, and too few managements do it well. As noted before, consumers are becoming increasingly proficient in letting the establishment know their wants. Management's job is to receive the message and take appropriate action. Often, this responsibility can be formally delegated to public relations and/or community affairs officials. But such delegation does not relieve other management personnel of the responsibility to listen and communicate in an effort to influence the hospital to reflect the needs of the broad spectrum of the community.

In recent years, consumer interest has been concentrated on the more visible outreach activities of health care institutions. The neighborhood health center, the community mental health service, or specific educational programs are good examples of such satellite endeavors. It is often satisfying to the consumer to have these efforts directed by independent boards, with full policy-making authority. It is sometimes feasible to separately incorporate these more easily defined and remote activities. Such a provision provides maximum community control and, at the same time, maintains a close association, in terms of management, between the satellite and the parent organization. Troublesome, petty issues are kept from the parent corporation at a considerable savings of time and tempers. When separate incorporation is not possible or feasible, advisory boards with delegated powers may be used to help make the consumer feel a part of the policy-making process and help make these institutional activities responsibe to the community.

However, the price to be paid for separate corporations and strong advisory committees must be considered before such programs are launched. In regard to services rendered, strong, autonomous groups will have little identification with the home team. As a result, mutually beneficial activities may fail to develop, duplication of service may occur, and quality standards in the satellites may suffer. Public stands, statements, and campaigns may be launched that are contrary to the policies and interests of the parent institution. When this takes place, the price the home institution pays for community responsiveness may be too high.

Consumers who are intent on making institutions more alert to their desires should fully exploit already available means. If the people inform the government of their wishes, the government can promote institutional reaction. The government's power of licensure, inspection, standard-setting, financing, and public evaluation can correct almost any situation, even in the most recalcitrant organizations. The interested consumer can soon learn how best to use this tool. From time to time government officials, because of potential political gains, will support consumer demands in order to gain visibility as friends of the people. In addition, the consumer of health care can also use the cumulative power of accreditation agencies, various consumer groups such as the Blue

Cross and Blue Shield plans, union organizations, and neighborhood associations to make his voice heard. The consumer is associated with many organized groups that are skilled and effective in speaking with the power of many for the desires of one. This type of influence on the governance of the hospital is of the utmost significance.

As consumers demand more participation in and responsiveness from health care institutions, the administrative hierarchy may evidence increased apprehension. Administration may feel that such participation can undermine deliberately balanced power centers and administrative authority. In most instances, this anxiety is not well-founded. Community input is merely one of many power elements that must be dealt with. The experienced administrative staff should be well-equipped to handle this latest power element, since it has already had experience in balancing and coordinating some 20 or 30 such influences. It does not seem that one more can be that damaging, and to act as if it could suggests an influence that is exaggerated. Such misgivings could propel this new type of participation to a level of importance that might not be achievable under other circumstances.

An alert administrative organization can cope with this new element, as it has with more traditional ones. It still has administrative understanding of financial affairs, has generalized administrative competence, has access to information sources, and serves as a channel of communication. New consumer participation will not rob the administration of these essential management tools. In addition, allowing the consumer to participate will afford administration a firmer base position, strengthened by expanded judicial and arbitration roles. Although improved community participation in policy-making may not make it easier to administer the respective units initially, it should, in the long run, provide a simpler and more satisfying operation.

The combination of inertia and complacency that is characteristic of far too many hospital organizations makes the suggestion of caution unnecessary as it applies to changes geared toward achieving a more broadly governed institution. However, for the few who may be caught up in the flow of social change (either as leaders or followers), it should be noted that good will and good intentions are not enough. Skill, judgment, and patience are required. Issues to be faced are: Who is the consumer? Who can truly represent the community? Can community representatives become identified with the establishment without being contaminated by it and thus losing their credibility with the community? Some representatives can manage their duties without jeopardizing their local standing; others cannot. If the latter situation occurs, and it frequently does, many new problems can be expected.

POWER BASE

The opportunistic representative may well use his new association with the establishment of a power base for new achievements. There is nothing terribly wrong with this if it does not corrupt his representative role. However, all too often it does, and this then becomes a serious deterrent for the organization. At other times the only way newly involved representatives can achieve and maintain visibility is to radicalize their positions and to establish non-negotiable positions. Such action often identifies them as symbols of the deprived and neglected.

Other characteristics of the consumer role in governance of the hospital can be equally trying. Many individuals entrusted with this responsibility have little organizational experience and no understanding of delegation of authority and the implied responsiblity each assumes when becoming a part of the establishment. Their motivation may be superb, but if they do not possess the necessary skill and knowledge to cope with their new role, major dilemmas can be anticipated.

Some organizations, the United Fund of Philadelphia for one, have recommended that agencies associated with it should rotate board members at least every six years. Upon initial examination, this suggestion seems valuable. However, after further consideration of this policy, it would seem that the handicaps it imposes upon multi-million dollar enterprises with vast numbers of employes and complex policies make it undesirable both for the institution and the community. Trustees of such establishments often require three or four years to become proficient at discharging their trustee duties. The six-year rotation policy would cause the organization to lose his talent just as it was becoming of greatest value. It seems almost ironical to note that increasing pressures for broadening the governance base of hospitals by this kind of action come at a time when equally strong pressure is being exercised to establish life-time tenure for medical staff positions. It might well be asked whether or not it is consistent to keep the trustee group in rotation but, at the same time, keep the influential medical staff protected from change? Of course, much of this discussion becomes academic when hospital boards become more "in-house," made up of the organization's top management and medical staff officials.

SUMMARY

The need to provide a broader base for the governance of the hospital must be faced and met. To fail to recognize this need could well bring about radical and catastrophic change. However, meeting this need does not provide an excuse for abdication of power; rather, it calls for responsiveness on the part of the health care institution.

Increased participation in the governance of the hospital can and should be achieved in a variety of ways. What is valid in one place may not be valid in another. Changes in the composition of the board of trustees and in membership policies may be one way of achieving this goal. Committee participation is another good way of achieving better representation. Direct management and community communication can also be most helpful. In addition, the consumer has access to many third parties who can help make inroads into the most rigid health care establishments. Among these third parties are the Blue Cross and Blue Shield plans, government, accreditation agencies, and various quasi-governmental agencies such as planning bodies.

Hospitals have an obligation to be responsive. Most are doing a better job of this today than ever before in history. Even more effective efforts can be expected in the future. Adjusting and responding to periods of change are not much different from other administrative challenges. It is the job of those involved in administering health care institutions to meet these challenges. Their institutions and the people they serve will be much better because of it.

To What Degree Are Hospitals Publicly Accountable?

S. DAVID POMRINSE, M.D.

As any reader of the daily press can testify, interest in the affairs of hospitals in this country is increasing. Several reasons for this trend are the portion of the gross national product that is spent on hospital services; the recognition on the part of politicians of the public's concern; and the increasing demand by the general population for readily available, high quality hospital care—a demand increased by the Medicaid and Medicare legislation.

With this intensified interest, however, has come a discordant note—the public is questioning whether hospitals are indeed carrying out their proper function as well as they might; it has been suggested that hospitals—particularly voluntary hospitals— should become "accountable" to the public interest.

The definition of accountability, however, is unclear and never has been satisfactorily set forth. When the accusation is made that voluntary

Reprinted, with permission, from *Hospitals*, J.A.H.A., Vol. 43, February 16, 1969, pp. 41-44.

hospitals are not accountable, it usually carries the implication that the institutions have something to hide and are being, therefore, deliberately unaccountable. The accusers seem to suggest that the solution to the problem is simply to put hospitals in a goldfish bowl and thereby make them properly accountable.

To be "accountable" is to be "answerable"—to give full and complete information upon which decisions can be based or have been made. To have "authority" is to have the right to make decisions, to carry them out, and, most significantly, to have the right to err. To be "responsible" means to have something to lose, be it a job, money, or status.

As all administrators know, successful management requires that each of the above be present if an organization is to function well. At any level, one is answerable to his boss; the hospital as a whole answers to the total community. One can do nothing without adequate authority—but this implies that errors will be made. The good administrator will keep his error rate to a minimum; but if he never errs, he never acts.

No hospital can hope to be 100 per cent successful in meeting the demands of the public; to believe it could do so would be totally unrealistic. One cannot assume true "responsibility" for anything unless he simultaneously is willing to bet on the outcome. The stakes may be high or low, but if there is nothing at stake, decisions will not be based on sober reflections or an appraisal of the risks and, therefore, will not be the best possible decisions.

EXPOSED TO VARIOUS PUBLICS

Voluntary hospitals are uniquely exposed to the public view. Stated more accurately, it might be said that they are exposed to the view of the various publics with which the hospital comes in contact.

First, there are the patients, from which every hospital receives both compliments and complaints. A good hospital is sensitive to these comments and adjusts its services continually in accordance with suggestions made and observations recorded.

A second public is the staff; members of the medical staff as well as the employee staff of hospitals usually are encouraged to suggest improvements. The competent administrator is alert to the suggestions and demands, and will attempt to incorporate into the hospital program those suggestions that are feasible and in accordance with the general policy of the institution.

A third public is the hospital's board of trustees—the official representative of the community. Every administrator knows that much of the information input to the board of trustees often comes via the paths of social intercourse—cocktail parties, business lunches, rounds of golf, and so on. Certainly the concerned trustee makes sure that he gets the answers to questions that are raised and sees to it that programs are adjusted accordingly.

Another public is the reimbursement agency, which is interested primarily in the financial operations of the hospital, and which is free to conduct audits and ensure that the data recorded in the hospital books are accurate. It may and often does question individual expenditures and comment on accounting practices.

An increasingly significant public is government—at the federal, state, and local levels. Medicare authorities ensure that hospital reimbursement is in accordance with their policies. Thus, hospitals must be prepared for audits by the general accounting office of the federal government. Such agencies as the state health department are free to conduct hospital inspections, make recommendations, and enforce them in order to asure that quality standards are met. Regional planning councils can decide that particular programs should be allocated to particular hospitals; they are being encouraged by federal and state laws to put teeth into their decisions. Finally, the local health and welfare departments have a keen interest in the operations of the hospital and conduct such inspections and audits of care as are appropriate.

DO HOSPITALS RESPOND?

The authority and opportunity for observing hospitals' functioning are clearly present. But do these agencies and groups really carry out their function? Obviously, the answer to this question will vary from agency to agency, and from locality to locality. A more specific question is: Are hospitals responding to the public interest in their operations and providing the necessary information upon which hospital functioning may be judged?

A recent count at one institution has shown that there are 105 different reports to, or inspections by governmental agencies, in addition to 38 reports to voluntary agencies, which have addressed themselves to one or another aspect of the hospital in the course of just one year. The fire department, the plumbing department, the building department, and the health department all inspect various areas of the hospital.

Blue Cross, Medicare, and Medicaid check the financial figures. The

Joint Commission on Accreditation of Hospitals and the residency review committees of the American Medical Association inspect professional activities. The parking lot is licensed, the gift shop audited, and the rehabilitation workshop approved. The press calls frequently and expects an immediate response to its queries.

Trips through the institution are arranged for the children of donors, future nurses' clubs, and visiting firemen. The hospital story is presented in a house organ to a mailing list that includes all employees, medical staff members, trustees, and thousands of others in the community, including the press. Annual reports are prepared and thousands of copies are distributed.

HOSPITALS PUBLISH FACTS

Despite this tremendous visibility, a well known hospital critic was quoted recently in the newspaper as saying, "I know more about General Motors than I do about Mount Sinai, three blocks down the street." Could the reason for this astounding confession be that he is more interested in the progress of his General Motors stock than in the program of a nearby hospital?

Are public corporations as open, however, about disclosing operating information as hospitals? Indeed, a frequent complaint of security analysts is that they are unable to learn about the earnings of separate divisions within corporations. Hospitals, on the other hand, publish the facts about the utilization of all their facilities by all classifications of patients.

Corporations quickly patent for their own benefit scientific discoveries, while hospitals publish their discoveries widely for the benefit of everyone. An identification badge is needed to get into most industrial plants; one need only ask to be shown any part of a hospital. Industry seeks to mold public acceptance of its products through advertising; hospitals attempt to meet community desires for service by shaping their programs in accordance with the needs and expressed wishes of their publics. The nature of industry is to compete for markets; at a growing rate, hospitals are joining together to plan programs on a rational economic basis, making maximum use of scarce personnel, equipment, and money.

WHO IS THE PUBLIC?

Who then is the public in "public accountability?" In spite of diligent literature review, this author has been unable to learn precisely what is meant by the term "public." Presumably, it means government—but government at which level?

In New York State the Department of Health has been assigned responsibility for supervision of hospital operations; yet the city government is attempting to maintain some control over these operations. Several agencies in city government have a very specific and useful interest in hospitals. Those agencies specifically interested in building, fire, construction, licensing, maternal and child care, air pollution, sanitation, and so on, have a proper and responsible interest in what goes on in the hospital, and they are exerting it.

To what part of governmental structure then are hospitals not accountable? The use of tax funds is reviewed by financial auditing agencies at the state and federal levels. General program accountability and planning of new facilities and major new programs is reviewed by regional planning agencies.

Authority, however, is in the hands of the board of trustees where, by law, it belongs. One can only surmise that what is called "accountability" actually is a cryptic term for "control."

As long as reporting is complete and honest, the public can determine whether its needs are being met efficiently and effectively. In other words, those who cry for public accountability really want to be in a position to make decisions and to have the authority to operate the hospitals. To claim that hospitals are not publicly accountable implies that the only additional involvement of "the public" would be in making the detailed decisions that govern the hospitals' operation.

VOLUNTARY VS. PUBLIC HOSPITALS

This author believes that the cry for public accountability is part of an effort to turn voluntary hospitals into public hospitals. The history of public operated hospitals, however, suggests that such a move clearly would be regressive.

The condition of the municipal hospitals in New York is widely known. In other cities, there has been less publicity but it is obvious that the public hospitals are certainly not comparable to voluntary hospitals in the quality of their performance. In addition, public hospitals are finding that they cannot operate efficiently because of the innumerable restrictions bound up with governmental control. Is this the direction voluntary hospitals should take? If the goal of the American hospital system is to provide high quality care at the lowest possible cost, then the history of the public system does not lend any encouragement to moving toward increasing governmental control of operations.

The innovative possibilities in the voluntary system are vital and necessary to the constant improvements of America's hospitals. The responsiveness of the voluntary hospitals to the wishes of its publics is an assurance that hospitals will adjust their programs to the people's wishes—something they can do much more easily than governmental institutions. The principle of freedom of choice that has been built into Titles 18 and 19 gives the general public the right to choose the type of medical service and hospital care that it desires. For example, since the enactment of these Titles, New York has seen an increase in the census of voluntary hospitals and a decrease in the census of public hospitals.

BOARDS OF TRUSTEES

But perhaps this formulation is too severe. Perhaps what is being called for is a more accurate representation of members of the "community" on the boards of trustees. Traditionally, boards of trustees have been made up of leaders of the business and professional communities. Involvement of minority groups has been relatively small and, generally, boards of trustees are self-perpetuating and tend to appoint the people they know and work with to fill vacancies in their membership.

The trustees are then representative of only a segment of the total community—but it is the only segment that can assume true responsibility for the operation of health programs; this group of community leaders can back up their decisions with influence, status, and money. To put the power of decision over the expenditure of millions of dollars and thousands of employees in the hands of those without the necessary education and experience is certainly not in the best interest of the community. Professional staffs are hardly likely to accept direction from those whose judgment is not based on proven ability. The complexity of decision making faced by all hospitals hardly makes their boards a place for elementary schooling in management.

It may be argued that the poor should sit on hospital boards because they stand to lose as much as anyone if improper decisions are made; they can lose their lives and their health. But this is equally true of persons of all economic and social strata.

PUBLIC CANNOT BE IGNORED

This does not mean, however, that all segments of the community should *not* have a voice in formulating the hospital's program. The hospital cannot ignore the wishes of its public anymore than a commercial enterprise can ignore the wishes of its market. Hospitals must listen to their clientele, perhaps by structuring segments of *all* groups in the community—not just the rich and the poor—into advisory committees that will channel the wishes of the populace into the stream of formal decision making in the hospital. Hospitals cannot ignore the less vocal and the less organized and pay heed only to those who profess to speak for particular groups. The techniques of market research are worth exploring in order to be sure that what we are told by "community leaders" is what people really want. It is important to remember, however, that sensitivity to the desires and needs of the community is not equivalent to offering control to any except those most capable of exercising control.

HOSPITALS MUST MAKE DECISIONS

The essence of the voluntary hospital system has been its ability to adapt to changing social, economic, and scientific conditions in a responsive and responsible fashion. Hospitals must and should live in the proverbial goldfish bowl; decisions should be exposed to public criticism and comment. Those decisions, however, should be made by the hospitals themselves, or their ability to react to change will be lost and the consuming public will pay the price of a hospital system that will be unable to adjust to its needs.

The irony of the demand for control of the voluntary hospital by those less capable of leadership is that the hospital will become increasingly inefficient and unable to meet legitimate health needs; the very people clamoring for control will suffer most from the institution's inability to perform properly. In most instances, government has been careful to preserve the unique character of the voluntary hospital. Therefore, hospitals must not be stampeded into giving up what has proven successful for an alternative that has not demonstrated its worth. As funds are increasingly obtained from governmental sources, hospitals must give the government what it has a right to expect for its money, but also must be sure that planning and decision making remain in the hands of the boards of trustees, advised by their medical staffs and their administrations.

In summary, hospitals must continue to accede to the demand for public accountability, but authority and responsibility must remain within the hospitals' realm.

Medical Care As A Right:
A Refutation

ROBERT M. SADE, M.D.

The current debate on health care in the United States is of the first order of importance to the health professions, and of no less importance to the political future of the nation, for precedents are now being set that will be applied to the rest of American society in the future. In the enormous volume of verbiage that has poured forth, certain fundamental issues have been so often misrepresented that they have now become commonly accepted fallacies. This paper will be concerned with the most important of these misconceptions, that health care is a right, as well as a brief consideration of some of its corollary fallacies.

RIGHTS—MORALITY AND POLITICS

The concept of rights has its roots in the moral nature of man and its practical expression in the political system that he creates. Both morality

Reprinted, with permission, from The New England Journal of Medicine, V. 285. December 2, 1971, pp. 1288-1292.

and politics must be discussed before the relation between political rights and health care can be appreciated.

A "right" defines a freedom of action. For instance, a right to a material object is the uncoerced choice of the use to which that object will be put; a right to a specific action, such as free speech, is the freedom to engage in that activity without forceful repression. The moral foundation of the rights of man begins with the fact that he is a living creature: he has the right to his own life. All other rights are corollaries of this primary one; without the right to life, there can be no others, and the concept of rights itself becomes meaningless.

The freedom to live, however, does not automatically ensure life. For man, a specific course of action is required to sustain his life, a course of action that must be guided by reason and reality and has as its goal the creation or acquisition of material values, such as food and clothing, and intellectual values, such as self-esteem and integrity. His moral system is the means by which he is able to select the values that will support his life and achieve his happiness.

Man must maintain a rather delicate homeostasis in a highly demanding and threatening environment, but has at his disposal a unique and efficient mechanism for dealing with it: his mind. His mind is able to perceive, to identify percepts, to integrate them into concepts, and to use those concepts in choosing actions suitable to the maintenance of his life. The rational function of mind is volitional, however; a man must *choose* to think, to be aware, to evaluate, to make conscious decisions. The extent to which he is able to achieve his goals will be directly proportional to his commitment to reason in seeking them.

The right to life implies three corollaries: the right to select the values that one deems necessary to sustain one's own life; the right to exercise one's own judgment of the best course of action to achieve the chosen values; and the right to dispose of those values, once gained, in any way one chooses, without coercion by other men. The denial of any one of these corollaries severely compromises or destroys the right to life itself. A man who is not allowed to choose his own goals, is prevented from setting his own course in achieving those goals and is not free to dispose of the values he has earned is no less than a slave to those who usurp those rights. The right to private property, therefore, is essential and indispensable to maintaining free men in a free society.

Thus, it is the nature of man as a living, thinking being that determines his rights - his "natural rights." The concept of natural rights was slow in dawning on human civilization. The first political expression of that concept had its beginnings in 17th and 18th century England through such exponents as John Locke and Edmund Burke, but came to its brilliant debut as a form of government after the American Revolution. Under the leadership of such men as Thomas Paine and Thomas Jefferson, the concept of man as a being sovereign unto himself, rather than a subdivision of the sovereignty of a king, emperor or state, was incorporated into the formal structure of government for the first time. Protection of the lives and property of individual citizens was the salient characteristics of the Constitution of 1787. Ayn Rand has pointed out that the principle of protection of the individual against the coercive force of government made the United States the first moral society in history.[1]

In a free society, man exercises his right to sustain his own life by producing economic values in the form of goods and services that he is, or should be, free to exchange with other men who are similarly free to trade with him or not. The economic values produced, however, are not given as gifts by nature, but exist only by virtue of the thought and effort of individual men. Goods and services are thus owned as a consequence of the right to sustain life by one's own physical and mental effort.

If the chain of natural rights is interrupted, and the right to a loaf of bread, for example, is proclaimed as primary (avoiding the necessity of earning it), every man owns a loaf of bread, regardless of who produced it. Since ownership is the power of disposal, [2]every man may take his loaf from the baker and dispose of it as he wishes with or without the baker's permission. Another element has thus been introduced into the relation between men: the use of force. It is crucial to observe who has initiated the use of force: it is the man who demands *unearned bread* as a right, not the man who produced it. At the level of an unstructured society it is clear who is moral and who immoral. The man who acted *rationally* by producing food to support his own life is moral. The man who expropriated the bread by force is immoral.

To protect this basic right to provide for the support of one's own life, men band together for their mutual protection and form governments. This is the only proper function of government: to provide for the defense of individuals against those who would take their lives or property by force. The state is the repository for retaliatory force in a just society wherein the only actions prohibited to individuals are those of physical harm or the threat of physical harm to other men. The closest that man has ever come to achieving this ideal of government was in this country after its War of Independence.

When a government ignores the progression of natural rights arising from the right to life, and agrees with a man, a group of men, or even a majority of its citizens, that every man has a right to a loaf of bread, it must protect that right by the passage of laws ensuring that everyone gets his loaf - in the process depriving the baker of the freedom to dispose of his own product. If the baker disobeys the law, asserting the priority of his right to support himself by his own rational disposition of the fruits of his mental and physical labor, he will be taken to court by force or threat of force where he will have more property forcibly taken from him (by fine) or have his liberty taken away (by incarceration). Now the initiator of violence is the government itself. The degree to which a government exercises its monopoly on the retaliatory use of force by asserting a claim to the lives and property of its citizens is the degree to which it has eroded its own legitimacy. It is a frequently overlooked fact that behind every law is a policeman's gun or a soldier's bayonet. When that gun and bayonet are used to initiate violence, to take property or to restrict liberty by force, there are no longer any rights, for the lives of the citizens belong to the state. In a just society with a moral government, it is clear that the only "right" to the bread belongs to the baker, and that a claim by any other man to that right is unjustified and can be enforced only by violence or the threat of violence.

RIGHT—POLITICS AND MEDICINE

The concept of medical care as the patient's right is immoral because it denies the most fundamental of all rights, that of a man to his own life and the freedom of action to support it. Medical care is neither a right nor a privilege: it is a service that is provided by doctors and others to people who wish to purchase it. It is the provision of this service that a doctor depends upon for his livelihood, and is his means of supporting his own life. If the right to health care belongs to the patient, he starts out owning the services of a doctor without the necessity of either earning them or receiving them as a gift from the only man who has the right to give them: the doctor himself. In the narrative above substitute "doctor" for "baker" and "medical service" for "bread." American medicine is now at the point in the story where the state has proclaimed the nonexistent "right" medical care as a fact of public policy, and has begun to pass the laws to enforce it. The doctor finds himself less and less his own master and more and more controlled by forces outside of his own judgment.

For instance, under the proposed Kennedy-Griffiths bill,[3] there will be a "Health Security Board," which will be responsible for administering the new controls to be imposed on doctors, hospitals and other "providers" of health care (Sec. 121). Specialized services, such as major surgery, will be done by "qualified specialists" [Sec. 22(b)(2)], such qualifications being determined by the Board (Sec. 42). Furthermore, the patient can no longer exercise his own initiative in finding a specialist to do his operation, since he must be referred to the specialist by a nonspecialist—i.e., a general practitioner or family doctor [Sec. 22(b)]. Licensure by his own state will not be enough to be a qualified practitioner; physicians will also be subject to a second set of standards, those established by the Board [Sec. 42(a]. Doctors will no longer be considered competent to determine their own needs for continuing education, but must meet requirements established by the Board [Sec. 42(c)]. The professional staff of a hospital will no longer be able to determine which of its members are qualified to perform which kinds of major surgery; specialty-board certification or eligibility will be required, with certain exceptions that include meeting standards established by the Board [Sec. 42(d)].

Control of doctors through control of the hospitals in which they practice will also be exercised by the Board by way of a list of requirements, the last of which is a "sleeper" that will by its vagueness allow the Board almost any regulation of the hospital: the hospital must meet "such other requirements as the Board finds necessary in the interest of quality of care and the safety of patients in the institution" [Sec. 43(i)]. Hospitals will also not be allowed to undertake construction without higher approval by a state agency or by the Board (Sec. 52).

In the name of better organization and co-ordination of services, hospitals, nursing homes and other providers will be further controlled through the Board's power to issue directives forcing the provider to furnish services selected by the Board [Sec. 131(a)(1),(2)] at a place selected by the Board [Sec. 131(a)(3)]. The Board can also direct these providers to form associations with one another of various sorts, including "making available to one provider the professional and technical skills of another" [Sec. 131(a)(B)], and such other linkages as the Board thinks best [Sec. 131(a)(4)(C)].

These are only a few of the bill's controls of the health-care industry. It is difficult to believe that such patent subjugation of an entire profession could ever be considered a fit topic for discussion in any but the darkest corner of a country founded on the principles of life and liberty. Yet the Kennedy-Griffiths bill is being seriously debated today in the Congress of the United States.

The irony of this bill is that, on the basis of the philosophic premises of its authors, it does provide a rationally organized system for attempting to fulfill its goals, such as "making health services available to all residents of the United States." If the government is to spend tens of billions of dollars on health services, it must assure in some way that the money is not being wasted. Every bill currently before the national legislature does, should, and must provide some such controls. The

Kennedy-Griffiths bill is the closest we have yet come to the logical conclusion and inevitable consequence of two fundamental fallacies: that health care is a right, and that doctors and other health workers will function as efficiently serving as chattels of the state as they will living as sovereign human beings. It is not, and they will not.

Any act of force is anti-mind. It is a confession of the failure of persuasion, the failure of reason. When politicians say that the health system must be forced into a mold of their own design, they are admitting their inability to persuade doctors and patients to use the plan voluntarily; they are proclaiming the supremacy of the state's logic over the judgments of the individual minds of all concerned with health care. Statists throughout history have never learned that compulsion and reason are contradictory, that a forced mind cannot think effectively and, by extension, that a regimented profession will eventually choke and stagnate from its own lack of freedom. A persuasive example of this is the moribund condition of medicine as a profession in Sweden, a country that has enjoyed socialized medicine since 1955. Werkö, a Swedish physician, has stated: "The details and the complicated working schedule have not yet been determined in all hospitals and districts, but the general feeling of belonging to a free profession, free to decide — at least in principle - how to organize its work has been lost. Many physicians regard their own work now with an apathy previously unknown."[4] One wonders how American legislators will like having their myocardial infarctions treated by apathetic internists, their mitral valves replaced by apathetic surgeons, their wives' tumors removed by apathetic gynecologists. They will find it very difficult to legislate self-esteem, integrity and competence into the doctors whose minds and judgments they have throttled.

If anyone doubts that health legislation involves the use of force, a dramatic demonstration of the practical political meaning of the "right to health care" was acted out in Quebec in the closing months of 1970.[5] In that unprecedented threat of violence by a modern Western government against a group of citizens, the doctors of Quebec were literally imprisoned in the province by Bill 41, possibly the most repressive piece of legislation ever enacted against the medical profession, and far more worthy of the Soviet Union or Red China than a western democracy. Doctors objecting to a new Medicare law were forced to continue working under penalty of jail sentence and fines of up to $500 a day away from their practices. Those who spoke out publicly against the bill were subject to jail sentences of up to a year and fines of up to $50,000 a day. The facts that the doctors did return to work and that no one was therefore jailed or fined do not mitigate the nature or implications of the passage of Bill 41. Although the dispute between the Quebec physicians and their government was not one of principle but of the details of compensation, the reaction of the state to resistance against coercive professional regulation was a classic example of the naked force that lies behind every act of social legislation.

Any doctor who is forced by law to join a group or a hospital he does not choose, or is prevented by law from prescribing a drug he thinks is best for his patient, or is compelled by law to make any decision he would not otherwise have made, is being forced to act against his own mind, which means forced to act against his own life. He is also being forced to violate his most fundamental professional commitment, that of using his own best judgment at all times for the greatest benefit of his patient. It is remarkable that this principle has never been identified by a public voice in the medical profession, and that the vast majority of doctors in this country are being led down the path to civil servitude, never knowing that their feelings of uneasy foreboding have a profoundly moral origin, and never recognizing that the main issues at stake are not those being formulated in Washington, but are their own honor, integrity and freedom, and their own survival as sovereign human beings.

SOME COROLLARIES

The basic fallacy that health care is a right has led to several corollary fallacies, among them the following:

That health is primarily a community or social rather than an individual concern.[6] A simple calculation from American mortality statistics[7] quickly corrects that false concept: 67 per cent of deaths in 1967 were due to diseases known to be caused or exacerbated by alcohol, tobacco smoking or overeating, or were due to accidents. Each of those factors is either largely or wholly correctable by individual action. Although no statistics are available, it is likely that morbidity, with the exception of common respiratory infections, has a relation like that of mortality to personal habits and excesses.

That state medicine has worked better in other countries than free enterprise has worked here. There is no evidence to support that contention, other than anecdotal testimonials and the spurious citation of infant mortality and longevity statistics. There is, on the other hand, a good deal of evidence to the contrary.[8,9]

That the provision of medical care somehow lies outside the laws of supply and demand, and that government-controlled health care will be free care. In fact, no service or commodity lies outside the economic laws. Regarding health care, market demand, individual want, and medical need are entirely different things, and have a very complex relation with the cost and the total supply of available care, as recently discussed and clarified by Jeffers et al.[10] They point out that " 'health is purchaseable', meaning that somebody has to pay for it, individually or collectively, at the expense of foregoing the current or future consumption of other things." The question is whether the decision of how to allocate the consumer's dollar should belong to the consumer or to the state. It has already been shown that the choice of how a doctor's services should be rendered belongs only to the doctor: in the same way the choice of whether to buy a doctor's service rather than some other commodity or service belongs to the consumer as a logical consequence of the right to his own life.

That opposition to national health legislation is tantamount to opposition to progress in health care. Progress is made by the free interaction of free minds developing new ideas in an atmosphere conducive to experimentation and trial. If group practice really is better than solo, we will find out because the success of groups will result in more groups (which has, in fact, been happening); if prepaid comprehensive care really is the best form of practice, it will succeed and the health industry will swell with new Kaiser-Permanente plans. But let one of these or any other form of practice become the law, and the system is in a straitjacket that will stifle progress. Progress requires freedom of action, and that is precisely what national health legislation aims at restricting.

That doctors should help design the legislation for a national health system, since they must live with and within whatever legislation is enacted. To accept this concept is to concede to the opposition its philosophic premises, and thus to lose the battle. The means by which nonproducers and hangers-on throughout history have been able to expropriate material and intellectual values from the producers has been identified only relatively recently: the sanction of the victim.[11] Historically, few people have lost their freedom and their rights without some degree of complicity in the plunder. If the American medical profession accepts the concept of health care as the right of the patient, it will have earned the Kennedy-Griffiths bill by default. The alternative for any health professional is to withhold his sanction and make clear who is being victimized. Any physician can say to those who would shackle his judgment and control his profession: I do not recognize your right to my life and my mind, which belong to me and me alone; I will not participate in any legislated solution to any health problem.

In the face of the raw power that lies behind government programs, nonparticipation is the only way in which personal values can be maintained. And it is only with the attainment of the highest of those values—integrity, honesty and self-esteem—that the physician can achieve his most important professional value, the absolute priority of the welfare of his patients.

The preceding discussion should not be interpreted as proposing that there are no problems in the delivery of medical care. Problems such as high cost, few doctors, low quantity of available care in economically depressed areas may be real, but it is naive to believe that governmental solutions through coercive legislation can be anything but shortsighted and formulated on the basis of political expediency. The only long-range plan that can hope to provide for the day after tomorrow is a "nonsystem"—that is, a system that proscribes the imposition by force (legislation) of any one group's conception of the best forms of medical care. We must identify our problems and seek to solve them by experimentation and trial in an atmosphere of freedom from compulsion. Our sanction of anything less will mean the loss of our personal values, the death of our profession, and a heavy blow to political liberty.

REFERENCES

1. Rand A: Man's rights, Capitalism: The unknown ideal. New York, New American Library, Inc. 1967. pp. 320-329
2. Von Mises L: Socialism: An economic and sociological analysis. New Haven, Yale University Press, 1951, pp. 37-55.
3. Kennedy EM: Introduction of the Health Security Act. Congressional Record 116:S 14338-S 14361, 1970
4. Werko L: Swedish medical care in transition. N Engl J Med 284: 360-366, 1971
5. Quebec Medicare and Medical Services Withdrawal. Toronto, Canadian Medical Association, October 19, 1970
6. Millis JS: Wisdom ? Health? Can society guarantee them? N Engl J Med 283:260-261, 1970
7. Department of Health, Education, and Welfare. Public Health Service: Vital Statistics of the United States 1967. Vol. II, Mortality. Part A. Washington, DC. Government Printing Office, 1969. p. 1-7

8. Financing Medical Care: An appraisal of foreign programs. Edited by H. Shoeck. Caldwell, Idaho, Caxton Printers, Inc. 1962

9. Lynch MJ. Raphael SS: Medicine and the State. Springfield, Illinois, Charles C. Thomas, 1963

10. Jeffers JR. Bognanno MF. Bartlett JC: On the demand versus need for medical services and the concept of "shortage." Am J Publ Health 61:46-63, 1971

11. Rand A: Atlas Shrugged, New York, Random House, 1957, p. 1066

IMPLEMENTATION OF CONSUMER PARTICIPATION

The readings in this section discuss a variety of issues which are crucial to the implementation of consumer participation in various health care settings. They are intended both to convey the underlying subtleties and complexities of this phenomenon and also to serve as a reference for administrators in dealing with the initiation of consumer programs.

Johnson stresses the importance of stable board-of-trustee structures. The key aspect of hospital adaptation to consumer needs is the attitude and conduct of the medical staff. Without physician support, meaningful change is impossible.

Glogow discusses the advisability of shared control of public health services. Participation by citizens will open a system previously closed to consumer intervention. Suggested mechanisms include election of citizens to health department policy-making boards and shared decision-making between health professionals, elected officials, and board members.

Burke outlines five strategies employed by health institutions in adapting to consumer participation. Strategies include education-therapy, behavioral change, staff supplement, co-optation, and community power.

Fauri examines factors which have limited consumer participation in the past. The primary barriers are related to the conflicting roles of health professionals and their patients. This clash is viewed as inevitable and must therefore be resolved in delivery settings.

Galiher, Needleman, and Rolfe provide a conceptual grid which specifies opportunities for consumer participation at local, state, and federal levels. Planning, financing, regulatory, and delivery programs are discussed. The sets of skills required for prospective participants at each level are also analyzed and related to a continuum which defines degrees of citizen intervention.

Hochbaum discusses consumer participation in health planning, particularly from the perspective of the disadvantaged citizen. He contends that merely providing a platform for the expression of problems is an insufficient response. He also delineates contributions which could be made by social scientists.

Perlmutter emphasizes the need for a new model of institutional change which takes account of lay and professional roles. Previous inclusion of consumers in special programs can be expanded to more general concern with good results.

Evans examines the issue of standards for participation and their impact on area-wide planning programs. Emphasis is on the composition of policy boards with respect to the proportion of provider, minority, and special interest members.

Giving The Consumer A Voice
in the Hospital Business

EVERETT A. JOHNSON

In the folklore of administration, two age-old chestnuts are used to explain the current interest in broadening representation of hospital boards of trustees. One old saw says put the complainer into a responsible spot, and he will shortly drop the role of critic for that of defender. The other old chestnut says that he who is critical of an organization should get into the power structure and work from within to create change.

Standing alone without qualification both tenets are more destructive than useful. Each is true in special circumstances, but as generalizations both are false. Unfortunately many of today's government bureaucrats and hospital administrators can't separate sound administrative theory from unsound administrative folklore.

The first adage assumes that a critic will participate, understand, and contribute to the cause. The facts are, though, that in many circumstances people refuse to participate, understand, and contribute after appointment because their loyalties are elsewhere. In the process, critics

Reprinted with permission from *Hospital Administration*, V. 15, 1970, pp. 15-26.

who fail to perform satisfactorily simply weaken the existing representative functions and policy decisions. How many noncontributors can a board absorb before deterioration sets in?

The second adage assumes that a person on the inside has the necessary skills and understandings to provide new leadership, to gain acceptance for new ways of doing things, and to evoke support from other members of the board. Realistically, people gradually grow in their skills and experiences and cannot be leaders without certain necessary attributes.

These realities of participation in large scale organizations do not imply either good or bad outcomes for broader community representation. They merely say that the goal of wider effective community leadership is not easily achieved. To be poor, or black, or a union card carrier, or a member of the new left, are inadequate credentials for changing established policies from within through a seat as a hospital board member. If these are the only qualifications for board membership, it should be realized that the achievement of new program directions will be more readily accomplished from without by techniques of direct confrontation than from within.

Naive social engineers have been busy recently around the country erecting new organizational structures based on majority consumer interests. In Model Cities programs, Office of Economic Opportunity projects, and Comprehensive Health Planning Activities, the federal push has been to implement this current rage in administrative folklore.

PRESENT LIMITATIONS OF BOARDS

With two years of experience in programs emerging from these legislative acts, many professional people's efforts have reluctantly and gradually been withdrawn. The legislative goals are worthwhile, the notion of consumer participation reasonable, and program output low. Staff work in these new programs has been confused, misdirected, and inept, while board meetings have been endless and repeated criticisms of existing agencies and programs through one meeting after another.

Good intentions and the purest of idealism are not the substance from which effective boards and programs appear. An effective board is developed over time and is not achieved by the accident of its creation.

In the hospital world there have been many failures in the attempt to effectively widen hospital board representation, even though there are a few boards that have successfully accomplished it. Before exploring the ways in which the effectiveness of a board can be increased by broader representation, some thoughts about present typical limitations of hospital boards should be noted.

In the past two decades in the United States, it is quite clear that the size of the middle class has been tremendously expanded. Their value system and demands for health care are typified by the many hospital and physician moves to the fringe areas of cities. Here traditional practices of hospital operation and ways of delivering health care have been finely tuned and the age-old customary practices of medicine protected.

In the city, meanwhile, hospitals have faced aging buildings, advancing medical technology, dwindling supply of new physicians entering practice in their area, rising demands for health services, discontinuities of patient care; all continually increasing everybody's frustrations.

Both outlying and city hospitals have been equally struck with the impact of inflation and manpower shortages. The consumer, both organized and unorganized, has responded with increasing criticism. Much of the criticism has been imperfect, imprecise, ignorant of the relevant facts of hospital operation, and yet fundamentally expressive of a real desire for improved medical services. The answer to relevancy in health care has been a belief that wider board representation will produce the needed changes. Organized medicine's newly heightened sense of insecurity in this situation has been to respond by believing, like the others, that relief can be obtained by representation on the hospital board.

If all of these interests ever manage to arrange board membership, the usual ability of administrators to predict future board action will largely be memory. So, too, will the harmony, goodwill, and effectiveness of past board meetings.

OPERATING CHARACTERISTICS OF BOARDS

The basic issue today is how to increase the relevance of hospital care to the community and yet maintain effective, cohesive hospital boards of trustees. Before modifying existing organization structures, awareness of several operating characteristics of boards should be fixed.

One is that a board is composed of people who bring to its work their own habits, personalities, prejudices, and past experiences. Their individual attributes are not altered because they are now board members. Abrasive personalities are still irritating when working in a group, just as race baiters and haters continue to ply their viewpoints in and out of meetings.

However, if a board is seen only as a group of individuals, each with his own set of attributes, any insights into group action are lost. When people become part of a board, each one establishes in his own mind, and then works out gradually his relationship with other members of a board. The added dimension, in addition to individuality, is the individual relationship within the group—and they may change each time a member is changed or added.

A fairly common example of this relationship is occurring with greater frequency these days. This is the meeting where the successful middle class executive finds himself on the same board as a man dressed in work clothes, necklace, turtleneck, topped off with sunglasses and beard, who talks and curses without restraint, and continually projects the image of being ready to throw a Molotov cocktail. Or the reserved, quiet-speaking physician, meeting the new poverty leadership, dressed in simple dresses, with lumpy, bright colored sweaters telling him how it really is when they try to get medical care for their children.

In both instances the group relationships are fascinating to watch as they develop and shift over time in committee work; where at times the community builder and the town burner find themselves on the same side of an issue—and its effect on their understandings of each other.

A fundamental characteristic of board operation is that individual personalities in the group must be able to accommodate to each other if there is to be an effectively functioning unit. The board must generate for itself a unique set of qualities, of morale, of acceptable and unacceptable behavior if it is to move an organization toward its program goals.

When an individual attends board meetings where a few members ostentatiously treat him as a misguided, misinformed community idiot, the group will not become effective for solving hospital problems; even though it may be useful therapy for insensitive members publicly working out their own personal hangups. One of the more common examples of this problem is seen in the way some physicians unfortunately attempt to work with hospital boards as representatives of the medical staff.

A simplistic notion about board operation is that 51 per cent of the votes cast for any motion is democratic and a reasonable way for all red-blooded Americans to make organizational policy. No concept about board operation is further from reality. To be effective, a board must reach a consensus which will reflect as broadly as possible as many diverse interests as possible represented in the board in the final draft of a new policy. It is not the stakes in any one issue that typically wrecks the effectiveness of a board but most often the cumulative effects of prolonged division without effort to compromise and modify policy actions.

To accomplish consensus in a board, considerable organizational sophistication is necessary in its members. Many new program boards of the last few years are suffering a generation gap in reverse; older, cooler heads are missing in these new councils and with them the values learned through previous organizational experience. In some new boards, brokering of votes is seen as the way to power, and the naive notion that all of their future rides on the number of votes to be cast aye and nay on the next motion before the house is the clarion call to be answered. They have not learned that there is a tomorrow and that new issues call for new alliances within the board. They have not learned that in consensus there is effective progress.

OPTIMIZING THE COMMON GOOD

One other caveat of effective board operation needs review. Too often inexperienced boards believe that a chief executive officer must work with them and overlook the need for them to also work with him. They overlook the fact that they can impinge on his rights and responsibilities only if they are willing to damage the total organizational effort. Authority does arise out of expertise and professionalism and does place restraints on board action.

Effective, experienced executives do not need continual psychological support, but they do need consistency and predictability from a board if their work situation is to be personally satisfying. Executives are as human as board members but experienced enough to use and control emotions to achieve support for organizational goals. Being human they occasionally err and find that they lose control of a problem because of their loss of emotional control.

If a board is to be a valuable asset, it must achieve several organizational ends. The first is to bring to bear on major policy decisions the collective wisdom of the board to optimize the common good. There must be a reasoned weighing of alternative policy decisions and a board climate conducive to thoughtfulness if the best choices are to be made. Another board purpose is to secure advance support for new program decisions. When new programs are instituted without broad support, the odds for failure are generally significantly higher. If a board does not have confidence in a new program, why should the potential user of the new service take a chance on the outcomes when his potential loss may be much higher than that of a board member? A final board purpose is to achieve continuity of policy, so that confidence in the work of the organization develops through stability of performance.

CRITERIA FOR EFFECTIVE PERFORMANCE

The one ultimate criterion by which a board must be judged is on the success of the programs of the organization. How many people get well through a trip to the hospital? How many persons are saved from an early death? How many patients are freed of pain? How many are returned to productive activities? Each industry has its own set of goals. These are some of the goals in the hospital field.

With the criteria for effective performance of a hospital board defined, the ramifications of new consumer representation can better be evaluated. For many the need to infuse new relevancies in hospital boards is typified by Cicero's comment on a friend, "He remained the same, but the same was no longer fitting."

In the drive to develop new relevancies in institutions and organizations of "The Establishment," a simple, but true observation is often ignored; that the definition of quality is in the eye of the beholder. That is, expectations about hospital care vary by social and economic levels. The poor expect access to medical care; the black, equal treatment; the union, preferred attention; the middle class, broad spectrum care programs; the upper class, immediate availability; the government, lower cost care. Each expectation to some degree must be compromised to meet someone else's expectation at the focal point, the individual hospital.

As hospital board membership is broadened, the clash of expectations can be expected to significantly increase. Today most hospital boards are a homogeneous group of citizens of similar backgrounds and common expectations and by and large represent the health desires of the increasing middle class in America. They have not in the past, nor now, reflected the needs of the less affluent groups in American society.

WHY NOT BROAD REPRESENTATION?

To broaden representation is to probably increase intra-board conflict and also run a substantial risk of lowering organizational and administrative effectiveness. The new kind of board members often show a lack of ability to compromise, fail to grasp the overall perspective of the agency, and demonstrate a lack of balance in their judgment. The modus operandi seems to be all or nothing at all, with emotion and petulance as the format.

In this setting, the organizational life expectancy of the chief executive officer is unpredictable, and the emotional trauma he endures generally seems to be above and beyond the call of duty. Capable executives do not for long accept interference with operations, sub rosa interventions with personnel, instability in board policy, and personal abuse.

The social engineer's concept of broader representation in hospital boards, as the best way to increase activity and programs of health care, is a fallacy. What they realistically desire is the implementation of a health program that will better serve the disadvantaged groups in society. To achieve this goal, the needs of the lower class must be presented at the board level with sufficient power to create the initiative for new programs or the rearrangement of existing programs.

Minority representation of itself in a hospital board will not change the direction of existing programs. It is almost impossible to believe that the disadvantaged could gain majority control of all hospital boards. Since hospital and health matters are largely in the hands of the conservative elements of our society, and likely to remain so, it appears that unless the situation is clearly desperate, majority control of hospital boards will not pass to the new left representatives.

This state of affairs does not mean that health care programs are satisfactory in the United States. They are not satisfactory. The poor do not receive adequate medical care; blacks do have limited access to medical and hospital care; there is a great deal of disjointed health care that is inefficiently and ineffectively organized from the standpoint of the consumer. Many unmet health care needs exist. The knowledge to develop and deliver improved health services exists. Yet the gaps and discontinuities remain and traditional habits and mores go on undisturbed, while the ignorant and the abused continue to be born, to grow, and to age in poor health.

With the poor in wealth and health still with us in our modern world, and if consumer representation of their interests within the hospital structure will probably decrease their lot, where do we look for a better way to focus their voice?

PHYSICIANS MUST COOPERATE

A continual surfacing of the inadequacies of health care programs within hospital board rooms will not of itself generate significant change. The blocks to major program changes are too large to be easily overcome. Even dedicated, skilled boards and hospital administrators seldom can openly tackle and attempt to modify or remove long-held traditions by the practitioners of medicine. The primary resistance to needed change resides in physicians, rather than trustees and administrators.

Hospitals deliver medical care only through physicians. The most effective health care management in the country is useless without a physician component as part of the total available controllable resources. Apparently much of the reasoning about broader consumer board representation ignores the reality of the division of control between hospitals and physicians. If public schools have generated great controversy between school superintendents and faculties, how much less success will hospitals have without the power of the payroll? Because of the financial independence, as well as the solidarity of physicians, few neighborhood health centers have been launched outside of university medical center control. A shortage of cooperation between hospitals and physicians substantially reduces the ability of hospital administration to develop new programs.

It is for this reason that both minority and majority representation of the new consumer interest on hospital boards can and will be stymied. The route to improved medical care lies in altering the traditional attitudes of organized medicine, to reflect the real-world of the seventh decade of the twentieth century. The voice of the medically untreated or mal-treated expressed through the hospital will not create this change. Since the end of World War II, the will and power of medical staffs have much more frequently seen their views prevail than have those of the hospital or the community.

This pessimistic view does not mean that a hospital board should not appoint or elect representatives of the broader consumer representative. It does mean that whenever such a person is considered for nomination, the test of acceptability should be the same test as for other trustees: intelligence, motivation, spirit of goodwill, loyalty, and reputation. Also it implies that no miracles can be anticipated as a result of such appointments.

The typical administrative ploy to handle representation without disruption by authority is to create advisory boards of committees. This device prevents the boat from being rocked, yet allows temperatures of the agitators to be taken without substantial risk. An advisory appointment from the standpoint of both the hospital and the consumer is undesirable. The consumers will recognize that their role lacks authority, while the hospital will appear to be promising more change than its concern can generate.

Another usual administrative strategy, given a probable failure of board membership or advisory committee representation, is the use of supra-organizational voice or control. Here the total control spectrum above the hospital structure ranges from total control by ownership, to control of specified operating decisions, to establishment of minimum standards through licensure.

Each step in this continuum has its pros and cons, but the same basic dilemma remains. Without control over the medical staff, the provision of health services cannot be extended or amended by a hospital unless physicians support such changes. A governmental takeover may successfully control and direct existing medical practice, but, short of a totalitarian approach, it cannot force physicians into new activities. If this is true, it means that new health programs need the support of the medical profession more than the support of hospitals if new programs are to be launched to fill existing care gaps.

The fundamental issue then is not having an articulate voice of the consumer in hospital affairs but to have one in medical affairs. The tackling of this question has so far been avoided by our friendly social engineers. Perhaps its implications are so close to home that they fear starting a new snowball rolling that will later engulf their professional freedoms. If the poor, the handicapped, and the minorities are to receive better care, medicine must participate.

Since the existing deficiencies in health care programs are mostly inner-city and rural in location, the return of the physician to these areas is basic to any improvement in medical services. The neighborhood health center concept appears to be an appropriate way to do this. However, someone must initiate the organization, relate it to other health institutions, and find physicians to staff it. Outside of the largest metropolitan centers and university-related centers, few centers have been developed. This is because of the greater strength of medicine rather than hospitals in small and medium size cities. The folkways of private practice and non-institutional medical services predominate.

IS CRISIS INEVITABLE?

To conceive a plan that integrates most aspects of medical care into a coordinated total is difficult to do when its premise must be based on either non-cooperation or overt hostility from organized medicine. Since medicine is economically composed of multiple small enterpreneurial units that interrelate directly with the consumer, resistance to innovation is difficult to overcome. It is obvious that any plan developed must be voluntary in character and attract the cooperation of the physician, either through altruism or economics, if it is to be stable and successful. Consumer representation has a right to be present, heard, and felt in the new approaches to health care. Physicians have the same need. Hospital administration has this need only to the extent that it participates in the community and larger health care issues. However, if physicians refuse to recognize the legitimacy of interests other than their own, it is impossible to construct a workable model for new services—and the existing problems will go on, and on, until a crisis occurs and control is removed from medicine.

On the other hand, where there is no organized hostility from physicians to new health programs, a workable organizational structure can be developed. The issues are then who is to take the initiative to develop new programs and how will they be funded. At this point in the development of the Great Society there seems to be no shortage of sponsors, but only that of enough money to fund new programing.

BASIC SCHISM TO OVERCOME

An ever increasing awareness of the present gaps and inadequacies in health care is the root factor in creating a growing demand for broader representation on hospital boards. The definitions of need are real, while the proposed remedy is unreal. If organized medicine is sympathetic and sufficiently concerned, existing boards and administrators will generally respond in a like way and will initiate and manage the needed programs. Where physicians are antagonistic to expanding health care programs, no amount of broader consumer representation will be able to initiate and maintain new hospital services.

What is in reality being looked at is the basic fact that the traditional organization structure of a hospital, with its division of function and power between medical care and administration, is in actuality a fair weather form of organization, ill-suited to handle serious internal differences of opinion. Power is so distributed within the structure that one group can block the other and vice versa—and the unmet health needs continue to go on and on. Until this basic schism is compromised and overcome, or the traditional customs of medicine are substantially modified, general distribution of needed programs of care will not take place.

CHALLENGE OF UNMET NEEDS

In closing it should be noted that the conclusions reached are unfortunate for the poor in health. If choice rather than experience reigned, my desires would have led to the end that broader community representation would bring about the establishment of needed new programs of health care. As long as humanitarian motives prevail in hospital administration, the in-generation of administrators will struggle to initiate programs to meet the unmet needs in America. The challenge to do so was well expressed by Eric Hoffer in *The True Believer:*

> The discarded and rejected are often the raw material of a nation's future. The stone the builders reject becomes the cornerstone of a new world. A nation without dregs and malcontents is orderly, decent, peaceful, and pleasant, but perhaps without the seed of things to come. It was not the irony of history that the undesired in the countries of Europe should have crossed an ocean to build a new world on this continent. Only they could do it.

Community Participation and Sharing in Control of Public Health Services

ELI GLOGOW

A large segment of the population is discontented with the role of public health departments. This discontent is expressed by other health professionals as well as those whose discipline is public health. Among the questions being raised are: What's wrong with public health? Why have health departments become so out of touch with the times, so out of the mainstream of health matters? Why is the leadership so apathetic? What's going to be left for health departments if more of their functions are taken over by other agencies? Why aren't health departments more involved in the provision of medical care services or of mental health services? Why don't they do a better job about environmental health and automobile safety? The list could be increased because one hears such questions throughout the nation.

Health departments have been described as systems characterized by excessive entropy, a concept that systems theorists define as a law of nature in which organizations move toward disorganization and death[1]. To fight entropy, say the theorists, organizations must resist becoming

Reprinted with permission from *Health Services Reports*, V. 88, 1973, pp. 442-448.

closed systems; organizations must import new energy in the form of new people, new ideas, and new programs. These theorists state that as time goes on, organizations become conservative; their members pursue safe, uncontroversial paths and become more concerned with the security of their employees.

Persons concerned about the mission of public health claim that policymaking boards of health represent the establishment's point of view. These boards direct departments to pursue establishment-approved programs. When a dynamic health department impinges on the domain of either private medical practice or private industry, pressure is exerted on the health officer. The result is a retreat to cautiousness. Too often the chastised professionals hesitate to initiate new programs because they fear alienating their professional superiors. Survival becomes the dominating force.

A combination of external forces, such as the elected public officials, appointed health commissioners, and private interests—together with cautious, survival-oriented health department professionals—have contributed to the present static conditions of public health.

This static condition is being recognized. The leadership in the American Public Health Association is attempting to remedy it[2], but the task is not easy, and increasing opposition is evident among members who are resisting change. Recent editorials in the APHA's "The Nation's Health"[3] have revealed that some members are leaving the association because they are experiencing a "loss of professional status." One member wrote, "I'm being driven to the corner of our professional organization by consumers." Another says the association has become "a consumers' lobby", and has abandoned scientific programs. However, these complaints are not the real issue.

The issue is that in its attempt to break out of the old, traditional, conservative model, the new leadership is attempting to open up the relatively closed system of public health. These leaders are introducing new inputs by listening and relating to other groups in their respective constituencies. These groups include the consumers, the poor, the minorities, and other previously uninvolved segments of society. The APHA is taking strong positions on issues such as national health insurance. In short, the leadership is attempting to revitalize the public health system.

DECENTRALIZATION AND CITIZEN PARTICIPATION

Among the solutions being offered for the revitalization of health departments is some form of decentralization, community control, or consumer participation. Proponents of this approach believe that health department bureaucracies must share some of their power with the citizenry, particularly with persons who previously have not been represented in decision-making bodies. The proponents point to accumulating evidence of a movement both in the United States and abroad for people to have a greater voice in their work[4], education[5], church[6], and lives in general[7]. They predict that this trend toward participatory democracy will continue and the subsequent force can energize public health, thereby bringing it back into the mainstream of health. To explore this movement, there is a need to clarify such much-confused terms as decentralization, community control, community participation, and community involvement.[8].

Traditionally, decentralization may be used synonymously with administrative decentralization. Decentralization refers to delegation of authority from higher to lower levels within an organization or unit of government. Federal offices are created or street-level bureaucracies are established. The objective of such decentralization is to bring government closer to the people, but not to delegate authority to entities outside the formal structure of government.[9].

Conversely, political decentralization refers to the delegation of authority not only to lower levels within the formal government hierarchy but also to groups outside the government. Apparently administrative decentralization is markedly different from political decentralization. Administrative decentralization implies retention of power and authority with the formal government unit, whereas political decentralization mandates the sharing of authority with persons outside government[10].

Community control or neighborhood control may be viewed as a form of political decentralization. In its extreme version, "control" is assumed to have literal meaning in that the local unit seeks autonomy while at the same time asserts a claim to the fiscal and taxing resources of the wider community[9a].

In terms of a health agency, community control has been described as (a) the allocation of the all important planning, policy, and operational responsibilities to broadly representative neighborhood health boards with locally responsible neighborhood health administrators, and (b) the power of the local community to hire and fire all staff including professionals and to control all departments including the clinical services[11].

The terms citizen involvement, participation, or consumerism refer to a variety of devices which allow the individual access to the institutions of government; in this instance, health departments. These devices may be viewed as a continuum of authority, power, and control being shared by citizens and official agencies. This continuum ranges from token citizen involvement to the most extreme form of community control, which all but excludes involvement of governmental or agency representatives.

In the general study of decentralization and participation, I have found Eisinger's model to be particularly useful[12]. He presents a rather complex paradigm, the heart of which is control sharing. He describes control sharing as a form of administrative and political organization of municipal service agencies in which the authority to make policy decisions about service levels and general administrative standards is shared. Among the decision makers are professional bureaucrats, elected officials, and democratically selected citizens representing geographic neighborhoods or particular client groups. Another crucial aspect of his concept is the "formally guaranteed presence of democratically selected citizen representatives or client representatives on bureaucratic policy making boards."

HEALTH DEPARTMENTS VS. DECENTRALIZATION

Proponents of a decentralized, control-sharing scheme for health departments believe it is one of the ways to regenerate public health. They point out that the decentralization of health department services, which began as early as 1915, was administrative: more authority was delegated to public health administrators at the local level[13-15].

These proponents claim that although nonprofessionals from the community are members of the board of health, these persons have been carefully selected by local government officials and have not been elected by their constituencies. This concept of democratic selection is a key aspect of Eisinger's control-sharing model.

Furthermore, proponents say that citizen involvement usually has been in uncontroversial programs, such as immunization campaigns, chest X-ray surveys, community sanitation campaigns, and health education activities. Seldom have citizen groups radically changed the direction of health departments from health education and prevention of communicable disease to politically hot issues, such as the delivery of medical care services, mental health services, or air pollution control programs.

Advocates of decentralized control sharing admit a number of "activist health departments"[16] are involved in dynamic, innovative programs. However, most health departments are concerned with carefully circumscribed, noncontroversial activities.

FOUR POSITIONS

In reviewing the growing literature on decentralization and citizen or consumer participation, I have found no overt opposition to consumer or citizen involvement. It is the degree of citizens' participation that becomes the subject of concern[17-22]. I have attempted to delineate four positions within this subject as follows.

Participation is good. This position, accepted by almost everyone, represents the ethos of participatory democracy. To oppose it is to admit being totalitarian, and few would dare. Entire programs are built on the participation concept. Programs such as the Office of Equal Opportunity's neighborhood health centers, the Demonstration and Model Cities Act, and the Comprehensive Health Planning Law require a majority of consumers to constitute their board membership.

Community control is better than participation. Advocates of community control say participation is good but that it is not enough; control is the answer. Their position may be illustrated by the following demands on one community by advocates of community control[23].

- Self-determination in health care planning (both services and facilities)
- Removal of all outside-appointed administrators and staff working in the community
- Immediate cessation of health care facility construction pending review by a community-appointed review board
- Publicly supported health care provided for short-term illness and preventive medicine (including elimination of all fee-for-service remuneration), that is, free health care for all
- Health education program for all members of the community
- Community control over health care facilities (including hiring, firing, salaries of personnel, and construction)
- Total support from community and extra-community organizations and individuals.

Community control is not enough. The third group comprises persons concerned with the limitations of community control. These critics warn of the danger of participation for the sake of participation, achieving accountability with no increase—perhaps even a decrease—in productivity or efficiency[24]. They claim that community control is concerned mainly with administrative problems and suggest that the real power sources must be reached in order to effect significant changes in the health system.

These people warn that community control will fall far short of its objectives unless it becomes a broader struggle for popular, democratic control of all public institutions and the economy[11,25,26]. They feel the movement must go further and escalate its demands.

The case has yet to be made. This group represents an increasing number of persons voicing concern about whether decentralized, control-sharing models work. In a recent issue of the American Behavioral Scientist which was devoted entirely to urban decentralization and community participation, a number of contributors raise flags of caution[9]. One contributor reports that little evidence can be found supporting or refuting the proposition that greater participation in local governance improves services[10].

Another author concludes that neither decentralization nor citizen participation (nor neighborhood control) are waves of the future and that these systems or structures are not likely to be either durable or widely adopted[27].

A third contributor writes that "already some early supporters of decentralization measures have begun to move away from their initial positions, and, as disadvantages accumulate with existing experiments, there may likely be a return to the virtues of professionalism and strong central policy direction"[9b].

In a nationwide study of citizen participation in Model City programs, Dinerman reported that only 30 percent of the Model Cities directors who responded to her questionnaire described their experience with citizen involvement as being "very effective"[28]. Most respondents evaluated resident participation as being only "somewhat effective" in stimulating needed changes in community services and programs.

Persons in this group raise the issues of benefits in relation to costs and wonder whether the benefits are worth the foreseeable disadvantages. These persons are concerned about the dangers of factionalism being created within neighborhoods and between neighborhoods competing for scarce resources. This faction worries about "alleged leaders" who profess to speak for the communities and about the dismally low percentage of neighborhood residents who vote for representatives to local boards. The group fears the lack of organization, the inefficiency, and the dangers of eventual disillusionment and hostility among local residents who discover their health problems may not have been significantly affected by the community's participation.

CRUCIAL SIDE BENEFITS

It may be too soon to determine if decentralized, control-sharing mechanisms result in improved services. A number of studies are now in progress which should provide much needed information[29]. More time may be required before consumers can develop the needed technical expertise to make the proper decisions affecting their community. However, the comments of E. Kelty, a National Institute of Mental Health official who has had considerable experience with community-controlled organizations, are revealing. In a personal conversation on April 4, 1972, he said: "As a result of their involvement in health programs, there are now low income consumers who can stand up and talk to professionals and who are quite sophisticated about the whole planning process."

There are those who feel that the desire for improved public services may be only part of the rationale for control sharing. They claim that even if higher quality services are not produced, social and psychological benefits will accrue. These rewards, such as reducing the feeling of powerlessness and alienation, may be as important as the provision of direct health services[12,30].

An entire profession, public health education, has been built on the evidence that citizen participation in planning and carrying out health programs yields acute awareness of health problems, increased use of health services, and—in many instances—prevention of disease. In the final analysis, say the proponents of decentralization and community control, unless major changes in services and their delivery are attempted, there may not be too much left for public health departments to do.

One thing appears fairly certain. Barring a backlash toward a repressive political state, one can predict that the movement by people to have a greater voice in their lives will continue and will probably gain momentum. Citizen participation appears to be here to stay[20,31].

IMPLICATIONS FOR ADMINISTRATION

I began this paper stating there was considerable discontent with the state of public health and reported that one solution being offered was some form of a decentralization, power sharing, or community control. Although there is no consensus as to which form is best, I did say that the participatory democracy theme seems to be pervading most institutions and will likely continue to do so. Widespread practice of participatory democracy, I believe, is a healthy development and a force which administrators could use to revitalize public health.

My major point is that the combination of external forces such as conservative local government, local medical societies, and other private interests—in concert with conservative bureaucracies within health departments—have helped create the status-quo situation in which public health now finds itself.

I believe that public health administrators can effect changes by using new social forces whether they be within or outside the health department. The outside forces are those persons who until now have had little to say about decision making, that is, consumer groups, minorities, uninvolved segments of the middle class, and young professionals going into private law or medical practices. The forces within are the new professionals and the nonprofessional workers entering public health eager to do meaningful work.

Many of these new workers are client centered and advocacy oriented: they have a value system that fits neatly into a progressive mission for public health. Such a mission would provide direct medical services for all people—not just poor people. These services might include contraception or abortion and deal with subjects currently considered controversial but which directly affect the public's health.

In no way am I suggesting that public health administrators ignore the traditional holders of power such as local government officials, private industry, and private medicine. This would be folly. These groups are important in this pluralistic society. Administrators will have to work with all groups, but such cooperation will require certain knowledge and skills, some of which I will discuss.

1. Administrators will have to realize that their departments must be more truly open systems[1a]. No longer will administrators have the luxury of running their departments as relatively closed corporations in which the decisions affecting the community's health are made exclusively by a board of health, a group of administrators, a professional staff, or any combinations of these groups. More frequently decisions will have to be based on community needs—not the convenience of the staff. This change will necessitate altering the ratio of time that administrators spend inside their work unit to the amount of time spent outside the unit. There will be a definite shift in the direction of "outside" activities.

2. Administrators have to establish improved mechanisms for feedback not only within their organizations, but for their client groups as well. Feedback must be set up for their patients, patients' families, and other clientele groups. Adequate feedback is not autogenic; it must be engendered by careful planning.

3. System theorists state that organizations must have sensing devices reaching into the environment if they are to survive. Most health departments have been attuned to the established power sources, such as local government, private medicine, and private interests. However, the administrator will have to extend his awareness to those groups who have not been adequately represented. Yet he will have to be aware that there are dangers in interpreting statements of so-called community

leaders—leaders who pretend to represent their communities but who in reality may be speaking for themselves.

4. Just as accountability has become a key issue in public education[24,32,33], so may it be in public health. Administrators in all likelihood will be accountable not only to the recognized power sources, but to the emerging power groups such as the minorities, welfare rights representatives, and consumer groups.

5. The administrator must be aware that the health department's outputs are going to be increasingly scrutinized by its community's constituencies in terms of efficiency and, more important, its effectiveness. Efficiency may be thought of as the "amount of resources used to produce a unit of output"[34], but it may not necessarily be related to the quality of output. Measuring effectiveness will be thornier, because it necessitates studying the agency's outputs in terms of its goals. Serious questions will be raised by the emerging community groups concerning the relevance and quality of these goals and, equally important, the agency's value judgment.

6. The administrator will have to become more knowledgeable and skillful in dealing with conflict. Most present-day administrators come from the middle class and find it difficult to deal with the hostility, verbal abuse, and militancy of the indigenous community[35]. On the basis of my personal observations of numerous such confrontations, a safe prediction is that as militant groups demand more services, the traditional purveyors of services will protest.

The administrator will be right in the middle and will require considerable skills in negotiation and bargaining to resolve conflicts. Effective involvement of poor people in community decision making will ultimately require the institutionalization of bargaining mechanisms, just as collective bargaining arrangements have become the normal practice in labor-management relations[36].

7. In addition to their own feelings, administrators will have to deal with those of individuals in community groups, members of boards of health, and of their staffs. Whether relating to minority groups or to members of the youth counter-culture, both within and outside their agencies, administrators will find that these groups express their feelings more freely and are reluctant to suppress them.

8. Expertise in group dynamics will be another requisite. Increasingly administrators will find themselves working with groups of all kinds, sizes, and functions. Administrators are now using terms such as task force, study groups, autonomous work groups, project management, and matrix organization. All of these terms imply the concept of working in teams or small groups.

Bennis and Slater[37] point out that in the very near future there will be a plethora of temporary organizations in our society. These organizations and groups will be continuously forming, dissolving, and being replaced by new ones. Administrators will have to be able to relate to these groups quickly. They will not have the luxury of gradually developing working relationships.

9. The skillful use of politics, which has been described as the ability to influence the actions of others, will be increasingly required in a participatory, control-sharing model. In the past, political activity traditionally revolved around elected officials and the more powerful private and public interests. However, additional segments of society are entering politics, exerting pressures, and making demands. The administrator will truly be the person in the middle, pressed between the private and public providers of health services and the vocal, organized recipients.

10. Administrators will also require a thorough understanding of the health industry, their agencies' functions, and the newer technological developments. These developments include computerization, information systems, planning methodologies, and performance budgeting techniques. Although these are grouped together, I am not suggesting they are of secondary importance. They are part of the required vital tools of the profession.

You might comment after reading the list of recommended knowledges and skills, that no single administrator is likely to have them all. You may be right! If Bales and other investigators[1b] are correct in stating that the totality of leadership attributes are rarely found in a single person, then perhaps the administrator's job is to develop a leadership team which has these knowledges and skills. This will necessitate that he share control and power within as well as outside his organization.

Whether he builds a leadership team or attempts to develop his own skills, I suggest that the wear and tear on the nervous system of administrators who work in participatory, control-sharing agencies will be enormous. In view of (a) the stress and hazards involved in satisfying the demands of competing power groups and (b) the increasing tendency of professionals to follow their profession rather than accept a life-long career in one particular agency[38], the administrator's job tenure in any one position may be limited, perhaps to 4 or 5 years. By that time, he may want to change jobs or have the chance to "recharge his batteries," much like faculty members do in the university sabbatical system. This will necessitate enlightened and basic changes in civil service procedures. Financial limitations and tradition will be difficult to deal with, but it is hoped that they will not be impossible to change.

This paper is not intended to discourage administrators from working in participatory, control-sharing agencies. Admittedly, the problems will be numerous. However, if health departments are again to become relevant, vital agencies, they must more vigorously attempt to become participatory and control-sharing.

SUMMARY

The considerable discontent with the present state of public health suggests that a major cause is that health departments have become relatively closed systems. The combination of conservative decision-making bodies outside the health department—such as elected public officials, private medical and other private interests—in concert with bureaucratic, security-conscious leadership within the departments has contributed to the present state in all too many health departments.

New segments of the population, such as the consumer, the minorities, the poor, must be brought into the departments of the decision-making process. Decentralization, community control, and other citizen participation models are discussed as possible ways of revitalizing health departments.

One model of citizen participation was stressed. It contained the following concepts.

1. The community's democratic selection of its representatives to policy-making boards for the health department.

2. Sharing the authority to make policy decisions among the health professionals, elected officials, and the democratically selected citizen representatives.

Whether citizen participation will result in improved services cannot be discerned at this time. A number of studies in progress should contribute much needed data. However, it is asked whether some of the side benefits accruing from citizen participation, such as the combatting of alienation and powerlessness, may not be as important as the improvement of services.

Although no one model of citizen participation or control-sharing was identified as optimal, I believe that some variation of the model is needed if public health is to become relevant again. Administrators who will be working in a participatory, control-sharing model should be aware of the difficulties they will face and the knowledge and skills which will be required for effective administration.

REFERENCES

1. Katz, D., and Kahn R.: The social psychology of organizations. John Wiley and Sons, Inc., New York, 1966, p. 21; (a) p. 59; (b) p. 313.
2. Kimmey, J. R.: Renew commitment to role of leader in health changes. The Nation's Health, January 1972, p. 1.
3. Kimmey, J. R.: Backed into the corner . . .! and other misconceptions. The Nation's Health, February 1972, p. 1.
4. Emery, F. E., and Thorsrud, E.: Form and content in industrial democracy. Some experiences from Norway and other European countries. Tavistock Publications Limited, London, 1968.
5. Gibbs, J. R.: Dynamics of leadership in selected readings. In Behavioral science and the manager's role, edited by W. Eddy et al. National Training Laboratory Institute for Applied Behavioral Science, Washington, D.C., 1969, pp. 123-135.
6. Zahn, G.: The great Catholic upheaval. Saturday Rev 54: 24-27, Sept. 11, 1971.
7. Berkley, G. E.: The administrative revolution. Notes on the passing of organization man. Prentice-Hall, Inc., Englewood Cliffs, N.J., 1971, pp.140-145.
8. Burns, E. M.: A critical review of national health insurance proposals. HSMHA Health Rep 86: 111-120, February 1971.
9. Smith, B. L. R.: Introduction to urban decentralization and community participation. Am Behav Scient 15: 3-14, September-October 1971; (a) p. 7; (b) p. 13.
10. Haider, D.: The political economy of decentralization. Am Behav Scient 15: 108-129, September-October 1971.
11. Jonas, S.: A theoretical approach to the question of "community control" of health services facilities. Am J Public Health 61: 916-921, May 1971.
12. Eisinger, P. K.: Control sharing in the city. Am Behav Scient 15: 36-51, September-October 1971.
13. Purdom, W.: An evaluation of decentralized public health administration. Am J Public Health 57: 509-517, March 1967.
14. Thomas, W. C., Jr., and Hilleboe, H. E.: Administrative centralization versus decentralization and the role of generalists and specialists. Am J Public Health 58: 1620-1632, September 1968.
15. Stotzfus, V.: Evaluation of the decentralization process by employees of a state health department. Public Health Rep 85: 919-927, October 1970.
16. Bellin, L. E.: The new left and American public health—attempted radicalization of the A.P.H.A. through dialectic. Am J Public Health 60: 973-981, June 1970.
17. Brieland, D.: Community advisory boards and maximum feasible participation. Am J Public Health 61: 292-296, February 1971.
18. Citizen participation in local health programs. HSMHA Health Rep 86: 330, April 1971.

19. Galiher, C. B., Needleman, J., and Rolfe, A. J.: Consumer participation. HSMHA Health Rep 86: 99-106, February 1971.
20. Notkin, H., and Notkin, M.: Community participation in health services: A review article. Med Care Rev 27: 1178-1201, December, 1970.
21. Parker, A. W.: The consumer as policy-maker: Issues of training. Am J Public Health 60: 2139-2153, November 1970.
22. LaNove, G. R., and Smith, B.: The political evolution of school decentralization. Am Behav Scient 15: 73-93, September-October 1971.
23. Kunnes, R.: Community control of community health. The New Physician 19: 28-33, January 1970.
24. Riessman, F., and Gartner, A.: Community control and radical social change. Soc Policy 1: 52-55, May-June 1970.
25. Aronowitz, S.: The dialectics of community control. Soc Policy 1: 47-51, May-June 1970.
26. Beck, B.: Community control: A distraction not an answer. Soc Work 14: 14-20, October 1969.
27. David, J.: Decentralization, citizen participation, and ghetto health care. Am Behav Scient 15: 94-107, September-October 1971.
28. Dinerman, B.: Citizen participation and social services. Regional Research Institute on Social Welfare, University of Southern California, Los Angeles, p. 21. Mimeographed.
29. Levens, H.: Organizational affiliation and powerlessness: A case study of the welfare poor. Soc Problems 16: 18-32, September 1968.
30. Community mental health centers evaluated. Behav Today 3: 1, Mar. 13, 1972.
31. The American city manager: An urban administrator in a complex and evolving situation. Public Admin Rev 31: 16, January-February 1971.
32. Wilson, C. E.: Year one at I. S. 201. Soc Policy 1: 10-17, May-June 1970.
33. Learning and the need for assessment. Los Angeles Times, Apr. 2, 1972, Sec G, p. 6.
34. Etzioni, A.: Modern organizations. Prentice-Hall, Inc., Englewood Cliffs, N.J., 1964, pp. 8,9.
35. Moore, M. L.: The role of hostility and militancy in indigenous community health advisory groups. Am J Public Health 61: 922-930, May 1971.
36. Brager, G. A., and Jorris, V.: Bargaining: A method of community change. Soc Work 14: 73-83, October 1969.
37. Bennis, W. G., and Slater, P. E.: The temporary society. Harper & Row Publishers, Inc., New York, 1968, p. 74.
38. Bennis, W. G.: Changing organizations. McGraw-Hill Book Co., New York, 1966, p. 25.

Citizen Participation
Strategies

EDMUND M. BURKE

The participation of citizens in community planning, public as well as private, has increased rapidly in the past few years to the point where it is now a fairly common and frequently praised practice. Federal legislation and, more telling, the demands of citizens themselves, have combined to make citizen participation an essential requirement in any urban project. Yet, nothing in community planning to date has caused more contention. In city after city, program after program, citizen participation is the principal source of confusion and conflict.

Urban renewal agencies are a case in point. They have been subject to constant criticism for their citizen participation practices. Even the few which have conscientiously attempted to involve citizens at the grass roots level find their motives suspect.[1] The poverty program, committed to citizen participation from the start, is another and more publicized example. Its difficulties over citizen participation have involved Congressmen, Office of Economic Opportunity (OEO) officials,

Reprinted with permission of The Journal of the American Institute of Planners V. 35, 1968, pp. 287-294.

mayors, community organization workers, citizens, and even the Bureau of the Budget. The resulting imbroglio now is being blamed for the recent congressional antagonism to the Community Action Program (CAP). Nor, surprisingly, are private agencies, based on the principle of voluntarism, immune from attack. Mobilization for Youth in New York City, as well as other Ford Foundation-financed "gray area" projects have stumbled over the application of citizen participation and have been forced to curtail program goals. Why has this happened?

DILEMMAS OF CITIZEN PARTICIPATION

Part of the difficulty stems from society's idealized value premise concerning citizen participation, coupled with an inability to make it work in policy-making. Citizen participation is part of our democratic heritage, often proclaimed as a means to perfect the democratic process. Stated most simply, it views the citizen as the ultimate voice in community decision-making. Citizens *should* share in decisions affecting their destinies. Anything less is a betrayal of our democratic tradition.

Yet, even its most ardent supporters admit that citizens cannot participate in all decision-making functions. Questions of national security are the most extreme examples. Decisions requiring technical competency may be others. On what basis, though, are decisions defined as technically outside the purview of the citizen?

The answer is not easily found. Indeed, there may not be one. For example, when neighborhood groups insist on participating in local school issues, including selection of the school principal—is that citizen participation? Or as Fred Hechinger, education editor of the *New York Times*, describes it, "citizen control"?[2] The question is perplexing because many of those currently sympathetic to the New York City citizens abhorred attempts of other citizen groups who, during the McCarthy period, demanded their kind of participation in school affairs.

Moreover, arrayed against the objectives of citizen participation are those of experts. Jealous of their own prerogatives, they may be unwilling to admit nonprofessionals into the decision-making arena. In New York, for example, a $3.5 million legal aid project funded by OEO was put in jeopardy because the legal profession refused to allow the poor to have a direct voice in policy-making.[3]

But this, of course, is the basis of the dilemma—the demand both for participatory democracy and expertise in decision-making. Certainly it is not possible to maximize both value preferences. Accommodations have to be made. Generally, value conflicts—the conflict between freedom and control is one example—tend to be resolved pragmatically. Mechanisms are developed to minimize differences and conditions are used as criteria for determining when and how to maximize one value over another.

Probably the most troublesome area of all is the choice of strategy objectives for citizen participation. Commonly advocated as serving fairly specific objectives, citizen participation is often predicated less upon value premises than upon practical considerations. In many cases, this is what makes it acceptable. It can, according to some claims, rebuild deteriorating neighborhoods, devise realistic and better plans, pave the way for the initiation of the poor and the powerless into the mainstream of American life, achieve support and sanction for an organization's objectives, end the drift toward alienation in cities, halt the rise in juvenile deliquency, and recreate small town democracy in a complex urban society.

This suggests that citizens can be used as instruments for the attainment of specific ends. Citizen participation, in other words, is a strategy. But the ends are sometimes conflicting. In one case citizen participation is advocated as an administrative technique to protect the stability or even the existence of an organization; in another, it is viewed as an educational or therapeutic tool for changing attitudes; in still another case, it is proposed as a means for assisting an organization to define its goals and objectives.

To imply that citizen participation is a single, undifferentiated, and overriding strategy is misleading. It is more accurate to speak of several strategies of citizen participation, defined in terms of given objectives. These objectives will be limited by available resources, as well as the organizational character of community activities, particularly community planning. Because planning operates through formal organizations, any strategy will be influenced by organizational demands—the necessity for coordinated efforts, the orientation toward purposeful (ideally, rational) action, and the demands of the environment, which, for public agencies, are often the requirements of extra-governmental jurisdictions. Thus, the relevancy of a strategy depends both upon an organization's abilities to fulfill the requirements necessary for the strategy's effectiveness, and upon the adaptability of the strategy to an organizational environment.

The intent of this paper is to analyze citizen participation not as a value, but as the basis for various strategies. The more common uses of citizen participation will be reviewed, indicating the assumptions, conditions, and organizational requirements of each. Five strategies will be identified: *education-therapy, behavioral change, staff supplement, cooptation, and community power.*

EDUCATION-THERAPY STRATEGY

A frequently proclaimed but rarely viable strategy of citizen participation focuses upon the presumed need for improvement of the individual participants. Accomplishing a specific task is irrelevant; rather, the participants become clients who are the objects of treatment. Consequently this strategy has often been defined as an end in itself.

One focus is education. In this context the act of participation is held to be a form of citizenship training, in which citizens working together to solve community problems not only learn how democracy works but also learn to value and appreciate cooperation as a problem-solving method. This would strengthen local government, spur community development, and create a sense of community or community identification.

Utilizing participation in community affairs as an educational device has had a profound and controversial impact on the practice of community organization employed by social workers. Early writers advocated participation not as the means but as the goal of community organization. At this stage there was a strong social reform orientation attached to community organization, and one of the pioneers in the field, Eduard Lindeman, termed it the Community Movement.[4] Later writers continued this emphasis but referred to participation as the "process goal" of community organization. Murray Ross, one of the principal spokesmen of this school of thought, explains that the aim of community organization is to help communities develop their own capacities to solve problems. Achievement of planning goals is secondary.[5]

More recently this view has come under criticism. Some maintain that process is secondary—in fact, not a goal at all but only a means. Cooperative attitudes, learned through the medium of participation, are preliminary to problem solving, and therefore are the means by which tasks are successfully undertaken.[6] One writer has suggested that in practice this takes place automatically—the goal of integration or process is abandoned as the demands of achieving specific tasks arise. "Broadly based decision-making must be replaced by decision-making by a few, who then sell the task objective to others. The process of encouraging people to make their own decisions as to what is good for them thus gives way to the process of convincing them of what a change agent or a small group of 'leaders' thinks is good for them."[7]

Another way to focus this strategy is to use participation therapeutically as a means for developing self-confidence, and, indeed, self-reliance—an underlying theme, incidentally, of the citizen participation objectives of both urban renewal and poverty programs. Individuals, according to this logic, will discover that by cooperating with their neighbors they can bring about changes affecting their community. More significantly, they will inspire each other, communicating an elan of hope and self-confidence. The participants will learn that they can reform their own lives: or, according to the hopes of OEO, turn away from the self-defeating and despairing culture of poverty; or, according to the Department of Housing and Urban Development (HUD), increase their sense of responsibility for their dwelling unit.

However meritorious the aim, there appears to be considerable difficulty in implementing this strategy. Admittedly, social group workers use participation as a device to achieve therapeutic or educational objectives. Then, too, those working with citizen groups report that positive changes do occur among individuals participating in community projects. Oscar Lewis, the anthropologist, has suggested that organizing the poor and giving them a sense of power and leadership through participation has been one method of abolishing the subculture of poverty in certain countries, notably Cuba.[8] Black Power advocates, as well, adopt as one of their premises that the organization of the black community will bring about the self-confidence and hope that American society has consistently denied its Negro citizens. But the formal and deliberate organization of citizens for this purpose has rarely been tried, and if so, seldom for any appreciable time.

One such attempt was in Cincinnati more than fifty years ago. Called the Cincinnati Social Unit Plan, it organized a number of neighborhood districts and involved citizens in major health planning programs. The program engendered criticism from professional groups—chiefly medical—and local government officials. Some held the view that the citizens became too self-reliant. "There are still those who do not trust the voice of the people," commented Eduard Lindeman at the time.[9]

Mobilization for Youth in New York, a prototype of the Community Action Agencies, is another attempt, and similar in many respects to the Cincinnati program. It defines participation as a means for increasing the independence of individuals in deprived areas. "Participation by adults," according to the Mobilization for Youth project, "in decision-making about matters that affect their interests increases their sense of identification with the community and the larger social order. People who identify with their neighborhood and share common values are more likely to control juvenile behavior."[10] But, like the Cincinnati program, it has run into difficulty with public officials and many of its goals have been emasculated.

What frustrates the use of this strategy in community planning is the inability to accommodate it to organizational demands. The focus is upon the means; participation is the overriding objective, not the accomplishment of goals or group tasks. The participants, therefore, must be determiners of decisions and policies, even to the point of allowing them to make unwise decisions or to create conflict and controversy. If, for example, the aim is to build self-reliance into the poor, any attempt to deter or inhibit their role in decision-making will only reinforce their alienation and their belief that they are incapable of making decisions. Public officials in Cincinnati or New York would not take such chances. Similarly the Bureau of the Budget, governed by norms of efficiency and performance, has discouraged the use of this strategy by local anti-poverty agencies.[11]

BEHAVIORAL CHANGE STRATEGY

Group participation has been found to be a major force for changing individual behavior. Individuals tend to be influenced by the groups to which they belong and will more readily accept group-made decisions than lectures or individual exhortations to change. This has led to a strategy of participation which, although somewhat similar to the *education-therapy* strategy, is sufficiently different to require a separate classification. The strategy is deliberately change oriented and is aimed at influencing individual behavior through group membership. It is a strategy commonly associated with community organization practice and more recently with increasing importance in certain schools of management science.[12] Moreover, it is a strategy reflected in much of the urban renewal literature on citizen participation, and, in fact, is even enunciated in a President's Housing Message to Congress.[13]

Briefly, the objective is to induce change in a system or subsystem by changing the behavior of either the system's members or influential representatives of the system. The group is seen as a source of influence over its members. Therefore, by focusing upon group standards—its style of leadership, or its emotional atmosphere—it is considered possible to change the behavior of the individual members. The group itself becomes a target of change even though the goal may be to change individual behavior.[14] This particular emphasis distinguishes this strategy from the *education-therapy* strategy, for though many of the techniques may be similar the objective is different. Whether an individual personally benefits from participating in the process is not necessarily relevant. The focus is upon the task and upon helping the group accomplish the task goal.

Two major premises underlie the *behavioral change* strategy. First, it has been found that it is easier to change the behavior of individuals when they are members of a group than to change any one of them separately. Second, individuals and groups resist decisions which are imposed upon them. They are more likely to support a decision and, equally important, more likely to assist in carrying it out if they have had a part in discovering the need for change and if they share in the decision-making process. Participation in the decision-making process, in other words, can create commitment to new objectives.

The effectiveness of this strategy, however, depends upon the existence of certain conditions. In the first place, the participants must have a strong sense of identification with the group, and feel assured that their contributions and activities are meaningful both to themselves and to the group. There must, too, be some satisfactions or gains from participation, either through personal and group accomplishments or from the mere fact of the association with other members. The awareness of the need for change, and consequent pressure for change, must come from within the group as a shared perception. Facts, data, and persuasion are not enough.

There is a necessity, too, for participants to be actively involved in the decision-making process. The making of the decisions, the working through of the problem, so to speak, are the dynamic factors that change behavior. Communication channels, consequently, need to be open and undistorted. "Information relating to the need for change, plans for change, and consequences of change must be shared by all relevant people in the group."[15]

Planning agencies, particularly publicly supported ones, find it difficult to fulfill these conditions. Even though committed to the strategy, as many often are, intra- and extra-organizational demands often dictate a change in strategy. The complexity of many planning projects and more important, the commitment of planners themselves, obstruct the citizen from becoming actively involved in decision-making. Citizens frequently complain that they are unable to understand the planners and consequently unable to become committed to a policy or goal they do not understand.

Extra-organizational demands have the effect also of closing off communication channels to the citizens. Organizations faced with adhering to performance norms, such as budget deadlines, discover that they are unable to apply the strategy. The demands for submission of program proposals (for example, the initial planning period in the poverty program is six months) or the priority demands emanating from a national agency, such as HUD or OEO, precludes the possibility of involving citizens for the purpose of changing their behavior. Local poverty agencies' staff complain that their time is spent in selling proposals to citizens to gain their support. They have neither the time nor the sanction to effectively foster group deliberation and initiative, however much they would like to.

A further difficulty is relating the participant group of other influential or decision-making centers of the community. It is rarely possible to include all members of a system in a community planning project. Frequently, then, the planning organization is dealing with system representatives. The group becomes not merely a medium of change, but also an agent of change—an action group designed to influence much larger systems. One example would be a representative neighborhood renewal committee attempting to influence other residents and city officials to improve its neighborhood area. But it is not always possible to assume that those involved are in a position to carry out the group's intentions. For the strategy to be effective in community planning, therefore, the participant must not only commit himself to a course of action, but also be in a position to commit others. This has been a vexing problem in community planning. It is not uncommon to involve someone who has little or no influence in the group he represents, or who may not be truly representative of his group.

If, on the other hand, the system representatives can influence change in their own reference groups, the strategy is a highly effective model for planned change. Experiments in industry with this strategy have been quite persuasive.[16] Moreover, a group highly committed to a change objective has proven to be a more effective change agent than an equivalent number of individuals.

STAFF SUPPLEMENT STRATEGY

Probably one of the oldest and certainly one of the most prevalent reasons for citizen participation is the simple principle of voluntarism—the recruitment of citizens to carry out tasks for an organization which does not have the staff resources to carry them out itself. This is a strategy basic to voluntary associations. Hospitals, family casework agencies, recreation services such as the YMCA and the Scouts, and fund-raising agencies rely upon citizen volunteers to perform many essential agency functions. In some instances, agencies depend entirely upon citizens to achieve their objectives. The clearest example is the voluntary fund-raising agency.

In community planning this strategy has been used to supplement the expertise of the planning agency's staff with the expertise of particular citizens. Basically, this is what Nash and Durden proposed in their suggestion to replace the planning commission with citizen task forces.[17] Moreover, it is a strategy widely used by Welfare Councils and a premise which underlies the Welfare Council's reliance (overreliance, some suggest[18]) on the committee approach to social planning. The assumption of the Welfare Council is that its own staff need not be experts in substantive planning issues, rather they should be experts in knowing how to involve and work with citizens who are the presumed experts.

The objective of the strategy is to exploit the abilities, free time, and/or the expertise of individuals to achieve a desired goal. Ideally, it is a procedure whereby the citizen volunteer is matched with the specifications of the task. Interestingly, some agencies actually write up detailed job descriptions for volunteer roles. Much attention, therefore, has to be given to perfecting techniques for recruiting and holding volunteers. Incentives to stimulate willingness to participate become crucial because of the desire to recruit specific individuals.

The use of skilled volunteers as supplementary staff is easily compatible with the requirements of many organizations. It is assumed that the volunteer is in agreement with the organization's objectives and is recruited to assist in carrying out those objectives. Few citizen participants are actually involved in policy-making roles. Scout leaders, case aides, and fund-raising solicitors, for example, are recruited to carry out the policies and directions of the organization. Incidentally, it is this auxiliary role which the Bureau of the Budget prefers for the poor in the poverty program.[19]

There are opportunities in community planning, nevertheless, for the participant to play a significant role in policy-making, and where in fact, this is the assumption upon which he is recruited.[20] The particular expertise of the citizen participant—a juvenile court judge in a study of delinquency, a public welfare recipient in an analysis of poverty, or a public health doctor in an air pollution study—is supposed to assist in determining policy. There is the possibility, however, that the citizen's expertise can become merely a sanctioning element; that is, a symbol through which in actuality the staff's voice becomes policy. But that is another strategy—*cooptation*—and is discussed later.

It is difficult to assess the usefulness of the participation of skilled volunteers in community planning. The overall strategy depends, of course, upon the classical notions of rationality in planning, about which there is now considerable doubt.[21] On many issues, particularly in welfare, urban renewal, and city planning, there are few "correct" decisions. The absence of any valid data, and more important, the ambiguity of assigning values, creates a situation in which decision-making arises out of bargaining, negotiation, and compromise. The advice of an expert, whether he be citizen or professional, often becomes merely another opinion. And this is a decided limitation in relying upon this strategy exclusively in community planning. Additional strategies need to be employed which take into account the politics of decision-making or are aimed at overcoming value differences.

COOPTATION

Another citizen participation practice is to involve citizens in an organization in order to prevent anticipated obstructionism. In this sense citizens are not seen as a means to achieve better planning goals nor are they seen as partners in assisting an organization in achieving its goal; rather, they are viewed as potential elements of obstruction or frustration whose cooperation and sanction are found necessary. This strategy, *cooptation*, has been defined as "the process of absorbing new elements into the leadership or policy-determining structure of an organization as a means of averting threats to its stability and existence."[22]

Cooptation is neither a new technique nor does it apply only to voluntary or welfare organizations. Corporations, for example, elect representatives of banking institutions to their boards of directors to provide access to financial resources. Politicians have been notably imaginative in this art. For instance, in order to ward off predictions that his administration would be fiscally irresponsible, President Kennedy appointed a highly respected Republican as Secretary of the Treasury.

Cooptation can take two forms, both of which are applicable to organizations involving citizens. One is employed in response to specific power forces. Certain individuals are considered to have sufficient resources or influence—financial, decision-making, legislative—to vitally affect the operation of the organization. To capture this influence or at least neutralize it, not only are they brought into the organization, but, more significantly, they are included at the policy-making level because their influence is crucial to the continuation of current organizational policy. This has been termed "informal" cooptation, and its key characteristic is that it is a technique "of meeting the pressure of specific individuals or interest-groups which are in a position to enforce demands."[23]

Although informal cooptation has obvious advantages, it also exerts its own toll. Choice becomes constrained. Those coopted will want to share in influencing policy and thus become one more definer of organization policy. Stability and security may be gained by cooptation, but frequently at a price. An organization will thus have to weigh the benefits against the costs.

A more prevalent practice of welfare and planning organizations is to rely upon what has been termed "formal" cooptation. It is a device for winning consent and legitimacy from the citizenry at large. The underlying belief is that the need the organization purports to serve is not in itself sufficiently persuasive to gain community support. Thus, groups who reflect the sentiments of the community are absorbed into the organization in order to gain legitimacy. Clergymen, for example, are inevitably involved in community projects because they bestow credibility upon the projects. Other groups reflecting community sentiments, who consequently are invariably involved, are representatives of labor, business, the professions, and women's organizations.

Formal cooptation also describes the practice of setting up and maintaining communication networks in a community. Any organization needs to establish reliable and readily accessible channels of communication through which information and requests may be transmitted to all relevant segments and participants. An organization depending upon community support and sanction is obliged to relate itself to the community as a participant. A common method is to tap into already existing citizen groups—neighborhood organizations or block clubs, for instance. In this way the local citizens, through their voluntary associations or committees, become identified and committed to the program and, ideally, the apparatus of the operating agency.[24]

The participants' ability to affect policy, according to Philip Selznick, is the basis for the distinction between informal and formal cooptation. Informal cooptation implies a sharing of power in response to specific or potential pressures. Formal cooptation, on the other hand, merely seeks public acknowledgement of the agency-constituency relationship, since it is not anticipated that organizational policies will be put in jeopardy. What is shared "is the *responsibility* for power," explains Selznick, "not the power itself."[25]

It is not possible to assume, however, that voluntary groups formally coopted by an organization will be willing to remain passive with respect to policy. Where citizen groups are in general agreement with the goals of the host agency, as may have been the case in Selznick's analysis of the TVA, the observation may be applicable. But with changing conditions and possible disagreement on goals, the citizen group may endeavor to capture or at least influence the policy-making centers to insure that policies are made in their interest.

Urban renewal is an example. On the whole, renewal agencies have tended to adopt the formal cooptation strategy. Relationships are established with neighborhood groups or block committees which serve both as a means for sanctioning renewal objectives and as a network of communication, especially in project areas marked for rehabilitation. Citizen groups, however, soon resist the role of sanctioning agents and information carriers, and push for more of a voice in planning decisions. Consequently, local urban renewal agencies have been hard pressed to establish procedures for citizen involvement, turning to trial and error applications of different practices.[26]

Yet, despite the usual disparaging connotation attached to cooptation it does provide a means for achieving social goals. Certain groups not normally included in community policy-making are given an entrance into the decision-making arena. Moreover, because it provides overlapping memberships, it is also a device that increases the opportunity for organizations to relate to one another and, thus, find compatible goals. From the organization's viewpoint, it provides a means for giving "outsiders" an awareness and understanding of the problem it faces.[27] At the same time, the strategy is an administrative device. Facilitating the achievement of social goals is incidental. The aim is to permit the limited participation of citizens as a means of achieving organization goals, but not to the extent that these goals are impeded.

COMMUNITY POWER STRATEGIES

Power may be defined as the ability to exercise one's will even over the opposition of others. Individuals are capable of obtaining power and influence through the control of wealth or institutions. Whether such power can be exercised in all instances, or whether a small group can control all community decisions is a matter of dispute. Not disputed, however, is the fact that centers of power do exist outside the formal political structure of a community and such centers are influential in shaping community decisions.[28]

Most community organizations are interested in exerting influence. Frequently organizations come into being exclusively for the purpose of bringing their will to bear on community decisions. There are two strategies of citizen participation based on theories of community power, both designed to exploit community power. The first is to capture influentials by involving them as participants in the organization in order to achieve organizational objectives. This is the informal cooptation previously explained.

Another significantly different strategy accepts the premises of community power theories, but not the conclusions. Change, it is suggested, can be caused by confronting existing power centers with the power of numbers—an organized and committed mass of citizenry. In effect, a new center of power is created, based not upon control of wealth and institutions but upon size and dedication.[29] This type of organization has the ability to obtain accommodation from existing power centers, both from its inherent strength and its choice of tactics.

Demonstrations, boycotts, and picketing are the common weapons of such mass organizations. Negotiation on issues is inevitable, but negotiation from strength is a prerequisite. The power structure must first be put into a position of willingness to negotiate and this occurs only after they have been pushed to do so. "When those prominent in the status quo turn and label you an agitator," says Saul Alinsky, the chief ideologist of the conflict-oriented strategists, to his organizers, "they are completely correct, for that is, in one word, your function—to agitate to the point of conflict."[30]

The conflict strategy works best for organizations committed to a cause rather than to specific issues or services. In securing the involvement of individuals identified with the basic cause, the organization serves as the unifying vehicle for achievement of individual aims. There is, then, little necessity to include the participants in the goal-defining process. Agreement is assumed. But on specific means to achieve the goal, disagreement may arise. Because the participants are emotionally involved in the ends, detached, pragmatic analysis of alternatives is difficult. Concerns are immediate and give rise to impatience, which, coupled with emotional involvement, can often lead to internal squabbling and dissension. Such conflict over means can immobilize an organization and lead to schisms. Certain race relations agencies have exhibited this difficulty.

Moreover, the effectiveness of the strategy appears limited in duration. Maintaining citizen interest appears to be the chief difficulty. The organization has only its goal, its idealized purpose, to sustain interest and create satisfactions. It is difficult to maintain interest in idealized goals over long periods of time. The emotional commitment required is too personally enervating. Often the leader of the organization is forced to depend upon exhortations or the manufacturing of crises to recharge interest. Membership dwindles, or frequently the organization changes, tending to rely less upon conflict tactics and more upon cooperation. New classes of participants, reflecting community sentiments or power forces, are invited to join. Goals are modified and the organization becomes undistinguishable from other service-oriented organizations.

CONCLUSIONS

It is apparent that the effectiveness of a particular strategy of citizen participation depends upon certain conditions and assumptions peculiar to itself; likewise each strategy has its own advantages and limitations. The principal difficulty is in adapting a strategy or strategies to the demands of the particular type of organization and the environment within which it functions. Not all strategies are appropriate for all organizations. Conflict-oriented strategies, as many local anti-poverty agencies have demonstrated, are inappropriate in governmentally sponsored programs which demand coordination and cooperation.

A strategy of conflict appears best suited to social reform organizations which are privately supported, or, even more advantageous, self-supporting. Most disadvantaged groups seeking social change have had to depend upon either their own resources or the resources of groups highly sympathetic to their cause. The civil rights struggle is one good example; organized labor is another.

The *behavioral change* strategy and the *staff supplement* strategy appear to be the most appropriate for community planning. The latter permits the planning agency to employ on a voluntary basis the expertise of community individuals. Citizens are recruited for their particular talents—knowledge of the problem (and this can include people who are affected by the problem itself, such as clients of social welfare agencies), skill in publicity and promotion techniques, influence with community decision centers, and representation of community sentiment groups. Such people are recruited into the organization and encouraged to contribute their specialized knowledge to the solution of problems, functioning as full-fledged organizational participants.

The *behavioral change* strategy would appear to be useful in overcoming what is commonly referred to as the "politics" of the planning process. Given the debatable preference characteristics of planning goals and the free market concept of competing community organizations, it would seem advisable to employ a strategy of participation aimed at accommodating various interests. The *behavioral change* strategy has the advantage of subjecting value preferences to a dialogue, allowing them to be aired within the context of the planning process. Other involved organizations are also encouraged to participate in order to allay their fears, gain their advice, and seek their cooperation.

Obviously, this implies a more purposeful approach to citizen participation than is commonly assumed by planning agencies. One issue, of course, is the ability of the staff to work with citizen groups. The appropriateness of any strategy of citizen participation will depend in large measure upon the capabilities and knowledge of the staff to implement it. A strategy of *cooptation*, for instance, requires skill primarily in administration—relating citizen participants to the organization in such a way that they will not interfere with organization goal achievement. Power-conflict strategies appear to demand leadership of a particular type; often a charismatic leader is needed. He has to be skillful in exhorting his followers, giving them a sense of purpose, and helping them to identify with the goals of the organization.

The behavioral change and staff supplement strategies, on the other hand, require knowledge and skill in handling the dynamics of individual and group behavior.[31] While constantly seeking to maximize rationality, the staff needs to be sensitive to the individual differences of participants, enabling them to contribute to the planning process. The staff also must be able to analyze community systems in order to locate decision centers, identify representatives of community sentiment groups, and suggest individuals who can contribute knowledge and information to the solution of a problem. Moreover, the staff role is the direct antithesis of the executive leadership role. Although direction often is warranted, the aim is to give the citizen a sense of participation and an opportunity for leadership. The intention is to work with citizens in a collaborative process in much the same way that David Godschalk and William Mills suggest.[32]

Finally, there is the issue of organizational commitment to, but limited grasp of, citizen participation. The objective in this paper has been to provide an analytical understanding of citizen participation, in its various forms and functions. Clearly, understanding the particular conditions requisite for the success of a particular strategy frequently is a source of difficulty which contributes to the confusion and contention over the efficacy of citizen participation in general. Not clear about strategy implications of citizen participation, many planning organizations find a gap between what they purport to do and what they actually can do. Federally sponsored programs, such as urban renewal, the poverty program, and model cities, are a case in point.

Federal agencies at the national level, constrained by Congressional critics and bureaucratic practices, are forced to specify priorities and program guidelines, inhibiting participation by citizens on the local level. In turn, local staffs are often reduced to grinding out programs for Washington's approval. Many have been disillusioned and demoralized.[33]

Whether or not this is an inherent conflict is difficult to say. At this time it seems so. Yet, it is likely that within the constraints imposed on organizations at both national and local levels a new strategy of citizen participation may evolve. Too many federal agencies are too committed to the general principle of citizen participation not to find a solution.

To do so the premise that citizen participation is self-evident has to be discarded. Planning agencies must be more precise about what they mean by citizen participation, how they intend to implement it, what agency resources will be used to organize and involve citizens, and what voice citizens will have in planning decisions. This may mean a redefinition of planning agencies' goals toward a new focus where a citizen group assumes the responsibility for defining the goals and aims of the planning agency. But it also may mean less contentious citizen participation.

NOTES

1. Conflict and controversy is also found among staff members within urban renewal agencies. See "Citizen Participation in Urban Renewal," *Columbia Law Review*, 66 (March 1966), 500-505.
2. Fred M. Hechinger, "I.S. 201 Teaches Lesson on Race," *The New York Times*, September 25, 1966, p. E9.
3. "Lawyers for the Poor" (editorial), *The New York Times*, December 12, 1966.
4. Eduard C. Lindeman, *The Community* (New York: Association Press, 1921), pp. 58-76.
5. Murray G. Ross, *Case Histories in Community Organization* (New York: Harper & Bros., 1958), pp. 10-11; and Murray G. Ross, *Community Organization* (New York: Harper & Bros., 1955), pp. 13, 21-22, 48-53.
6. Bernard Coughlin, "Community Planning: A Challenge to Social Work," *Social Work* (October 1961), 37-42.
7. Roland L. Warren, *The Community in America* (Chicago: Rand McNally & Co., 1963), pp. 329-330.
8. Oscar Lewis, *La Vida* (New York: Random House, 1966), pp. xlii-lii.
9. Eduard Lindeman, "New Patterns of Community Organization," *Proceedings of the National Conference of Social Work, 1937* (Chicago: The University of Chicago Press, 1937), p. 321. See also, Roy Lubove, *The Professional Altruist* (Cambridge: Harvard University Press, 1965), pp. 175-178.
10. Mobilization for Youth, Inc., *A Proposal for the Prevention and Control of Delinquency by Expanding Opportunities* (New York: Mobilization for Youth, Inc., 1961), p. 126.
11. *The New York Times*, November 5, 1965, p. 1.
12. See, for example, Douglas McGregor, *The Human Side of Enterprise* (New York: McGraw-Hill Book Co., 1960).
13. John F. Kennedy, *Housing Message to Congress*, March 1961.
14. Dorwin Cartwright, "Achieving Change in People: Some Applications of Group Dynamics Theory," *Human Relations*, IV (1951), 387.
15. *Ibid.*, p. 390.
16. See L. Coch and J.R.P. French, Jr., "Overcoming Resistance to Change," *Human Relations*, 1:4 (1948), 512-532.
17. Peter Nash, and Dennis Durden, "A Task Force Approach to Replace the Planning Board," *Journal of the American Institute of Planners*, XXX (February 1964), 10-22.

18. Robert Morris, "Social Work Preparation for Effectiveness in Planned Change," *Proceedings of the Council on Social Work Education* (New York: Council and Social Work Education, 1963), pp. 166-180.
19. *The New York Times, loc. cit.*
20. This also holds true to some extent if the citizen is recruited to serve on a board of directors.
21. Richard S. Bolan, "Emerging Views of Planning in an Emerging Urban Society," *Journal of the American Institute of Planners*, XXXIII (July 1967), 233-245.
22. Philip Selznick, "Foundations of the Theory of Organization," *American Sociological Review*, 13 (February 1948), 34.
23. *Ibid.*, p. 35.
24. Philip Selznick, *TVA and the Grassroots* (Berkeley: University of California Press, 1953), pp. 224-225.
25. *Ibid.*, pp. 34-35 (his emphasis).
26. Edmund M. Burke, "Citizen Participation in Renewal," *Journal of Housing* (January 1966), 18-21.
27. James D. Thompson, and William J. McEwen, "Organizational Goals and Environment: Goal Setting as an Interaction Process," *American Sociological Review*, 23 (February 1958), 28.
28. For an excellent summation of power and influence see Dorwin Cartwright, "Influence, Leadership, Control," in James March, ed., *Handbook of Organizations* (Chicago: Rand McNally and Co., 1965), pp. 1-47.
29. Advocacy planning appears also to stress the concept of community power as a strategy of chance. The power the advocate planner is stressing, however, is the power of knowledge—the technical apparatus that he can offer local interest groups which thus enables them to gain concessions from City Hall. See Lisa R. Peattie, "Reflections on Advocacy Planning," *Journal of the American Institute of Planners*, XXXIV (March 1968), 80-88.
30. Quoted in Charles E. Silberman, *Crisis in Black and White* (New York: Vintage Books, 1965), p. 335.
31. Staff requirements for implementing the client-oriented strategy are difficult to define. In fact, the advocates of using participation as an educational or therapeutic device have not been too clear on the requirements of the strategy itself. More emphasis has been placed on its merits than on its utility and consequences in community planning. Conceivably this is why it tends to be vitiated in practice.
32. David R. Godschalk and William E. Mills, "A Collaborative Approach to Planning Through Urban Activities," *Journal of the American Institute of Planners*, XXXII (March 1966), 86-95.
33. For an unintentional indictment of citizen participation in the poverty program see Memorandum to Participants in ABCD (Boston) Staff-Community Conference, held on January 7, 1967, entitled "Evaluation of Conference" (mimeographed, February 10, 1967), p. 4.

The Limits on Consumer Participation in Public Social Programs

DAVID P. FAURI

Social programs and the movement for client or consumer participation which grew and prospered during the 1960s now seems to be in decline as the Federal Administration searches for new alternatives. This thus appears to be a period in which to review where we have been. In this article we will examine factors which experience has shown to limit the participation of consumer-client groups.

Organizations which plan and deliver social services are, like other purposive organizations, molded by assumptions which often operate without recognition. These assumptions and resulting institutional structures place responsibility for control, guidance, and authority within the organizations themselves, with consumers of the organizational products and services placed outside the organizations. Organizational theorists and management specialists have been concerned for some time with the development of participative internal structures and improvement of working environments. This focus, while often beneficial, has usually not included recognition of the roles consumers might

Reprinted with permission of *Public Welfare*, V. 31, 1973, pp. 16-24.

play within organizations. Consumers of social services have remained outside the organizations providing the services and are usually not involved in structuring them. Thought is rarely given to an alternative pattern of relations between organizations providing services and the consumers of these services. Consumers are usually well represented by pressure groups and associations of special interests which are truly effective. These groups have lacked power with which to bargain in the political-administrative environment, and have thus played a limited role in the conceptual development and implementation of social service programs. Responsibility for control, guidance, and modification of service delivery systems has rested in the legislative process and in the administrative environment of governmental bureaucracies.[1] Consumer ability to influence these patterns is the same as, or perhaps less than the ability of the general public to exert influence. This has meant that consumers, like anyone else, must participate through democratic participatory mechanisms, including voting and political party membership and activity, or through other alternatives external to these organizations such as protest movements, demonstrations, and local community development organizations. It is my position that interactions between those providing and those consuming the services are strongly influenced by assumptions concerning how program agencies should be organized and how employees act toward consumers. We should be aware of these guiding assumptions when considering the alteration of interaction patterns of organizations and consumers.

HISTORICAL FACTORS

The present widespread utilization of the public sector to provide social services, as compared to the private and voluntary sectors, has meant that organizational patterns have been heavily influenced by governmental, political, and administrative structures. The history of government social programs is a long one, with major growth in this country coming at the time of the Great Depression.

THE LEGACY OF THE GREAT DEPRESSION

In 1935 the Social Security Act thrust the Federal Government into a major role in providing care and services to needy persons. The social philosophy which was built into American Governmental policy at that time drew heavily upon much earlier thinking inherited from Britain and the colonies. A basic intention of the assistance programs established under the Act was the provision of minimal requirements of needy children, needy old persons, blind individuals, the unemployed, and families with deceased fathers. These were the "deserving poor" facing conditions of poverty beyond their control. This rationale represented a compromise between the Judeo-Christian tradition of recognizing and providing charity for the needy and the Calvinist concept of the poor having only themselves to blame for their condition. The deserving poor were to be identified through the application of a means test and eligibility standards. Those who could work were to do so if jobs could be found. As public social welfare utilized public monies, funds were to be spent with frugality, and the Protestant Ethic of hard work and self-support were not to be undermined through excessive public charity. As in the Elizabethan Law of Charitable Uses, government prescribed how charity would be dispensed and under what conditions and in what form it would be given. The planning and administration of social programs thus became a public matter, and bureaucracies employing professionals from many fields were created to conduct these functions.

INSTITUTIONALIZING CHARITY

Charity has become institutionalized, as have social action programs. Even private contributors now are encouraged to work through organizations such as the Community Chest, and large private resources are channeled through private foundations. Assisting one's neighbors has as a result been moved a step away from the pre-industrial, person-to-person assistance. Profes-social programs thus become a public matter, provide the services.

Present-day public social services reflect the social values of earlier periods, just as much of present-day life does. The public administration of public social programs, whether the public and professionals employed in the programs are aware of it or not, are conducted with strong guidance from the past. Puritan moral values, which taught that financial success in this world is a sign and reward of ethical superiority and that failure is the result of idleness and wickedness, are still influential.[2] The public administrator involved in such programs is asked to carry out a societal mandate to help reform those not fitting into the accepted pattern for gaining salvation, although salvation today is economic salvation rather than religious salvation.

TO STRENGTHEN THE WORK ETHIC

American society is still work-oriented, and work is generally looked on as not only providing a living but also as a source of personal satisfaction and growth as well as a measure of social status and meaningful activity. Social programs created to assist those in the "culture of poverty" were intended to help the less fortunate, but they also strengthened the work ethic and the capitalistic economy. Program responsibility is placed with professionals who may well reflect these values in their own conduct. The consumer is conceived of as the person for whom the programs, and the effort of the society, are intended, and through the efforts of program professionals they are the recipients of the best intentions of the larger society.

In such a system the client is not in a position to exert much influence over what the programs intended to benefit him actually deliver. The political power and influence of the poor or culturally deprived are low, and their organizational experiences are limited. Administrative systems are not open to any great degree to their participation, and this reinforces the tendency for others, namely program professionals, to plan and implement for the client group with the best intentions of the larger society, in which the clients play a very limited role.

BUREAUCRATIC LIMITATIONS

Bureaucracy, in its formal sense (rather than in the popular usage denoting excessive multiplication of functions, concentration of power in administrative bureaus and excessive governmental "red tape"), has its roots in Max Weber's ideal-type construct which enumerates fundamental categories of rational legal authority.[3] The Weberian ideal-type construct approach argues that bureaucracy is the most technically effective method of organizing work to achieve efficiency. Of Weber's categories, there are three which particularly function to restrict opportunities for participation by consumers of social program services. They are: 1) organization of official functions bound by rules; 2) specified spheres of competence of officials; 3) the principle of hierarchy in organization structure.

AN OVEREMPHASIS ON RULES

In the first item, rules themselves need not necessarily be restrictive of participation; rather, the manner in which organization employees utilize rules is critical. Rules are necessary to the group working toward common goals, but in bureaucracy they can become dysfunctional when emphasized so much that their enforcement overshadows organizational goals.[4]

The exercise of bureaucratic rules concerning consumers can become overly authoritarian. Rigidity of behavior and domineering attitudes of officials are encouraged by the sanctity of rules. An official's status in an organization may rest in part on demonstrated ability to apply organizational rules precisely and objectively to consumers. Rules may prevent the opening of organizations to participation by consumers by building a wall of rules difficult to cope with, which may alienate persons who are not members of the bureaucracy. Rules may encourage authoritarian behavior by officials and may produce rigid attitudes towards consumers, encouraging an "us" and "them" atmosphere. Feelings of a "we" atmosphere—we the officials and the consumers working for agreed upon goals—is unlikely to exist when bureaucratic rules dominate organizational relationships.

As bureaucracies tend to be composed of middle-class persons, rules are apt to reflect middle-class values and structure the response of the middle-class bureaucrat to lower-class consumers.[5] For example, organization rules often require delays in decisions so issues can be "cleared" or so "things can be done right." While serving the organization well, this is likely to conflict with lower-class values which encourage immediate responses rather than postponement of final decisions. This is not to suggest such rules should be eliminated, but attention should be given to integrating organizational rules and consumer values, and participation of consumers within organizations is one way of approaching this problem.

The second item to be considered as restrictive of opportunities for consumer participation is the existence of specified spheres of competence in bureaucracy. This is directly related to the subject of professionalism (considered in a separate section), for it encourages and necessitates the presence of professionalism in organizations. Spheres of competence result from specialization and differentiation of functions in large, complex organizations. Knowledge is the basis of competence, and control on the basis of knowledge is a key element in making bureaucracy rational and superior to other organizational forms. Spheres of competence encourage the growth of increased knowledge within the bureaucracy and resulting increases in power. If a consumer wishes to become involved in the details of his case, he may lack the "competence" to understand the details, for this is the responsibility of the bureaucrat. If he should acquire an understanding of the details, he may then be threatening to the officials and may open himself to rude treatment or the documents relating to his case may become classified or "lost." The concept of spheres of competency implies certain persons—the officials—are qualified to deal with specialized matters on which they are expert. This should not be totally condemned, for it provides expertise necessary in complex organizations. It opens the door to abuses, however, since it encourages the development of areas of power from which others may be excluded.

THE "PROJECT TEAM"

The "project team" concept offers a partial solution to the dysfunctional aspect of spheres of competency. The concept has been employed in the aerospace industry, in N.A.S.A. and in research corporations. It allows competency to be utilized without building power into permanent parts of the organization controlled by those having the competency. Project teams are created to meet certain defined problems and limits are set on the time devoted to a particular problem. This limits the life of task groups and moves competency around within the organization. The major limitation of this mode of operation is that task groups and time limitations are most readily employable in organizations dealing with unique problems or with a wide variety of situations. Research institutions and major problem-solving operations dealing with technological hardware, such as defense or space operations, can adopt this approach as they work with time deadlines and move from problem to problem. The use of project teams in situations requiring considerable routine and less creative work is more difficult. The idea suggests, however, that these teams may be an ideal vehicle for including consumers in public social service organizations. Defining social problems and planning new services requires the ability to deal with unique problems in a set amount of time, and project teams would likely be suitable in such situations.

The third item of rational legal authority of the Weberian ideal-type construct to be examined here is the principle of hierarchy. The problem raised for the consumer of organizational services by the principle of hierarchy is that he has access only to the lower rungs of the hierarchial ladder. He may even be seen as the ground upon which the ladder rests—that is, lower than the bottom rung of the ladder. Hierarchy can potentially be used to keep the consumer in his place, limiting his participation in organizational matters. If he raises questions, he can be put off with the comment that, "such and such will have to be cleared" with a higher authority. Hierarchy can be used as a weapon and for self-protection ("That's not my responsibility, I don't have the authority for it, you'll have to talk to . . .").

Such instances are the manifestations of the hierarchy principle in operation in which accountability and responsibility rest on the shoulders of individuals in specific organizational roles. The system implies the roles, and by implication those placed in these roles are in a juxtaposition of inferior/superior. It is difficult to imagine how organizational consumers could participate in organizational decision-making as anything less than inferiors. Consumers would seem to hold the lowest "office" possible, and it is unlikely they would readily be accepted within an organization when organizational employees are hindered from accepting one another as equals due to hierarchial role identities.

THE TENDENCY TO DEPERSONALIZE

When individuals are categorized into hierarchial roles depersonalization of relationships between people is encouraged. If employees interact on a depersonalized role-to-role basis, we might expect them to also conduct similar relationships with consumers seeking help from the organization or attempting to participate in it. Merton comments on this in discussing bureaucratic structure and personality.

> "Since functionaries minimize personal relations and resort to categorization, the peculiarities of individual cases are often ignored. But the client who, quite understandably, is convinced of the 'special features' of his own problem often objects to such categorical treatment. Stereotyped behavior is not adapted to the exigencies of individual problems. The impersonal treatment of affairs which are at times of great personal significance to the client gives rise to the charge of 'arrogance' and 'haughtiness' of the bureaucrat."[6]

THE ARROGANCE OF LOW-STATUS OFFICIALS

The air of "arrogance" and "haughtiness" may be induced by the discrepancy between the position held by the bureaucrat in the hierarchy and his position with reference to the public.[7] Often the organizational representative having most frequent or initial contact with the public holds low organizational status. If dominated by superiors, a person in such a role might tend to give similar treatment to those even lower in the order—the consumers.[8] Even if consumers are invited to participate, they will still be low men on the totem pole and in poor position to exert influence or maintain self-respect. Robert Michels, writing in the early part of the century, commented on what he considered to be the negative effects on the individual of hierarchial relationships. "The dependence upon superior authorities characteristic of the average employee suppresses individuality and gives to the society in which employees predominate a narrow petty-bourgeois and philistine stamp."[9] The result of this system, as he interpreted it, was to create, "a mania for promotion, and obsequiousness towards those upon whom promotion depends"; and "arrogance towards inferiors and servility towards superiors."[10]

A rational modification to hierarchy would encourage organizational employees to act in a more personal and open manner toward fellow employees and consumers. Participative management, Theory Y management techniques and organizational development methods have been applied to bureaucratic organizations, but while they tend to tone down dysfunctional elements such as hierarchy, they do not make structural changes in authority relationships.

Kirkat has proposed a consociated ideal-type organization construct which employs a "multivalent authority structure" in place of permanent hierarchy.[11] Leadership is geared to particular problems, project teams are employed and time limitations force restructuring of authority with the initiation of new problems of new time dimensions. Such an organizational pattern may not be useful for all organizations, but it does suggest one possible alternative organizational form for meeting the negative aspects of hierarchy.

Orion F. White's article on the dialectical organization suggests approaching the principle of hierarchy with its defined roles and layers of authority through a dialectical method in which roles are identified nonhierarchically.[12] In this approach, organizational roles would be fluid and authority would be allocated functionally and equally, resulting in lateral authority relations. Staff relations would consciously be designed on a principle of "nondominance" in which individuals would not possess or develop authoritative positions. In this type of arrangement, administrative responsibility in differing functional areas with differing agency members areas, allowing no one person to control all administrative matters and with policy being arrived at through a balance of power situation among the staff.

Proposed alternative organizational patterns are perhaps more numerous than their actual operation in the public sector, for experimentation is difficult to bring about, difficult to evaluate and difficult to move beyond the experimental stage. Most of all, traditional bureaucracy is geared to self-preservation and maintenance of the status quo so that intrusion into its operations by non-believers is unwelcome.

ECONOMY AND EFFICIENCY

Managing government affairs in as efficient and economical a manner as possible is a long standing tradition of American democracy, even though our history is full of abuses of public trust to achieve private gain. Of factors which may prevent or limit the development of consumer participation in social service programs, the desire (or the demand) for economy and efficiency may be the most crucial. Participation requires professionally trained personnel and specialized, skilled technicians or bureaucrats to stand aside or slow down while less well-trained and less-skilled persons become involved in the working of organizations, possibly slowing down decision-making.

Economy in public programs suggests that the public purse must be protected through the expenditure of the least number of dollars necessary to get a job done. It is a rational approach to utilizing scarce resources for the great variety of governmental programs and services. Efficiency refers to the method by which economy should be achieved. Efficient use of resources (men, materials, and money) will save money and result in greater output for each dollar expended.

The potential conflict between participation and the tradition of economy and efficiency is illustrated by Alan Altshuler in his work on community control.[13] Concentrating on large cities and black community groups, Altshuler identifies a major argument against participation in public program policy formation by any group of lay citizens—most citizens value efficiency more than they value participation.

Economy and efficiency in the management of government programs appear on the surface to be good for all, and it is accepted as fact by many Americans. Demanding that public programs implement these values is a means of protecting the public purse, and this is seen as beneficial to everyone since taxes are paid by most everyone. Government which is efficient and which conserves resources is often thought of as the best government. Verbalization of these feelings has helped win many an election. Usually we do not consider the secondary results of this value, and new approaches to decision-making on the local level must pass the test of this value.

THE TAXPAYER'S VIEW

To the middle class, which carries the major tax burden, each tax dollar saved adds to expendable personal income. The values of economy and efficiency are as a result strongly supported, helping to preserve the status quo, and this is an important secondary result of these values. Programs which encourage participation of consumers in decision-making do so with the reservations of the middle class which foots much of the tax bill. Asking these taxpayers to tolerate a slower decision process and nonprofessional administrative activity so that poor people might influence government programs is asking them to go against an ingrained tradition. This is difficult to sell, since it can be interpreted as employing their taxes to support someone else's participation.

A second class problem built into the economy and efficiency syndrome is that the middle class, having a distaste for welfare and those who may utilize welfare benefits during a good portion of their lives (rather than only on an emergency basis) are unwilling to see additional monies expended, even indirectly, to support corrupt life styles. Corrupt life styles involve, from this point of view, not working and depending for support on transfer payments from the public till. Middle-class values concerning life styles, personal income and employment for gainful ends reinforce the demand for economical and efficient governmental programs, especially in the area of welfare and public expenditures on the disadvantaged.

PROFESSIONALISM

The specialization required to deal with societal and organizational complexities induces us to consider many functions as requiring professional competency. This results in requirements for professional training for some administrative positions. For example, many public health directors hold M.D. degrees as a requirement of a position which is largely administrative. Such requirements are often accepted as logical and beneficial on the assumption that a professional in a given field can best deal with problems of that field. This is assumed to provide better administered public services. But as we shall see, the trend for professionalism can conflict with the development of consumer participation. The following three item definition serves to summarize the basis of professionalism.[14] First, professionalism is based on the authority of knowledge. This is specialized, not generalized, knowledge acquired through extensive specialized training. However, the fact that professional knowledge is specialized does not prevent people from equating it with general knowledge and superior intelligence. A favorite statement of new car salesmen is, "A number of doctors in town drive our cars," which evokes the status and intelligence attributed to M.D.s. Second, professionalism is service-based, person-to-person provision of expertise to solve specific problems. When an individual must meet critical needs, such as health, legal or educational requirements, he seeks assistance from a professional in these fields, requesting service on a one-to-one basis. This is not to say that professionals do not operate in group settings or on anything but a one-to-one basis, but generally their service is provided directly to consumers on a person-to-person basis. Third, the personal nature of the service provided by the professional requires interpersonal interaction involving trust and confidentiality. The client, patient, or patron places himself in the hands of the professional in the expectation and trust that the professional will base his actions on what is best for the consumer. A relationship of trust and confidence is assumed in the person-to-person application of professional knowledge.

One additional factor should be mentioned in identifying the parameters of professionalism. The traditional professions of law and medicine are often contrasted with the semiprofessions. (Theology and university teaching are also classified as traditional or full professions. One must question placing university teaching in this category as being self-aggrandizement by those who study and write about professions from university teaching posts.)[15] Although the traditional professions and the semiprofessions can be distinguished, present purposes are served by lumping together the traditional and the semiprofessions.[16] They all exhibit the authority of knowledge, a personal service base and interpersonal interaction involving trust and confidence between professional and client.

AN ORGANIZATIONAL FOCUS

Many of today's professionals are organization-based. They work in organizations and depend on organizations for their income. This seems natural and we expect it, given the organizational dominance of our society. The professional so employed is in a position to use his abilities in assisting the organization in its problem functions, and he is in a position from which he may find himself relating to a variety of clients and working on numerous problems, or individual cases, during a working day. In addition, he frequently works in an organizational setting rather than in individual practice, especially when considering public programs.

CLIENTS AS "CASES"

Under these conditions, the danger exists of the professional becoming task-oriented rather than person-oriented. Personal involvement takes time, and if the professional employee is expected to carry so many cases per day, per week, or per month, he may think of himself as having so many "cases" rather than people to serve and limit the time available for each. It may become necessary to treat people in an impersonal, abstract manner in order to accomplish the work at hand. Professional judgment may be invoked in determining what is best for the client with the client expected to depend on the professional for this determination. Add to this the complexities of bureaucratic rules and the client is put into a situation of dependency.[17] The situation is then ripe for patronizing treatment of the client, and the path of least resistance for the client may be to go along with such treatment, thereby reinforcing it.

Professionalism, when practiced in an organizational environment, can change the ideal of a person-to-person, confidential relationship of the professional and the client. The ideal professional relationship is one in which the professional helps the client with what the client would like to accomplish. In an organizational situation, the professional may have to serve organizations' wishes along with those of the client, diverting the traditional professional relationship. For example, the organization may specify that clients may be assisted in only certain ways and not in other ways, and it may require the professional to prescribe what action will be taken to meet certain problems without offering the client alternatives.

"YES SIR—YES DOCTOR!"

Many persons in professional roles, conscious of communication problems with consumers, can recall situations in which the consumer had been so conditioned to status differences between themselves and professionals that person-to-person communication was impossible. This condition is reflected in constant "yes sir," or "yes doctor" responses. If the professional attempts to break this cycle, the consumer, conditioned to expect abstract professionalism, may consider the professional to be acting "unprofessionally." Even the slightest sort of person-to-person communication, let alone participation, becomes difficult in such a patronizing environment. A situation of inherent inequality between the status of the professional and the dependency of the consumer hardly lends itself to the development of participation.

Smith cites the results of a survey undertaken for the National Advisory Commission on Civil Disorders to support the contention that condescending attitudes are prevalent in professional conduct in the public sector. Seventy-eight percent of urban social workers responding to the survey believed a major part of their responsibility was to "teach" the poor how to live.[18]

PROFESSIONALISM AS A BARRIER

Tolstoy, in The Death of Ivan Ilych, perceptively described the professional confrontation of a magistrate with an M.D.[19] Faced with serious illness, the magistrate recognizes, yet cannot surmount, another professional's patronizing manner and secretive attitude. This short novel should be required reading for all professionals in training.

Ivan Ilych recognizes the important air of the doctor double talk, the jargon, the impersonalness—"always in the same way, for everybody alike," professional correctness and interpersonal incompetence; and yet he accepts it. He knows his role, just as he would expect a prisoner in his courtroom to know his role. He cannot interact on a personal, person-to-person, basis with his doctor; he cannot participate in understanding, let alone in solving, what is in fact the beginning of his own death.

The phrase "always in the same way for everybody alike" is a perceptive statement of the ideal functioning of bureaucracy and points up the problem of professional services delivered in an impersonal manner. Professional service involving the ideal of service on a person-to-person basis is hard to maintain if professionalism itself, in the form of impersonal behavior, interferes with person-to-person interaction. Professionals operating in bureaucratic settings can easily become overly impersonal, employing the bureaucratic ideal of equal treatment and over using their professional "face." Like Ivan Ilych, the consumer can go along, saying at most, "We poor people probably often put inappropriate questions. But tell me in general—is there anything that can be done?"

We are so conditioned to the importance of professionalism that we use terms such as nonprofessional, paraprofessional or semiprofessional to distinguish those qualified in a field from those less qualified or unqualified. Even film reviews will note when a nonprofessional is involved in professional activities; "As Micol's grandmother, a non-professional named Inna Alexies turns in a superbly moving portrait of old age."[20] We do not expect a nonprofessional to participate professionally in a field reserved for experts, let alone do it superbly. The expectation in an age of specialization is that we will operate only in roles for which we are trained.

An additional factor to recognize is the tendency for professions to develop employment preserves. Control of access and entry to professional fields serves not only to help ensure high standards of service but also helps to limit the supply of a resource for which there is usually considerable demand. This helps keep prices up in the typical high-demand, low-supply situation. Protecting the client by maintaining high entry standards also protects the profession from deterioration of its economic position. An often cited example is the low output of American medical schools in relation to the need for medical doctors. Encouraging participation of consumers in organizations employing professional services conceivably could be seen as a threat to professional control of these professional matters.

THE CHALLENGE TO PROFESSIONAL AUTHORITY

Consumer participation, in asking professionals to share decision-making with consumers, questions professionalism's right to determine what is best for the client. Professional authority is coming to be less taken for granted in meeting social problems as professionals are not accepted as having sole authority, and their expertise is challenged as limited since they usually do not experience life conditions similar to those of the consumers of their services.[21]

This in itself may not be enough to bring about change but professional behavior is coming to be judged not only by consuming groups but also by professionals in other fields as they come to realize the shortcomings of their profession in dealing with complex, interrelated problems which cannot be solved by one profession alone. Outside judgment is coming from both consuming groups and other professional groups as they look at one another's work. This situation of increasing functional interdependence has been identified by Frederick C. Mosher who states, "As the focus of specialisms has narrowed, the boundaries around social problems have broadened and fuzzed. A consequence is that few professions can now claim total competence to handle basic problems even within those functional areas in which they once were recognized as exclusive monopolists."[22]

THE INEVITABILITY OF INTERACTION

This interrelatedness forces a rethinking of the interaction of professionals with one another and with clients. We can no longer assume a traditional role of authoritative expertise for the professional in social service matters. It may be more appropriate to look on the professional in social service organizations in a collegial sense—collegial not only with other professionals in the same field but collegial with consumers and with other employees of the organization. Professionalism may turn out to be less limiting to the development of consumer participation in public social programs than either bureaucracy or economy and efficiency because of the challenges to professionalism from consumers and from the professions themselves.

NOTES

1. It has been suggested that bureaucracies and middle-class values are very compatible and exclude lower-class (consumer) values. For example ... "minimum attention is given to socializing clients into the bureaucratic norms because bureaucratic norms run counter to (or at best ignore) lower-class norms and values." Gideon Sjoberg, Richard A. Brymer and Buford Farris, "Bureaucracy and the Lower Class," *Sociology and Social Research* (April, 1966), p. 330.
2. For a classic analysis of the Puritan attitude toward poverty and its impact on Western society see R. E. Tawney, *Religion and the Rise of Capitalism* (New York: Harcourt, Brace and Co., 1926).
3. Max Weber, "The Essentials of Bureaucratic Organization: An Ideal-Type Construction," translated by A.M. Henderson and Talcott Parsons, *The Theory of Social and Economic Organizations* (New York: Oxford University Press, 1947), pp. 329-40.
4. In the words of Robert Merton, "Adherence to the rules, originally conceived as a means, becomes transformed into an end-in-itself; there occurs the familiar process of displacement of goals whereby 'an instrumental value becomes a terminal value.' " Robert Merton, "Bureaucratic Structure and Personality," *Reader in Bureaucracy,* edited by Robert K. Merton and others (Glencoe, Ill.: The Free Press, 1952), p. 365.
5. Sjoberg, Brymer, and Farris, *op. cit.,* p. 335.
6. Merton, *op. cit.,* pp. 368-69
7. *Ibid.,* p. 369.
8. Victor Thompson, *Modern Organizations* (New York: Alfred A. Knopf. 1961), pp. 129-137.
9. Robert Michels, *Political Parties* (New York: Dover, 1959), p. 189. English translation first published in 1915.
10. *Ibid.*
11. Larry Kirkhart, "Public Administration and Selected Developments in Social Science." *Toward a New Public Administration,* edited by Frank Marini (Scranton, Pa.: Chandler Publishing Co., 1971), pp. 127-64.
12. Orion F. White, "The Dialectical Organization: An Alternative to Bureauc-

racy." *Public Administration Review,* XXIX, No. 1 (January-February, 1969), pp. 32-42.

13. Alan A. Altshuler, *Community Control: The Black Demand for Participation in Large American Cities* (New York: Pegasus, 1970).

14. William J. Goode, "The Theoretical Limits of Professionalization," *The Semi-Professions and Their Organization,* edited by Amitai Etzioni (New York: The Free Press, 1969), pp. 266-313.

15. Goode, *ibid.,* places theology and university teaching among the four great professions.

16. Etzioni, *ibid.,* p. vi, uses the term semi-professions for the newer professions. Weber, *op. ct.,* used the term "heteronomous."

17. Michael P. Smith, "Alienation and Bureaucracy: The Role of Participatory Administration," *Public Administration Review,* XXXI, No. 6 (November-December, 1971), pp. 658-64.

18. *Ibid.,* p. 661.

19. Leo Tolstoy, "The Death of Ivan Ilych," *The Death of Ivan Ilych and Other Stories* (New York: The New American Library, 1960), pp. 121-22.

20. *Time,* XCIX, No. 3 (January 17, 1972), p. 54.

21. S. M. Miller and Martin Rein, "Participation, Poverty, and Administration," *Public Administration Review,* XXIX, No.1 (January/February 1969), p. 21.

22. Frederick C. Mosher, "The Public Service in the Temporary Society," *Public Administration Review,* XXXI, No. 1 (January/February 1971), pp. 47-62.

Consumer Participation

CLAUDIA B. GALIHER
JACK NEEDLEMAN
ANNE J. ROLFE

Health affairs have been moving rather rapidly from a largely private affair to a matter of public policy. Accompanying that movement has been an emerging consumerism still largely without a defined role and function, largely without the acceptance and support of health professionals, and also lacking a base in the larger consumer body. In order to fulfill the potential of consumerism for changing and improving the health care system, it needs nurturing and developing by consumers themselves; but it also needs the support and encouragement of health professionals. Consumer input at all levels in all agencies is needed to develop a more effective and responsive health care system.

If one considers the mandates of various government health programs, they all depend upon a large pool of informed citizens in health affairs. It would seem logical, therefore, that an office of consumer health affairs be established at an appropriate level in government health activities. Comprehensive health planning, in fulfilling its mandate for a majority of consumers at the State level and for areawide agency boards

Reprinted with permission of HSMHA Reports V. 86, 1971, pp. 96-106.

to be similarly constructed, seems to have an especially high level of need for an informed consumer health constituency. Comprehensive health planning might, therefore, be encouraged to increase and broaden the thrust of its activities in consumer participation.

A multitude of factors are responsible for the rapidly emerging prominence of consumers in the health care system—higher educational levels of the general population, greater expectations derived from improved communication, a somewhat higher standard of living (or expectation of a higher level of living), and frustrations which develop when the demand and ability to purchase health services do not equal the ability of the system to supply services and frequently not the quality of service desired. Additionally, the slow growth in the development of new ideas and programs to meet increasing needs, the general cultural acceptability of "militancy," and the more political nature of health services today are all important factors in the emergence of the consumer role in health.

Consumer participation, especially in ghetto communities, has become an important force for change. In some cases, it is even perceived as a serious problem to professionals in the health field. The ghetto consumer has sought power within the very structure of the medical care system and demands a substantial role in policy development and a role in governing health care institutions. Because of the strength of these demands, sometimes backed by Federal money, and his insistence on change, the consumer on the one hand poses serious threats to the health professional and on the other hand provides the potential for improvements of health care in a relatively short time.

WHAT IS CONSUMERISM?

Consumer participation is citizen involvement . Citizen involvement in health is neither a new concept nor does it have a single objective. In the past, well-to-do members of a community gave their time, usually as members of boards or trustees of hospitals, to insure that the community had health care. Some ethnic groups provided institutions for care of their own people. In other related parts of the health system, such as health planning agencies and insurance plans, the "participating" consumers were, and still are in some cases, from the middle and upper classes of the community. They were chosen because of their position, money, and business knowledge. More recently, in some areas of the country the upper class businessman and the union leader have also been encouraged to participate.

Up to now, citizen board members have largely not encroached on the planning for the delivery of health services but have participated mostly in areas of lay expertise, such as fund raising. The health professional has largely dominated health-related decision making. Thus, who shall get health services, where they shall come from, and how they shall be provided rarely rests in the hands of the consumer. Professional satisfaction with a program rather than consumer satisfaction has been the measure of success.

Even in the neighborhood health centers of the Office of Economic Opportunity, where maximum feasible participation was mandated, an appraisal by Sparer and co-workers[1] showed that consumer involvement varied. Seven neighborhood centers were rated high in the degree of involvement (actual participation of the consumer group in policies, practices, and operational decisions), nine rated moderate, and 11 rated low.

Demand for consumer participation is arising mostly in ghetto areas and somewhat in middle-class areas and is devoted almost exclusively to gaps in health care and to dissatisfaction with service and with the manner in which service is rendered. Heretofore, these have been solely professional decisions. This involvement is both strong and frankly political. Whereas the fundraising role is almost dead, the new ghetto consumer has the potential to influence the direction of Federal and State moneys.

Early in 1969, President Nixon requested that the Secretary of the Department of Health, Education, and Welfare study the problems of Medicaid and related programs and make recommendations to improve these programs. By July of that year, a task force[2] was in operation.

It was determined very early that the problems of Medicaid or Medicare, or both, lay beyond the walls of such specific programs. Rather the problems existed within the current health system, and significant changes in our system of delivering care were required.

It was noted by the task force that "not only do millions of consumers get care on a hit and miss basis or lack access to care except in medical crises, but virtually all consumers lack access to the decision making machinery that can bring about change. Few institutions and programs include representatives of every day users of their services on policy-making or governing boards in spite of their non-profit and presumedly community character"[2].

A basic tenet of the report (and of this paper) is that "greater consumer involvement in decision making is required to overcome deficiencies in the health system . . . and to achieve better management of resources . . . without substantial consumer input, health institutions can become excessively self serving and, in fact, tangential to even fundamental community health problems. Also, without consumer input, user identity with service can deteriorate and inappropriate use can occur. Perhaps it should be added that, as in the management of other community institutions, for example, education, the fact that the consumer 'wants in' is a valid reason for involvement in its own right"[2].

Yet staff research in this area demonstrated no national means of providing the consumer the assistance he needs to become a positive force for the improvement of national health care services and no means for bringing the consumer and provider together to work jointly. This observation should not be interpreted to mean that in individual cases and in special instances consumers have not been in roles of power in the health system or that the consumer does not take part in health system decisions, but these instances are rare in the national picture.

WHO IS A CONSUMER?

"Who is a consumer" is frequently a cloudy issue. In recent deliberations of the Task Force on Medicaid and Related Programs, the consumer was defined as "any user of the health care system." Since users reflect certain social, economic, racial, and geographic characteristics, the task force recommended that a "participating" consumer must also reflect these characteristics [2].

In ghetto areas, as is true in other communities, not every person participates directly in programs affecting his community. The ghetto consumer is frequently represented by an organization whose leaders and most of whose staff originate from the immediate community. There may also be various volunteers (VISTA, and so forth) from outside the community as well as other part-time or full-time salaried staff and consultants from outside the community who act as advisers and who, in many cases, guide the community organization to action.

Consumer groups usually state that they are supported by the community and feel that they voice their discontent. In most instances, motives are good. They seek to improve health care in the community and, in many cases, they know what's wrong with a facility. They come, however, usually with little or no organizational capability and very little knowledge of health. These consumer groups are usually distrustful of the health establishment and in turn are usually not trusted by the establishment[3].

CHANGE

A variety of factors are moving us toward a greater role for consumers. The consumer role in three government programs—the Juvenile

Delinquency Program of the Department of Health, Education, and Welfare; O.E.O.'s Community Action Program; and more recently, the Model Cities Program of the Department of Housing and Urban Development—offers interesting comparisons.

Consumerism has evolved from a minor role in the public-private policy-shaping function of the Juvenile Delinquency Program's community leadership coalition to more significant participation in policy formulation in Community Action Program activities—and it has further progressed to a more dominant position in the Model Cities Program. This program sometimes places city government and black neighborhoods in adversary relationships, with each having a degree of independent authority over planning and program development.

The Juvenile Delinquency Program offered the "previously unheard" consumer what might be labeled token participation. O.E.O. programs were encouraged to achieve "maximum feasible participation." The Model Cities Program represents an evolution of the consumer role to a "must be heard" status both within organized neighborhoods and in its claims on the attention of city government.

More important, and specifically in the health area, comprehensive health planning requires at least a majority of consumer representatives on comprehensive health planning councils. In most cases, however, there is little evidence that mandating consumer participation has truly achieved the participation of consumers, especially the "previously unheard" consumer.

There are increasing attempts to permit consumers to participate in policy making at all levels. Even though not entirely successful, in many cases it has been realized that a board of trustees of a hospital made up entirely of persons who no longer live in a community usually cannot voice the needs and desires of that community. In his inaugural address as President of the American Hospital Association, Dr. Mark Berke said[4]: "For all of us, the question now is how to involve consumers in a meaningful way. We need to get some input from such groups, and to gain from them knowledge and understanding of our problems for these problems are, in the final analysis, the problems of the consumers."

In line with Berke's comments, the Catholic Hopital Association has recently issued a "Board of Trustees Guide" which stresses community representation as a desirable element in trustee membership[5.]

OPPORTUNITIES FOR PARTICIPATION

The Urban Coalition in its "Rx for Action"[6] has recommended "that information about the community, the various bodies in the community in which the people can participate *as members,* and the nature of organized efforts be catalogued and made available to all citizens, particularly neighborhood groups representing the poor." The Coalition has further suggested that this function could best be performed by the comprehensive health planning agency.

Opportunities for consumer participation in varying organizational settings with varying needs for policy determination, advice, technical assistance, monitoring, and evaluation postulate the need for consumers of varying sophistication and varying experience.

Figure 1 suggests that the experience needed to make appropriate inputs into a local hospital board, community consumer services committee, neighborhood health center, or voluntary agency differs from that needed to plan or advise on State or national programs; more important, perhaps the reverse is true. Hence, the Medicaid task force recommended that "organizations and institutions involved in planning, purchasing, and delivering health services should provide for majority consumer participation in deliberations on the nature of those services, and at least one-third of that majority should be made up of users of the health care program or facility involved"[2].

From this statement, it would follow that there are both broad and particular consumer interests to be considered; for example, the American Hospital Association's "consumers" would be both broadly representative of potential hospital users and might also include some recent actual users.

Opportunities for consumer participation might be looked at in the light of a "Chinese box" in which the most effective consumers emerge from a system which fosters their development.

Prewitt[7] uses the Chinese box to describe the process by which our political leaders are chosen, but his box might be adapted to a health-political system. Such a system would require that certain consumer functions be performed in behalf of those who receive health care at local, State, and national levels.

Figure 2 postulates a planned system of producing informed consumers chosen from all those who are served, phased through a series of experiences on varying levels, from which those who have the most to contribute and who have personal charisma would emerge.

The figure also postulates that each program will have its own consumer selection criteria based on functions as defined legally, by charter or bylaws. Also operating would be other selection criteria such as socioeconomic representation and the selective effect of personality and skill. As the opportunities for participation grow fewer, many are called but few are chosen.

Achievement of the status of health consumer leader or of top spokesman for health consumers at the national level could not happen without the experience, desire, and significant personal effort on the part of consumers.

Until consumer participation in health affairs is a more frequent and planned phenomenon, it would appear to remain haphazard in its development, depending upon those who have reached an awareness of their inequity of access to health care to bear the brunt of evolving a larger role for consumers. In "Rx for Action"[6], the Urban Coalition has suggested that encouraging and cherishing consumer participation in total is a necessary function of the planning process if change and improvement is to take place in health affairs. If, therefore, comprehensive health planning would undertake to strengthen the consumer's role in health affairs, development of this role might not remain haphazard. With councils and boards at the State and areawide levels required to have a majority of consumer representatives, comprehensive health planning agencies—more than any others—need experienced and effectively functioning consumers.

Planning dominated largely by the professional, as in the past, has not achieved its promise. Planning dominated by the consumer is too new to be measured against results. It seems obvious, however, that the degree to which the consumer discharges his perceived role, "help to identify problems and inadequacies in medical care, suggest solutions, and help to design and implement new policy will represent the degree to which change in health care is accomplished"[2].

DEGREES OF PARTICIPATION

There is a critical difference between going through the ritual of participation and having power to affect the outcome of the process. Arnstein[8] poses a ladder pattern of participation as one means of sorting out what is meant by participation[fig. 3]. The ladder postulates degrees of responsibility. Unless consumers have been designated responsibility or have assumed responsibility for outcomes in the decision making process, the full impact of their potential may not be realized.

STAFF SUPPORT

Experiences with community action programs, comprehensive health planning, and other groups indicate that the nature of staff support given to orienting board members (and consumer members specifi-

**Figure 1. Theoretical opportunities for consumer participation
at local State, and Federal levels**

Local	State	Federal
Planning and Coordination Functions		
Areawide comprehensive health planning	State comprehensive health planning	National Advisory Council on Comprehensive Health Planning Programs
Hospital planning	Hill Burton	Hill Burton
Other planning councils	Other planning councils	Other Federal advisory councils
Financing Functions		
Medicaid	Medicaid Advisory Committee	Medical assistance advisory committee
Medicare	Medicare Advisory Committee (some States)	Health insurance benefits Advisory Council
Private insurance	. . . .	Health Insurance Council
Prepaid group practices	. . . .	Group Health Association of America
Organization and Delivery Functions		
Hospital boards	Hospital associations	American Hospital Association
Nursing homes	Nursing home associations	American Nursing Home Association
Home health care	. . . .	(Proposed)
Neighborhood health centers	. . . .	Office of Economic Opportunity
Prepaid group practices	. . . .	Group Health Association of America
. . . .	. . . .	Veterans Administration
Indian health	. . . .	Indian Health Service
Migrant health	. . . .	Migrant health program
Regulatory Functions		
. . . .	Facility and personnel licensure	. . . .
Environmental health	Environmental health	Environmental health

Figure 1. Theoretical opportunities for consumer participation
at local State, and Federal levels — continued

Local	State	Federal
Voluntary and Professional Health Agencies		
Health and welfare councils	State councils	United Health Foundations, Inc. (non-Federal)
Medical society	State associations	American Medical Association (non-Federal)
Hospital association	State association	American Hospital Association (non-Federal)
Public health society	State association	American Public Health Association (non-Federal)
Voluntary health agencies	State association	National associations

cally) has much to do with the quality of consumer participation. Taking this factor into consideration, the Medicaid task force recommended that: "State and local government should establish staff capacity for inaugurating and promoting educational programs for consumers. Health care agencies including hospitals should also be encouraged to undertake similar activities. Licensing organizations that are working closely with health care institutions on other matters should assist these institutions in providing for consumer participation in policy matters relating to service"[2].

CONSUMER TRAINING

Many voluntary agencies have provided orientation programs for new board members with varying degrees of success. Since the development of programs requiring consumer participation, such as the neighborhood health center, Model Cities, and comprehensive health planning, more consumers are being given training. Such training has brought into focus a "new" consumer, not the familiar typical volunteer or yesterday's board member of the health agency. The low-income consumer appears characterized by a direct approach to problems, speaking out on issues, a lack of tolerance with professionals' methods of doing business, and intensely strong and personal involvement with the issues at stake.

Figure 2. The Chinese box — a pool of consumers

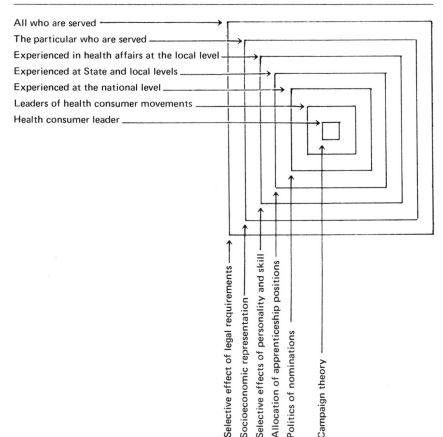

The degree of feeling and hostility which can be generated was reported in a study of the training program for consumers in policy-making roles in health care projects[9]. "Some felt that medical professionals unnecessarily asserted the sanctity of the medical professional. One board member quoted a doctor as saying to him, 'You better remember you are working with doctors, not a bunch of carpenters.' "

Professionals, generally, were criticized for using complicated, technical language to express simple points: "Professionals rattle off this hogwash; half the time I don't know what's going on." Or in the words of other board members, "Doctors can rattle on for hours; if you try to ask a simple question, they just take it and go on and on. We asked our

Figure 3. Arnstein's ladder of participation

8	Citizen control	
7	Delegated power	Degrees of citizen power
6	Partnership	
5	Placation	
4	Consultation	Degrees of tokenism
3	Informing	
2	Therapy	Nonparticipation
1	Manipulation	

director to stop using long words because we just don't understand"[9].

Moreover, "an effective representative board will always be involving new groups and its activities and the issues facing the boards are constantly changing." Training should not be viewed as a "one-shot stabilizing device but an ongoing process"[9].

EXTENT OF CONSUMERISM

Thus far, the thrust for greater community participation has had its major impact on the public school system. The community is asking for an unfreezing of that lethargic system administratively and politically and for a shift from peer accountability to community accountability. It has been suggested that the demand for accountability should lead to new methods of evaluation and quality control, integrating in a comprehensive way a variety of approaches. A further effect could be demand for active participation within the school system by teachers, students, and paraprofessionals. The major goals are to make institutions more relevant to the needs of the neighborhood and to make agencies more accessible and service more available.

A major hypothesis is that a strong community voice will sensitize the various human service institutions to potential neighborhood reactions, bringing about anticipatory reaction to community demand and producing a new and more responsive atmosphere and tone in the agencies. Whether this will happen remains to be seen. What is clear is that consumers are seeking ways to change human services.

While pointing out the impact that a community voice may have on the human services system, Reissman and Gartner[10] suggest that "bringing soul to the system does not necessarily improve its efficiency, though it may change its atmosphere and character; that the unfreezing of the equilibrium of human service does not guarantee improvement; it provides an opening for such improvement." The test remains ahead. To avoid many of the basic dangers, Reissman and Gartner call for specific policy changes at the national level, suggesting that local community interests must be connected clearly to larger national and international issues because the basic problems of our society originate and the basic control of resources lies at the national and centralized level.

PROVIDER TRAINING

Most, if not all, persons who see the need for shifts or changes in health care systems—aside from the problem of learning to work with consumers—suggest that there is a need for training professionals on policy-making and advisory boards. Parker, co-author of a report on training consumers in policy-making roles, states that professionals "have as much, if not more, need for training as the low-income consumer representatives"[9].

Little information exists with respect to the training of professionals to participate on policy-making and advisory boards. In many organizations, such as comprehensive health planning agencies at the State and areawide levels, orientation or board member training appears to be subsumed as part of an ongoing operation rather than an area which requires specific planning.

There is a wealth of material available on how to get a group to work together effectively. The degree to which such information is being used in specific situations when there has been no major thrust nationally to orient boards, neighborhood health centers, and comprehensive health planning groups is not documented. There are some clues, however.

In a series of informal interviews with CHP board members, one chairman of a CHP council indicated that, as the new chairman, he intended to seek out those members of the council least known to him and least vocal in the activities of the council and determine their interests and relevant experiences. If these interests are not expressed voluntarily, he plans to make an attempt to draw them out by providing an atmosphere in which they can express their views.

Another areawide CHP council first organized a consumer group, which in turn was given the responsibility for developing criteria for selection of provider members and orienting such provider members to perceived health needs. An advisory committee charged with reviewing grant applications recently suggested that all CHP agencies be required to submit annual reports on their orientation activities.

POTENTIAL FOR CHANGE

In some of its deliberations, the Medicaid task force panel concerned with consumer participation perceived the unique role of the consumer as being (a) to assure that decisions of policy-making health bodies are based on awareness of the needs and interests of consumers, (b) to provide a continuing liaison with the population served, and (c) to monitor the delivery of health services from the point of view of the consumer as to effectiveness and cost. It is essential to spell out the role of the consumer, both to enable him to fulfill his responsibility and function and to enable the providers to accept the consumers' input[11].

It is also essential to define precisely the unique role of the health professional in providing technical expertise. Similarly, it would seem useful to spell out those areas of joint responsibility for policy development and advisory activities. Furthermore, it would seem useful to differentiate clearly, in charges to boards and committees, their roles in decision making or their advisory activities.

Effective decision making by boards or committees does not come by accident. Consumer participation is but one aspect of a board's effectiveness. It can only happen if roles are clearly defined, if orientation to function is a continuing process, if staff have clearly defined roles to nurture it, and if the process is traceable in the activities of the agency at whatever level. What needs to be done to make consumer participation fulfill its potential seems clear. Whether it will get done remains to be seen.

ACCOMPLISHMENTS

It is too early to measure what the new consumerism is accomplishing in health affairs. Some impact is traceable but the lack of a clearly defined responsibility for consumer affairs in health by any agency hampers a full accounting. Some impacts are reported with irritation, other impacts with satisfaction. The interviews with comprehensive health planning agencies reported previously indicate that in certain councils consumers have been successful in moving consumer health problems to a higher priority. The National Welfare Rights Organization has recently been in a dialog with the Joint Commission on Accreditation of Hospitals, pointing to a consumer role in hospital affairs. Advisory committee members of O.E.O. neighborhood health centers have formed a National Patient Rights Organization which has announced and is promoting a consumer manifesto. Medicaid task force staff members report that most organizations and agencies in the health field are talking about consumer participation. Consumer organizations have been formed to undertake functions which existing organizations would not.

Whether consumer participation in health will remain a spotty, little known entity or whether it will become a full-fledged element of a changing political and organizational scene which is more responsive and relevant in all human services remains to unfold. What is clear is that the health professional needs the consumer to achieve a relevant and responsive health care system.

REFERENCES

1. Sparer, G., Dines, G. G., and Smith, D.: Consumer participation in O.E.O. assisted health centers. Amer J Public Health 60: 1091-1102, June 1970.
2. Report of the Task Force on Medicaid and Related Programs. U.S. Government Printing Office, Washington, D.C., 1970.
3. Wilson, J. Q.: Planning and politics: Citizen participation in urban renewal. American Institute of Planners Journal 29: 242-249, November 1963.
4. Berke, M.: The president's inaugural address. Hospitals 44: 61-70, Mar. 16, 1970.
5. Board of trustees guide. Catholic Hospital Association, Chicago, 1970.
6. Rx for action: Report of the Health Task Force. The Urban Coalition, Washington, D.C., October 1970.
7. Prewitt, K.: From the many are chosen the few. American Behavioral Scientist 13: 169-187, November-December 1969.
8. Arnstein, S.R.: A ladder of citizen participation. American Institute of Planners Journal 35: 216-224, July 1969.
9. Meisner, L., Parker, A., Austin, L., Orr, C., and Ortega, M. .L.: A training program for consumers in policy-making roles in health care projects. School of Public Health, University of California, Berkeley, May 1970.

10. Reissman, F., and Gartner, A.: Community control and radical social change. Social Policy 1: 52-55, May-June, 1970.
11. O'Donnell, E.J., and Chilman, C. S.: Poor people in public welfare boards and committees: Participation in policy-making? Welfare in Review 7: 1-10, May-June 1967.

Consumer Participation in Health Planning: Toward Conceptual Clarification

G. M. HOCHBAUM

Consumer participation, which has its roots in concepts and ideas advanced and stressed for many years by behavioral scientists, health educators, and others, has suddenly become the focus of attention by the other health professions. As is the fate of many such newly discovered concepts, it is being greeted with attitudes ranging from total rejection and dubious caution to overoptimistic enthusiasm, and is embraced by some as though it were a poisonous snake, by others as though it heralded an era of social harmony and of perfect health services for all.

No careful and objective student could fail to recognize that this concept holds both great promise and many risks, and that it has to evolve through many trials and mutations before it will emerge in forms which lend themselves to any real assessment of its worth. Then, and only then, will it be possible to evaluate its strength and its weaknesses, and its ultimate contributions to the health and welfare of our communities. The final result will be either to discard it altogether, or—more

Reprinted with permission of The American Journal of Public Health V. 59, 1969, pp. 1699-1705.

likely—to adopt it with some modification as a method which under certain conditions, and for certain purposes, can help to realize at least some of the hopes we now place into it.

But it behooves us at this time of our initial and often clumsy trials with this approach not to be swayed either by exaggerated expectations or by hostile rejection—both born of emotional bias—but to observe and evaluate it rationally and with all the knowledge and tools available particularly from the behavioral sciences. It is especially important at this stage to analyze the social processes that take place in the interaction between the groups that confront one another in "consumer participation"—the representatives of the "consumers" and the representatives of the health professions—for it is in this interaction where the hazards lie, but also where help with the achievement of our goals may be found.

I would like to discuss certain problems which frequently arise in this interaction.

CHANGES IN OUR SOCIETY

We have witnessed over the past few years some radical changes in the structure and nature of our society. Segments of our population, which until recently have played a passive role, are demanding full and equal access to all the resources and services that our society is capable of providing—many of which these people have been at least partially deprived up to now. I am thinking primarily of our urban black population, of other minorities, and of the poor in general. We have been trying to respond to these demands by making more and better health services available to them by locating health centers within their neighborhoods, and by removing economic barriers for the utilization of health resources and services.

If accessibility of sufficient high-quality health services to the disadvantaged were the only issue at stake, these steps should logically be able to satisfy the demands of these disadvantaged as long as we carried them out effectively and on a large scale. But accessibility is not the only issue. Indeed, it is not even the most important issue.

Behind these demands by our disadvantaged citizens, and behind their demands for better educational job opportunities, and for a voice in the affairs in our society—behind all of these demands lies an awakened and steadily growing need and desire to live, to feel like, and to be treated as fully equal citizens of our society.

For a person with such a need and such a desire it is not enough to be given what he wants. He feels an urge to have something to say about *what* is given, *where*, and *in what ways* it is given. He wants to know that he has at least some control over such things which, after all, affect his health and welfare and his very life.

Therefore, some kind of participation in health planning—or for that matter in planning for a variety of other community programs—is of great importance to many of these people for its own sake, as a visible symbol of their equal human rights, quite apart from the more tangible beneficial health results that may stem from such participation. But this fact tells us also that it is not enough for the authorities to patiently listen to the views and ideas expressed by the representatives of the people before the authorities reach decisions—even when these decisions take such views and ideas into account.

DEMAND FOR PARTICIPATION

To put this differently: The demand for participation in planning on the part of the disadvantaged (especially of the more vocal and militant segments) cannot be satisfied for long if we offer them merely a platform to express their views but reserve the right for final decisions for ourselves. Their demands can be satisfied only if they feel that they share in the decision-making process itself. Failure to satisfy these demands can have very serious consequences not only for health services themselves, but equally for community politics and race relations.

It is this question of sharing in the *decision-making process* (rather than of merely participating in planning discussions) which is a potential source of problems and friction. The reason is that each of the two groups which confront one another—the health professionals and the spokesmen of the consumer population—may bring different and conflicting attitudes and expectations to their joint meetings. The health professionals probably feel that *they* are the experts when it comes to people's medical care needs and to methods for meeting these needs. They may be willing to listen to the consumer spokesmen, and even to make allowances for some of their special wishes and preferences, but are often unlikely to give up their own authority to make final decisions even on these wishes.

The consumer spokesmen, on the other hand, may feel justified in claiming a far greater slice of the issues to be decided than the professionals are inclined to yield. As mentioned earlier, these spokesmen may view the confrontation with the professionals and authorities as a test for their newly won political and racial ambitions, extending far beyond their more limited desire to merely assure better health services for their people. Therefore, they may demand and expect a share even in decisions concerning aspects which they are not equipped to judge and handle, although they may be fully aware of this lack of competence. For example, in one such actual case, consumer spokesmen insisted on certain types of medical personnel to be on duty in a planned neighborhood health center in order to be ready at any time to provide medical care for certain specific medical problems. The health professionals rejected the demand. They argued that such problems occurred only relatively rarely, that even when they did, they would not represent emergency cases, and that they could be handled more efficiently by referring patients elsewhere. These arguments fell on deaf ears despite their obvious soundness. A great deal of hostility was aroused on both sides. The health professionals were perplexed and angered by the apparent unreasonableness and stubborness of the consumer representatives, and the latter saw the episode as evidence that so-called "consumer participation" was just a cover-up for continued refusal of equal health services for the black community.

What had actually happened was this. The consumer spokesmen honestly believed, though erroneously, that all health facilities in the more affluent white communities have such personnel and offer such medical services. As far as these spokesmen were concerned, they only demanded the same for their own clinic. In other words, the question of whether such services were actually needed was really irrelevant to them. But they attached great importance to these services as symbols of equity with the more affluent white society.

In the light of this, the strategy by the health professionals in the planning group would have been better if they had not argued against the demand only on the basis of its medical virtues or lack of virtues. An attempt should have been made to demonstrate to the consumer representatives the fact that health facilities in affluent white communities do *not* as a rule have such medical personnel and services, that those patients who require such services are usually referred elsewhere, and that therefore the demand was not justified *on the basis of the concept of equity.*

NEED FOR COOPERATION

This somewhat oversimplified example illustrates the frequent and disruptive problem that arises when two such groups look at the same issue from two quite divergent points of view without being aware of this fact. While the health professionals are usually primarily concerned with the medical care aspects and argue their own views on the basis of *medical care* considerations, the consumers are equally or more concerned with the *social, political,* and *racial* aspects and argue their case correspondingly, usually to the irritation and total consternation of the professionals in the group. Unless the fact is understood by the latter, and unless they learn to cope with it, much time can be lost, a good deal of hostility can be aroused on both sides, and the end result may be very disheartening.

The example also illustrates a second problem that should be anticipated and understood. As pointed out earlier, the spokesmen of our disadvantaged population groups, especially the more vocal and militant spokesmen of our urban black communities, demand to an increasing extent a real and substantive role in the actual decision-making process. In fact, they often demand to be *the* ones who make the decisions and regard the health professionals as persons whose job it is to meet these demands merely by making their skills and competencies available. This view is of course in conflict with the views of even those generally flexible and liberal professionals who are perfectly willing to allow the lay sector in the planning group to make all sorts of decisions on nonmedical and nontechnical matters, but who still reserve professional and technical decisions for themselves.

Alan Mayers has used "decisional territory" to describe the scope of issues on which a given group lays claim for being entitled to make the decisions. The two sectors in the planning group—the consumers and the professionals— each bring their own decisional territories to the confrontations. One can visualize these territories graphically as two overlapping circles. One encompasses all the issues for which the professionals claim the sole right to make decisions since they feel such decisions require special expertise which only they possess. The other circle contains all the issues for which the consumers claim the right to make decisions. The area formed by the overlapping of the two circles represents the potential battleground because both groups lay claim to it.

Such an overlap of the two decisional territories is probably unavoidable and must be expected. Sometimes it may be reduced if the two groups succeed in reaching some prior agreements as to the boundaries of their respective territories. But this solution is not always feasible and does not always work.

It is very important and necessary for the professionals to understand *why* lay members of the planning body insist on determining technical issues which they are clearly not equipped to judge. In this confrontation between consumers and providers of health services, the burden of understanding the other and the burden of exhibiting the skills and the often superhuman patience and tolerance necessary to cope with such conflicts, rest clearly primarily with us, the health professionals.

TRAINING CONSUMERS AND PROFESSIONALS

It is on *this* point that I slightly disagree with those who place their emphasis on needs to train merely the consumer representatives in planning skills, on certain technical aspects of the health area, and in other related matters. Without denying the need for such training, we must place still greater emphasis on the need to train the *professionals* so that they develop the understanding and skills required for resolving the conflicts inherent in such confrontations.

Let me summarize the main points made so far:

1. We must recognize and accept the fact that it is the *consumers* of health services who are the final and proper judges of what kinds of services they want, how they want them delivered, what form they should take, and in what setting they should be provided. It is only on the medical and other technical details that the health professions have any exclusive right to make decisions. This leaves, of course, the gray area of overlap which is the primary source of conflict.

The main problems arise from two facts. The first is that the health professions have traditionally usurped the absolute right to be the final arbiters on *all* issues pertaining to health and are usually unwilling or unable to surrender this right. The second fact is that because of the emotions engendered by the social and racial revolution, consumer groups are often unable or unwilling to accept even reasonable limits to *their* decisional territory and therefore demand at least symbolic rights to make decisions also on some issues beyond their competency.

2. It has long been a basic principle of health education that the people with whom we work should be involved at early stages of planning. But today's vogue of "consumer participation" has primarily grown out of political rather than educational concerns. It is seen as a means to help the disadvantaged guide their newly emerging aggressive demands for equal rights and greater power into constructive channels and to calm our restive communities.

We have learned from work in industrial psychology that participation of employees in management decisions does hold the promise of more ready acceptance of managerial innovations. Also quite plausible claims for greater utilization of health services following consumer participation in the planning of such services have been made in several instances. Yet I know of no really convincing or even persuasive evidence that such consumer participation is resulting in health services which are any better and more effective than health services that are planned by professionals who make a concerted effort to learn about, understand, and appreciate the characteristics and needs of the people to be served. In fact, I suspect, that often the opposite is true. Joint planning by consumers and providers can easily lead to compromises between conflicting opinions, to dilution of standards, and thereby to *less* adequate services. Nonetheless, we must first find ways to accomodate the political, social, and racial issues and to satisfy these reasonably well in the eyes of our target population. To the extent to which we succeed in this, we should be able to develop a better basis for constructive consumer participation in planning with diminishing conflicts on the respective decisional territories. To repeat, we must deal with the social, political, and racial issues *before* we can generate the proper attitudes on *both* sides for more effective joint health planning.

PROBLEM OF COMMUNICATION

There is still another problem which seems to arise whenever a group of people—whether they come from the consumer population or from the professional sector—get together to discuss the subject of consumer participation. This problem is one of communication and stems from the fact that the term "consumer participation" has been used freely and carelessly to describe a wide spectrum of modalities of the underlying concept. A short time ago I witnessed a rather heated and prolonged dispute over the desirability or undesirability of such consumer participation. After a while it became clear that each member of the group was talking about a different thing although all used the same term. When each person was asked to write privately on a piece of paper what his concept or mental image of "consumer participation" was, and the several responses were compared, this fact was dramatically brought home, and resulted in a much more orderly and productive discussion from then on. In fact, to everyone's surprise, there was much less real disagreement than the preceding discussions seemed to reflect.

The question, then, as to what consumer participation really means, needs constant clarification and, in turn, gives rise to other highly important questions.

For example, what is meant by "consumers"? Are consumers only those who obtain services within a given delivery system, or also those who do not, yet obtain their services from some other delivery system such as the private sector of medicine? Do we include as "consumers" even those who do not yet, but hopefully will obtain services at some later date? Does the term "consumer" apply *equally* to the individual with a broken finger who comes to a clinic into which he has never set foot so far and probably will not set foot again for a long time if ever, as well as to the individual who conscientiously comes for his yearly check-up in addition to seeking medical advice whenever appropriate reasons exist? If we include any other persons, in addition to those who *actually* obtain health services from a specified delivery system, the term "consumer" has a misleading connotation and should be dropped.

What do we mean by "participation"? If consumer representatives are permitted to express their needs, wishes, and complaints but the decisions as to what to do about these rest with the professionals, is this participation? Or does the term imply an actual sharing of decision-making power?

The term "consumer participation" implies the selection of spokesmen for the consumer population. Who are they to be and how are they to be selected? Should they be the more educated and knowledgeable members of the population, those who are likely to bring the best understanding of the issues involved to the planning? If so, can they be selected by the lay population or must they be identified on the basis of their qualifications as determined by professionals? Are the better educated and more affluent members of, say, the urban black ghetto really true representatives, or are they almost as far removed from the people for whom they are to speak as are the professionals themselves? Or should these representatives be selected from the very segments of the population which heretofore have been its most disadvantaged? If so, would they not be so uneducated, so naive about health services and about planning, and so incompetent as to be unable to contribute meaningfully to the planning? Moreover, would attempts to communicate between them and the professionals be so difficult as to be almost futile?

ANSWERS AND OBJECTIVES

These are only some of the questions with which we need to struggle. Each of them may have one best answer or it may have several answers depending on context and situation. The trouble is that in discussions on consumer participation each person carries with him a certain image of his concept of the term—an image that is a mosaic of his own private and implicit answers to these questions and one that may be different from that of some others in the group. It is not always necessary to resolve all such differences and reach complete consensus as to any one specific set of answers. But it is necessary for each person in the group to make his own "image" explicit in order to avoid the confusion of a dialogue in which similarities and differences between persons' concepts are obscured by everyone's use of the same but undefined terms, thereby giving rise to apparent but not necessarily real agreements or conflicts.

A very similar problem is often generated by the question of *why* we should advocate consumer participation in the first place. What are the objectives which we try to pursue by it, what specific purposes is it to serve? Is it to bring about more effective delivery of more appropriate and better health services through assuring their greater accessibility to those who find it difficult now to obtain such services? Is it to assure that the services provided are in accord with the needs and desires of the consumer population *as felt by them*? Or do we aim at larger goals of which the actual delivery of health services is only a part? For example, do we hope that consumer participation will lead to a greater awareness of health matters on the part of the population, to increase motivation to improve their own health status, to a spilling over of the educational effects of the services provided into the realm of people's personal health habits and practices? Do we also see consumer participation in *health* planning as an effort coordinated with participation in planning for housing, education, job training, and other community problems, and leading to the political, economic, and social motivation of population groups which have heretofore been relatively passive, naive, and helpless in the face of the community power structure? Is there also the more or less implicit hope that such participation will lead to a calming of the increasing turbulence in our restless cities?

Depending on one's views of these goals and purposes, different approaches, methods, and procedures in consumer participation will have to take prominent positions. Especially when the question of evaluation is raised, different criteria and measurements would be appropriate, and disagreements concerning these may be less a function of disagreements concerning the values of the several possible criteria and measurements than a function of disagreements concerning goals and purposes. Again, if these latter remain only implicit and are not explicitly clarified, it will be difficult if not impossible to discuss such matters rationally and to reach consensus.

SUMMARY

The problems discussed in this paper are only a few of those that must be considered. They have been selected for attention because I believe them to be fundamental and crucial to the future of consumer participation. The concept of consumer participation in the planning of consumer health and welfare programs, while not new, is only now entering into the arena where the future of our society is being forged. As we struggle with the concept itself and with ways of translating it into operations, we must be sensitive to the fact that we are treading on uncertain ground and are groping for new ways of dealing with problems as old as human history. Precipitous commitments to specific solutions can have exceedingly serious consequences. We must be willing to analyze and evaluate on a continuous basis both the concept and its various operational counterparts as they change with time and experiences; and we must do so in the light of theoretical considerations as much as against the purposefully planned accumulation of reliable observations and concrete data.

It is this last requirement—that of rigorous, factual, and objective study and evaluation—which I believe to be of paramount importance. It is here where social scientists should and can make their most significant contributions because the question is predominantly a social and not a medical one.

I do not mean to imply by this that an evaluation of biomedical results is not also needed, but the process by which such results are to be achieved is a social one of which the actual medical procedures are only a part. In fact, when we look at some of the most disturbing health problems of the disadvantaged such as, for example, infant mortality, there is considerable evidence that they have social and behavioral components that contribute more to these problems themselves than the biomedical components. Thus the effectiveness of health services dealing with such problems must be assessed against consumers' behavior as well as against such traditional measures as the number of people treated or reduction in morbidity and mortality among consumers.

Thus the importance of social science to an evaluation of consumer participation, as a means to improve health services and the welfare of our communities in general, is beyond doubt. But social science can make constructive contributions only if social scientists approach the questions raised in this paper as true scientists who are objective and nonpartisan—whatever their own personal feelings are about the disadvantaged and about the nature of the political, economic, or social issues involved. And they can make such contributions only if they are permitted to carry out objective, nonpartisan studies, and if the results are considered by the health and the political leadership—even if these results should run counter to preconceived notions and to wishful thinking.

Social scientists represent, of course, not the only professional group that can play this role, and they cannot do so without close cooperation with other professions. Nonetheless, they probably come closest to meeting the professional and technical requirements for reliable and objective investigations both of the concept of consumer participation in the planning of health services and of the various operational systems based upon it. But whoever may carry out such scientific investigations, these are desperately and urgently needed. Only with their help can we hope to learn whether, under what conditions, for what ends, to what extent, and in what forms the concept of consumer participation has real social value, or whether its continued encouragement will bring about a chain reaction which may intensify other problems or even generate new ones in our communities.

After all, it is entirely possible that out of our present, often fumbling experiments with the concept, there will emerge elements of more effective health services delivery systems. On the other hand, we must guard against welcoming the concept precipitously out of a feeling of frustration, even of futility concerning our present systems, much as a cancer patient—whose confidence in legitimate medical resources has been shaken—may turn to Krebiozen merely because it is claimed to have some special healing powers not possessed by traditional medicine.

It must be admitted that as of now the tendency to embrace consumer participation in planning and especially in decision-making is not based on much demonstrable and objective evidence as to its actual results. But too much is at stake to allow this trend to continue unchecked unless and until we have more factual knowledge on which to judge and plan a development which could irrevocably change our health care and even our entire social system.

Citizen Participation
and Professionalism:
A Developmental Relationship

FELICE PERLMUTTER

The discussion of citizen participation in policy-making, centered largely on the experience of publicly funded community programs, has raised many questions, has yielded less than satisfactory results, and has clearly indicated that the rationale for citizen involvement has been confused and frequently pragmatically or opportunistically determined (Kubey, 1970).

Furthermore, as human services have shifted in emphasis from a total concern with individual adjustment to an added concern with institutional change, much attention has been paid to the implications of this shift vis-a-vis manpower utilization. While much of the initial discussion centered on community organization programs in social work, the impact of this shift, both philosophical and practical, subsequently affected the wide spectrum of human service agencies both in the voluntary and public sector. As a result of the antidelinquency and poverty programs new professional roles were identified, such as enabler, broker, advocate, activist (Grosser, 1965). A second major concern

Reprinted with permission from *Public Welfare* V. 31, 1973, pp.. 25-28.

was the utilization of nonprofessionals, and the literature is replete with discussion of the new careers programs. While the original interest was largely related to the assumption regarding the effectiveness of having people serve as helpers who were close to or had themselves experienced the problems of the client population (Perlmutter, 1965), a second and not unimportant aspect was the value of the service for the helping person himself (Reissman, 1965). In addition, the manpower implications of the new careers programs were of importance from the public policy point of view.

This paper will discuss the relationship between the nonprofessional and the professional, with a focus on the issue of citizen participation. The central thesis is that the respective roles of and relationships between the nonprofessionals, as policy makers, and the professional staff are not static and permanent but must be viewed dialectically. The experience in social welfare will be used to support the argument which is analytically framed by a model of social agency change (Perlmutter, 1969).

LAY INVOLVEMENT IN POLICY PLANNING

The involvement of nonprofessionals on the policy level in social welfare antedates the existence of the profession itself. The fact of concerned citizens organizing welfare services for various groups in need is too well documented to require further discussion. The important point to be made, however, is that the major pattern adopted in the United States is one of noblesse oblige, in which citizens involved in the formation of social agency programs have traditionally been from the upper class; the literature calls attention to the participation of high-status citizens as the lay group involved in policy formation (Ross, 1953). A tension exists between the layman and the professional; boards are viewed as instrumentalities primarily concerned with the fiscal operation of the agency and not for their knowledge of the particular agency's technical competence which is viewed as the professional's appropriate concern (Auerbach, 1961). The consequences of this historical pattern was the establishment of a static relationship between the lay policy makers and the professionals within a traditional context of service which led to the following formulation:

" . . . professionals must not become 'captives' of their clientele and surrender to them the power to determine the nature of the service offered (Blau and Scott, 1962)."

However, the social programs of the 1960's raised the urgent question concerning the participation of citizens in the planning of their own programs and hopefully is the legacy left by these programs (Levitan, 1969). The old roles and relationships were no longer acceptable whereby the professional unilaterally offered a service to the client; the involvement and participation of the constituents were essential.

The experience of self-help organizations provides an important field of study and can serve as a corrective to this traditional stance. There has been little examination of the experience of self-help, mutual-aid organizations as relevant to the development of professional services. The major lesson to be learned from these organizations concerns their use of professionals: *technical experts are used for specific problems as determined by the membership* (Katz, 1965, 1970). Furthermore, it is quite clear that in mutual-benefit associations (such as unions, fraternal organizations) the group is organized by the membership to meet its own interests; policies and procedures are determined by the group itself through its elected representatives. These examples of participatory democracy are consequently of heuristic value.

Since the involvement of the lay community in policy-making is traditional in social work, the major current issue in this field consequently is not the form of participation, advisory or policy-making, but rather who are the lay people and what is their role. A theoretical model of agency development accommodates important elements of both the service and the mutual-benefit organization but a differentiation in emphasis is made, appropriate to the agency's stage of development.

DETERMINING LAY AND PROFESSIONAL ROLES

An historical evolutionary model of social agency development posits three developmental stages in the life of a social agency: self-interest, professionalism and social interest. The model assumes an open system and views the agency in its social-environmental context. While the model specifies eight variables as crucial to an understanding of the agency, the variable of interest in this presentation is the "organizational elites," defined as consisting of the nonprofessionals as the lay policy-makers, and the professional staff. This theoretical model suggests that the role of the two groups of elites will vary according to the stage of development of the agency as follows.

In the initial self-interest stage the elan of a social movement exists as a group of citizens respond to unsolved and pressing social problems, frequently related to a subgroup that is not accorded equal treatment. The participation of the elites in this stage most approximates that of the self-help, mutual-benefit organizations with their emphasis on the specific needs and problems of their members. The lay board of directors is in a singular position of power for a variety of reasons: first, it has been instrumental in the formulation of the service and its definition of its mission; second, it is prestigious in relation to the community whose support is being sought; third, it selects the first administrator and staff with the intent of a clear-cut implementation of the agency's objectives in handling the pressing social problem.

Conversely, the position of the staff is weak because of the organizational requirements at this stage. The creativity and aggressive innovation rests with the board, whereas the staff operates as implementers of the agency's service. The question of professional competence is of less importance than the commitment and concern to get the job done; educational experience and training are accordingly given less attention than in the subsequent stages. For example, agencies for retarded children, primarily concerned with delivery of service rather than with quality and standards, frequently utilize nonprofessionals for their staff (Katz, 1961).

By contrast, the second stage of professionalism occurs when the pressing external problem has abated and the agency can now focus on the quality of its service, an internal rather than an external orientation. Because of the emphasis on the technical problems, the function of the elites reverses as the lay policy group *chooses* to give the ascendant role to the professional staff. The professional staff, using a body of knowledge and professional skill, operates relatively independently of the lay board of directors. (It is during this stage that the displacement of organizational goals is most likely to occur, as the professional focuses on techniques.)

The social interest or third stage of agency development occurs again within the social-economic context of the larger society. A new social problem arises directly related to that which stimulated the formation of the agency and requires that the agency reassess its position vis-a-vis the larger community. It can either remain internally and professionally oriented (and fixated), or it can respond to new and urgent needs of the broader system. The requirements of the elites again change in response to the different emphasis: the lay participants on the board must now again be actively involved in decisions related to a new definition of agency mission, and cannot leave the professionals in charge.

It is crucial that the lay members of the board be selectively recruited to help the agency move into each successive stage. While pressure from external groups is important for this development as part of the changing environmental context, an elite *inside* the organization must provide the stimulus for internal change.

A relationship is thus postulated between the developmental stages of the organization and its utilization of elites.

> It seems evident that the proper assignment of personnel and the diagnosis of administrative troubles will gain from a better understanding of the relation between personnel orientations and organization life history. . . . The selection of key personnel requires an understanding of the shift in problems that occurs as the organization moves from one stage of development to another. And for best results the participants should be able to recognize the phase through which they are passing. (Selznick, 1957).

If an evolutionary model of social agency development were part of the knowledge base of the professional in understanding the organizational context of his practice (just as developmental personality theory underlies an understanding of the client), the role of the professional would be appropriately conceptualized and more comfortably performed. The issue of client control would not pose a problem since the role of the professional would be related to the developmental needs of the organization. Thus, in the self-interest stage the professional would be the instrumentality through which the client's objectives would be fulfilled, a relationship clearly established in self-help organizations. The lay board could then choose to move the agency system into the second, professional, stage if a more sophisticated service were desired.

For example, a community-organized medical clinic in its first stage of development would be concerned with meeting the basic needs of its community on a quantitative basis and would not wish to leave the decisions regarding the distribution of services and the organization of the program to the physicians. Once the basic needs were met and the structure of the services established, however, the needs for higher quality care would require greater professional authority.

The central point is that the stage of development of the agency would determine the appropriate role of its elites, both the policymakers and the professionals. Rather than becoming a competitive venture based on power and conflict the choices would be more analytically and rationally determined in terms of agency direction and change.

DILEMMAS AND ISSUES

The utilization of past or potential consumers of service in self-help groups on both the policy and service delivery level has been important in retaining the vitality and flexibility of these organizations. However, it must be noted that the groups have usually been organized around specific problems of individuals at risk and are treatment oriented (e.g.,

Association for Retarded Children, the Polio Foundation). The utilization of these elites in agencies oriented to social and institutional change has not been sufficiently explored to justify assumptions of effectiveness.

Mogulof (1965) has suggested that lay participation in policy bodies is related to the commitment of social work to institutional change and that if "American social work will revert to the concept that presses for personal adjustment . . . rather than structural change . . . the poor will no longer be chosen for boards. . . ." This assumption must indeed be systematically tested since there is some evidence in the literature that, in fact, the opposite relationship obtains.

For example, in the San Francisco Neighborhood Legal Assistance Foundation, a Federally financed, community-controlled legal service agency, a conflict emerged between the radical white lawyers of the central office who were committed to social change and the black lawyers in the neighborhood offices who were focused on meeting the individual claims and grievances of the community clients.

> The goal of community control had been institutionalized in the autonomous neighborhood offices, while the aim of institutional change was embodied in the Main Office legal staff. It was obvious that the growing antagonism between the two structures in large measure represented a conflict between the two goals. The lawyer-founders had been wrong in assuming that control by the client community was a necessary condition, let alone compatible with a program of institutional change. . . . (Carlin, 1970).

Consequently, this evolutionary model facilitates the selective recruitment of lay people based on the requirements of the agency's stage of development. Whereas the first stage of self-interest requires that the lay group which determines the mission of the agency is the ascendant elite with a vested interest in the program, the role and participation of a different group of members for lay policy-making is required in the second stage of professionalism. Similarly, in moving to the social-interest change orientation of the third stage, a more "cosmopolitan" group of policy-makers is suggested in contrast to the "local" orientation of the earlier group.

Another issue must be raised: does a program conceived, organized, and operated by professionals under public funding follow the same developmental pattern? Specifically, can the role of lay citizens be the same as that of the elites in the self-help tradition? The tension in many of the public programs (e.g., Community Mental Health Centers) can be elucidated by an application of the theoretical model as follows: whereas the community expectation is one of participation appropriate to the first, self-interest stage of organizational development, the professionals in these programs are operating in the context of the second stage of professionalism. There is an incompatibility of roles and relationships in these two different stages; consequently, an understanding of the organizational requirements would help define appropriate role performance.

CONCLUSIONS

Our rapidly changing field of human service places great demands on all parts of the system as a variety of strategies are required to meet its objectives. While decisions regarding the utilization of lay people and professionals have been haphazardly made and frequently dysfunctional to the service developed, a theoretical model of agency change can serve as the basis for decision-making in regard to the complex issues relating to policy formulation and service development.

NOTES

Arnold J. Auerbach. "Aspirations of Power People and Agency Goals," *Social Work,* Vol. 6, No. 1 (January 1961).

Peter M. Blau, and Richard W. Scott. *Formal Organizations* (San Francisco: Chandler Press, (1962).

Jerome E. Carlin. "Store Front Lawyers in San Francisco," *Transaction,* Vol. 7, No. 6. (April 1970).

Charles F. Grosser. "Community Development Programs Serving the Urban Poor," *Social Work,* Vol. 10, No. 3 (July 1965).

Alfred Katz. *Parents of the Handicapped* (Springfield, Ill.: Charles C. Thomas Press, 1961).

Alfred Katz. "Application of Self-Help Concepts in Current Social Welfare," *Social Work,* Vol. 10, No. 3 (July 1965).

Alfred Katz. "Self-Help Organizations and Volunteer Participation," *Social Work,* Vol. 15, No. 1 (January 1970).

Sumati N. Kubey. "Community Action Programs and Citizen Participation: Issues and Confusions," Vol. 15, No. 1 *Social Work,* (January 1970).

Sar A. Levitan. *The Great Society's Poor Law: A New Approach to Poverty* (Baltimore: John Hopkins Press, 1969).

Melvin B. Mogulof. "Involving Low-Income Neighborhoods in Antidelinquency Programs," *Social Work,* Vol. 10, No. 4 (October 1965).

Felice Perlmutter and Dorothy Durham. "Using Teenagers to Supplement Casework Service." *Social Work,* Vol. 10, No. 2 (April 1965).

Felice Perlmutter. "A Theoretical Model of Social Agency Development," *Social Casework,* Vol. 50, No. 8 (October 1969).

Frank Riessman. "The Helper Therapy Principle," *Social Work,* Vol. 10, No. 2 (April 1965).

Aileen D. Ross. "The Social Control of Philanthropy," *American Journal of Sociology,* 58 (1953).

Philip Selznick. *Leadership in Administration* (Evanston, Illinois: Row, Peterson and Co. 1957).

Representational Standards in Comprehensive Health Planning

RICHARD D. EVANS

INTRODUCTION

Since 1961 when one of the earliest "consumer majority" recommendations for areawide health planning boards appeared in a widely circulated report, the health industry and other segments of our society have progressively extended this form of "democracy by hierarchic fiat."* Such efforts to extend the principle of interest group involvement at all levels and for new types of activities, including planning and administrative as well as general policy-making, have been the center of considerable debate as to their effective results. These developments, and the innovations in federal, state, regional, and local relations that are presently emerging from the "New Federalism," suggest the continuing need for systematic analyses of this policy issue.

*The initial emphasis was, of course, on health facility planning. See Reference 1.

Reprinted with permission of *The American Journal of Public Health* V. 64, 1974, pp. 549-556.

This report describes selected results of an empirical, comparative study of the application of federal and state policies in seven areawide and 10 subarea comprehensive health planning organizations.† These organizations were formed following the passage of the Comprehensive Health Planning and Public Health Services Act of 1966 (P.L. 89-749), in which Congress established comprehensive health planning as a federally supported activity. Comprehensive health planning integrates physical, mental, and environmental health services planning at all jurisdictional levels through a "partnership" of consumer-provider and governmental-private interests. The areas included in this study range from the highly urbanized New York City, to a primarily rural region with a relatively small urban population. Extensive data were collected on the characteristics and roles of approximately 540 areawide comprehensive health planning board members, and a somewhat reduced range of data on 246 members representing 10 "subarea" boards (county jurisdictions in this instance) within a single comprehensive health planning area. The average areawide board size was 77, with a range of 55 to 125. The subarea boards averaged about 25 members each.

Before proceeding to the analysis, however, it is important to place the concern for representational "standards" in its broader context: the creation of areawide comprehensive health planning (CHP) agencies and the specification of organizational and program standards can be interpreted as an attempt to implement social-structural change at the regional level of the Federal system. Robert Mayer has suggested that such change can occur in three interdependent ways:[2]

- When the group of actors, among whom the basic roles and statuses are allocated, is significantly changed;
- When there is a change in the combinations of roles, through obsolescence or an introduction of new roles into the social system; and/or
- When there is a redistribution of rewards and obligations among the various roles within the social structure.

Further, social-structural change may occur either at the macro or micro levels. At the macro level the constituent elements that are changed are the region's component social structures or subsystems. At the micro level, the constituent elements are individuals.[2] The development of comprehensive health planning illustrates each of the three modes of social-structural change, and at both the macro and micro levels.

†The areas included in the analysis are located in New York State.

As suggested above, the focus of this paper is limited to three rather fundamental policy issues arising from the attempt to create social-structural change in areawide comprehensive health planning organizations. Specifically, to what degree is the combination of actors who are represented in the system at the micro level consistent with the hierarchically imposed standards? That is, have the representational policies actually been implemented, and, if not, what are the problem areas? Second, what effect can regional decentralization, in the form of subarea comprehensive health planning boards, be expected to have on local compliance with these policies? And finally, what patterns of representation could be expected by relying on local discretion and eliminating existing federal and state policies (as in certain elements of the New Federalism)?

The answers to these questions do not, of course permit a final judgment as to the net impact of such policies on the program outputs of the areawide comprehensive health planning process. Later analyses from this study will, however, provide empirical data on the relationship between formal representation and the actual participation and influence of the different types of board and staff members, including the minority/disadvantaged, physicians, hospital representatives, environmentalists, local government officials, and others.

THE STANDARDS

Congressional legislation and the administrative regulations of the federal Comprehensive Health Planning Service, require each areawide agency to establish a council or board whose membership shall include representatives of local government, hospitals (including Veterans Administration hospitals) and other health care facilities, practicing physicians, home health care, the appropriate Regional Medical Program, and the consumers of health services. In addition to requiring that a majority of the board (or council) and its Executive Committee be consumers, "the council shall be generally representative of all geographic portions and socioeconomic groups, including the minority groups, of the area."[3]

The Region II office of the Comprehensive Health Planning Service has operationalized the latter standard by informally recommending a minimum of 20 per cent minority and/or disadvantaged representatives on the council or board. The 20 per cent standard is based on a position paper issued by the Region II Regional Health Advisory Committee. The stated rationale was that "representatives of disadvantaged populations ought to be present in numbers sufficient to have an impact upon deliberations beyond that of token participation."[4] The 20 per cent proportion was presumed to be the minimum "threshold" at which this would occur.*

Finally, in an attempt to assure compliance with the full intent of the comprehensive health planning legislation, the New York State Health Planning Commission† has further elaborated the representational standards which areawide agencies in that state must meet. In order to prevent dominance by any one group, no greater than 20 per cent of the board membership can represent any single major sector of the health care system. And, to assure the adequate inclusion of local government, mental health and mental retardation, and environmental health, each of these groups must be represented by at least 10 per cent of the Board.[5] Both federal and state regulations allow a single board member to represent more than one interest group, however.

CONSUMERS AND PROVIDERS

The relationship of an individual to the health system, and thus his perceived constituency, is defined most broadly in terms of whether he is a "consumer" or "provider" of health services. Federal administrative regulations define consumers as persons "whose major career occupation is neither the organization, financing or delivery of health services, nor the teaching of or research in health sciences."[3] The "consumer majority" requirement has been the only numerically specific representational standard in Congressional legislation. It has been suggested that the language found its way into the 1966 legislation during a review session with a U.S. Senator. When observing the general statement regarding consumer representation in the draft bill, he asked "Why not a consumer majority?"‡ Since the civil rights movement and the antipoverty program had set in motion heightened expectations for citizen participation, and established health and welfare organizations were

---

* Later reports from this study will empirically test this assumption.

† This state-level comprehensive health planning agency was created by the Governor pursuant to section A of Public Law 89-749, and is thus often referred to as the "A" agency. Areawide agencies are provided for in Section B of this Act, and in the parlance of the field are referred to as "B" agencies.

‡ Florence Fiori, Director of the Region II Office of Comprehensive Health Planning Service, is the source of this information.

increasingly supporting the concept, there apparently was no compelling reason to debate the point.§

Several issues were observed in the areawide agencies' application of the consumer majority criterion, however. Those to be discussed here include the constituency implications of the voluntary affiliations of a board representative (e.g., who does a consumer, who is also a hospital trustee, represent?); the constituency implications of a representative's location in the "organizational hierarchy" of his or her occupation; the reluctance to accept environmental professionals as "providers" of health services; and the use of an ex officio membership category which falls outside the present federal and state representational specifications.

The constituency implications of a board member's other voluntary associations have already received much attention and the arguments need not be detailed here. One of the assumptions underlying "consumer" representation in health decision-making is, of course, that "providers" tend to use restrictive decision criteria—such as institutional maintenance and occupational self-interest—which at times will be in conflict with the application of more consumer-directed decision criteria. This problem arises quite naturally as a result of their own immediate self-interest and the direct or indirect influence of their "significant others." The debate over whether a member of a hospital board of trustees or the president of a hospital auxiliary is a consumer or provider centers on how strictly one wishes to apply this underlying principle of the policy.

The present federal definition of a "consumer" is clearly limited to a consideration of occupation, and it thus includes such members as the hospital trustee and the hospital auxiliary president if their major occupation is not health administration, research, or teaching. And, the comprehensive health planning agencies in this study fully embraced this interpretation—to the extent that 11 per cent of those board members informally perceived by agency staff as representing hospitals on the CHP Board were nevertheless classified as consumers (on the basis of occupation) in the application of the consumer majority standard. The data from this analysis indicate that those perceived as representing

---

§ The political winds were not all blowing in the same direction, however. During that same year (1966) the Green amendment responded to the complaints of city governments and granted them the option of taking over the private nonprofit community action agencies which typically ran the antipoverty programs. Also, the model cities legislation of that year pointedly called for "widespread citizen participation," not "maximum feasible participation" as specified in the Economic Opportunity Act of 1964, and it explicitly recognized the final authority of city hall. See Reference 6.

hospitals but also classified as consumers included mostly members in business occupations—commerce, manufacturing, and finance. The remainder were in non-remunerative positions such as an unemployed woman hospital trustee; or a retired person with strong affiliations with the local hospitals, including in one instance a retired hospital administrator.

The second constituency question arises from the location of a board member in the organizational hierarchy of his occupation. For example, a Commissioner of Social Services in New York State has responsibility for major health-related programs such as Medicaid. While some agencies classified such representatives as providers, others interpreted his location in the organizational hierarchy to be sufficiently removed from such activities as to warrant his classification as a consumer representative on the comprehensive health planning boards.* Similarly, a governmental program coordinator responsible for major health services was classified as a consumer representative by one agency.

Third, even greater discrepancies existed in the agencies' application of the consumer definition to environmental professionals—perhaps at least partially a result of the general uncertainties involved in the environmental dimension of the comprehensive health planning formula. The manager of a local water board, an environmental lab professional, a city engineer, a consulting environmental engineer, and other such professionals were often designated as consumer representatives.

As a percentage of each agency's membership, the total number of the latter two types of "marginal" consumer-provider classifications ranged from 0 to nearly 6 per cent. The agency average was 2.8 per cent, and in one case these members were sufficiently numerous to cause the consumer proportion to fall to less than 50 per cent of the board.

A much more serious source of variation among agencies was found to arise from the use of ex officio memberships, however. Federal and New York State policies did not include this type of member in their representational guidelines. Five of the seven areawide agencies therefore utilized this membership classification, with the ex officio membership ranging in size from 2 to 56 per cent of the regular memberships of these agencies.

Further, since eight of every 10 ex officio members were found to be providers (and none were ethnic minority and/or disadvantaged), the

---

* One agency designated a white Commissioner of Social Services as a consumer representing the minority/disadvantaged.

impact of such a membership category on the required "consumer majority" was very substantial for several of the agencies. For example, including all members in the analysis caused one agency's reported "60 per cent consumer majority" to drop to a "45 per cent consumer minority!"

MINORITY AND/OR DISADVANTAGED

The areawide comprehensive health planning agencies' performance in the inclusion of ethnic minority and/or disadvantaged members† was, despite a great deal of rhetoric on this issue, quite poor. Somewhat surprisingly, even according to the areawide agencies' own classifications (obtained from staff interviews) and excluding ex officio members, only two of the seven agencies met the 20 per cent informal standard set by Region II, and one was as low as 7 per cent. The average proportion for the seven agencies, including ex officio members, was 14 per cent.

Further analysis indicates the expected predominance of consumers in the category of minority/disadvantaged—88 per cent were consumers, with an individual agency range of 83 to 100 per cent. Alternatively, one might examine the status of the minority/disadvantaged within the consumer and provider groups taken separately: approximately one-quarter of the consumers were minority/disadvantaged, compared to 3 per cent of the providers.

Given the informal position of the Region II Comprehensive Health Planning Service that lower socioeconomic groups should be represented on the boards directly and not merely by upper income "advocates," in this study's determination of disadvantaged representation the agency staffs were asked to designate specifically those members that they considered to be economically disadvantaged personally. Also, since all agencies are required to include a brief vita on each member in their applications for federal funding, the "occupational status" of nearly all of the agency members was determined. This variable is an attempt to measure one dimension of the status of an individual in the social structure. The procedure is to assign a status "rank" of one through seven to a person's occupation, based on a detailed guide developed by August Hollingshead.[7,8] For example, a bank president or

---

† Note that this "and/or" category includes any member who is either an ethnic minority (American Indian, black or Spanish-speaking), or economically disadvantaged, or both. The "and/or" convention is frequently dispensed with in referring to the "minority/disadvantaged."

TABLE 1. Economic Status by Occupational Status for Areawide Agencies

Occupational Status*	Reported Economic Status†					
	Advantaged		Disadvantaged		Totals	
	No.	%	No.	%	No.	%
High						
1	243	54	3	7	246	49
2	164	36	13	28	177	35
3	38	8	16	35	54	11
Midrange						
4	8	2	5	11	13	3
5	0	0	2	4	2	0.4
6	0	0	5	11	5	1
Low						
7	0	0	2	4	2	0.4
Totals	453	100	46	100	499‡	100

*As interpreted from members' curriculum vitae.
†As classified by agency sources.
‡This survey represents 93 percent of the 540 board members of the seven areawide agencies.

a physician would receive a rank of one; middle managers and lesser professionals a two; small business owners and voluntary agency staff who are not professionally trained or are of low organizational status are assigned a rank of three; clerical workers a four; skilled manual workers a five; semi-skilled workers a six; and unskilled laborers the lowest rank of seven.

Comparing the occupational status of the areawide members designated disadvantaged with the remaining members (the "advantaged"), then, one observes an expected pattern of divergence (Table 1). Only 7 per cent of the disadvantaged are found in the top occupational rank as compared to 54 per cent of the advantaged.

On the other hand, viewing these data from a different perspective, further examination indicates that fully 70 per cent of the areawide members designated as economically disadvantaged by agency sources are in the upper three of the seven occupational status levels. Since income is expected to be positively correlated with occupational status, this suggests that as many as 70 per cent of those members designated as economically disadvantaged may in fact represent middle and upper income families.

While specific cases can always be cited such as the white Commissioner of Social Services "representing" the minority/disadvantaged, fortunately it is possible to pursue this seeming paradox more systematically by examining the actual income levels of those "disadvantaged" members who responded to a mail questionnaire sent to all board members (see Table 2).* Of the 18 "disadvantaged" members in this sample (see Population Breakdown B, Table 2), 17 were consumers and one was a provider (see Breakdown C). Of the 17 consumers, 13 were minority and four were of majority ethnicity (D). The single provider in the sample designated as economically disadvantaged (C) was of minority status.

Finally, proceeding to Breakdown E to examine both the "social class" and the "household incomes" of these 18 members, it is discovered that few are in fact economically disadvantaged. Over one-third of these members are in the upper two social classes (occupational status and education combined). And, individual household incomes of these members range from $4,000 to $40,000, with most $13,000 or more!

Since middle to upper class blacks predominantly "represent" the minority/disadvantaged,† with few lower class blacks or whites as CHP members, the question arises as to the role of "white middle class America" in the comprehensive health planning process. In the political arena, this numerical "majority" has, of course, received special attention recently. If it is assumed that occupational staus levels three, four, and five (see Table 1) generally comprise the middle class,‡ it is apparent that only 14.4 per cent of the total CHP membership falls into this category. Of these, one-third are minority and 7 per cent are providers. Thus, despite their numerical predominance in the citizenry at large and increasing importance politically, only 9 per cent of the total membership are middle class white consumers.

---

* Since Hollingshead's index of social class will also be included in the socioeconomic profile of these members, the sample in Table 2 will necessarily be restricted to those members who not only indicated their approximate household income, but also their years of education on the questionnaire. The social class index has been developed by Hollingshead as a combination of the person's occupational status and his educational rank. The procedure is to weight the occupation and education variables seven to four, respectively. Then, after adding the two numerical quantities, the result is classified into four categories of "social position"—I, II, III, and IV. Here the term "social class" is substituted for "social position" as it is more commonly used.

† The actual proportion is 72 per cent.

‡ Level two would therefore generally comprise the upper middle class, level one the upper class, level six the lower middle, and level seven the lower class. These are, of course, only rough approximations.

TABLE 2—Socioeconomic Characteristics of the "Disadvantaged"

Population Breakdown

A — Total Population

B — Economic Status
- Advantaged
- Disadvantaged (n = 18)

C — Consumer-Provider Status
- Consumer (n = 17)
- Provider (n = 1)

D — Ethnicity
- (under Consumer) Majority (n = 4)
- (under Consumer) Minority (n = 13)
- (under Provider) Majority (n = 0)
- (under Provider) Minority (n = 1)

E — Individual's Social Class / Household Income

Consumer — Majority (n = 4)

Individual's Social Class	Household Income
I	$13,000
III	6,000
	4,000
IV	4,000

Consumer — Minority (n = 13)

Individual's Social Class	Household Income
I	$25,000
	40,000
	25,000
	25,000
	17,500
	13,000
	13,000
III	17,500
	17,500
	10,000
IV	6,000
	10,000
	6,000

Provider — Minority (n = 1)

Individual's Social Class	Household Income
III	$17,000

OTHER COMMUNITY INTERESTS

As already indicated, the involvement of other specific community interests in comprehensive health planning has been of concern to both federal and state policy-makers. The representations of local government, mental health and mental retardation, and environmental health were considered sufficiently problematical by the New York State Health Planning Commission to warrant an explicit policy of 10 per cent minimum board membership for each. Home health care and Regional Medical Program representations have been subsequently required by Congressional legislation, although the "consumer-majority" criterion has been the only Congressional standard with an explicit numerical minimum.

While concern for a minimally acceptable threshold of representation for these groups has been voiced, the 1970 federal regulations also warn that the board should "not be weighted toward any one (interest), such as hospital administrators, public health officials, or private practitioners."[9] And the New York State regulations operationalize this caveat by placing a "20 per cent maximum" limit on the representation of any single major sector of the health care system.

In order to allow a fully comparative perspective, an assessment of the community interests with which each of the 540 areawide board members was most closely associated was made using a fairly detailed classification scheme (Table 3). Provision was also made for second and third representational classifications for each board member where such were felt to be significant—we therefore are able to provide the "cumulative" representation for each group.

These data were collected from interviews with upper level agency staff. The tabulated results were therefore not subjected to the usual "numbers game" wherein secondary membership classifications are carefully evaluated to ensure a multidimensionally "balanced" membership roster. That is, if you need a home health care representative to meet the federal requirement, but your total board membership is at its maximum, the solution might be to find someone (perhaps already on the board) who can be classified as representing two or more interests, one of which is home health care.

First, considering those community interests whose adequate representation is considered problematical by federal and state authorities, it is apparent that the areawide agencies have had particular difficulty in integrating the environmental health and home health care elements into the representational mix. Environmental health's cumulative board representation was only 4.3 per cent. Interestingly, this pattern was

TABLE 3—Representation of Community Interests

Community Interest	Cumulative Representation*
	%
Business	7.4
Commercial	3.0
Manufacturing	3.3
Finance and insurance	1.1
Church-related	1.7
Civic associations	1.5
Communications media	0.7
Community-at-large	8.9
Education	10.6
General	6.4
Medical schools	2.0
RMP	2.2
Environmental health	4.3
Foundations	0.2
Government	7.6
Central executive	3.9
Legislative	3.7
Health facilities (major)†	13.3
Hospitals	10.7
Long term care	2.4
Health insurance	1.7
Health professions	19.0
Physicians	11.1
Nurses	2.0
Dentists	1.9
Other professionals	3.9
Paraprofessionals	0.2
Health services privately organized	0.6
Housing	0
Judiciary	0.4
Labor unions	3.1
Lawyers (organized)	0.7
Mental health and mental retardation	6.3
Planning/coordination/fund raising	10.6
Health facilities	1.5
Development or "comprehensive"	4.3
Social (general)	4.3
N.Y.S. Health Planning commission	0.6
Political party	1.1
Public or community health	7.0
Education emphasis	1.7
Services and education combined	4.8
Home care primarily	0.6

Public safety	0
Social Services/welfare/group work	4.6
Sociocultural groups	13.5
Elderly	0.7
Minority and/or disadvantaged‡	12.4
Rural	0.4
Youth	0

*Each figure was derived by dividing all designated member representations by a base of 540 total areawide members. Since one member may represent up to three different interests, the total will not equal 100 per cent. Note also that the reference here is to "representation," not occupation. Ex officio members are included.

†Includes unspecified health facility representatives.

‡Includes representatives from neighborhood health centers and freestanding clinics, model cities, OEO community action programs, and other groups generally representing minority and/or disadvantaged interests. In this classification schema the members were not specified as minority/disadvantaged themselves, however.

reflected in the agencies' inattention to environmental health programs, as well, and the lack of staff specialists in the environmental area. Home health care was a negligible 0.6 per cent, with only three of the seven agencies designating a member as representing such interests. Also the representations of the other mandated community interests, local government and mental health and mental retardation, are below New York standards.

Contrariwise, the representations of the physicians and hospitals are substantially greater. These groups constitute an average of approximately 11 per cent each on the boards, for a total of 22 per cent.

Including all health-related professions together, their representation totals 19 per cent. Similarly, aggregating hospitals, long term care institutions, health centers and clinics, health facility planning, and hospital insurance groups, we find a health facility contingent of approximately 18 per cent.

Finally, including medical school and Regional Medical Program representatives with health professionals would result in an areawide proportion of 23 per cent for this group. Including these representatives with the broadly denied health facility interests would result in a total of 22 per cent for the latter.*

* The New York State Guidelines define a "major sector of the health care system" more narrowly than this, however. Certainly these subgroups would not be expected to present a unified position on most health issues.

Comparing these comprehensive health planning board representations to the population mix as a whole, the 1970 Census of Population reports approximately 1 per cent of all New York State employed persons 16 years old and over as "physicians, dentists, and related practitioners," and 1.7 per cent other (nonpractitioner) health professionals and technicians.†

SUBAREA BOARDS

Five of the seven areawide agencies studied either had subarea (county or district) boards or councils, or they were in the process of developing such. This analysis included 10 such boards in one area, with a total of 246 members. Nine of the subareas are predominantly rural, while one contains a major metropolitan complex. Here we will briefly summarize these data in terms of the issues raised above.

The subarea boards clearly demonstrated a more substantial commitment to the spirit of the "consumer majority" policy, with an aggregate consumer proportion of 59 per cent as compared to 50.2 per cent for the areawide agencies. No subarea board utilized the ex officio membership classification—whereas five of the seven areawide agencies had used this device, and in some cases as a means of securing more providers on the board.* As for "marginal" consumer-provider classifications, the same rate was found for the subarea boards as for the areawide boards—approximately 3 per cent.

The subarea board members are substantially lower in average occupational status and income than the areawide board members. For example, 22 per cent of the subarea members are middle class white consumers, compared to only 5 per cent of the respective areawide agency members. And, while the subarea members report an average family income of $18,000, the respective areawide agency members average a rather remarkable $40,000!† It is apparent that the characteristics of the subarea board members more closely approximate the characteristics of general population—the "grassroots" constituency, if you will.

Despite the subarea boards' much stronger commitment to con-

---

† Health administrators are not included in these figures, however. See Reference 10.

* It should be remembered, however, that while 10 subarea boards are included, these were all within one area. Since the areawide agency for this area did not utilize the ex officio category, other groups of subarea boards would need to be included in order to generalize about this variable.

† The sample size for the subarea members is 75, and the sample size for the areawide agency members (relevant to these subarea boards) is 38.

sumer dominance (at least numerically) and their lower occupational status and income, the minority/disadvantaged fared only slightly better at this level in absolute terms. Nine per cent of the subarea members were perceived to represent the ethnic minority and/or disadvantaged, as compared to 7 per cent for the respective umbrella areawide agency, and an average of 14 per cent for all seven areawide agencies.

SUMMARY AND CONCLUSIONS

We have attempted to evaluate certain aspects of the local experience with the representational policies established by both federal and state governments. The results of this analysis at least partially document the nature and extent of the difficulties encountered with these standards at the local level, and the adaptive mechanisms that are consequently utilized.

A "consumer majority" was found to be only a tenuous reality for most areawide agencies when the twin issues of consumer definition and ex officio membership were considered. And in one extreme case, a "60 per cent consumer majority" was reduced to a "45 per cent consumer minority" when the provider-dominated ex officio members were included.‡

While the reported representation of minority and/or disadvantaged groups fall well below the Region II "20 per cent" recommendation, the real poor (especially low income whites) are found not only with an inadequate quantity of representation, but a representation that largely relies on middle and upper income members presumably serving as benevolent intermediaries, or (at best) "advocates" for the disadvantaged. Individual household incomes of those members designated as economically disadvantaged ranged from $4,000 to $40,000, with most $13,000 or more.

While the Region II Comprehensive Health Planning Service informally advocates the "direct" representation of the poor, and the 1970 federal regulations specify that, with regard to all interest group representatives, an "effort should be made to ensure that they indeed represent those interests,"[9] this study indicates that in actual practice the poor have generally not been represented by poor people at the areawide level of comprehensive health planning.

Furthermore, although the subarea boards demonstrated a stronger commitment to the "consumer majority" concept, and subarea members more closely approximated their "grassroots" constituency in terms of

---

‡The actual roles of the ex officio members will be analyzed in a forthcoming report.

occupational status and income, in absolute terms the minority/ disadvantaged fared only slightly better at the subarea level than at the respective areawide level.

It is suggested that the subarea's moderate level of minority and/or disadvantaged representation is largely explained by the lower level of urbanization, and consequent lower proportion of ethnic minority population in the predominantly rural subareas in question.§ For most comprehensive health planning boards, the ethnic minority groups are heavily depended upon for "disadvantaged" members since: (1) poor whites have been less likely (proportionately) to become involved in comprehensive health planning; and (2) white middle class agency staff are more likely to incorrectly classify middle class minority persons as economically disadvantaged.

Table 2 above provides some evidence for the latter conclusion (see Population Breakdown E). As for the observation regarding poor white involvement, it was found that only 3 per cent of all areawide agency members represent "poor whites," while twice that number of board members represent poor minority persons. This sharply contrasts with a statewide population ratio of nearly two poor whites for every poor minority person.

Since fewer ethnic minority residents are available for comprehensive health planning membership in the outlying subareas, the above factors would tend to restrict the relative representation of both ethnic minorities and the disadvantaged at the subarea level. Further, the lower average status and income on the subarea boards would tend to make the economically disadvantaged more difficult to identify. Despite these factors, the subarea boards did report a minority/disadvantaged representation of 9 per cent, as compared to the respective areawide proportion of 7 per cent. Relatively speaking, then, the subarea minority/ disadvantaged representation exceeds that of the respective areawide agency by a substantial margin.

The conspicuous lack of middle class white consumers in the respective areawide agency, only 5 per cent, is also found to be significantly improved at the subarea level with 22 per cent.

The conclusion suggested by these data is, then, that the policy of encouraging subarea organizations can offer some very tangible results in increasing the representation of "all geographic portions and socioeconomic groups, including minority groups, of the area."

---

§ The average minority population for those counties outside the major metropolitan center of the region is 2.4 per cent, as compared to 7.9 per cent for the central county and 17.6 per cent for the central city. See Reference 11.

Finally, the effect of local discretion in determining what interests will be represented on the areawide comprehensive health planning boards can be assessed from two vantage points. First, examining the one membership category not covered by federal or state policies, eight of every 10 "ex officio" members were providers. Second, substantial disparities were observed in the areawide agencies' compliance with both the letter and the spirit of existing guidelines—and these were consistently in the direction of continuing the dominance of the traditional health system interests.

A frequent observation of those familiar with other community change efforts is that "the prevailing forces in a community capture new programs."[12] While such a conclusion cannot be established without a careful examination of the actual participation and influence patterns in comprehensive health planning, the representational patterns described above give cause for serious skepticism.

Furthermore, the data presented on the workings of local discretion suggest that the prospects for such an arrangement achieving the goals embodied in federal and state representational policies are not reassuring.

REFERENCES

1. Joint Committee of the American Hospital Association and the Public Health Service. Areawide Planning for Hospitals and Related Health Facilities, p. 14. U.S. Government Printing Office, Washington, D.C., 1961.
2. Mayer, R. R. Social Planning and Social Change. Prentice-Hall, Inc., Englewood Cliffs, New Jersey, 1972.
3. U.S. Federal Register, Vol. 37, No. 160, p. 16619. August 17, 1972.
4. Willie, C., Noroian, E., Simms, G., and Harris, J. Why and How to Involve People of Disadvantaged Circumstances in Governing Boards of Comprehensive Health Planning Agencies. April 23, 1969 (mimeographed).
5. New York State, Health Planning Commission. Federal-State Guidelines for Operational Grants for Comprehensive Health Planning. March 26, 1968 (mimeographed).
6. Marris, P., and Rein, M. Dilemmas of Social Reform: Poverty and Community Action in the United States, Ed. 2. Aldine Publishing Company, Chicago, 1973.
7. Hollingshead, A. Two Factor Index of Social Position. Privately published, New Haven, 1957.
8. Hollingshead, A., and Redlich, F. Social Class and Mental Illness, pp. 398-407. John Wiley and Sons, New York, 1958.
9. U.S. Department of Health, Education, and Welfare, Public Health Service, Division of Comprehensive Health Planning. Project Guide for Areawide

Comprehensive Health Planning: Policy Statement and Information for Applicants. January, 1970.

10. Bureau of the Census, Census of Population: 1970. General Social and Economic Characteristics, Final Report PC (1)-C34. Table 54. New York.

11. U.S. Bureau of the Census, Census of Population: 1970. General Population Characteristics, Final Report PC (1)-B34. Table 16. New York.

12. Marshall, D. R. The Politics of Participation in Poverty, p. 75. University of California, Berkeley, 1971.

RESEARCH ON CONSUMERISM

If the phenomenon of consumerism in the health care sector is to be fully understood, measures of the participation process must be developed and studies which employ these measures executed. The articles presented in this section present methodologies and report on completed studies.

Anderson and Kerr observe citizen groups associated with Model Cities programs. They measure the degree of consumer involvement and responsibility and the content of meetings by observation and review of relevant documents. Characteristics and attitudes of participants are also examined. Relationships between participants and group activities are suggested.

Partridge and White present a methodology which focuses on consumer input into allocative decisions of neighborhood health centers. Topics discussed at joint consumer-staff meetings are coded and analyzed to exclude non-allocative discussions. Limitations of the analytic approach are presented.

Douglass attempts to show relationships between participants' organizational affiliation and their attitudes within the decision-making process. Data have been collected by personal interview and content-analysis of minutes.

Sparer, Dines and Smith take advantage of a nation-wide data base but have to rely on a simpler measurement system than other studies. They are able to record patterns in the organization of consumer groups, the role of staff support, and the extent of participation.

Metsch and Veney show relationships between three levels of concern. They create three variable categories: the social context of the program, structural aspects of the advisory boards under study, and outcome measured by the level of consumer-provider interaction and administrative response. Relationships between these variable sets are demonstrated with a multiple regression technique.

Citizen Influence in
Health Service Programs

DONNA M. ANDERSON
MARKAY KERR

INTRODUCTION

Citizen participation in decision-making about the provision of
health services is not a new concept. In 1917 an attempt was made in
Cincinnati to incorporate a complex plan of community participation in
the actual governance of a health center and other community services.
Even earlier efforts, though limited, can be found around this period in
several other cities.

During the 1950s the concept of citizens participating in decision-
making reappeared in the urban renewal programs. It became more
widespread through the Juvenile Delinquency and Youth Crime Programs and the Ford Foundation gray area projects in the early 1960s and
OEO Community Action Programs authorized by Congress in 1964. As
evidenced in the literature, increased citizen participation was accom-

Reprinted with permission of The American Journal of Public Health, V. 61, 1971, pp.
1519-1523.

panied by confusion, doubt, conflict, and dissatisfaction on the part of both consumers and providers.

In order to learn more about citizen participation, the Institute for Interdisciplinary Studies has undertaken an exploratory study of citizen participation in decision-making in the delivery of health care services. We directed ourselves to three questions: Do consumers of health services actually participate in decision-making? What is the nature of that participation? What is the relationship of certain external factors to the nature of participation? The study, as a part of the U. S. Public Health Service, Health Services Research Center grant, is designed to find out about the process of participation, rather than the effect of citizen participation on the quality of health care services.

METHODOLOGY

As a result of three months of informal observation of eight citizen groups in the Twin Cities Metropolitan area, ranging from groups associated with private or public hospitals to Model Cities Programs to prepaid group practice clinics, three criteria evolved for making a final selection of groups we would ask to participate in the study. The criteria were developed on the basis of achieving a mix in terms of:

 a. the group's approach to delivering health services to a geographically defined population;
 b. the general socioeconomic status of group participants;
 c. the formal authority or amount of influence of the group in decision-making.

We contacted seven groups by telephone and mail and sought to obtain their cooperation for the four-month period of August 1 to November 30, 1970. We gave both written and oral assurances to the groups, that all information gathered would remain confidential. Furthermore, we agreed to provide participating groups with both specific and general findings upon completion of the study.

Five of the seven groups contacted agreed to participate in the study. One group was not scheduled to meet regularly during the period of study and the second group did not see how observation of their group would contribute to the study objective. However, on short notice we were able to obtain the cooperation of a sixth group.

Characteristics of the Citizen Groups

Five citizen groups are associated with units providing health services to a defined population and include an advisory committee to a public general hospital, and community-controlled clinics in a minority populated neighborhood and University neighborhood; the sixth group is concerned with planning for adequate health care services to its neighborhood population. Two groups appoint their members, one group elects part of the membership and appoints the remainder and in three groups, members volunteer to serve. Two groups meet monthly, three groups meet bimonthly, and one group meets either weekly or three times a month. Chairmen were elected in three groups, appointed in one group, and determined by consensus in two groups. The health centers of three goups receive either partial or total federal funding for operation, while two groups operate their health center from contributions and donations. One group receives federal and local funds for planning health-service programs.

From our review of small group observation literature, particularly the Bales Interaction Process Analysis, and preliminary observation of citizen groups, we isolated three areas that we wanted to look at. We felt that the extent of participation by citizens in a group was determined by: (1) degree of involvement, (2) amount of responsibility assumed, and (3) content of group meetings. Basically, what we wanted to get from observation of a group's meetings was: who talks, how long they talk, the form of what they say, and the nature of what they say.

Who Talks

In order to determine who talks in a citizen group, we developed categories for group membership that would reflect the various roles of all the groups in the sample. These membership categories include chairman, other officer, group member, program staff, professional health, nonmember, and unfamiliar.

How Long They Talk

One of the alternative methods for recording group interaction that we examined was the MIDCARS (Minnesota Interaction Data Coding and Recording System) system; developed by Richard Sykes, Ph.D. at the University of Minnesota. This system was designed to record interaction by a role category every 15-30 seconds. Because of time and budget factors, instead of using an interaction recorder instrument, we decided to develop an observation form that would be divided into five-minute time units. Interaction observed by membership category in each five-minute segment is recorded for the duration of a citizen meeting. What this means is that for each five-minute period, we can roughly determine the number of interactions and between whom.

Form

In addition to how long citizens talk in their meetings, we wanted to get at the forms of interaction for what they say. We identified five possible forms: statement, question, formal report, proposed solution, and other.

Items

We classified the nature of what citizens say into two broad areas: procedural and issue-oriented. Procedural items relate to group maintenance, in general, or process during the meetings, and they specifically include the ways in which a group goes about handling its problems and issues. Items were classified into formal priorities, direction, formal proceedings, evaluation, and miscellaneous. Issue items relate to the dimensions of the health program, community programs, problems, or politics. Included are items which relate to both the provision of health services and the planning for provision of health services in a neighborhood or area. Within this issue category, items are classified into medical technical, human quality, administrative, community-related, and miscellaneous. Also, we record in group meetings effects of the nonsubstantive items or actions such as applause, laughter, or jokes.

For any citizen group meeting, we will determine whether citizens or program staff or professionals dominate a meeting and the general issues for discussion. In all groups, the relative frequency of items on the observation form will be computerized and will allow us to make comparisons between the participating groups.

In addition, information about a citizen meeting, such as starting and closing times, arrival time of leadership, most frequent and influential participants, unusual happenings, and impressions of observers, is recorded on a meeting summary sheet.

Observation of group meetings is conducted by nine trained observers. Two people are assigned to follow one group for the purpose of increasing inter-observer reliability. Observers were trained in two large group sessions, and then in small group sessions according to the need and time of the individuals. The training included practice coding exercises and discussion about the form and items on the coding form.

Preliminary data from observations derived from the meeting summary sheet are presented in Table 1.

We have found that certain factors independent of interaction and content of meetings may have significant effects upon the nature of participation. Individual participant characteristics and attitudes naturally seem to be two relevant factors. Significant differences in opinion between providers and citizens could force a group to focus on internal conflict rather than on the provision of health services.

To gather data about individual characteristics and attitudes, we devised an opinion poll. Several measures were developed to elicit information about various aspects of participant attitudes. The opinion poll included five sections: (1) selected demographic data; (2) attitudes toward citizen participation measured by a favorability scale; (3) ranking of 13 outcomes of participation in sets of paired comparisons to indicate outcomes preferred by participants; (4) reference group measured by a semantic differential scale in which a favorability rating is given by each participant to the provider group and to the consumer group with choice of group being indicated by strength of rating; (5) role perception as indicated by selection of an activity as a responsibility of the citizen group or of the program staff (service provider).

Both providers and consumers were used to pretest the poll. Each section was timed and the entire poll took approximately 15 to 20 minutes, varying with the individual. Some changes were made after the pretest to gear the language of the poll to a level understandable by anyone who would fill it out. We learned that some participants from the ethnic neighborhood group were unable to read English. To make it easier for members of that group to complete the poll, to maintain good relations with the group, and to insure results of the poll, we made available a Spanish translation.

During the first two weeks of October, the poll was distributed by observers at the citizen group meetings. Members were encouraged to complete the poll as a group activity during the meeting. However, in accordance with the concept of citizen participation, each group decided when the poll would be filled out. Many completed the poll at the meeting, others took them home to return them by mail in self-addressed stamped envelopes that we provided.

Other factors seeming to impinge on the nature of participation are structural characteristics. Specifically Neil Gilbert suggests in his book, *Clients or Constituents*, that the location of a group with respect to the existing political and administrative structure is crucial as far as that group's ability to maintain strength and influence social change. Related to the area of developing and maintaining a power base are matters of community accountability, methods of selecting members for citizen groups, etc. Also, citizen participation is viewed as a process. In this respect, the sophistication of a group to deal with concepts of health-service delivery evolves over time, as the group works with health care issues.

In order to examine the relationships of situational characteristics to

Table 1. Preliminary Data from Group Observation Summary Sheets, September through October, 1970

Group	Number of meetings	Average meeting attendance	Subject areas discussed
Group 1 (Model Cities)	8	23	Prepaid group health insurance for neighborhood, hiring health-planning staff, questionnaire of health needs of senior citizens, drug education proposal, five-year health plan, emergency care program
Group 2 (Health Center in predominantly black neighborhood)	3	31	Use of medical students at health center, selection of new members, committee structure, nominees of professionals to serve on Board, attending public health association conference, how to keep a group working together
Group 3 (Neighborhood health center)	3	15	School hot lunch program, clinic questionnaire, consumer health board training program, election of officers and committee priorities, publicity of clinic services, transportation services, newsletter to families in neighborhood, new advisory committee members
Group 4 (Advisory committee to public general hospital)	5	27	Cost accounting between public and private hospital, awareness & prevention committee report, programs of city health department, home health services, needs for ambulatory care, relationship to comprehensive health planning, how to get input of community health needs, teaching hospital, county mental health program, new childrens' hospital, hospital bed needs report
Group 5 (Community-controlled health center in University neighborhood)	5	6	Mobile unit service for aging population, funding & resources, veterinarian service, clinic space, operating costs, clinic hours, pharmacy service

Group	Number of meetings	Average meeting attendance	Subject areas discussed
Group 6 (Community-controlled health clinic in Mexican-American community)	5	28	Babysitting services, nutrition services, obtaining medical equipment for health center, building a coalition with blacks, clinic hours, dental services, emergency room services at public hospital, community health survey, self-determination for Chicanos

the nature of participation we gathered information about groups through a review of their formal documents. We sought to determine any requirements, limitations or specific authority that might be stipulated, as well as information about the population served by the citizen group. The latter characteristic has implications for representation, method of selection and size of the group.

Assorted Preliminary Opinion Poll Results

The following results are based on a 48.8 per cent return of opinion polls. Eighty-two opinion polls have gone out to five of the six groups cooperating in the study. Of those who have responded, 17 were consumers, 22 were providers with 11 of the providers participating as citizen group members. Twenty-one of the respondents were male, 18 were female. However, the women sampled are more regular meeting-attenders than the men. Seventy-two per cent of the women attend every meeting, and 57 per cent of the men attend every meeting. Related to meeting attendance, our results so far indicate that 83.3 per cent of those who attend every meeting travel less than three miles to get there. Forty-one and seven-tenths per cent of those who attend every meeting walk, 37.5 per cent drive their own car, 16.7 per cent ride with someone else, and the remainder ride bicycles. None of the respondents indicated use of buses, taxis or any other form of transportation.

Results of the role-perception activity list indicate greater consensus on certain items than the authors expected. For each of 8 items, respondents were to indicate who should have responsibility for the activity—program staff or citizens. If the respondent felt the responsibility should be shared, he was to mark both program staff and citizens. Based on 33 responses, the three activities polling the most agreement about who should carry out responsibility for the activities were:

1. Hold offices within the group. Seventy-one per cent of all respondents felt citizens only should hold offices. This constitutes 76.2 per cent of the providers and 63.6 per cent of the consumers who marked this item.

2. Have control over the money to be spent in the health program. On this item, 58.3 per cent of the consumers who responded felt citizens should control funds and 52.4 per cent of the providers felt the same way. Another 30.3 per cent of all respondents felt both citizens and program staff should control funds.

3. Have responsibility for coordinating the health program with other community programs, agencies or activities. Fifty-four and sixth tenths per cent of all respondents agreed that only program staff should be responsible for this activity. Another 21.2 per cent felt citizens should have sole responsibility for the activity and 24.2 per cent felt both program staff and citizens should have responsibility.

For the other items, the results were more spread out indicating more disagreement about responsibility. The other five activities listed in the poll were:

1. Determine which health services the community should have

2. Provide information to the public about health services available in your community

3. Have final approval for hiring health program staff

4. Prepare coffee or refreshments for meetings

5. Gather information about what kinds of health problems there are in the community.

Aside from the study design, data collection, and data analysis, several items of interest to researchers, program planners, etc., have become apparent. First, of little surprise, the resistance to polls or questionnaires, by whatever name, is more than substantial. We approached the group participants by explaining the purpose of the poll and answering any queries from group members. Our response rate so far has been about 50 per cent for each of the five groups polled. A follow-up letter to group members may increase our return. The sixth group was polled just a week ago. Those results will be included in a final report.

The second issue is a moral-ethical question for research. By way of background, two of the groups cooperating in the study requested reimbursement for their participation. These requests came after the groups had agreed to cooperate and project funding was already established. It should be noted that both of the groups are funded primarily through contributions and donations with little, if any, federal, state, or local tax support. Some of our study staff indicated a desire to contribute their time and skills to the groups and in order to avoid potential biasing of results, we requested involvement be delayed until the completion of the study.

At this time, we would like to raise the issue and pose a question about which we have mixed feelings: Should future research and program development studies incorporate into project budgets financial reimbursement for primarily non tax-based study participants?

SUMMARY

The citizen participation study consists of three major parts: the group observations, the opinion poll, and the formal document review as related to the six citizen groups cooperating in the study. For each group and across groups, the relationships in which we are interested are those between structural characteristics, characteristics of citizens and providers, and the immediate group situations in which they are interacting.

ACKNOWLEDGMENT

The authors wish to express thanks to Margaret Paul, Citizen Participation Study staff member, for her substantive contribution to both the study and this paper.

Community and Professional Participation in Decision Making at a Health Center

KAY B. PARTRIDGE
PAUL E. WHITE

Creation of a design for investigation of the content and process of community participation in a neighborhood health center is a challenge. We shall describe the methods used in a longitudinal study of the participation by the community and professionals in decision making at one health center. First, the history of community participation and some revelant theoretical considerations will be reviewed. Second, the impact of the particular study setting on the selection of study methods will be analyzed. Finally, the ways in which the relevant data were obtained and how these data were categorized will be described.

In previous reports on community participation, numerous problems have been identified, including those emanating from the interaction of the community and professionals. Davis and Tranquada have reported on areas of conflict at the Watts health center.[1] These authors emphasized the conflicts arising from differences in goals, the difficulties in joint decision making, and differences in perceptions of reality.

Reprinted with permission of Health Services Reports V. 87, 1972, pp. 335-342.

Goldberg and co-workers have mentioned problems arising from the interaction of members of the community and professionals, as well as from the degree of representativeness of participants and the degree of control to be exercised by the community.[2]

Zurcher, in "Poverty Warriors," describes in detail the stress and strains on the Economic Opportunity Board of the Office of Economic Opportunity of Topeka, Kansas, resulting from the interaction of the poor and near-poor.[3] He repeatedly emphasizes the impact that the process of participation had on all members of the governing board. Zurcher further states that "... the dynamics of [of board meetings] reflected a fission or fusion of world views and the travails of socialization." Articles on the growth and development of individual health centers include stories of difficulties and disagreements, as well as of the learning that goes on as the community becomes involved in the administrative aspects of the center.[4-10]

In order to understand more clearly the factors and forces at work in the participation of the community and professionals, it is helpful to identify the elements of the situation and their interrelationships. Briefly, persons with different backgrounds, personalities, and goals become part of a health center because they are serving with a particular group (board or council). Each group, under specific conditions and constraints, evolves a way of behaving within that group and toward other elements of the health center. This group interaction, across time, provides a particular experience for the group members and produces specific outcomes or results, which in turn affect future events.

We analyzed over time the relationship of three major variables to the perceptions and participation of members of these groups. The first was the status of the participant, specifically, whether professional or nonprofessional. The second variable considered was the setting in which participation occurred, that is, as a member of the board or the advisory council. Traditionally, the board, being located at the apex of the organizational hierarchy, has the final and most authoritative voice on policy matters. The advisory council, in contrast, is given a consultative role as the name implies.

The outcomes of interaction were an important final consideration. Participation in a successful group experience has been shown to have a positive effect on group members.[11,12] In our study, participation was defined as interaction on allocative decisions, that is, on decisions affecting resources. Therefore, it could be hypothesized that the more decisions a group made, the more meaningful would be its interaction; also, that the increased decision making would lead to an increase in perceived satisfaction, influence, and competence among the group members.

HYPOTHESES

The following hypotheses were framed:

1. Professionals on the board or advisory council of a health center perceive themselves as more competent and influential than do nonprofessional group members.

2. Professionals on the board or advisory council will report more satisfaction with their participation than will nonprofessionals.

3. Participants of the group (board or advisory council) which makes more decisions to allocate resources will report more competence, influence, and satisfaction than will members of a group making fewer allocative decisions.

4. Participants of the group which makes more allocative decisions will report more consensus on goals and view other group members as more supportive of their views than will members of the group which makes fewer decisions.

THE SETTING

The study was conducted from October 1968 to March 1970 in a health center that had been established by prolonged, persistent efforts of a group of mothers from the community. Lengthy negotiations with numerous organizations resulted in the creation of a community corporation to establish and run the health center. A tripartite arrangement provided equal representation for a community agency, a local university, and a group health organization on a governing board of 12 members. The board was expected to perform the traditional duties of a board and was the final authority on policy and other matters.

An advisory council, composed of 10 professionals and 10 community residents, was created because no community member of the board qualified as a "consumer" as defined and required by the Office of Economic Opportunity. The role of the advisory council, never specifically delineated, was to provide a mechanism for communication with, and involvement of, the community. Although the health center's bylaws of incorporation did not provide for an advisory council, the grant application showed such a council as reporting to both the medical director and the board.

METHODS

Data for the study were obtained from interviews, observations and reports of meetings, and other written communications. The investigator interviewed all members of the board and council and three key members of the staff in early 1969 and again one year later to collect descriptive data on each person and elicit his views on selected aspects of the health center.

The investigator obtained data on the content of board and council meetings by direct observation and detailed notation of the proceedings. For meetings that she was unable to attend, the official minutes were analyzed. A tape recorder was not used for two reasons. The advisory council objected to its use at its meetings. Moreover, use of a tape recorder at community meetings in another neighborhood had proved completely unwieldy. Background noise was high, identification of speakers was difficult, especially during lively discussions, and the tape recorder frequently jammed or failed.

Written communications by, or received by, the two groups under study (including memorandums and letters to and from the project director, the administrator, and chairman of the board) were also reviewed.

While previous research and theories about community and professional participation, in part, dictated the questions chosen for investigation, experience in this particular research setting greatly influenced the selection of the techniques used for obtaining answers to questions. The factors which influenced decisions on methodology deserve mention beause similar decisions are faced each time attempts are made to do research in an action setting.

First, research of this type must conform to the pace of the organization under study. From a methodological point of view, it would have been preferable to delay data collection until numerous methodological dilemmas were resolved. We decided, however, to field the investigation in the first months of the health center's existence so as to learn as much as possible about the initial forces that would affect subsequent community involvement. Consequently, the investigator observed board and council meetings before having answers for many questions on methodology.

Uncertainty about the reception that the investigator would receive also affected the methodology. After 21 months of contact with the health center, it is difficult to recall the initial insecurity felt by participants and investigator alike as to what was going to happen. Although the board and council had formally agreed to permit the research and to cooperate in any way possible, for these groups to experience the presence of a silent outsider or to answer a series of questions without a prior inkling of their content was another matter.

The advisory council, more than the board, expressed doubts and second thoughts about the advisability of participating in the study. Their dilemma was succinctly described by their chairman, who said,

"We're still walking through the woods. Why don't you come back and study us when we've got a role?" Because of the uncertainty felt by everyone, the early months of the investigation were kept as low-keyed and nonthreatening as possible.

Because of these very uncertainties, however, the investigator often needed to be present at the health center. To learn as much as possible about the center and at the same time become a visible, accepted element in the setting, she attended numerous community meetings and talked with many persons connected with the center. Toward the middle of the study period, it was possible for her to reduce contact to only the council and board meetings. By the time of the initial interviews (approximately 6 months after the start of the study), the investigator was known and accepted by many of the council and board members. This acceptance facilitated a more informal atmosphere at interviews and helped in getting complete responses to open-ended questions.

The choice of the open-ended type of questions to obtain key portions of the interview data was also dictated by the study setting. First, in relation to items such as goals of the health center and roles of the groups, the investigator did not feel she could anticipate potential answers well enough to formulate forced-choice questions. Second, it was believed that respondents might give what they believed was an "appropriate" answer on a multiple-choice question, but one which could mask their own feelings. Third, the rapidity of events and the desire to do "before and after" interviews precluded the preparation of a sensitive, closed-ended instrument for the interviews.

Another factor that shaped the investigation was the necessity of preparing a questionnaire for interviews which could be used comfortably both with experienced professionals, knowledgeable in their fields, and with respondents who were new to both health affairs and research. Insofar as possible, therefore, simply phrased questions were used and complicated approaches avoided.

Finally, although the broad rubric of participation in allocative decision making was identified early as the key focus of the study, it was not clear initially what sort of information—in view of research constraints—could be obtained from board and council meetings. Therefore the investigator attended the initial meetings to observe and record as much as possible of the discussion and activities. Only after many meetings and repeated study of their content did the following categorical analysis evolve.

ANALYSIS OF DATA

Content of meetings. As stated, the essential element in participation in the health center, as defined for our study, was allocative decision making. Raw data on meetings, consisting of almost verbatim accounts of proceedings at the board and council meetings were analyzed. The first step in such analysis was the identification of each issue or topic discussed during the meeting. Some examples of topics include a progress report from the training director, a discussion of the need for a drug addiction program, and the setting of a date for the next meeting. Often one broad topic subsumed several subtopics which were coded individually.

After separate topics were identified, it was possible to code several dimensions for each issue—the type of issue, how long it was under discussion, what action was taken, whether or not it was related to health center resources, who initiated the topic, and whether or not the topic was on the agenda. The last two dimensions—initiator of the topic and its status—reflected to what extent different categories of topics were included formally in the meeting format and which were initiated without being on the agenda and by whom.

An important measure of meaningful participation was the percentage of topics discussed that affected resources. A second index of participation was the number and types of decisions each group made. The final disposition of each topic was noted. Alternative outcomes included acceptance, rejection, tabling, assignment for study, and no decision—when one was needed. The last category included issues which were presented to the board or council for a decision, but on which no action was taken.

The crucial element in analyzing the content of meetings was the establishment of a satisfactory coding system for the topics themselves. In the days before community participation, most decisions made within a health center would have been encompassed by the three categories: medical-technical, administrative, and interorganizational relationships. With the advent of emphasis on "maximum feasible participation," however, lay persons and consumers have become involved so that the topics discussed and the considerations that affect decision making have been altered.

The extent and manner in which laymen were to participate in health center matters was never clearly delineated by the Office of Economic Opportunity. As operational instructions, such general guidelines as, "The Neighborhood Health Council shall participate in such activities as the development and review of applications for OEO assistance, the establishment of program priorities, the selection of the project director . . ." were ambiguous.[13] The individual health center—with its professional and lay persons—had to evolve ways of incorporating community input.

Participation of members of the community in the formal health center setting has added new dimensions to the topics and issues discussed at meetings of the board and advisory council. Analysis of the topics and issues discussed needed to reflect these additions. Six major categories resulted:

1. Medical-technical
2. Administrative
3. Interorganizational relationships
4. Community and medical-technical
5. Community and administrative
6. Community and interorganizational relationships

In addition, two other categories relating to the operation and maintenance of the board and advisory council were set up. The definitions of these topics, because they were critical to our analysis, are explained in detail.

The first traditional category, medical-technical, relates to medical standards of practice. This category, based on the definition of technology of medicine elucidated by Levine and co-workers[14], refers to the medical aspects of a professional's role, such as the ability to diagnose illness, to use the proper treatment, or to do surgery. Included were topics such as techniques of treatment, drugs to be carried in the pharmacy, and professional qualifications of applicants for staff positions.

Administrative topics deal with organizational efficiency. Billing procedures, funding, health center construction, staff reports, and the budget are examples of issues which might be exclusively administrative.

An example of the interorganizational relationships of a health center would be its interaction with a health department or with professional organizations. Organizational realities require that an organization relate to the other groups and organizations around it. Topics included under this heading were working with a ctiy-wide coordinating committee, with the health department, or with professional groups.

Any time that a member of the group perceived an issue as affecting community interests, goals, resources, or needs and discussed it in that light, the topic was then categorized as a community topic. The discussant need not have been a layman or member of the community. For example, an administrative topic might have first been discussed solely from a traditional administrative viewpoint, but later in relation to its effect on the community. A discussion of the budget for the health center, for example, might have begun with an analysis of its personnel's fringe benefits (an administrative topic), but have been followed by a presentation of the pros and cons of augmenting the budget of the training department so as to allow more community persons to be trained (administrative topic in relation to effect on the community).

The medical-technical category in relation to the community might include a reference to the community's preference for injections instead of tablets in treatment. The category of interorganizational relationships in respect to their effect on the community covered topics such as coordination and interaction of the center with organizations representing the local community.

The interview—open-ended questions. Open-ended questions were used in interviews to elicit the participants' perceptions of the roles of their group (board or council), the goals of the health center. Responses to the open-ended questions were coded into categories based on a study of the responses to both the initial and followup interviews.

Group members were asked, "What do you think the (advisory council) (board) is supposed to do?" Following are the 11 code categories that were created to group their responses:

1. Advise
2. Make policy
3. Represent community needs and wishes
4. Represent the health center in the community
5. Serve as a community watchdog of quality
6. Respond to the community
7. Provide an opportunity for community involvement
8. Help in employment and training
9. Oversee management, the budget, and the achievement of goals
10. Miscellaneous responses about the group's composition
11. Role not clear.

The first two categories reflect the broad, nonspecific views of each group's role that were given by many respondents. Categories 3 through 9 were for expressions of more specific purposes. Numbers 3 through 7 reflect the liaison duties of relating the health center to the community and vice versa. Varying postures and activities vis-a-vis the community are provided for in each category.

One category was for miscellaneous responses related to the composition of the group rather than to its role, and a final category was for persons who said that the role was not clear or defined. The number of responses falling into these last two categories is one index of the difficulties group members had in understanding their group's role.

Responses to three separate questions provided data on the goals of the health center as seen by the respondents. The questions were: What do you think the health center should do for the people in the neighborhood? What services do you think should be available? What long-term results or outcomes are you looking for from the health center? Eight categories of responses resulted:

1. Deliver health and medical care
2. Provide social services
3. Serve as an economic and social stimulus to the community
4. Teach the community
5. Employ and train people for the center and community
6. Serve people with dignity and warmth
7. Serve as a demonstration project
8. Offer an opportunity for community participation.

The first and most obvious purpose of the health center was the delivery of health or medical care. Responses such as "get a healthier community," "do preventive care," "treat the sick," and "reduce mortality" were put under this heading. A second category was used for responses related to the delivery of social services, such as welfare counseling and help with a person's social problems.

The third category of goals related to providing a social and economic stimulus to the community. Not only employment was included here, but also intangible hopes, such as creating pride and serving as a nucleus of community organization and spirit.

A fourth category was for goals related to health education and those related to sharing health knowledge and values with patients and the community. The fifth was a role in the employment and training of people, both to meet the needs of the health center and of the community. The sixth purpose assigned to the health center was that of serving people with warmth and dignity. Convenience, accessibility, and concern were cited as legitimate expectations.

The seventh category was that of serving as a demonstration project, being a model for other health centers. This category included responses concerning the testing of theories of medical care in real life. A final category of goals related to offering the opportunity for community participation.

This system of categorization made it possible to identify changes in the respondents' views of their health center's mission as well as shifting views among lay and professional subgroups about its goals.

The interview—areas of decision. A second portion of the questionnaire solicited participants' perceptions of their ability and influence on 11 areas of decision. Some of these decision areas included topics mentioned in the OEO guidelines for health centers as appropriate concerns for advisory councils. Other topics had been used by Schwartz in his study of community participation in group practices.[15] To discuss these topics, varying degrees of professional, administrative, and community expertise were required. The 11 areas of decision were as follows:

1. Setting eligibility limits
2. Handling complaints from patients of the center
3. Formulation of employment policies
4. Deciding which programs were most important—or should have the most emphasis
5. Selection of the medical director
6. Evaluation of the care being given
7. Choosing persons for nonprofessional positions, such as secretaries, aides, drivers, and so forth
8. Setting fee scales to be charged at the center
9. Working closely with community groups and residents
10. Setting the health center's hours
11. Approval of the annual budget.

The areas of decision were presented as topics which might come before the respondent's group for a decision. The respondent, who was to assume that his group had to discuss each issue and reach a decision, was asked to state the following for each area.

1. How much influence do you think (community people) (professionals) like yourself will have on the final decision?
2. On which topic do you feel most able to make a decision; on which topic do you feel least qualified?

The first question about influence was intended to evoke the respondent's general view of his potential contribution and influence in the decision making process. The second was designed to demarcate the areas of decision in which the participants might be most predisposed to participate.

LIMITATIONS OF DATA

The data as gathered and conceptualized present a number of limitations. Ideally, information on the participation of the health center's staff in decision making should have been included. Interviews with members of the staff and an analysis of the content of staff meetings would have been revealing. Also, data gathered from meetings of the advisory council and the board present only one aspect of the total decision-making process. Discussions and decisions at meetings are only the tip of the iceberg and do not reflect the multitude of activities carried on outside of meetings to accomplish the group's goals.

In any study in which the data are based on oral sources, such as the notes on meetings used in our analysis, questions arise as to accuracy and completeness. Such questions are even more likely to be raised if the meetings are of the type that are often characteristic of community participation since such meetings may become unruly at times, and the subjects introduced may not be directly related to the meetings' purposes. Use of a second observer, of tape recorders and projectors, or of both, would strengthen the reliability of a study in which notes on such meetings were used. Unfortunately, however, the context of community-oriented studies does not always lend itself to such approaches.

The principal focus of the study was community participation in the allocative decision making of a health center. To evaluate that phenomenon it was necessary to determine what and how many allocative decisions were made and by whom. It was also necessary to identify, insofar as possible, what influence a respondent's status and role had on his perceptions of his influence, competence, and satisfaction. The impact of the respondents' participation in allocative decision making on their perceptions also had to be analyzed.

The data gathered indicated how many decisions were made by each group at each of its meetings and how many of those decisions actually affected the distribution of resources. Shifting areas of interest between the council and board could be identified. It was also possible to see how and where each group came to grips with the task of identifying its role and its relationship to others in the health center situation. Information became available on the shifting membership within the groups and how group members changed their views of their contributions to the council or board and of the potential contribution of their group to the health center. The second round of interviews reflected the impact of a year's experience in decision making on participants' perceptions.

In spite of some limitations, the methodology described appears to produce useful data and insight into community participation at a health center and should be useful to persons interested in studying this subject. Results of the study in which the methodology was used will be reported subsequently.

REFERENCES

1. Davis, M. S., and Tranquada, R.E.: A sociological evaluation of the Watts Neighborhood Health Center. Paper presented at 96th annual meeting of the American Public Health Association, Nov. 16, 1968, Detroit, Mich.
2. Goldberg, G. A., Trowbridge, F. L., and Buxbaum, R. C.: Issues in the development of neighborhood health centers. Inquiry 6: 37-47, March 1969.
3. Zurcher, L. A.: Poverty warriors. University of Texas Press, Austin, 1970.
4. Falk, L. A.: Community participation in the neighborhood health center. J Natl Med Assoc 61: 493-497, November 1969.
5. Gordon, J. B.: The politics of community medicine projects: A conflict analysis. Med Care 7: 419-427, November-December 1969.
6. Hochbaum, G. M.:Consumer participation in health planning: Toward conceptual clarification. Am J Public Health 59: 1698-1705, September 1969.
7. Kent, J. A., and Smith, C. H.: Involving the urban poor in health services through accommodation—the employment of neighborhood representatives. Am J Public Health 57: 997-1003, June 1969.
8. Parker, A. W.: The consumer as policy maker— issues of training. Paper presented at the 97th annual meeting of the American Public Health Association, Nov. 11, 1969, Philadelphia, Pa.
9. Sparer, G., Dines, G. B., and Smith, D.: Consumer participation in OEO assisted neighborhood health centers. Paper presented at the 97th annual meeting of the American Public Health Association, Nov. 13, 1969, Philadelphia, Pa.
10. Wise, H. B., Levin, L. S., and Kurahara, R. T.: Community development and health education: I. Community organization as a health tactic. Milbank Mem Fund Q 46: 329-339, July 1968.
11. Zander, A.: Group aspirations. In Group dynamics, edited by D. Cartwright and A. Zander. Harper and Row, New York, 1968.
12. Thibaut, J. W., and Riecken, H. W.: Some determinants and consequences of the perception of social causality. In Readings in social psychology, edited by E. Maccoby, T. Newcomb, and E. L. Hartley. Henry Holt and Company, New York, 1958.
13. Office of Economic Opportunity (Health Services Office): The comprehensive neighborhood health services program guidelines. U.S. Government Printing Office, Washington, D.C., March 1968.
14. Levine, S., Scotch, N. A., and Vlasak, G. J.: Unravelling technology and culture in public health. Am J Public Health 59: 237-244, February 1969.
15. Schwartz, J.: Medical plans and health care. Charles C Thomas, Springfield, Ill., 1968.

Representation Patterns in Community Health Decision Making

CHESTER W. DOUGLASS

In order to understand better the dynamics of the community decision making process it would be helpful to know to what extent the people in that process are representatives of community groups and how these representation patterns affect their actions during the decision making process. Specifically, what is the nature of a participant's organizational affiliation, the nature of his representation of that organization, and the orientation of his attitudes within the decision making process? Considerations of community representation and its consequences are important in the creation of planning bodies that are charged with developing interorganizational cooperation in meeting the needs of residents.

From a background of community organization efforts, social workers have gained insights into the nature of representation and the importance of different kinds of representation. Murphy (1954) in his development of community organization practice, has defined the *formal*

Reprinted with permission of The Journal of Health and Social Behavior V. 14, 1973, pp. 80-86.

representative as being that representative who has the "... approval by formal vote of his organization, either by an executive committee or board vote or by the responsible administrative authorities of the agency." This representative speaks for his agency on all deliberations.

Two other kinds of representation can be derived consequentially from Murphy's definition. These are *informal* and *type* representation. The informal representative is the representative who does not have approval by vote from the executive bodies or the administrative authorities of his agency. He does not speak for his agency in the deliberations. He acts as liaison between his agency and the deliberating body. A type representative is one who is associated with an agency or group only in so far as he personally is a member of that agency or group. He neither speaks for the agency nor acts as liaison to the agency. Using these definitions of organizational representation, participants in the community health planning process in the present study are classified according to whether they are a formal, informal, or type representative.

As part of a comparative analysis of eight Model Cities health programs, the representation patterns of the most influential decision makers were studied. The Model Cities process combines the demands of neighborhood residents, the inertia of the status quo of City Hall, and the money and administrative guidelines of the federal government. Hence, representation patterns in a decision making process of this kind become a crucial concern.

An attitudinal measure of representation was also obtained, namely, the role of the participant as perceived by the participant. Role is defined by a determination of a participant's view of his own action as representing consume∙ interests or provider interests. It was expected that formal representatives would act on behalf of the organizations they formally represent. Contrastingly, it was expected that type representatives would act on behalf of their own attitudes and perceptions of their role. Informal representatives were expected to act partly on behalf of their own attitudes and partly on behalf of the interests of the organizations they represent. Therefore, type representatives were expected to show less congruence between their organization affiliation and their self perceptions of their role. However, formal representatives were expected to show a consistency between their organizational affiliation and their perceived role. Hypothesis 1 states the expected relationships.

> Hypothesis 1: As organizational representation varies from formal to informal to type, the consumer or provider self perceptions of participants tend to be less associated with the consumer or provider status of their organizational affiliation.

Health Services Attitudes. Bachrach and Baratz (1962) have suggested that perhaps a community ethos contributes to the situation in which certain issues or alternative solutions do not get raised for discussion. If the participants hold such a guiding set of beliefs or attitudes, this factor may be associated with the nature of their input in the decision making process and ultimately the orientation of the resulting policies. If the attitudes that correspond to this behavior could be adequately diagnosed, the representation patterns may begin to take on greater meaning. Therefore, in order to provide a more precise indication of the orientation of participants toward the delivery of personal health services, a health services attitudes index was constructed. A measure of attitudinal orientation on a consumer oriented-provider oriented scale provides a method of refining the differences among the participants (Porter, 1969; Mohr, 1966).

The constructs that form the basis for the health services attitudes index (HSAI) concern the extent to which consumers ought to be involved in the planning and administration of services and the degree to which health services should be oriented toward the recipients of those services. The 12-item scale consists of statements concerning four health issues: (1) consumers' rights to health services; (2) the relative convenience of services to consumers; (3) the desired level of consumer influence in health planning; and (4) the desired level of consumer influence in administrative control of operational programs. (A copy of the entire health services attitudes index is available upon request from the author.) A consumer orientation on the HSAI is evidenced by a cluster of attitudes concerning these four parameters that would support the notion that convenient health services are a right, and that consumers ought to have a major voice in: (1) defining the need for health services; (2) the planning for those services; and (3) the administrative control of operational programs.

Type representatives were expected to show less congruence between their organizational affiliation and their health services attitudes, while formal representatives were expected to show a consistency between their organizational affiliation and their health services attitudes.

> Hypothesis 2: As organizational representation varies from formal to informal to type, the consumer or provider health services attitudes of participants tend to be less associated with the consumer or provider status of their organizational affiliation.

Hypotheses 1 and 2 imply an association between the participants' self perceptions as consumer or provider oriented actors and their health services attitudes. Hence, the corollary:

> Corollary to Hypotheses 1 and 2: The consumer-provider orientation of participants' self perceptions and the consumer-provider orientations of their health services attitudes are consistent regardless of type of representation.

The organization with which each participant is affiliated (for the purposes of health planning) is defined as a consumer or provider organization in the same manner that the participants have been defined. That is, if an organization uses the majority of its resources to deliver or finance health services, it is a provider organization. If not, it is a consumer organization. The participant's self perceived orientation is decided by his response concerning the interests he feels he is speaking for regardless of his organizational affiliation. For example, if the respondent is a doctor representing a hospital, but sees himself as an advocate for the Model Cities resident, his self-perception is scored as consumer oriented.

METHODOLOGY

The present study is concerned with the decision making process that produced the health program in eight cities in Michigan that have received Model Cities grants from the U.S. Department of Housing and Urban Development. Data concerning program characteristics were collected by means of content analysis of Model Cities documents. Four cities produced health programs that tend toward the establishment of innovative programs under new administrative arrangements (interpreted as consumer oriented). In contrast, the other four cities produced health programs that appear to expand previously existing health services programs within their existing administrative structure (interpreted as provider oriented).

Sampling. Initial interviews in each city were held with four key participants based on their position during the decision making process. During the one and a half hour interview with these initial respondents, measurements were taken concerning the repsondent's involvement with the first year health plan decisions, as well as the respondent's perception of the major participants in the decisions in question. Each of the initial respondents was given the opportunity to name the participants whom they felt were most influential in the decisions that resulted in his city's first year plan. If a participant was: (1) named as being highly influential by any one of these first four respondents or (2) named by more than two people as having been at all influential, he became part of the sample to be interviewed. Throughout all subsequent interviews, names were added to the sample according to these two criteria. The samples range from 10 to 14 respondents in each city, resulting in a total study sample of 95. The data concerning the characteristics of participants were collected by means of personal interviews.

Variables. Four characteristics of the participants in the decision making were studied. The nature of representation and the participant's perceived role were defined above. In addition, participants were defined as consumers or providers. Consumers receive health services and providers are concerned with the delivery of health services. A participant was determined to be a provider if his most common position (50 per cent or more of his income) was associated with the provision or financing of health services. Conversely, a consumer is that participant who receives less than half his income from the health services industry. Nearly all participants in the study received either 100 per cent or more of their income from health industry activities and thus could be clearly classified as consumers or providers.

The attitudes held by each participant toward the delivery of health services were also studied. The constructs that form the basis for the health services attitudes index (HSAI) were outlined above. The health services attitude index (HSAI) used a Likert-type summated scaling procedure that was initially constructed by obtaining expert judgment on items as an *a priori* check on content validity. Possible scores on the index ranged from 12 to 72. When analyzed for a relationship with dichotomous variables, the HSAI scores were divided at the median. Most participants are likely to have displayed some degree of combination between consumer orientation and provider orientation. Therefore, HSAI scores above or below the median indicate that these participants tended to be more of one type than of the other. Respondents with scores less than 25 (the median) were interpreted as tending to be consumer oriented, respondents with scores of 25 or greater were interpreted as tending to be provider oriented. (See Krech, Crutchfield, and Ballachey, 1962.)

Thirty-two judges were obtained to rate 22 items according to their consumer versus provider orientation. On the basis of these judgments, 12 of the original 22 items were selected for inclusion in the HSAI. In obtaining judgments there is an underlying assumptiion that the attitudes of the judges are independent of the scale values of the statements (Edwards, 1957).

The 32 judges represented approximately equal numbers of consumers, doctors, and other providers (not doctors). The consumers included individuals from various social and economic classes, the doctors included physicians and dentists in private practice and academia, and the other providers were employed by community health agencies and the University of Michigan School of Public Health. The Pearson correlation coefficients are: doctors and consumers (.97), doctors and other providers (.99), and consumers and other providers (.98). There-

Table 1. Number of Respondents by Class of Representation,
Self Perception, and Organizational Affiliation

	Class of Representation					
	Formal		Informal		Type	
	Organizational Affiliation:		Organizational Affiliation:		Organizational Affiliation:	
Self Perception	Cons.	Prov.	Cons.	Prov.	Cons.	Prov.
Consumer oriented	25	2	13	15	6	12
Provider oriented	0	14	0	8	0	0
	$\chi^2 = 32.8$ ($p < 0.001$)		$\chi^2 = 2.58$ ($p > 0.10$)		n.a.	

fore, the apparent agreement on the scale values of statements obtained from respondent's similar to those in the study sample, supports the content validity of the health services attitudes index.

Reliability. An item analysis was performed in which a correlation coefficient was computed to show the relationship of each item to the summated score of the entire scale. That is, how well is the item measuring what the scale itself is measuring? The health services attitudes index showed inter-item correlation coefficients that were nearly all significant at the .01 level. Single item correlations with the summated score showed coefficients ranging from .57 to .91. The split-half reliability coefficient of the index was also computed. The resulting reliability coefficient was .90. The scale therefore exhibited the requisite consistency to measure a unidimensional construct.

FINDINGS

In the text of Hypothesis 1, Table 1 displays the relationships between self perception and consumer-provider organizational affiliation in the three classes of representation. A chi-square statistic was used to compare the proportion of representatives from consumer organizations whose self perceptions are either consumer or provider oriented with the proportion of representatives from provider organizations whose self perceptions are either consumer or provider oriented. The chi-square for formal representation is 32.8, for informal representation 2.58, and for type representation the chi-square cannot be computed. This trend in the data suggests that a participant's self perceived role is

Table 2. Number of Respondents by Class of Representation,
Health Services Attitudes, and Organizational Affiliation

Health Services Attitudes Index	Formal Organizational Affiliation:		Informal Organizational Affiliation:		Type Organizational Affiliation:	
	Cons.	Prov.	Cons.	Prov.	Cons.	Prov.
Consumer < 24	15	3	8	13	6	8
Provider ⩾ 25	10	13	5	10	0	4
	$\chi^2 = 6.74$ ($p < 0.01$)		$\chi^2 = 0.30$ ($p > 0.50$)		n.a.	

(Class of Representation spans Formal, Informal, Type)

not related to his organizational affiliation if he is an informal or type representative. Rather, the orientation of his perceived role is related to his organizational affiliation only if he is a formal representative.

However, on closer inspection of the data it is evident that representatives who were affiliated with consumer organizations consistently felt that they were consumer oriented in their actions during the decision making process. There is no variation in the association between organizational affiliation and self perception as representation varies from formal to informal to type for representatives of consumer organizations. Therefore, Hypothesis 1 is supported only for representatives of provider organizations.

An alternative method of comparing these variables across the three classes of representation is by looking at proportion of provider representatives who are consumer oriented. This proportion should increase as representation changes from formal to informal to type if Hypothesis 1 is to be supported. The ratios, using Table 1, are 0.12 for formal, 0.65 for informal, and 1.0 for type representatives, which means that as representation changes from formal to informal to type, there is a tendency for these participants to be more consumer oriented. Hence, formal representatives of provider organizations are likely to be provider oriented in their behavior during the decision making process. Informal and type representatives of provider organizations tend to act in terms of their own consumer or provider oriented self perceptions.

In the test of Hypothesis 2, Table 2 shows that the relationships between health services attitudes and consumer-provider organizational affiliation decrease in a manner similar to the analyses of Table 1.

The chi-square for formal representation is 6.74, for informal 0.30, and for type cannot be computed. This trend in the data suggests that a participant's health services attitudes are not related to his organizational affiliation if he is an informal or type representative. However, if representation is formal, the orientation of his health services attitudes tend to be highly associated with his organizational affiliation.

The proportion of provider representatives who are consumer oriented and the proportion of consumer representatives who are provider oriented were analyzed for Table 2. If these proportions increase as representation changes from formal to informal to type, Hypothesis 2 will be supported. The ratios for provider representatives are 0.23 for formal, 0.57 for informal, and 0.67 for type representatives. These data show a tendency to increase, which means that as representation varies from formal to informal to type, there is a tendency for provider participants to be more consumer oriented. The ratios for consumer representatives are 0.40 for formal, 0.39 for informal, and 0.0 for type representatives. These data for representatives of consumer organizations fail to show any systematic relationship with health services attitudes as representation varies from formal to informal to type. Therefore, Hypothesis 2 (similar to Hypothesis 1) is supported only for representatives of provider organizations.

In the analysis of the data for both Hypotheses 1 and 2, formal representatives of provider organizations exhibit a consistent relationship between their organizational affiliation and their self perceived role or their health services attitudes. It seems, then, that the degree of formality associated with representation is predictive to the kind of input that the participant is likely to have. Providers who are formal representatives are more likely to yield an orientation that can be predicted by their organizational affiliation.

The findings of Hypothesis 1 and Hypothesis 2 imply a positive association between self perception and health services attitudes that will now be analyzed. This analysis will also serve as a check on the validity of the instrument used to measure these two constructs.

In the test of the corollary to Hypotheses 1 and 2, Table 3 shows the responses of the 95 respondents as they perceive themselves as consumer or provider oriented and the consistency of this response with their score on the health services attitudes index (HSAI). While the association is not perfect, a chi-square of 14.7 ($p < 0.001$) is of a high enough magnitude to support the corollary hypothesis that the measures on these two variables are highly related. This finding is important because it adds to construct validity of the HSAI, that is, the evidence that the scale measures the trait it was designed to measure.

Table 3. Number of Respondents by Health Services Attitudes
and Self Perception

Health Services Attitudes Index	Self Perception		Total
	Consumer Oriented	Provider Oriented	
Consumer 24	45	5	50
Provider 25	25	20	45
Total	70	25	95

x^2 = 14.73 (p < 0.001).

DISCUSSION

The citizen (consumer) participation literature generally deals with statements of normative positions or at most descriptions of the roles that consumers or providers played in a particular setting. The present study offers an analysis of the participants in a community health decision making process that goes beyond simple comparison of consumers and providers. A health services attitudinal index (HSAI) has allowed a finer discrimination within the provider and consumer groups.

The thesis presented at the outset of the paper postulated that the nature of a participant's representation is a factor that contributes to the kind of input he has in the decision making process. The findings show that providers who are *informal* and *type* representatives are more likely to yield a more consumer oriented input than their organizational affiliation might suggest. In this theoretical analysis, it is concluded that the nature of a participant's input is affected by the degree to which he speaks for the organization with which he is affiliated. If a provider formally represents his provider organization in a decision making process, he is more likely to be a provider oriented force in the process than if he were an informal or type representative.

In an applied setting, this finding has implications for those who are attempting to create interagency committees for the purpose of health planning. A requirement for a certain provider-consumer mix on a planning body will not ensure a policy output that is representative of this particular mix. If it is true that the decisions are dominated by the providers, differences in outcomes seem to be based on the orientation of these providers. If the selection of providers is made on a formal basis, this act tends to predict that the policy outputs of the decision making process will be made on the terms of the existing community health organizations. If the selection is not made on a formal basis, participants are likely to be chosen on the basis of their health services attitudes. Therefore, the selection of informal and type representatives is a critical factor in the planning process.

It has been found that providers who are informal or type representatives show a tendency to perceive their own role in such a way that it corresponds with their attitudes. If these attitudes are consumer oriented, innovative plans are more likely to result because the participants do not enter the decision making process with the official requirement to "speak for" any organization in the process. However, it must be recognized that the informal and type representatives could have been selected by people who wanted provider oriented providers to dominate the process. Therefore, informal and type representation is not a guarantee of a certain kind of input, but rather the result of a selection process that tends to allow participants to make decisions that are based on their own self perceptions and attitudes.

The mean HSAI of providers who are informal and type representatives in the four cities that tended to produce consumer oriented plans is 22.1. In contrast, the mean HSAI of this same group of providers on the four cities that tended to produce provider oriented plans is 32.4 — representing much more provider oriented attitudes. The orientation of the resulting programs seems to be reflected in the HSAIs of the providers who are informal and type representatives. This finding is significant in that it supports the conclusion that the method of selecting *informal* and *type* representatives is a major variable in the health decision making process. Future research focusing on the methods of selecting participants for comparable decision making processes is necessary in order to specify the elements of this crucial stage in the community decision making process.

CONCLUSIONS

Providers who are formal representatives are the most likely to yield an orientation in the decision making process that can be predicted by their organizational affiliation.

Providers who are informal or type representatives tend to act in terms of their own self perceptions and attitudes, which might be consumer or provider oriented.

Representatives of consumer organizations are consistently consumer oriented in their perceived roles and attitudes regardless of the nature of their representation.

The selection of informal and type representatives for a decision-making body is a critical stage in the health planning process.

REFERENCES

Bachrach, P., and M.S. Baratz. 1962 "Two faces of power." American Political Science Review 56 (December): 947-952.

Edwards, L.E. 1957 Techniques of Attitude Scale Construction. New York: Appleton.

Krech, D., R. Crutchfield and E. Ballachey. 1962 Individuals in Society. New York: McGraw-Hill.

Mohr, L.B. 1966 Determinants of Innovations in Organizations. Ph.D. Dissertation. Rackham School of Graduate Studies, University of Michigan.

Murphy, C.G. 1954 Community Organization Practice. Cambridge: Riverside Press.

Porter, R.A. 1969 Community Mental Health Planning Ideology of Organizational Participants in the Model Cities Program. Ph.D. Dissertation. Florence Heller Graduate School for Advanced Studies in Social Welfare, Brandeis University.

Consumer Participation In OEO-Assisted Neighborhood Health Centers

GERALD SPARER
GEORGE B. DINES
DANIEL SMITH

INTRODUCTION

As the nation sought to address the problems of poverty in the mid-sixties the Office of Economic opportunity (OEO) was established as an action agency to redress the imbalance in national priorities. The War on Poverty was to be fought under many service banners — jobs, education, legal assistance, and health. Each of these, however, was to be pursued under a more general operational flag — community organization.

While in many areas community participation has become an organizational goal without service objectives, each service program — Head Start, Legal Services, Health — was to assure consumer participation.

There has always been discussion — in OEO and elsewhere — among those interested in community organization. One school of

Reprinted with permission of *The American Journal of Public Health* V. 60, 1970, pp. 1091-1102.

thought has attempted to gather community residents together over issues of conflict and confrontation. In such programs, the issues may be real or imagined, but in either case they are used to arouse community interest, if not indignation. The principal work of such organization is to confront the power structure external to the community and to protest inequities.

The other school — call it the service orientation — tries to identify real needs in communities and, together with the community residents, organize into a meaningful structure which meets their basic needs. This may be seen most generally in the service-based community organization such as Head Start, Health, Legal Services. The difference in this theory of community organization is that, if successful, it will bring antipolitical groups together in a situation where compromise — political or otherwise — will help both parties (sides) to achieve what they want.

The end effect of the first school of thought, where there is an attempt to gather the community together over issues of conflict, can be and frequently is the establishment of a group calling for control that has nothing to control. Whereas, when the effect of organization can be put into community avenues to direct and control some of the factors that affect people's lives — family, education, legal and personal rights, health care, and housing — consumer participation has achieved its goals. Consumer participation in health programs is of particular interest because of the nation's current concern with the critical issues of medical care costs and organization, and the problems of poverty.

In the medical care arena, the passage of the Social Security amendments of 1965 included major emphasis on providing financing mechanisms for two population groups — Medicare (Title XVIII) for the aged, and Medicaid (Title XIX) for the medically indigent. These medical care financing costs soon skyrocketed to over $10 billion in additional state and federal outlays for health care. These contributed to the current crisis in medical care which is characterized by rising costs, rising public concern and rising expectations among consumers. The industry is further plagued by professional manpower resources that are insufficient and inadequately distributed.

These currents of change converged on the OEO-assisted Neighborhood Health Center (NHC) program legislation which stipulated that the program was:

> "1. To make possible with maximum feasible utilization of existing agencies and resources the provision of comprehensive health services . . .; and

2. To assure that such services are made readily accessible to the residents . . ., are furnished in a manner most responsive to their needs and with their participation . . ."[1]

The first objective was to test and develop new ways to deliver ambulatory medical care in a system which linked to other services. Early program planning also anticipated that Medicaid and Medicare funds could provide a financial base for these projects. The second objective was to increase utilization of servies while assuring resident participation in developing them.

As these events were taking place, a method of program planning and evaluation was being formalized. At the national level, that process sought to impose quantitative methods developed for analysis of military programs on other federal programs. Thus the emerging social programs in health, education, welfare, housing, and poverty, and their cadres of professionals, proceeded to develop cost-effectiveness ratios, input-output measures, and cost-benefit and impact studies.

The logic of analyzing data as a prelude to major public program decisions is inherently sound. The development of analytical methods for social programs is essential. Managers of these programs know too well that improved methods are needed for improved decision-making. But, in the surge to develop techniques to respond to management's demands for quantitative rationale to aid in making program decisions, too few voices have been raised cautioning that the technology is scant and perhaps inappropriate.

The economists say the NHCs should have an antipoverty consequence — but the technique for relating improvements in the poverty community to the intervention of the NHC has yet to be developed.

The medical care administrator wants an effective system at reasonable cost — but he cannot say compared to what. The techniques of measuring cost, quality, and effectiveness of health care are still rudimentary.

The medical and health officials say the NHC must have favorable impact on health status — but they have been unable to assess the impact of any system of medical care on changes in health status.

The sociologists say that community participation shoud result in improved community relations between consumers and institutions purporting to serve them,[2] or to achieve broader community goals,[3] but admit that research is needed to develop the understanding to make judgments about the processes.

Too few professional voices have been raised to suggest that the primary objectives — (1) access to an acceptable system of medical care and (2) consumer participation in public programs — are social goods that need no further justification.

We should strongly resist the urge to test socially desirable objectives by their purported secondary benefits, primarily because these benefits fit an input-outcome model. While it is important to support research on the relationships between desirable inputs and their secondary outcomes, it is equally important to proclaim the deficiencies of current technology to measure these secondary outcomes. It is incumbent on evaluators and researchers to support the notion that some socially desirable actions need no further justification. Citizen participation in public programs is one of these.

While it is likely that access and participation may lead to other social benefits, we should first measure the degree of accomplishment in achieving these two simple objectives. It is the purpose of this study to analyze some of the factors that relate to the degree of consumer participation.

METHODS

The findings presented here outline some of the OEO's experiences with consumer participation in Neighborhood Health Centers. The analysis will examine the factors that seem to be relevant to the issues of consumer participation.

The primary data presented come out of our contacts with Neighborhood Health Centers and their associated consumer groups that have taken place during project reviews conducted by OEO as part of a site appraisal process initiated about two years ago. A team of specialists in a variety of disciplines — including medicine, dentistry, nursing, business and management, manpower development and training, and consumer and community organization — have reviewed 27 centers. The team spends approximately two days on each site. Discussions and reviews are conducted with project staff, staff of the administering agencies, local hospitals, health departments, and medical, dental, and pharmaceutical societies and consumers.

The outline for the review of consumer participation follows the factors mentioned in the Neighborhood Health Center Guidelines. The guidelines state that:

> "The neighborhood health council shall participate in such activities as the development and review of applications for OEO assistance, the establishment of program priorities, the selection of the project director, the location and hours of center services, the development of employment policies and selection criteria for staff

personnel, the establishment of eligibility criteria and fee schedules, the selection of neighborhood resident trainees, the evaluation of suggestions and complaints from neighborhood residents, the development of methods for increasing neighborhood participation, the recruitment of volunteers, the strengthening of relationships with other community groups and other matters relating to the project implementation and improvement."[4]

Site-visit team members usually attend a meeting of the consumer group; collect copies of minutes of prior meetings; discuss operations of the project with the consumer group, its president or chairman and other members; review lists of group membership and the manner of election or designation to the group. The reports and findings from these contacts represent the basis for the following analysis. Project analysts in the Comprehensive Health Services Division of the Office of Health Affairs, who are in most intimate and frequent contact with the projects, have contributed their judgments on these factors where site-appraisal findings were lacking in specific detail. Other findings represent data reported by consumer specialists who have been used as consultants for the Consumer Affairs Office of the Office of Health Affairs.

This analysis examines the administrative and organizational status of the consumer group as these factors relate to the degree of involvement in project matters. These elements have both objective and subjective components. We can report objectively that a committee structure exists or does not. It is more difficult to rate the degree of adequacy of this and similar functions. The ratings used are generally a consensus of the OEO management and project staff involved in program monitoring. This is true of most such ratings presented. There is by no means unanimity on these ratings, although there is more uniformity than difference.

Ratings of degrees of consumer involvement, conflict, and personality factors were most difficult. The three groups of raters have markedly different contacts with projects. Project analysts deal mainly with key persons at the Neighborhood Health Center and of the consumer group. Their contacts are the most regular, through all phases of early program growth and development. The analysts are most knowledgeable about the projects but it is often difficult to remain objective about personalities and issues of consumer involvement. Consumer specialists usually become concerned with the most troubled centers at a time of crisis.

The limitations of the site-appraisal findings are that they are often based on only two days of contact as part of a broader review of the project. Consumer group meetings have sometimes been specially structured for the team. Rapport with consumers in brief encounters is often difficult to establish. Some advantages are that the site-visit process is structured, findings are presented in a similar pattern, site visits have rarely taken place during a period of active conflict, team members have rarely had prior contact with the project. Thus differences in judgments presented here are resolved in favor of the site-appraisal findings.

Definitions

Degree of involvement – This is a judgment related to the actual participation of the consumer group in the major and minor policies, practices, and operational decisions of the project. Activity levels of the consumer group, and aspirations of this group that have not resulted in an actual participation, are considerations but not the key to high ratings on this factor. Are they active partners in these processes during developmental and implementing phases?

Personality parameter – Each group — consumer and provider — is of course composed of personalities. Some are so outstanding as to be considered a primary agent in influencing the activities of this factor because it is important to the understanding of the dynamics of the process of consumer involvement. Leadership is unquestionably critical to group functioning.

Conflict – This is difficult to define. Consumer groups experience organizational difficulties, to a degree probably not unlike other groups. There are false starts, changes in leadership, heated discussions, and sometimes a complete disruption of group functioning. Difficulties internal to the group, and between the consumer group and provider representatives, have a similar range of experiences. Conflicts for this presentation are those internal or external relations that have disrupted group functioning or functioning between the groups.

FINDINGS

Administrative Relations and Involvement (Table 1)

Of the 27 centers visited from 1967 to date, 7 are rated high in the degree of consumer involvement, 9 moderate, and 10 low. No pattern is apparent that would relate the administering agency to the degree of involvement. Hospitals, health departments, and community corporations appear in each group. Only three group practices and four medical schools are represented. The structure of the consumer group is not critical; two of the three consumer boards have a high degree of in-

Table 1. Administrative Relations and Degree of Consumer Group Involvement

Center	Administering agent (1)	Consumer group structure A—advisory Bd—board (2)	Degree of involvement H—high M—medium L—low (3)
1.	Community corp.	A	H
2.	CAA	Bd.	H
3.	Medical school	A	H
4.	Health dept.	A	H
5.	Medical school	A	H
6.	Community corp.	A	H
7.	Hospital	Bd.	H
8.	Medical school	A	M
9.	Hospital	A	M
10.	Hospital	A	M
11.	Health dept.	A	M
12.	Hospital	A	M
13.	Medical school	A	M
14.	Group practice	A	M
15.	Health dept.	A	M
16.	Health dept.	A	M
17.	Health dept.	A	L
18.	Group practice	A	L
19.	Health dept.	A	L
20.	Health dept.	A	L
21.	Health dept.	A	L
22.	Community corp.	A	L
23.	Hospital	A	L
24.	Hospital	A	L
25.	CAA	A	L
26.	Group practice	A	L
27.	Community corp.	Bd.	L

volvement but the third board rates low. Five of the seven high-rated groups have advisory functions only, yet their actual function relative to program operational matters is indistinguishable from those two high-rated groups established as boards.

Organizational Status of Consumer Group (Table 2)

Five organizational components were scored for each center visited: committee structure and functions, status of by-laws, regularity of meet-

Table 2. Organizational Status of Consumer Group

Center	Committees (1)	Bylaws (2)	Regular meetings (3)	Elections (4)	Minutes 3—high 2—medium 1—low 0—none (5)	Total
			High			
1.	3	3	3	3	3	15
2.	3	3	3	3	3	15
3.	3	3	3	3	3	15
4.	3	3	3	2	3	14
5.	3	3	3	2	3	14
6.	2	0	2	2	2	8
7.	3	3	3	1	3	13
			Medium			
8.	3	0	3	3	1	10
9.	3	0	3	3	3	12
10.	0	3	3	1	2	9
11.	3	3	3	2	3	14
12.	3	3	3	2	3	14
13.	3	3	3	2	3	14
14.	2	1	3	2	3	11
15.	0	3	2	1	2	8
16.	1	2	3	3	3	12
			Low			
17.	3	0	3	2	3	11
18.	2	3	0	3	2	10
19.	2	3	3	1	3	12
20.	1	1	3	1	3	9
21.	3	0	3	1	3	10
22.	2	0	3	1	3	9
23.	2	0	2	1	2	7
24.	1	0	3	2	3	9
25.	1	2	1	3	1	8
26.	2	0	3	1	2	8
27.	2	3	3	1	3	12

ings, board election procedures, experiences, and availability and completeness of minutes. These are basic elements of organized groups, although their relevance to measures of success in group functioning is not clear. Each element, if it existed, was scored 1 (low), 2 (moderate), or 3 (high); and a zero if it did not exist.

Only one of the seven high-involvement groups scored less than 3 on more than one element. It scored 2 on four elements and zero on bylaws. Each of the others scored high (3) on each element except elections. For three of the seven high-rated centers, election procedure was the single factor preventing perfect scores.

Among the 27 centers, elections scored high (3) less frequently than any other factor. Only seven groups scored high on this factor.

Among the 10 low-involvement groups, suitable election procedures and adequacy of bylaws appear as the two factors most frequently scoring low. In 6 of these, bylaws were nonexistent. In only 3 of the other 17 groups with moderate- or high-involvement rating were bylaws nonexistent.

Committee organization is apparently a key element in group involvement in project operations. Of the 16 moderate and high-rated groups, 11 have the highest ratings. Of the 10 low-rated groups, only 2 scored high on the committee factor.

This analysis suggests the following:

    1. Consumer groups have had much difficulty in holding adequate elections and in establishing effective bylaws. These two elements appear to be influential in over-all assessments of organizational status of the group.

    2. Effectiveness of committee functioning is related to the degree of involvement in the operational aspects of the project.

Consumer and Provider Personalities as Related to Involvement of Consumer Group (Table 3)

The effect of outstanding personalities on group functioning is often important. Personalities perhaps as much as administrative or institutional arrangements have influenced relations between NHC staff and consumer groups. Outstanding personalities exist on both sides: 8 in consumer groups, and 16 in provider groups. Consumer group personalities are presumed to act on behalf of that group. The provider personalities can be characterized as provider or consumer group-oriented. Of the 16 provider personalities, 3 are identified with a strong consumer orientation; all identified with a highly involved consumer group. Only one of the ten low-rated consumer groups has an outstanding personality identified in that group. Four of the high-involvement groups have an outstanding member (usually the chairman or president). Two of the remaining high-rated 3 projects have an outstanding personality on the project staff (often the director) who acts in a positive way on behalf of consumer group involvement.

Table 3. Degree of Involvement Relative to Key Personalities Among Consumer and Provider

Center	Involvement prior to site visit	Consumer group personality No—O Yes—C	Provider personality C—consumer oriented P—professional oriented O—none
1.	H	O	C
2.	H	C	P
3.	H	O	P
4.	H	C	C
5.	H	C	P
6.	H	O	C
7.	H	C	O
8.	M	C	O
9.	M	O	P
10.	M	O	P
11.	M	O	P
12.	M	O	P
13.	M	C	P
14.	M	O	O
15.	M	O	O
16.	M	C	P
17.	L	O	O
18.	L	O	P
19.	L	O	O
20.	L	O	O
21.	L	O	P
22.	L	O	O
23.	L	O	P
24.	L	O	P
25.	L	O	O
26.	L	O	O
27.	L	C	O

Six of the moderately involved groups have a strong provider-oriented personality on the project staff.

Only one high-rated group has a strong provider personality without a high-rated consumer personality; that group is one of the three groups rated highest on organizational status.

This suggests that there is positive relationship between outstanding personalities and consumer group involvement. This may be equal in importance to group organization. Group organizational status appears related to the existence of an outstanding personality in the group.

A strong staff personality oriented toward providers tends to limit consumer group involvement. But if the strong staff personality has a positive consumer group orientation the involvement of the group in project operations is enhanced.

Consumer groups without strong leadership are less organized and less likely to be effectively involved in project operations.

Changes in Consumer Group Involvement — Related to Organizational and Personality Factors (Table 4)

The site-appraisal process provides a perspective on consumer involvement processes at only one point in time. The findings presented are drawn from that experience. Using other feedback and assessments of project analysts and consumer specialists we have rated current involvement degree. No change is seen for centers visited since March, 1969. Too little time has elapsed. None of the high-rated groups have changed.

Two groups rated as moderate and three low-rated groups have improved their degree of participation. In four of these, the degree of organization was rated higher than the degree of involvement. In the sixth group the visit took place over 15 months ago and there may have been improvements in consumer group organization function.

In the two cases where involvement has shifted from moderate to high, organization was high and strong personalities are found in the consumer groups. In one of these cases the current personality on the provider side is now consumer-oriented.

One other moderate-rated group was highly organized at the time of the site visit, but it was confronted by a strong provider personality. It has not improved its involvement rating.

Conflict (Table 5)

Of the 27 projects visited, 7 had experienced conflict related to the consumer group prior to the visit. In 3 groups, conflicts were internal to the group and, for the remaining 4, conflicts were between the consumer group and an external establishment — the project or the administering agency.

Of the low-rated groups, conflict was found only once and this was between groups rather than internal to the consumer group. Conflict often relates to involvement and these groups are more likely to be less active and less organized.

Table 4. Changes in Involvement Activity Related to
Organizational Status and Personalities

Center	Degree of involvement site visit (1)	Degree of organization (2)	Personality C—consumer P—provider (3)	Current assessment of consumer involvement (4)
1.	H	H	C	H
2.	H	H	C P	H
3.	H	H	P	H
4.	H	H	C C	H
5.*	H	H	C P	H
6.*	H	L	C	H
7.	H	H	C	H
8.*	M	M	C	M
9.*	M	H	P	M
10.	M	L	P	M
11.	M	H	P	M
12.	M	H	C P	H
13.	M	H	C C†	H
14.	M	M	O	M
15.	M	L	O	M
16.*	M	H	C P	M
17.*	L	M	O	L
18.	L	M	P	M
19.	L	H	O	M
20.	L	L	O	L
21.*	L	M	P	L
22.	L	L	O	L
23.	L	L	P	L
24.	L	L	P	M
25.	L	L	O	L
26.	L	L	O	L
27.	L	H	C	L

*Centers visited since March, 1969.
†Changed since site visit.

In none of these cases was the conflict considered to have significantly affected the operational status of the project although there were unquestionably a few close calls.

The conflict issue has been the most difficult to deal with. Obviously our analytical tools and perceptions need to be substantially improved before we can attempt to draw inferences from these events.

Each project hires a substantial number of persons from the com-

Table 5. Consumer Involvement as Related to Consumer Group and Staff Conflicts

Center	Degree of consumer involvement (1)	Conflict prior to site visit (consumer) I—internal E—external O—none (2)
1.	H	E
2.	H	O
3.	H	E
4.	H	O
5.	H	O
6.	H	O
7.	H	O
8.	M	I
9.	M	I
10.	M	O
11.	M	O
12.	M	I
13.	M	E
14.	M	O
15.	M	O
16.	M	O
17.	L	O
18.	L	O
19.	L	O
20.	L	O
21.	L	O
22.	L	O
23.	L	E
24.	L	O
25.	L	O
26.	L	O
27.	L	O

munity for a variety of jobs. These residents contribute to the capability of the project to be more responsive to community needs. Conflicts often develop among the newly operational staffs. It is difficult for a Washington-based management agency like OEO to judge differences in conflicts as they relate to staff and consumer group problems. Staff unrest has sometimes spread to the consumer group and conversely.

Much additional experience is required to understand the nature of these conflicts, to assess their influence on project and group function, and to determine desirable intervention or prevention steps.

We cannot assume that conflict is counterproductive. Sometimes major strides in consumer involvement and in project functioning have been an outcome of apparent conflict.

Other Issues

Our discussions with providers and consumers permit several generalizations to be made:

Providers strongly state they are unwilling to turn medical and professional matters over to the community group, but no consumer group that we have seen has claimed jurisdiction over clinical judgments.

Providers want to make judgments on professional qualifications of peers, consumers want to interview staff for "sensitivity" to the community.

Many providers feel genuinely comfortable with having the consumer groups participate actively in the establishment of personnel policies. They have already delegated much operational responsibility to the personnel committees of the consumer groups, particularly for the screening of jobs to be filled by community residents.

Program Matters

Many project directors and other members of the project staff see no barrier toward the discussion of programmatic issues with consumer groups. Hours of service including after hours coverage by medical staff has been the subject of discussions in many of the projects. In several projects, family or geographic priorities for early service by the project have been discussed with consumer groups. Where membership or enrollment in the project was restricted, community groups worked with the project in establishing priorities for earliest participation, i.e., the older families, the larger families, families with one or more individuals with chronic illness, and so on.

Budget and Grant Proposals

Discussions with project staff and project directors indicate that there were no general barriers to discussing project proposals and grants with consumer groups. Very often the lateness of preparation of grant proposals and tight deadlines for submission of these proposals to OEO have engendered a situation where the grants have been submitted to OEO prior to their discussion with the consumer group. In some instances, this has been explained as being due to the press of the deadlines which has precluded presentation before consumer groups that meet only once a month. There are few substantial barriers, from the standpoint of the providers, to discussion of the over-all grant proposal with the consumer groups and representatives of the consumer group. Often the budget and financial committees participate with project staff in the development of different phases of the project proposal.

Role of Consumer Group

While the analysis suggests that consumer group structure — as a board or as an advisory group — does not appear critical to group involvement in the project, there is a strong movement among consumer groups connected with NHC to establish themselves as boards and community corporations. This movement will unquestionably gather additional adherents, particularly among consumer groups. However, it is not clear whether consumer groups, established as boards of directors, can and do engage more effectively in policy decisions. There is a danger that incorporation can become a goal in itself for the community, whereas the real goal would more appropriately be participation in direction of program policy.

As programs mature, as they grow in size and complexity, judgments on these matters and the direction of solutions to these will fall into the hands of a small number of persons who are hired by the board because they possess the technical and community knowledge needed to deal with these problems.[5] While either a board of directors or an advisory group can and should remain in close touch with the operations, boards tend to be concerned with general rather than daily operations.

General

There are a number of anecdotal experiences which suggest that consumer participation can be an effective force in improving health services delivery. One consumer group was instrumental in establishing a policy that all medical staff should reside within the community, thereby being accessible to persons in the community after hours. This was in a basically black community. The project was successful in hiring four white physicians who moved into the community and have been residing in that community for over a year.

Another project established a policy that all medical providers would need to be fluent in Spanish within six months. This was discussed with physician applicants and only those were hired who would make an effort in learning Spanish. Physicians accepted positions in this center realizing full well that they were on probation until they could learn to speak Spanish.

In discussions with consumer groups, it was apparent some members were more knowledgeable about implications of what comprehensive family-oriented Neighborhood Health Centers could and should be to the community than were many of the individual practitioners who had only recently come out of other institutional or private settings. Community residents can and do understand these concepts of care, and no longer will accept less.

Low Participation

We should not end the study without expressing some concern for those centers where the level of participation is low. Eleven of the centers visited fall in that category. Of this number five are basically rural communities, three of which are located in the South. It is highly unlikely that there will be major progress in these five areas soon. Three of the other six groups located basically in urban settings have already increased their level of consumer participation.

While this study has been able to develop a relative ranking of degrees of participation of consumer groups, a very critical factor is missing: the preexisting potential for participation prevalent in the community as compared to the actual accomplishment. Some of the groups rated low or moderate in this analysis have made significant progress when measured against the political and social climate in their communities. The fact that poor consumers sit as equal voting members of groups in discussions with health department officials, and officers of the local medical and dental societies may be a sign of great strides in some communities. The fact that many of these consumers and some of the professionals are minorities sitting together for the first time may be an achievement that exceeds in significance the current assessment of consumer group involvement in the NHC projects.

SUMMARY

This study has analyzed some of the OEO experiences with consumer involvement in NHC projects. It has found that:

Consumer groups function better when they are better organized. Adequate elections and bylaws are key factors in organizing the consumer group. Strong leadership by a member of the group is important, but consumer group orientation on the part of project staff is also helpful and sometimes may substitute for group leadership.

A strong staff personality has a major input on enhancing or limiting group involvement.

The consumer group can function effectively whether it is a board or an advisory group. This issue has sometimes been the cause of group unrest and conflicts. It has been difficult to separate internal conflicts from external conflicts due, in some measure, to the success of projects in hiring community residents as staff. Disruptive conflict has not been a factor in most projects.

The widespread advocacy of consumer participation in service programs by residents of local communities by no means reflects general agreement regarding the goals of such participation, the forms it should take, or the means for its implementation. Although benefits to be derived from consumer invovlement are now discernible and some projects have become more responsive to community needs, the primary objective of resident participation in these projects has been achieved with varying degrees of success.

More rigorous in-depth study and analysis are needed to understand the social, political, cultural, and administrative forces that affect the issues and processes of consumer involvement. Such in-depth analyses, conducted by trained observers, are currently being initiated in two studies funded by PHS. We would hope that these studies will further illuminate these processes for managers, providers and consumers so that all can work more effectively together.

REFERENCES

1. Economic Opportunity Act of 1964, as Amended, Section 222(a)(4).
2. Hochbaum, G.M. Consumer Participation in Health Planning: Toward Conceptual Clarification. A.J.P.H. 59:1698-1705 (Sept.), 1969.
3. O'Donnell, E.J., and Chilman, C.S. Poor People on Public Welfare Boards and Committees, Participation in Policy-Making? Welfare in Review, U.S. Department of Health, Education, and Welfare, SRS 7,3: 1-10, 28-29 (May-June), 1969.
4. The Comprehensive Neighborhood Health Services Program, Guidelines No. 6128-1, Health Services Office, Community Action Program, Office of Economic Opportunity (Mar.), 1968, p. 6.
5. Michels, R. Political Parties: A Sociological Study of the Oligarchical Tendencies of Modern Democracy. Glencoe, Ill.: Free Press of Glencoe, 1959. (Known as the "iron law of oligarchy.")

A Model of the Adaptive Behavior of Hospital Administrators to the Mandate To Implement Consumer Participation

JONATHAN M. METSCH
JAMES E. VENEY

Consumer participation in the planning and management of social services has become a mandated component of governmentally sponsored and subsidized programs in recent years. The participation of consumers in the decision-making processes of these target organizations is legitimate and appropriate for several reasons: first, it is a mechanism for stabilizing the relationship between social service organizations and an external environment that can best be characterized as turbulent. Second, while in the past critical constituencies of social service organizations may have been professional and philanthropic, the general public, which brings resources to the organization (e.g., Medicare and Medicaid), provides teaching cases and a significant portion of needed manpower, must now be viewed as a principal constituency. Third, consumer participation keeps channels of communication with the community open and facilitates feedback on the acceptability and effectiveness of services. Finally, since consumer participation is included in the decision-making process of governmentally

Reprinted with permission of *Medical Care* V. 12, 1974, pp. 338-350.

sponsored planning agencies, input from consumers at the operating level should mitigate conflict when proposals for new programs and facilities undergo higher level review.

Since consumer participation is often mandated rather than voluntarily initiated by organizations, it would be unwise to assume that this mandate to implement consumer participation will be followed in time by a high level of consumer participation in the decision-making process. Literature identifies three types of organizational response to the mandate. These might be categorized as a normative response (shared values and norms between providers and consumers) generating cooperation, a utilitarian response (providers and consumers have complementary interests) generating contained conflict, and a coercive response (providers and consumers threaten one another) generating uncontained conflict.[17]

A normative response might be expected when the organization identifies itself as a community institution with an implied contract to serve its clients. Only planning with the community can relate services to needs and at the same time sensitize the community to constraints on the organization.[3,7,31]

A utilitarian response might occur when the community demands a role in decision making based on its subsidy to professionals using community equipment,[13] or its provision of teaching cases in training programs.[9] The organization may initiate consumer participation to attempt to understand consumer concerns at the local level before other agencies present the hospital's proposals for consumer review on Regional Medical Program or Comprehensive Health Planning agency boards.[2,12,36]

A coercive response might arise when members within the organization feel that enough conflict exists without involving consumers,[20] or when the feeling exists that only those who can back up their decisions with influence, money, or status should serve on boards,[29] or that services are too complex for consumers to understand or to help manage.[8]

Given this spectrum of potential organizational response patterns to the mandate to implement consumer participation in hospital planning and management, it is desirable to examine the adaptive behavior of administrators when such a mandate is promulgated.

PURPOSE OF THE STUDY

This paper develops a model of the adaptive behavior of hospital administrators to the mandate to implement consumer participation in planning and management. Since consumer participation is usually mandated rather than voluntarily initiated, legislating agencies need evaluative studies of administrative strategies of target organizations during the implementation phases of the process. Such studies will help determine if the adaptation to the mandate takes the form of cooptation of consumer representatives or steps that allow some degree of participation as called for in the directives. Studies will also improve the effectiveness of agency guidelines for participatory programs.

The model was developed to study the implementation phase (first year of activity) of consumer advisory boards established "to facilitate both the delivery and community utilization of ambulatory care" at 22 voluntary hospitals in New York City (19 were observed in the study). The boards were mandated by the city as part of a program of city/state subsidization of the deficits arising from amulatory care programs in the participating hospitals. Specifically, it was hypothesized that a predisposing variable (the attitude of the administrator toward consumer participation) and a set of contextual variables (describing the economic and social milieu of the organization as size and resources) are related to a set of outcome variables (describing levels of participation as measured by consumer/provider interaction, level of consumer input, and level of administrative response to consumer recommendations and requests). Also it was hypothesized that a set of implementation variables (describing the structuring of the advisory boards — whether there is a consumer or provider chairman, for example) is related to the set of outcome variables. This hypothesized relationship is shown in Figure 1.

The model is based on the frameworks offered by Pugh, Triandis, and Andersen[33,34,1] in that it identifies variable sets that are logically prior to one another. The purpose of delineating three broad variable sets is to identify a general framework within which researchers can direct studies of consumer participation. This is not to suggest that the variables conceptualized and measured within this study are the essential variables for all such research. The variables were selected because of knowledge of the study site, feasibility and accessibility, as well as theoretical appropriateness. Completion of the study itself suggested possible modifications of the variables and new variables such as consumer and provider representative attendance patterns, the number of consumer representatives on a particular advisory board, and the attitude of consumer representatives toward the target program. While further progress may best be made if researchers work within a similar broad conceptual framework, specific contextual, implementation, and outcome variables should be defined and operationalized in light of the program characteristics and setting under investigation. Where characteristics and setting are similar across study programs, the use of comparable variables would be appropriate.

INDEPENDENT   DEPENDENT

PREDISPOSING AND CONTEXTUAL VARIABLES $\longrightarrow$ IMPLEMENTATION VARIABLES[16] $\longrightarrow$ OUTCOME VARIABLES

PREDISPOSING VARIABLE

1. ATTITUDE OF THE HOSPITAL ADMINISTRATOR TOWARD CONSUMER PARTICIPATION[11,17,19]

CONTEXTUAL VARIABLES[30]

2. ADEQUACY OF SERVICES
3. CONTROL[18]
4. NUMBER OF FACILITIES
5. NUMBER OF BEDS
6. MEDICAL SCHOOL AFFILIATION
7. NUMBER OF OUTPATIENT VISITS
8. SUBSIDY
9. SUBSIDY AS PER CENT OF TOTAL EXPENSE
10. SUBSIDY AS PER CENT OF AMBULATORY CARE DEFICIT

SELECTION VARIABLES

11. CONSUMER REPRESENTATIVES[28,35]
12. PROVIDER REPRESENTATIVES

SOCIALIZATION VARIABLES

13. TRAINING[4]
14. PERMANENT CHAIRMAN[24]

15. CONSUMER/PROVIDER INTERACTION SCORES[5,22,23,25]
16. CONSUMER INPUT SCORE
17. ADMINISTRATIVE ACTION SCORE

FIG. 1. A model of the adaptive behavior of administrators to the mandate to implement consumer participation.

OPERATIONALIZATION OF THE MODEL

Predisposing Variable

The single predisposing variable under examination is the attitude of the administrator toward consumer participation. The writings of Etzioni,[17] Falkson,[19] and Chin and Benne[11] suggest a strong and direct relationship between attitude and the outcome of consumer participation in an organization. Falkson's research suggests that traditional programs (coercive) generate no participation, liberal programs (utilitarian) generate highly formalized citizen involvement with attempts to absorb clients into existing administrative processes, and radical programs (normative) develop fluid informal citizen involvement.

Contextual Variables

Contextual variables describe the economic and social milieu of an organization. Pugh and his colleagues[30] have delineated eight categories of contextual variables: origin and history, ownership and control, size, charter, technology, location, resources, and interdependence. Location and technology are assumed to be common to all the study organizations and not considered in the model as contextual variables.

The following contextual variables are considered. Table 1 gives comparative figures for these variables.

Adequacy of Services. Since consumer participation was initiated under the program to improve ambulatory care, it is essential to consider the extent to which the objective was met prior to the start of board activity (origin and history). Two of the 19 study hospitals were judged to have adequate ambulatory care services prior to the initiation of advisory board activity.

Control. All the hospitals involved in the study are voluntary institutions. This variable was included to explore the possibility that church-affiliated hospitals may differ from other nonprofit organizations as to outcome. The notion is based on the concept of the organization set[18] which suggests that as a partial social system, a focal organization depends on input organizations for various types of resources: personnel, materiel, capital, legality, and legitimacy. Church-related organizations have a different traditional organization set (e.g., Catholic Hospital Association, nursing order) than other nonprofit hospitals, which may have an impact on their dealings with a new set (health department, consumers). Eight of the hospitals under study are church-related institutions while eleven are categorized as "other nonprofit."

Table 1. Study Variables with Range and Mean Values for Each Variable

Variable	Range of Values	Mean
Attitude	Range: 4.50 to 9.62	Mean: 6.4389
Adequacy	2 hospitals identified as adequate; 17 identified as not adequate	
Control	8 church related hospitals; 11 other nonprofit hospitals	
Number of facilities	Range: 14 to 31	Mean: 23.53
Number of beds	Range: 237 to 1,168	Mean: 535
Medical school affiliation	11 with affiliation; 8 without affiliation	
Number of visits	Range: 22,129 to 295,016	Mean: 83,703.42
Subsidy	Range: $140,000 to $3,765,000	Mean: $811,294.74
Per cent expense	Range: 1.1 to 13.5	Mean: 3.9
Per cent deficit	Range: 15.9 to 164	Mean: 69
Consumer representatives	3 boards composed of patients 3 boards composed of community group representatives 13 mixed boards (patients and community group representatives)	
Provider representatives	12 chief executive officers attended meetings; 7 did not attend	
Chairman	14 consumer chairmen; 5 provider chairmen	
Training	4 boards had training; 15 did not have training	
Interaction score	Range: 1.11 to 5.14	Mean: 3.0984
Consumer input score	Range: 34 to 228	Mean: 114.1579
Administrative action score	Range: 6 to 102	Mean: 38.9474

Number of Facilities. This is a measure of number of services prior to the implementation of board activity (size). The number of facilities in the study hospitals ranged from a low of 14 to a high of 31.

Number of Beds. This is a measure of gross size of the hospital, since beds demand a significant portion of resources (personnel, money, administrative support) (size). The number of beds ranged from 237 to 1,168.

Medical School Affiliation. Teaching hospitals may place greater emphasis on comprehensiveness and quality of care as opposed to efficiency criteria and promote consumer participation to improve standards (charter). Eleven of the study hospitals have medical school affiliations; eight are not affiliated with medical schools.

Number of Outpatient Visits. The study program subsidizes a portion of the deficit of the participating hospitals' ambulatory care program. This variable measures the scope of the ambulatory care program (interdependence). The number of outpatient visits for 1970 ranged from 22,129 to 295,016.

Subsidy. This variable is the amount of the program subsidy for ambulatory care services for the first year of the program (interdependence and resources). The subsidy ranged from $140,400 to $3,765,600.

Subsidy as Per Cent of Total Expense. This is a measure of the extent to which the subsidy contributed to overall hospital expenses for a year (interdependence and resources). This variable ranged from 1.1 to 13.5 per cent.

Subsidy as Per Cent of Ambulatory Care Deficit. This variable considers the extent to which the subsidy contributed to the ambulatory care program deficit for the period immediately prior to board implementation (interdependence and resources). This variable ranged from 15.9 to 164 per cent (since the subsidy was based on forecasted ambulatory care deficit, one hospital was advanced a subsidy that exceeded 100 per cent of the actual deficit incurred).

Implementation Variables

The organizational phase of the implementation process was left to the hospital administrators to manage. Etzioni's discussion of organizational control structures[16] provides a conceptual framework for understanding administrator directed implementation. Etzioni suggests that organizational control (insuring that certain performances are carried out) is established through selection and socialization. He posits that effective selection reduces the need for socialization while an organization which accepts all individuals must rely heavily on socialization to generate organizationally beneficial behavior. It is of value to envision the implementation phase of consumer advisory boards as a selection/socialization process whereby different socialization and selection decisions by the administrator foster different kinds of participatory outcomes.

Selection Variables

Selection of Consumer Representatives. The literature indicates that consumers with previous participatory experience are more capable of contributing to input in the decision-making process.[28,35] For the purpose of this study, consumers on each board were classified as recipients of care (three boards), representatives of community organizations with previous participatory experience (three boards), and mixed (consumers form both of the previous categories) (13 boards).

Selection of Hospital Representatives. Since the satisfaction of many consumer requests requires an allocation of organizational resources, it was determined whether or not the Chief Executive Officer of the hospital (the chief allocator) attended the advisory board meetings. In 12 cases, the Chief Executive Officer attended the meetings, while in seven cases he did not.

Socialization Variables

Training. Bales and his associates[4] have identified "uniformities in interaction" in the small group setting. In order to solve problems, groups must resolve the communications problems of orientation ("what is it"), evaluation ("how do we feel about it"), and control ("what shall we do about it"). Since many consumers are inexperienced as either group participants or with the mechanics of the health care system, training may provide some of the skills necessary to handle the phases of the problem-solving process. It was noted whether or not the consumer received a training program provided by a voluntary agency in the city designed especially for them. Only four of the 19 boards selected the training program during the first year of the program.

Selection of Permanent Chairman. The chairman holds a position of critical importance. March and Simon[24] speak of selective filtering at every boundary of an organization and the pivotal role of the individual who is in the position to transmit and elaborate information (uncertainty absorption). Thus we can readily assume that the chairman will interpret and disseminate information related to the board's activity in a manner congruent with his consumer or organizational orientation and will filter out information selectively based on his own perceived objectives for the board. It was noted, therefore, whether the chairman was a consumer or a provider representative. Fourteen boards had consumers serving as the chairman, five had hospital representatives as chairman.

Outcome Variables

The outcome variable set is composed of three variables in order to examine board development over time: a measurement of consumer/provider interaction and two substantive outcome scores. The variables were evolved from content analysis of advisory board minutes. While the study did not specifically consider the relationship between outcome of consumer participation and changes in the level of community health, the research did proceed with the assumption that consumer participation as a component of the planning and management of health services will promote innovation in the delivery of health services and increase target population utilization by improving the acceptability and accessibility of care.

Consumer/Provider Interaction Score. This variable is the ratio of consumer initiated observations to provider initiated observations. The measure was used based on the assumption that the integration of consumers into the organization is more advantageous than attempts to control their behavior.[22,23,25] Specific advantages are exemplified by less turnover of consumer representatives and need to appoint replacements who require orientation to organizational objectives and open communication channels which keep the administrator aware of the acceptability of services. This outcome measure ranged from 1.11 to 5.14.

Consumer Input Score. This variable is the weighted recommendations/requests made by consumer representatives. This outcome measure ranged from 34 to 228.

Administrative Action Score. This variable is the weighted administrative actions in response to consumer input. This outcome measure ranged from 6 to 102.

Several instruments and data sources were used to operationalize the model. Attitude was measured through a Thurstone-type equal appearing interval scale.[15] Adequacy was determined by evaluating health department site visit reports. The remaining contextual variables were culled from health department reports and the HOSPITALS Guide Issues. The implementation variables and the outcome variables were obtained through content analysis of advisory board minutes during their first year of activity. Specific methodological aspects of the study have been discussed elsewhere.[26]

STATISTICAL MANIPULATION OF THE DATA

Stepwise regression analysis was used to determine the extent to which the variation in each of the three dependent variables could be explained by the independent variables in the model. For each dependent variable the following regression analysis was employed: 1) The predisposing and contextual variables were entered and selected in order of importance, that is, contribution to r^2. Only those that were statistically significant were retained. The statistically significant contextual and predisposing variables were entered, followed by the implementation variables which were allowed to explain as much of the remaining variation in the dependent variable as they could. Again, only those that were statistically significant were retained. 3) Finally, both the statistically significant contextual and implementation variables

Table 2. Results of Regression Analysis

Dependent Variable: Interaction Score

Overall F Value: 2.75268   Alpha Level: < .1

Variables in the Equation

Variable	B	St. Error B	Beta	Partial F Value
Number of facilities	0.08858	0.04952	0.33933	3.200
Adequacy	-1.40692	0.80491	-0.38027	3.053
(constant)	1.16240			

Dependent Variable: Consumer Input Score

Overall F Value: 15.15913   Alpha Level: < .001

Variables in the Equation

Variable	B	St. Error B	Beta	Partial F Value
Per cent expense	-2474.47570	328.59399	-1.38701	56.708
Adequacy	183.03948	31.64417	1.07016	33.458
Attitude	41.34522	6.50505	0.90955	40.397
Mixed board	61.49326	11.91433	0.54455	26.639
Training	-62.79007	14.38912	-0.48767	19.042
Chairman	32.15098	12.38914	0.26972	6.735
(constant)	-127.37013			

Dependent Variable: Administrative Action Score

Overall F Value: 7.57690   Alpha Level: < .005

Variables in the Equation

Variable	B	St. Error B	Beta	Partial F Value
Adequacy	46.95667	16.22842	0.61409	8.372
Subsidy	-0.00001	0.00001	-0.39177	3.121
Consumer input	0.23714	0.07744	0.53045	9.378
(constant)	16.00372			

were entered followed by other logically prior dependent variables which were allowed to explain as much of the remaining variation in the dependent variable as they could (interaction score and consumer input score for administrative action score; interaction score for consumer input score; consumer input score for interaction score). Again only those that were statistically significant were retained. Table 2 summarizes the results of the regression analysis.

P Value	r^2 Each Step	r^2 Change
< .1	.11406	.11406
< .1	.25600	.14194

P Value	r^2 Each Step	r^2 Change
< .001	.08983	.08983
< .001	.15508	.06524
< .001	.33321	.17813
< .001	.60619	.27298
< .001	.81803	.21184
< .005	.88344	.06541

P Value	r^2 Each Step	r2 Change
< .005	.11851	.11851
< .1	.35389	.23538
< .001	.60245	.24856

DISCUSSION

Interaction Score

Two variables explained .256 of the variation in the interaction score among the 19 study boards. The number of facilities is directly related to the interaction score while adequacy is inversely related to the interaction score. It should be noted that the relationships are not strong and should be interpreted cautiously ($p < .1$).

The results fit into the framework of the first stage of the problem solving process as described by Bales.[4] In phase one of the process, orientation, the group seeks to agree on a "common cognitive orientation or definition of the situation." Both of the variables identified as predictors of the interaction score provide a common basis for understanding the problems to be discussed. A large number of facilities is very visible to consumer representatives. Similarly, inadequacy of services represents another common denominator upon which agreement can be reached and upon which the later phase of the problem-solving process, direction and control, can be based.

While interaction (orientation) is an essential part of the problem-solving process, high interaction in itself is not enough to account for successful movement through the next two phases of the process. This is demonstrated by the low correlation between the interaction score and the consumer input score of .244 (not significant).

Consumer Input Score

Six of the independent variables explain .883 of the variation in the consumer input score: per cent of total expense, adequacy, attitude, mixed board, training, and chairman.

The per cent of total expense absorbed by the subsidy is inversely related to consumer input. Since the per cent expense is positively correlated to the number of visits (.537, significant at the .009 level), it follows that a small per cent expense is indicative of a small ambulatory care program. Since the objective of the study program is to promote ambulatory care, we might expect greater consumer input from boards related to hospitals with small ambulatory care programs as a stimulus to move toward the objective.

Adequacy and consumer input are directly related. This relationship complements the one found between per cent expense and consumer input. While a low percentage of total expense may indicate the low priority given to ambulatory care programming generating consumer input, existing adequacy may be a signal that assessment standards will be high and that consumer suggestions for improvements are acceptable. Also, adequacy may mean that new resources can be used to expand services rather than to rehabilitate existing programs.

Attitude of the administrator toward consumer participation is positively related to consumer input corroborating the theoretical notion that a favorable attitude generates a favorable outcome.

Where consumer representatives are mixed (some patients, some representatives of community groups) consumer input is greater. A plausible explanation is that mixed boards have a sensitivity to problem situations provided by recipients of care and the capacity to articulate ideas through those representatives with previous participatory experience in other settings.

Training is inversely related to consumer input. It may well be that boards in training come to view training as an end in itself during the training period and this attitude generates a decrease in substantive activity in the short run. Administrators may promote training to avoid intense consumer involvement if they understand this possibility.

Where a consumer is chairman, the consumer input is higher than when a provider representative serves as chairman. This finding supports an intuitive notion that the chairman has a great deal of control over the advisory board process and should be a significant influence on outcome.

Administrative Action Score

Three variables explain .602 of the variation in the administrative action score: adequacy, subsidy, and consumer input.

The literature on innovation suggests possible explanations for the positive relationship between adequacy and administrative action and the negative relationship between subsidy and administrative action.

The favorable administrative action level where a condition of adequacy exists may be viewed as slack innovation. Slack innovation is said to take place when there are uncommitted and unspecified resources of appropriate personnel, finances, material, and motivation available.[33]

The negative relationship between subsidy and administrative action might be viewed as distress innovation, that is, a search for new solutions to the basic problem of organizational survival.[32]

The fact that 22 voluntary hospitals have contracted with the city for subsidy is an indication of a stress posture by some. While the larger hospitals in the program most probably have received subsidies (grants, demonstration project money, etc.), the smaller hospitals may have little historical experience with this type of interorganizational relationship. The larger hospitals may accept the subsidy and give only a moderate response while the smaller hospitals behave more radically since this is deemed appropriate behavior. This may be summarized as a situation of "regression toward the mean" where initial interorganizational contact generates extreme behavior but later contacts generate behavior closer to existing patterns.

Consumer input is positively related to administrative action, a finding in line with the notion of the advisory process as a stimulus to organizational change.

PATH ANALYSIS

In building the model and running the regression analysis, the underlying assumption was that contextual variables are prior to implementation variables which are prior to outcome variables. This sequence is intuitively logical since contextual variables describe the economic and social milieu of the organization prior to the implementation of board activity and the outcome of board activity is temporally after the structuring of the boards (implementation variables). This assumption was investigated using path analysis, a technique using the intercorrelation coefficients of the study variables, in order to determine if relationships between variables are direct or a function of some mediating variable or variables.[6] The desirability of testing this assumption became evident: 1) from the observation that while Pugh hypothesized a pattern of unidirectional contiguous relationships (A→B→C→D), Triandis posited contiguous relationships with two way directionality (A——B——C——D), and Anderson found noncontiguous one-way interaction (A B C → D)[30,34,1]; 2) by virtue of the fact that regression does not provide a statement of causal relations. Three different models were stipulated and tested:

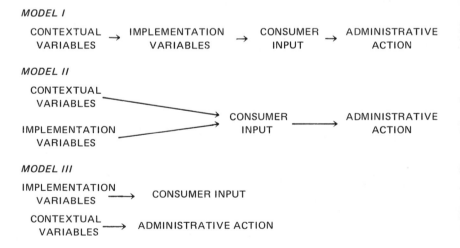

MODEL I

CONTEXTUAL VARIABLES → IMPLEMENTATION VARIABLES → CONSUMER INPUT → ADMINISTRATIVE ACTION

MODEL II

CONTEXTUAL VARIABLES
IMPLEMENTATION VARIABLES → CONSUMER INPUT → ADMINISTRATIVE ACTION

MODEL III

IMPLEMENTATION VARIABLES → CONSUMER INPUT

CONTEXTUAL VARIABLES → ADMINISTRATIVE ACTION

Model I suggests that prior variable sets constrain later variable sets to the end point where administrative action is a function of the contextual variables, the implementation variables, and consumer input. This model follows Pugh's basic hypothesis. Model II tests an alternative notion which assumes that the contextual variables and the implementation variables affect consumer input independently and that consumer input alone determines administrative action. The logic behind this model is that given certain contextual characteristics of the organization, the boards were nonetheless structured in a random manner. Since working with consumer advisory boards is new to administrators, it is realistic to test a model which assumes that even if the administrator wanted to control board activity through structural manipulation, guidance is not available to aid in the selection of implementation options that guarantee certain types of desired outcomes. Model III depicts the advisory board implementation process as composed of two distinct subprocesses. It suggests that implementation variables, or how the board is structured, explain the level of consumer input achieved, but that contextual phenomena (available resources, characteristics of the organization) determine organizational response to consumer input.

Testing of the three models indicates tht Model I best explains the relationships between the variable sets although it needs modification to be a true reflection of the intricacies of the implementation process.

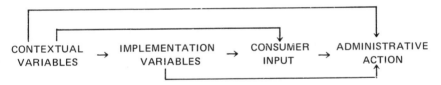

| CONTEXTUAL VARIABLES | → | IMPLEMENTATION VARIABLES | → | CONSUMER INPUT | → | ADMINISTRATIVE ACTION |

SUMMARY AND CONCLUSIONS

The project was undertaken with the goal of developing an empirical model of the implementation phase of consumer participation in order to identify significant manipulable variables as intervention points in the planning of programs involving consumer participation.

The theoretical notion that a consumer chairman promotes consumer participation is supported by the data and corroborated by findings in other recent studies.[10,14] It appears highly likely that provider representatives will be provider oriented if selected as chairman and their orientation will influence their boundary spanning behavior.

It was found in the research and confirmed by other study findings[10,14,19,21,27] that where consumer representatives are a combined group of recipients of services and community group representatives, input by consumers is increased.

This mix of consumer representatives may be appropriate only where the target institutions are voluntary organizations. The key individuals in generating consumer input are community group representatives with previous participatory experience. However, since patients self-select themselves to receive care at voluntary hospitals, the patients serving as consumer representatives legitimize the process of consumer participation. In situations where the entire community is the target (e.g., Model Cities) or where everyone in the community is a potential recipient of care (e.g., Neighborhood Health Centers), the selection of community group representatives alone may be satisfactory. Therefore, the consumer representative selection process should be appropriate to the consumer participation setting.

Four findings are stated as hypotheses because methodological problems during the research prohibit conclusive statements at this time.

The attitude of the administrator toward consumer participation is directly related to the level of consumer input achieved. This notion is confirmed by other studies[10,14,19] and suggests that educating administrators to the advantages of consumer participation may improve attitude and generate higher outcome.

Training does not automatically generate higher outcome.[27] Training may inhibit substantive activity in the short run if consumers see their training as their first objective. It may be used by administrators to socialize consumer representatives to organizational viewpoints as exemplified by emphasis on limited organizational resources. Different types of training (information giving vs. group process training) may generate different types of outcome.

Smaller programs are more responsive to the mandate to implement consumer participation than larger programs. The relationships between several of the independent variables and outcome indicate that smaller programs may be better targets for demonstration projects using consumer participation if a pattern of success is desirable.

In the study, adequacy was used as a measure of the extent to which the target orgnizations met the objectives of the program prior to the initiation of consumer advisory board activity. While two hospitals were categorized as adequate, the operational definition used in the study may conceal some important information. One of the two "adequate" hospitals was in the process of changing from a specialty hospital to a community general hospital. The high ranking of this hospital on both consumer input and administrative action may be a response generated to obtain community legitimation of its new role. In contrast, the other hospital characterized as "adequate" has a model outpatient program of long standing and scored low on both outcome measures. This suggests that consumer participation should be related to an objective and failure may be predicted where consumer participation is initiated without a specific purpose in mind.

Finally, path analysis indicates that implementation variables are independent predictors of outcome although higher outcome can be achieved where significant contextual variables are favorable. Thus the fact that a contextual variable is fixed does not prohibit intervening on implementation variables and consequently attaining a higher level of consumer participation.

IMPLICATIONS FOR ACTION

While this study was undertaken primarily to help move scholarly discussion of consumer participation away from a reliance on descriptive case studies and into the realm of conceptual and empirical model building, it is important to identify findings useful now to program planners. Our findings suggest that a consumer should be chairman in fact as well as in title. The consumer chairman should be articulate, somewhat knowledgeable about the health care scene, have the available time needed for the position, and be respected by other consumers and providers. Training programs should be tailored to the specific needs of the consumer representatives on the advisory board and not be generic to all boards (even within one program). Mechanisms must be developed for evaluating these programs.

While there is no precise formula for selection of consumer representatives, the program administrator should keep in mind the relationship between setting and selection options and the critical role that community group representatives seem to play in promoting successful board activity. Finally, there should be certainty that the objectives of the consumer participation program are clear to all provider and consumer participants and that some attempt be made to educate target program administrators as to the reasons for, and potential benefit from consumer participation.

REFERENCES

1. Andersen, Ronald: A Behavioral Model of Families' Use of Health Services. Chicago: Center for Health Administration Studies, 1968.

2. Ardell, Donald B.: Public regional councils and comprehensive health planning: a partnership? J. Am. Inst. Planners 36:397, 1970.

3. Bailey, David R.: A future course for boards of trustees. Hosp. Adminis. 14:76; 1969.

4. Bales, Robert F.: Some uniformities of behavior in small social systems. Sociological Research I — A Case Approach. Matilda White Riley, Ed. New York, Harcourt, Brace and World, Inc., 1963.

5. Barnes, Louis: Designing changes in organizational systems and structures. Systems and Medical Care. A. Sheldon, F. Baker, and C.P. McLaughlin, Eds. Cambridge, Mass., M.I.T. Press, 1970.

6. Blalock, Hubert M.: Causal Inferences in Nonexperimental Research. Chapel Hill: University of North Carolina Press, 1961.

7. Brieland, Donald. Community advisory boards and maximum feasible participation. Am. J. of Pub. Health 61:292, 1971

8. Brown, Ray E.: Changing management and corporate structure. Hospitals 44:77, 1970

9. Cathcart, H. Robert: Including the community in hospital governance. Hosp. Prog. 51:72, 1970.

10. Chenault, William W., and Brown, Dale K.: Consumer Participation in Neighborhood Health Care Centers — Volume I — Interpretive Report. Washington, D.C.: Department of Health, Education and Welfare, 1971.

11. Chin, Robert, and Benne, Kenneth D.: General strategies for effective change in human systems. The Planning of Change. 2nd ed. Warren G. Bennis, Kenneth D. Benne, and Robert Chin, Eds. New York, Holt, Rinehart and Winston, Inc., 1969.

12. Colt, Avery M.: Comprehensive health planning. Am. J. Pub. Health 60:1194, 1970.

13. deVise, Pierre: Planning emphasis shifts to consumers. Mod. Hosp. 113:133, 1969.

14. Douglass, Chester W.: Health Services Planning in the Urban Ghetto: A Comparative Analysis of Eight Model Cities Programs. Ann Arbor: School of Public Health Program in Health Planning, 1971.

15. Edwards, Allan C.: Techniques of Attitude Scale Construction. New York, Appleton-Century-Crofts, 1957.

16. Etzioni, Amitai: Organizational control structures. Handbook of Organizations. James G. March, Ed. Chicago, Rand McNally & Co., 1965.

17. ———: The Active Society. New York, The Free Press, 1968.

18. Evan, William M.: The organization set: toward a theory of interorganizational relations. Approaches to Organizational Design. J.D. Thompson, Ed. Pittsburgh, University of Pittsburgh Press, 1969.

19. Falkson, Joseph L.: An Evaluation of Alternative Models of Citizen Participation in Urban Bureaucracy. Ann Arbor: School of Public Health Program in Health Planning, 1971.

20. Johnson, Everett A.: Giving the consumer a voice in the hospital business. Hosp. Adminis. 15:15, 1970.

21. Kaplan, Marshall: The Model Cities Program — A Comparative Analysis of the Planning Process in Eleven Cities. Washington, D.C., Department of Housing and Urban Development, 1970.
22. Katz, Daniel, and Georgopoulos, Basil S.: Organizations in a changing world. J. Appl. Behav. Res. 7:343, 1971
23. Katz, Daniel, and Kahn, Robert L.: The Social Psychology of Organizations. New York, John Wiley and Sons, Inc., 1966.
24. March, James G., and Simon, Herbert G.: Organizations. New York, John Wiley and Sons, Inc., 1958.
25. McGregor, Douglas: The Human Side of Enterprise. New York, McGraw-Hill Book Co. Inc., 1960.
26. Metsch, Jonathan M., and Veney, James E.: Measuring the outcome of consumer participation, J. Health Soc. Behav. (in Press).
27. Mogulof, Melvin B.: Citizen Participation: The Local Perspective. Washington, D.C., The Urban Institute, 1970.
28. ———— : Coalition to adversary: citizen participation in three federal programs. J. Am. Inst. Planners 35:225, 1969.
29. Pomrinse, S. David: To what degree are hospitals publicly accountable. Hospitals 43:41, 1969.
30. Pugh, D.S., et al.: A conceptual scheme for organizational analysis. Adminis. Sci. Q. 8:289, 1963.
31. Rogatz, Peter: The health care system. Hospitals 44:47, 1970.
32. Shepard, Herbert A.: Innovation-resisting and innovtion-producing organizations. J. Bus. 40:470, 1970.
33. Thompson, Victor A.: Bureaucracy and Innovation. Birmingham, University of Alabama Press, 1969.
34. Triandis, H.C.: Notes on the design of organizations. Approaches to Organizational Design. J.D. Thompson, Ed. Pittsburgh, University of Pittsburgh Press, 1969.
35. Verba, Sidney: Small Groups and Political Behavior. Princeton: Princeton University Press, 1961.
36. Wells, Benjamin B. Role of the consumer in regional medical programs. Am. J. Pub. Health 60:2133, 1970.

Subject Index

Accountability, 106, 108, 147, 171
American Hospital Association
  Patient Bill of Rights, 13, 145
  Statement on Consumer Representation
    in Governance of Health Care
    institutions, 13
American universities, 76

Blue Cross and Blue Shield Plans, 131, 168
  public advisory committees, 145
Boards of trustees, 39, 165, 173, 176, 192
  193

Chinese box, 256
Citizens Board of Inquiry into Health
  Service for Americans, 13
Civil Rights movement, 94, 155
Client-centered approach, 210
Committee for Economic Development, 144
Community mental health centers, 284
Comprehensive Health Planning, 101, 135
  CHP Act of 1966, 288
  Region II Advisory Committee, 289
  Service (HEW), 289
Consumer
  control, 105, 243
  -provider interaction, 307, 318, 334, 367

Control-sharing, 206
Cook County Hospital, 133
Corporatization, 11

Debakey Report, 132
Decentralization, 204
Decisional territory, 271
Defining objectives, 65
Depersonalization, 241
Depression of 1935, 170

Emergency Medical Services Systems Act,
  84

Ghetto Medicine Program, 86, 90

Health Careers Guidebook, 124
Health Maintenance Organizations, 149
  HMO Act of 1973, 14
Health Policy Advisory Center, 13
Health Services Attitudes Index, 331
Health Systems Agencies, 14
  National Health Planning and Re-
    sources Development Act, 84
Hierarchy of motives, 27

Intangible objectives, 68

379

Author Index